Second Language Acquisition and the Younger Learner

Language Learning & Language Teaching (LL&LT)

The LL&LT monograph series publishes monographs, edited volumes and text books on applied and methodological issues in the field of language pedagogy. The focus of the series is on subjects such as classroom discourse and interaction; language diversity in educational settings; bilingual education; language testing and language assessment; teaching methods and teaching performance; learning trajectories in second language acquisition; and written language learning in educational settings.

Editors

Jan H. Hulstijn
Department of Second Language
Acquisition, University of Amsterdam

Nina Spada
Ontario Institute for Studies in Education,
University of Toronto

Volume 23

Second Language Acquisition and the Younger Learner. Child's play?
Edited by Jenefer Philp, Rhonda Oliver and Alison Mackey

Second Language Acquisition and the Younger Learner

Child's play?

Edited by

Jenefer Philp
University of Auckland

Rhonda Oliver
Edith Cowan University, Bunbury

Alison Mackey
Georgetown University

John Benjamins Publishing Company
Amsterdam / Philadelphia

™ The paper used in this publication meets the minimum requirements of
American National Standard for Information Sciences – Permanence of
Paper for Printed Library Materials, ANSI z39.48-1984.

Library of Congress Cataloging-in-Publication Data

Second language acquisition and the younger learner : child's play? / edited by Jenefer
        Philp, Rhonda Oliver, and Alison Mackey.
     p.   cm. (Language Learning & Language Teaching, ISSN 1569-9471 ; v. 23)
     Includes bibliographical references and index.
        1. Second language acquisition. 2. Language and languages--Study and teaching.
        I. Philp, Jenefer. II. Oliver, Rhonda. III. Mackey, Alison. IV. Title: 2nd language
        acquisition and the younger learner.
     P118.2.S4283   2008
401'.93--dc22   2008030302
ISBN 978 90 272 1984 8 (Hb; alk. paper)
ISBN 978 90 272 1985 5 (Pb; alk. paper)

John Benjamins Publishing Co. · P.O. Box 36224 · 1020 ME Amsterdam · The Netherlands
John Benjamins North America · P.O. Box 27519 · Philadelphia PA 19118-0519 · USA

Table of contents

List of contributors

Eva Alcón Soler
Department d'Estudis Anglesos
Campus de Riu Sec
Universitat Jame 1
Castellon de la Plana
Spain
alcon@ang.uji.es

Asta Cekaite
The Tema Institute
Linköping University
581 83 Linköping
Sweden
astce@tema.liu.se

Christine Dimroth
Max-Planck-Institute for Psycholinguistics
P.O. Box 310
6500 AH Nijmegen
The Netherlands
christine.dimroth@mpi.nl

Susan Duchesne
University of Wollongong
Bega Education Centre
PO Box 1020
Bega NSW 2550
Australia
sue_duchesne@uow.edu.au

Lyn Fogle
Department of Linguistics
Georgetown University
Box 571051
37th and O Streets, NW
Washington, D.C. 20057-1051
USA
erw2@georgetown.edu

ZhaoHong Han
Teachers College
University of Columbia
New York
USA
zhh2@columbia.ed

Junko Iwasaki
International, Cultural
and Community Studies
Edith Cowan University
Mount Lawley Campus
2 Bradford Street
Mount Lawley
Western Australia 6050
j.iwasaki@ecu.edu.au

Eun Young Kwon
Teachers College
University of Columbia
New York
USA
ek2110@columbia.edu

Chong Nim Lee
Centre for Applied Language Research
University of Southampton
Highfield
Southampton
SO17 1BJ
United Kingdom
C.N.LEE@soton.ac.uk

Patsy M. Lightbown
Department of Education
Concordia University
1455 de Maisonneuve Blvd. W.
Montreal, QC H3G 1M8
Canada
patsy.lightbown@verizon.net

Alison Mackey
Department of Linguistics
Georgetown University
Box 571051
37th and O Streets, NW
Washington, D.C. 20057-1051
USA
mackeya@georgetown.edu

María del Pilar García Mayo
Departamento de Filología Inglesa
y Alemana y de Traducción
e Interpretación
Universidad del País Vasco
Paseo de la Universidad 5
01006 Vitoria
Spain
mariapilar.garciamayo@ehu.es

Rosamond Mitchell
Centre for Applied Language Research
University of Southampton
Highfield
Southampton
SO17 1BJ
United Kingdom
r.f.mitchell@soton.ac.uk

Howard Nicholas
School of Educational Studies
La Trobe University
Victoria 3086
Australia
h.nicholas@latrobe.edu.au

Rhonda Oliver
Faculty of Regional Professional Studies
Edith Cowan University
South West Campus
Robertson Drive
Bunbury
Western Australia 6230
rhonda.oliver@ecu.edu.au

Jenefer Philp
Department of Applied Language Studies
and Linguistics
The University of Auckland
Private Bag 92019
Auckland 1020
New Zealand
j.philp@auckland.ac.nz

Kris Van den Branden
Centre for Language and Education
Katholieke Universiteit Leuven
Blijde-Inkomststraat 7
B-3000 Leuven
Belgium
kris.vandenbranden@arts.kuleuven.be

Joanna White
Department of Education
Concordia University
1455 de Maisonneuve Blvd. W.
Montreal, QC H3G 1M8
Canada
jwhite@education.concordia.ca

Introduction

Child's play?

Second language acquisition and the younger learner in context

Jenefer Philp, Alison Mackey and Rhonda Oliver
University of Auckland, New Zealand / Georgetown University /
Edith Cowan University

Research on second language acquisition (SLA) by children and adults is characterized by many different subfields and perspectives, both cognitive and social in orientation. Although children feature as participants in this research, it is relatively rare to find reviews or overviews of SLA that deal specifically with child SLA although there are a few important exceptions (early work by McLaughlin 1984, 1985; Vihman & McLaughlin 1982; Wode 1981 and more recent work by Foster-Cohen 1999 and Paradis 2007). This general lack of focus on children's SLA is somewhat surprising, considering that data from children as first language learners have often provided a basis and impetus for SLA theorizing. Among the best-known first language studies to prove influential was Brown's (1973) seminal work showing a predictable order of morpheme acquisition by children under the age of three, and Dulay and Burt's (1974) application of these findings to child SLA. Such research has not only contributed to a paradigm shift while acquisition research was distancing itself from behaviorist approaches, but also led to an important line of inquiry into developmental sequences which is still relevant today (see Goldschneider & DeKeyser 2001 and a review of these issues in King 2006). In classroom contexts, for example, Pienemann's (1984) early developmental sequence work research with Italian children acquiring German in elementary school – and, in particular, his argument that instruction will not enable language learners to skip developmental stages – has fueled a significant amount of research investigating similar questions in adult SLA.

So, what we see is that a number of leading approaches to SLA have been shaped by research originally carried out with children. For example, the interaction approach owes much to early work by researchers such as Wagner-Gough and

Hatch (1975), whose study of a five-year-old Iranian child highlighted the importance of forms *and* functions in the input and emphasized that conversation is a
forum for developing linguistic competence as opposed to simply practicing it (see
also Sato 1986). In adopting constructs such as recasts, clarification requests, negative evidence, and cognitive comparisons, interaction research has continued to
develop from roots found in first language acquisition research on child-directed
speech (e.g., Baker & Nelson 1984; Bohannon & Stanowicz 1988; Demetras, Post,
& Snow 1986; Farrar 1990, 1992; Nelson 1987).

With such considerations in mind, it is remarkable that, as Paradis (2007: 387)
notes, child second language acquisition has seldom been "studied as a subfield
with its own issues and questions separate from adult L2 acquisition on the one
hand, or bilingualism and educational outcomes on the other." Clearly, the fact
that ideas and findings in one area can *inspire* research in others does not mean
that these different areas should always be taken together. The primary goal of our
edited collection is to stimulate reflection about the unique nature of child SLA,
as well as some consideration of differences between younger children, older children and adolescents. The complex and contextualized portraits of young second
language learners which emerge in the 12 papers collected in this book suggest
that while some kinds of child SLA may typically be thought of as being as simple
(or as enjoyable and universally effortless) as "child's play", this is not the reality
for other younger learners (Foster-Cohen 1999; McLaughlin 1984). The question
mark we have placed in the title invites readers to consider this issue. This introduction aims to provide a brief overview of some key issues across research in child
SLA, focusing especially on issues featured in this volume of work. We define what
we mean by child SLA, reflect on why child SLA is of interest as a subfield, and
outline the main themes of the book as a whole.

Defining child SLA

Some researchers, taking a broad view of bilingualism (e.g., Baetens Beardsmore
1986; Grosjean 1998), consider child SLA to be a form of 'additive bilingualism',
differentiated by features such as history, stability, language functions, and use.
Other researchers, working from a range of perspectives (e.g., McLaughlin 1984;
Nicholas & Lightbown this volume; Schwartz 2004; Unsworth 2005), take the view
that child SLA is distinguishable from bilingualism according to relative onset. As
Schwartz (2004) argues, "In bilingual acquisition contexts, the grammars of two
languages are being worked out in tandem... [in L2 acquisition contexts] a child
begins acquiring a new language only after having previously created a grammar
that is (in most respects) complete" (p. 2). Conversely, De Houwer (1995) identifies bilingual acquisition among pre-school children as "the result of the very

early, simultaneous, regular and continued exposure to more than one language" (p. 222), from before the age of two.

Setting the lower boundary of SLA at an onset age of between 2–4 years old, these researchers agree that child SLA differs from first language acquisition on the one hand, and from adult language acquisition on the other, yet shares characteristics of each. Taking this issue further in the first chapter of our collection, Nicholas and Lightbown suggest that very young children (2–7 years old) differ from older children in the way they acquire a second language (see also McLaughlin 1984, 1985). As they point out, a considerable proportion of the child SLA literature deals only with young children, despite the fact that recognizing differences between children of different ages would obviously have implications for pedagogy as well as research.

This volume features research involving children as young as three (Kwon & Han), but also includes those of school age up to the period of early adolescence. Although they differ maturationally from younger children, older children also differ from adult L2 learners by virtue of cognitive, social, emotional and contextual factors. Research among adolescents has often been subsumed under adult L2 learning, particularly when making use of ideas from research on instructed language learning and individual differences (for overviews, see Dörnyei & Skehan 2003; Ellis 2004; Skehan 1989). In some areas, however, equating adolescents and adults may merit rethinking; accordingly, we include two chapters discussing research specifically focused on learners aged 12–14 (Alcón & García Mayo; White). Of course, individual differences emerge from the earliest stages of language acquisition and are relevant throughout life; however, given the somewhat steep maturational trajectory of children's cognitive and social development, the impact of these factors varies significantly over the course of childhood, adolescence, and adulthood.

Different periods in child SLA

Stages of childhood are often identified according to developmental changes which have been argued to correspond to qualitatively different ways of thinking (Berk 2006). These stages also largely follow divisions of schooling: Early childhood (between 2–7 years of age, when children are in preschool and the beginning grades); Middle childhood (7–11 years, in elementary or middle school); Early adolescence (12–14 years, in junior high school); and Later adolescence (15 years and older, in high school) (see, for example, Krause et al., 2003; Muñoz 2007). Such a delineation of stages characteristic of all children is not supported by all, especially those working within the area of educational psychology. For example, theorists differ as to whether development is seen as a continuous process or characterized by discontinuous stages, as well as whether development takes a unitary course or is dependent on context, e.g., schooling (Berk 2006). However, major characteristics of these phases of childhood are well documented, and some SLA researchers believe they can serve at least as a logical starting point for considering differences between younger and older child L2 learners (e.g., McKay 2006; Muñoz 2007).

In early childhood, for example, children are learning to think symbolically and are using language to represent objects, but they still do not think logically or understand the viewpoints of others. Piaget originally characterized this period as involving preoperational thought. Looking more closely at middle childhood, it becomes clear how distinct it is from early childhood. Children become more logical in their thinking and are able to categorize and organize objects, but are not yet abstract in thinking. They can, however, consider multiple aspects of a problem and imagine others' perspectives. Children at this age are increasingly adept at turn-taking, topic maintenance, and the pragmatics of making speech acts such as requests. As far as SLA is concerned, it is relevant to note that in middle childhood children already possess a highly developed L1 (or L1s), and their language is increasing in vocabulary size and grammatical complexity. They are acquiring greater metalinguistic awareness, which is reflected in their language play, including a delight in riddles and puns, and later, pedantic play contrasting literal versus illocutionary meanings. Their oral and written literacy is still developing, but they are exposed to a greater range of text types as they move through schooling. In addition, the experiences of context learning and socializing in middle childhood are different to those of their younger peers. For example, they typically spend longer in institutionalized settings, particularly in multiparty settings where there is a high ratio of peers to adults (e.g., school).

Similarly, early adolescence is distinct in character from middle childhood: cognitively, linguistically, and socially. Many L2 learners at this age have a greater capacity for abstract thought, including language analysis, and can draw logical inferences – a capacity which continues to develop in later adolescence, together with greater metalinguistic awareness across all domains – phonology, morphosyntax, the lexicon, and pragmatics (Berman 2007). In adolescence there is an increasing reliance on peers; adolescents spend more time with peers than with any other social partners (Berk 2006), and greater social networks and independence affect their contexts of interaction and L2 development. This is matched by consolidation of socio-cognitive abilities. Language use changes as social networks intensify and extend beyond home and school settings (Chambers 1995; Oliver, Haig, & Rochescouste 2005).

The uniqueness of the child learner

An examination of conversational data with children, like data presented in a number of the chapters of this volume, inevitably brings up features particular to child learners at different ages. For example, in the following excerpt, two 7-year-old children are working on a task in an ESL classroom in Australia. Certain features of their discourse unmistakably come from children; this is clear not only from the way that they disagree with each other, the threatened appeal to an adult, and the way that child 'A' switches quickly from the task at hand to self-entertainment. Teasing her partner, she playfully incants into the tape recorder, experimenting with different pitches as she imitates what a teacher might say.

Example 1

      B: Red
      A: Xx there's no red allowed to be on that
      B: Gonna tell the teacher
      A: Will you stop it... Will you stop it... Will you stop it right no::w [child is repeating in a funny voice to tape recorder]

                                (Philp, Oliver, & Mackey 2006: 15)

In a second example, in a similar context to the previous one, two 6-year-olds are working on a task-based activity which requires positioning objects in a hidden picture.

Example 2

      R: Pick up what? A bread?
      J: Huh?
      R: Pick up a bread?
      J: Um bread? No I don't have a bread.
           Have you a – oh sorry [Locates picture of bread] Um put it where?
      R: In the bread.
      J: Huh?
      R: In the table. Table.
      J: No I want to put in the – in the bread I like here. [Points to a different position for the bread].

                                  (from Oliver, in press)

Despite having negotiated and arrived at a mutually understood solution, child 'J' opts simply to do what he wants to do "I like it here." This sort of capricious response is not characteristic of adult-like behavior – particularly in a goal-driven task situation. While disagreements between participants, off-task behavior, and moments of contrariness sometimes occur in adult interactions, they are qualitatively different, for example, they are usually less confrontational. Interestingly, evidence like this suggests that children are less bound by the constraints of task conditions in their interactions, as well as by social norms. Indeed, as reflected in various chapters of this volume, task-based interactions in classrooms are not the only situations in which children choose not to follow "the script". Children's interactions are often flavored with the frivolity, spontaneity, enjoyment, and experimentation of language play, not to mention imaginative play (Cazden 1974). While such play may occasionally be present in adult interactions, we suggest it is markedly dissimilar in character and frequency.

Fortunately for children, in addition to the positive affective benefits of sharing this sort of enjoyment, research indicates that social and linguistic benefits may accrue as well. Socially, language play is often rewarded by the attention and approbation of peers (Cekaite & Aronsson 2005) and can serve to support affiliation between participants (Sullivan 2000). Games such as "let's pretend" routines may also permit children to assume new roles, provide practice opportunities, and nurture confidence in the L2 (DaSilva & McCafferty 2007). Linguistically, language play promotes manipulation of form and meaning, imitation, and repetition, and may increase saliency of form (Cekaite & Aronsson 2005; Cook 2000; Sullivan 2000). Moreover, because it is enjoyable, the affective strength of such play may potentially lead to deeper processing of the language (Broner & Tarone 2001; Cekaite & Aronsson 2005).

These ideas are further explored in this volume and are, we believe, a key area for further research involving children. What is already clear is that, in investigating and drawing generalizations about the ways in which interaction in a second language can facilitate acquisition, researchers must keep in mind that characteristics of peer and adult-child interaction might contribute to differences in the process of SLA for child learners. Children at varying stages have different levels of cognitive and social development compared to adults, as well as different types of relationships with peers and others, and these must be taken into account.

Why study child SLA?

In developing this project, an early question we asked ourselves was, "Where exactly do the similarities and differences between child and adult language acquisition lie?" We have just seen a brief illustration and explanation of one of these differences, in interaction, but this is probably the tip of the iceberg. Child-adult differences have also been addressed in the research literature with regard to rate and level of ultimate attainment (e.g., the critical period hypothesis) as well as with regard to the processes of acquisition (e.g., nativist accounts, work on developmental sequences and language transfer). We now turn to a short review of some of the major issues and findings in these areas.

Ultimate attainment

A significant amount of research involving younger L2 learners has revolved around seeking to explain age differences in rate and level of ultimate attainment: How and why is age a factor in success? What explains the uniform success of L1 acquisition compared to the wide disparity among L2 learners? (e.g., Long 2007) Why should adult SLA be affected to a greater extent than child language acquisition by such factors as the nature of the target language being learned, the quality of the input, and individual differences? (e.g., DeKeyser 2000) What explains gradient age effects on L2 attainment in phonology and morpho-syntax which have been found within the pre-puberty period? (e.g., Bialystok & Miller 1999; for review, see Birdsong 2005; Jia & Aaronson 2003; Paradis 2007).

The large body of empirical research that has investigated these questions straddles L1 and L2 acquisition research. The picture that emerges is one of greater success among children than adults, with differential effects of age according to linguistic domain (with the greatest effects tending to appear in phonology). There is considerable debate over the explanation for these age-related effects with much of it focusing on the question of whether there is a critical or sensitive period for second language acquisition, as there is for first language acquisition, after which time access to innate language learning capacities is unavailable (for reviews and positions, see Birdsong 2004, 2005; DeKeyser 2000; DeKeyser & Larson-Hall 2005; Hyltenstam & Abrahamsson 2003; Ioup 2005; Marinova-Todd, Marshall, & Snow 2000). Views supporting a critical period hypothesis (and some views of an innate language acquisition device, to be discussed below) suggest that child SLA is qualitatively different from adult SLA, although age limits are somewhat fluid and variable across different areas of language (age 7 is sometimes identified as a cut-off in phonology, whereas puberty has often been proposed as a cut-off in other domains, such as morphosyntax). Alternatively, the competition model (e.g., Bates & MacWhinney 1989; MacWhinney 2005) suggests that L1 and L2 acquisition processes are inherently similar, yet differ according to the learners' experience with another language. Both of these views, of course, leave room for differences between child and adult SLA.

Unsurprisingly, many researchers argue that socio-psychological variables, experience, and amount of input, rather than maturational factors alone (such as brain lateralization by puberty), account for the finding that age of exposure to a language is a strong predictor of success in acquiring it (Bialystok & Miller 1999; Birdsong 2005; Jia & Aaronson 2003). For example, in a 3-year longitudinal study of 10 L1 Chinese-speaking children (aged 5–9) and adolescents (aged 12–16) who had immigrated to the USA, Jia and Aaronson (2003) found age-related differences in language preference over time. The children aged 9 and under switched language preference to English within the first year, had English-speaking friends, and thus enjoyed a richer L2 environment. In contrast, the older children maintained their preference for the L1 over the 3 years of the study, had higher L1 proficiency, and had more Chinese-speaking friends and a richer L1 environment. The study provides evidence that child second language acquisition is "shaped by dynamic interactions of multiple factors. ... Cognitive, social and cultural variables interacted with each other and shaped... language preferences and hence language environments" (p. 156). Of interest here is how these cognitive, social and cultural variables are age-dependent in ways that suggest child SLA is distinctive.

Processes and mechanisms of acquisition

Related to the issue of ultimate attainment is whether child L2 acquisition relies on an innate language acquisition device and universal grammar (UG) (e.g., Lakshmanan 1994), or, alternatively, on general cognitive processes (Tomasello 1995, 1998), with lesser or greater levels of L1 entrenchment according to age (MacWhinney 2005). These issues have led to research comparing L1A with child L2A, and child L2A with adult L2A (Schwartz 1998, 2004; Unsworth 2005).

Another aspect of age-related effects on acquisition is the issue of language transfer, a process not often discussed specifically within the subfield of child SLA. With regard to child SLA, transfer is particularly interesting because, unlike simultaneous bilinguals, L1 is established, although not as entrenched as that of adult learners. For younger child learners in particular, transfer may occur in either direction due to the fragile nature of the L1 (see also work on language shift in this regard, Paradis 2005). Research in child L2 acquisition suggests L1 influence on phonology in particular (Flege 1999; Goldstein 2004), yet, for morphosyntax, developmental errors rather than L1 transfer have been argued to predominate (Dulay & Burt 1974; Jia 2003; Paradis 2005, see also Hakuta 1976).

Regarding developmental sequences, most work with child and adult L2 learners has suggested relatively little difference between the two age groups, specifically with regard to order of acquisition (e.g. Cazden, Cancino, Herlinda, Rosansky, Ellen, & Schumann 1975; Dulay & Burt 1973, 1974; Pienemann & Mackey 1993; Wode 1981; for review see Ellis 1994, 2008). Longitudinal studies, however, have indicated some differences in acquisition orders, and it has been proposed that L1 and social variables, such as interlocutor characteristics, may play a part (Hakuta 1976; Tarone & Liu 1995; Tarone in press). Given that a multitude of different theoretical positions (e.g., processability theory, emergentist accounts, generative research, etc.) are continuing to produce insights into how and when language learners acquire what they do, and given that the factors and findings highlighted by each approach must certainly interact in as yet little understood ways, it would be unwise to draw simplistic conclusions here. Clearly, the processes and mechanisms of child and adult language acquisition are similar in many but not all respects, and it is important to acknowledge that while certain aspects of human cognition may be constant across age, the complexity of *both* the human mind and the social environment cannot be ignored. A range of research approaches is needed to detail the interactions between a very wide variety of factors, to explore how they play out in the lives of individual children, and to begin to draw conclusions about child and adult SLA more generally.

Research approaches

Longitudinal studies, although relatively rare, are a vital source of data on child SLA. They provide evidence about changes in children's language over time in specific contexts, and/or on children's actual experiences in learning an L2 (Achiba 2003; Hakuta 1976; Jia & Aaronson 2003; Sato 1990; Toohey 2000; Wong-Fillmore 1976). This approach to research has been particularly valuable in helping us to better understand child language acquisition in its own right, and in drawing attention to the dynamic interactions between social, cognitive and environmental factors. For example, Achiba's (2003) description of the acquisition of requests in L2 English by a 7-year-old over 17 months provides a complex picture of pragmatic development, including variations according to interlocutor (e.g., peer vs. adult) and purpose. Wong Fillmore (1976) and Toohey (2000) provide multiple case studies of children aged 5–8 years learning English as immigrant children among L1-speaking peers. They point to individual differences in personality characteristics (e.g., outgoingness, assertiveness) and associated differences in sociability and opportunities for interaction with peers, which may partially account for differences in rate of acquisition (see also Wong Fillmore 1983).

The longitudinal approach described briefly above is, of course, complemented by research from a range of different theoretical and methodological paradigms that also take the linguistic, social and cultural environments of children as their focus. For instance, descriptive and experimental research carried out in a variety of classroom and non-classroom contexts has investigated the types of input and feedback or scaffolding that children receive, their opportunities for experimenting with and modifying language, and the social and cultural contexts of their interactions.

One currently popular approach to investigating SLA in both experimental and classroom settings is research exploring task-based interaction between L2 learners. The results of such studies suggest that for children, as for adults, meaningful communication with others is a key site for L2 development (Mackey & Oliver 2002; Oliver 1995, 1998, 2000, 2002, 2008; Oliver & Mackey 2003). Younger and older children alike are able to provide one another with feedback in response to nontargetlike utterances and, in turn, are able to modify their own utterances in response to such feedback from their peers. Researchers argue that processes such as noticing, comparison, and integration may (immediately or eventually) both facilitate comprehension of novel input and lead to improvements in L2 production (Ellis 1991). Moreover, the need to communicate with others encourages learners to grapple with the target language at a more challenging level (Swain 1995, 2000). Interestingly, research directly comparing the interactional processes of adults and children has indicated that, whereas more opportunities for modified output may occur in interactions between adults, more modified output is actually produced in interactions between children (Mackey, Oliver, & Leeman 2003). Further studies are clearly needed to explore other features of child and adult interactions.

Classroom-based research comes in a variety of forms and has produced a range of interesting and useful findings. Studies carried out among learners in intensive ESL and French immersion contexts, for example, have considered the effects of different types of instruction and corrective feedback on L2 acquisition and the production of targeted forms (e.g. Harley 1998; Lightbown, Halter, White, & Horst 2002; Lightbown & Spada 1990; Lyster & Ranta 1997; Spada & Lightbown 1993; White, Spada, Lightbown, & Ranta 1991). On the whole, this work has suggested benefits for early adolescent L2 learners in communicative classroom contexts.

In mainstream classrooms, descriptive work has recognized and highlighted the consequences for L2 development of the interactional opportunities afforded or denied by a child's peers, who present not only social advantages, but also constraints (Day 2002; Miller 2000; Perera 2001; Willett 1995). While the potential benefits of peer relationships are great, they are not universally advantageous (Berndt 2004). In language learning, peers can restrict opportunities for interaction, limit the identities available to the language learner, and bolster resistance to the second language (Day 2002; Toohey 2000).

In representing a range of approaches to child SLA research, the studies in this volume provide both a broad view and a variety of detailed, nuanced views of ways in which the distinctness and similarities of child and adult language acquisition can be investigated. All of the factors identified here (e.g., the benefits and constraints of peer relationships, learners' roles and identities, stages of cognitive development, characteristics of meaningful interactions such as feedback and opportunities for modified output, etc.) are relevant to both adult and child learners and can be explored through many of the same methods. At the same time, it is clear that the importance and effects of different factors vary across the lifespan;

not only will similar questions sometimes receive different answers when applied to adults versus children, but in many cases the questions themselves will have to be different. In the following concluding section, we identify three areas which look especially promising for research on child SLA.

Three aspects of child SLA

From the chapters collected in this volume three major themes have emerged which seem particularly likely to attract productive research and insights regarding child SLA. Though certainly not limited to these areas, we envisage an increasing interest in the importance of social context, continued investigations into methods of tailoring pedagogical approaches to the unique characteristics and ability profiles of children at different ages, and a growing understanding of the need for rich, detailed descriptions of the many and various factors which interact to impact a given child's L2 development.

The social context of L2 learning: Adult-child and child-child relationships

As already noted, the relationships children encounter are qualitatively different from those of adults, and the nature and importance of these relationships differ markedly over time as children develop and mature. In addition to factors associated with cognitive and social development, there are features of language use that are associated with the particular social contexts in which children engage (e.g., their homes, schools, and wider communities), not to mention the effects of children's various roles within these settings (e.g., as siblings, sons/daughters, grandchildren, nieces/nephews, strangers, students, peers, friends, etc.). These different settings and roles mean that children experience a complex range of relationships, needs, and obligations, and their experiences with the L2 change accordingly.

It is interesting, for instance, to consider how the varying equality and power relationships in which children find themselves might influence language acquisition. Unlike adult-child relations, peers tend to be relatively equal in their interactions, and their seeking of mutuality, particularly within friendship groupings, is reflected in their language use. This is not to say that peers do not engage in power positioning – much the reverse; because peers are relatively equal in power, negotiation of position becomes an important element in their interaction. This in turn contributes to shaping the role of peers in a child's second language acquisition, particularly in relation to the potential of peers to serve as teachers (Mercer 1995). Referring to social development, Hartup (1989; Laursen & Hartup 2002) distinguishes the different roles played by adults and by peers, using a metaphor of vertical and horizontal relationships (see also Berk 2006). Adult-child relationships are predominantly vertical; they "provide children with protection and security" and "[b]asic social skills emerge within them." In contrast, horizontal relationships "are the contexts in which children elaborate these skills with individuals who are more or less similar to themselves" (Hartup 1989:121). Accordingly, adult-child and child-child relationships are likely to serve different but complementary and interrelated functions in L2 development. While adults, caregivers, and teachers may provide more scaffolding and recasting of a child learner's language, and while they may work harder to support and negotiate language, a child's peers appear to provide contexts for practice. Further, children are active in their own development; they often choose roles for themselves, for their peers, and for those adults with whom they have relationships (Azmitia & Hesser 1993, cited in Schneider 2000; Furman & Buhrmester 1985). Hence, there is a clear need in child SLA research to consider the differential influence of peers and adults in child L2 development.

Pedagogy and child L2 learning: The importance of tailoring approaches

Language teaching books (e.g., Moon 2000; Slattery & Willis 2001) as well as language acquisition texts (e.g., Cameron 2001; Gibbons 2006) emphasize the need to match changes in cognitive maturity with changes in language teaching strategies, noting that teachers' scaffolding and feedback can and should be tuned to children's needs, both linguistic and cognitive. Correspondingly, another theme that emerges in this book, particularly in Section 3, is that different applications of pedagogy are appropriate for different ages. While this may sound obvious, there is relatively little discussion of this in the SLA literature. For instance, with the development of the ability to view language metalinguistically, older children are able to make use of their analytic abilities and to benefit from instruction that focuses more explicitly on the form and structure of a language. Harley and Hart's (2002) study of bilingual exchange students took a good first step to exploring these issues, specifically looking at aptitude as a variable in L2 development.

Detailed pictures of L2 development

An overarching theme of this volume concerns the importance of understanding the dynamic relationship of factors that exert influence over child L2 development. In order to come to a greater understanding of the processes involved in child SLA, it is clearly necessary to generate rich, detailed, holistic, and contextualized pictures of children in the process of learning a second language, particularly over time.

This volume

This edited collection includes theoretical work and empirical research findings in relation to child second language learning in different contexts from early to late childhood. The studies reported here include children who are learning a second language in the home, in school, or both, in contexts in which the language of instruction is the same as, or different from, that spoken by their own community. The languages being learned include English, Flemish, Japanese, Spanish, and Swedish. The children are learning with input from parents, peers, teachers, and the wider community, naturalistically and through formal instruction. Acquisition is considered from different perspectives, not only in terms of developing accuracy, fluency, and complexity with morphosyntax and lexis, but also with respect to uses of formulaic sequences, interactional moves, and linguistic means of integrating with specific communities of L2 users. Data collection methods range from ethnographic approaches to empirical pre-test/post-test studies, from longitudinal research to short-term investigations. Instruments include pedagogic tasks, pre- and post-tests, diaries, interviews, and observations of daily life. The studies in this volume utilize quantitative and qualitative approaches to the collection, analysis, and interpretation of L2 data. In short, a wide range of approaches to research concerning child L2 acquisition are represented, resulting in a collection that presents multiple perspectives. There are, inevitably, many elements of child SLA not covered in this introduction or this volume, and some that are touched upon to only a limited extent. Language play, for example, (Broner & Tarone 2001; Cekaite & Aronsson 2005), and the use of repetition, (Rydland & Aukrust 2005), are both characteristics intrinsic to children's production which seem likely to make an impact on L2 development and which deserve additional treatment in the literature.

As we have mentioned, the primary goals of this collection are to stimulate reflection about the unique nature of child SLA and to spark future research into some of the themes presented here, including a consideration of differences between younger children, older children and adolescents. With regard to the social context of the child, research could consider the differential influence of peers and adults for child L2 production and development. Concerning instructional contexts, further ethnographic and empirical research on classroom practices and their outcomes is needed. Finally, there is a need for longitudinal work that describes L2 development in children and takes account of the linguistic and social context of their learning. The research presented here provides a kaleidoscopic view of child SLA; we hope that future work will bring this view into sharper focus and explore child SLA with greater clarity – not only as child's play, but sometimes also as hard work, and always as uniquely lived experience. We next turn to a preview of the work collected here.

Organization of the book

The book contains four sections. The chapters in the first section provide overviews and a platform for the rest of the book. While data-based, they are more theoretical than the ensuing chapters on empirical research, which are differentiated according to age and context.

Section One: Characteristics of child SLA

The first section comprises two chapters, each of which presents a general idea about characteristics of second language acquisition that are particular to children. In the first chapter, **Howard Nicholas** and **Patsy Lightbown** argue for the distinctiveness of second language acquisition by very young children, aged 2–7 years, compared to older children, adolescents, and adults, and discuss the implications of this for L2 pedagogy for older and younger children. Both this chapter and the next by **Christine Dimroth** underline the significance of linguistic, social, and cognitive differences between children of different ages – for example, in strength of L1, knowledge of pragmatics and social relationships, and world knowledge, respectively. More specifically, Dimroth considers the contribution of age-related factors in the language learning experiences of two Russian sisters, one 8, the other 14 years old. In analyzing longitudinal data on their untutored acquisition of L2 German morphosyntax, Dimroth examines the impact of prior linguistic knowledge (both L1 and L2), motivation and identity formation, and state of cognitive development.

Section Two: Instructed language learning in the early years of education

Each of the chapters in this section reports on empirical research concerning children in a second-language or immersion setting in the early years of formal education (Kindergarten to grade 6). They offer cognitive and socio-cultural perspectives on language learning in these contexts, with the first two chapters reporting on observational data of individual children in day-to-day interaction with peers in school, and the last two exploring how classroom practices and teachers themselves can influence young children's interactions. **Jenefer Philp** and **Susan Duchesne** begin this section with an investigation of the ways in which a 6-year-old L2 learner in a first-grade mainstream class in Australia is supported by her peers. Their study highlights the interrelationship between social and linguistic goals, as well as the importance of peer interaction for child language acquisition. In the next chapter, **Asta Cekaite** presents data from two 7-year-olds in a mixed-age reception class for L2 learners in Sweden. Through exploring the learning affordances created by the social context of the classroom, Cekaite demonstrates how multi-party interactions, and the challenges involved in negotiating them, contribute to each child's development. **Rhonda Oliver, Jenefer Philp** and **Alison Mackey** then describe a quasi-experimental study examining the effects of teachers' instructions and guidance, when provided to the whole class or during pair-work, on task-based interaction among child L2 English speakers in an Australian primary school. In the final chapter of this section, **Kris Van den Branden** considers how classroom practices may actually inhibit negotiation of meaning during reading comprehension activities with 11-year-olds. In his study of eight 5th grade classes in Flemish primary schools, he finds a reluctance on the part of the students to ask for help when confronted with unknown words, and explores how teachers might encourage in children not only a willingness to read for comprehension, but also an inclination to seek to resolve comprehension difficulties through negotiation.

Section Three: Instructed language learning in later years of education

The third section presents research carried out among young adolescents in second- and foreign-language settings, inviting consideration of how instructed language learning may differ for adolescent learners in junior high and high school, and, compared to adult L2 learners in, for example, university settings. In the first chapter, **Eva Alcón** and **Maria del Pilar García Mayo** examine the incidence and effectiveness of incidental focus on form in a foreign language classroom in Spain with 12 L1 Spanish- and/or Catalan-speaking learners of English, aged 14–15. The data suggests that, for these students, noticing and successful uptake of corrective feedback are more likely when the problem is indicated by the student than when it is anticipated by the teacher. Focus on form in this context led predominantly to noticing of lexical items and promoted their accurate use in the short term. Next, **Joanna White** considers how young adolescent L2 learners might benefit from the resource of the teacher or, more specifically, how they benefit from explicit instruction. Her chapter reviews three pedagogical intervention studies targeting English possessive determiners: two in intensive ESL classes with 12-year-olds, and one comparing 14 year old learners in regular EFL programs in Quebec and Catalonia. Her findings support the view that adolescent learners benefit from explicit form-focused instruction. However, in addition to teaching context, the learners' L1 backgrounds, motivation, learning styles, and readiness to acquire the forms exert an influence on the effectiveness of instruction.

Section Four: Child SLA at home and in the community

The final section of this book presents empirical research carried out in home and community contexts. Largely made up of case studies, the aim of this section is to contribute to our understanding of how SLA occurs in the sorts of naturalistic contexts in which much second language learning by children takes place. First, **Junko Iwasaki** describes a 21-month longitudinal study of a 7-year-old child, from a family of L1 English speakers, who is acquiring Japanese as a second language in a Japanese school in Australia. Using a processability framework (Pienemann 1998), the author investigates the naturalistic acquisition of the L2 in this context. **Rosamond Mitchell** and **Chong Nim Lee**'s chapter reminds us of the importance of family life in L2 learning through an examination of conversations between three L1 Korean siblings, their mother, and their grandmother at home in England. The data explored here spans a period of nine months and includes episodes of home literacy, such as reading aloud, and play, including "playing school". **Lyn Fogle** similarly focuses on the contribution of home life to child L2 learning. Her data comes from two families in the United States, each with two children adopted from Russia, and she explores the language of one child from each family, aged 6 and 8. Examining the children's mealtime conversations with their father and sibling over three months, Fogle is able to investigate the nature of parental scaffolding of young children's discourse. Her findings suggest differential outcomes of the fathers' interactional strategies on the children's language production and participation in conversation. Finally, **Eun Yong Kwon** and **ZhaoHong Han** present the results of a 26-month longitudinal investigation of language transfer in the L1 and L2 production of a 3-year-old Korean child in the United States. The data suggest bidirectional language transfer as the child moves back and forth between learning environments (Korea and the United States) and caregivers (Korean-speaking and English-speaking adults).

References

Achiba, M. 2003. *Learning to Request in a Second Language: A Study of Child Interlanguage Pragmatics.* Clevedon: Multilingual Matters.

Azmitia, M. & Hesser. J. 1993. Why siblings are important agents of cognitive development: A comparison of siblings and peers. *Child Development* 63: 430–444.

Baker, N. D. & Nelson, K. E. 1984. Recasting and related conversational techniques for triggering syntactic advances by young children. *First Language* 5: 3–22.

Bates, E. & MacWhinney, B. 1989. Functionalism and the Competition Model. In *The Crosslinguistic Study of Sentence Processing*, E. Bates & B. MacWhinney (eds), 3–73. Cambridge: CUP.

Baetens Beardsmore, H. 1986. *Bilingualism: Basic Principles.* Clevedon: Multilingual Matters.

Berk, L. E. 2006. *Child Development* (7th ed.). Boston: Pearson Education.

Berman, R. 2007. Language knowledge and use across adolescence. In *Blackwell Handbook of Language Development*, E. Hoff & M. Shatz (eds), 347–367. Malden MA: Blackwell.

Berndt, T. J. 2004. Children's friendships: Shifts over a half-century in perspectives on their development and their effects. *Merrill Palmer Quarterly Journal of Developmental Psychology* 50: 206–223.

Bialystok, E. & Miller, B. 1999. The problem of age in second language acquisition: Influences from language, structure and task. *Bilingualism: Language and Cognition* 2: 127–145.

Birdsong, D. 2004. Second language acquisition and ultimate attainment. In *The Handbook of Applied Linguistics*, A. Davis & C. Elder (eds), 82–105. London: Blackwell.

Birdsong, D. 2005. Understanding age effects in second language acquisition. In *The Handbook of Bilingualism: Psycholinguistic Approaches*, J. Kroll & A. de Groot (eds), 109–127. Oxford: OUP.

Bohannon, J. N. III & Stanowicz, L. 1988. The issue of negative evidence: Adult responses to children's language errors. *Developmental Psychology* 24(5): 684–689.

Broner, M. & Tarone, E. 2001. Is it fun? Language play in a fifth-grade Spanish immersion classroom. *The Modern Language Journal* 85: 363–379.

Brown, R. 1973. *A First Language*. Cambridge MA: Harvard University Press.

Cameron, L. 2001. *Teaching Languages to Young Learners*. Cambridge: CUP.

Cazden, C. 1974. Play with language and metalinguistic awareness: One dimension of language experience. *Urban Review* 7: 28–39.

Cazden, C., Cancino, H., Rosansky, E. & Schumann, J. 1975. *Second Language Acquisition Sequences in Children, Adolescents and Adults*. Final Report. Washington DC: National Institute of Education.

Cekaite, A. & Aronsson, K. 2005. Language play, a collaborative resource in children's L2 learning. *Applied Linguistics* 26: 169–191.

Chambers, J. K. 1995. *Sociolinguistic Theory*. Oxford: Blackwell.

Cook, G. 2000. *Language Play, Language Learning*. Oxford: OUP.

DaSilva Iddings, A. & McCafferty, S. 2007. Carnival in a mainstream kindergarten classroom: A Bakhtinian analysis of L2 learners' off-task behaviours. *The Modern Language Journal* 91: 31–44.

Day, E. 2002. *Identity and the Young English Language Learner*. Clevedon: Multilingual Matters.

De Houwer, A. 1995. Bilingual language acquisition. In *The Handbook of Child Language*, P. Fletcher & B. MacWhinney (eds), 219–250. Oxford: Blackwell.

DeKeyser, R. M. 2000. The robustness of critical period effects in second language acquisition. *Studies in Second Language Acquisition* 22(4): 499–533.

DeKeyser, R. & Larson-Hall, J. 2005. What does the critical period really mean? In *The Handbook of Bilingualism: Psycholinguistic Approaches*, J.Kroll & A. de Groot (eds), 88–108. Oxford: OUP.

Demetras, M. J., Post, K. N. & Snow, C. E. 1986. Feedback to first language learners: The role of repetitions and clarification questions. *Journal of Child Language* 13: 275–292.

Dörnyei, Z. & Skehan, P. 2003. Individual differences in second language learning. In *The Handbook of Second Language Acquisition*, C. J. Doughty & M. H. Long (eds), 589–630. Malden MA: Blackwell.

Dulay, H. & Burt, M. 1973. Should we teach children syntax? *Language Learning* 23: 245–258.

Dulay, H. & Burt, M. 1974. Natural sequences in child second language acquisition. *Language Learning* 24: 37–53.

Ellis, R. 1991. Grammaticality judgments and second language acquisition. *Studies in Second Language Acquisition* 13: 161–186.

Ellis, R. 1994. *The Study of Second Language Acquisition*. Oxford: OUP.

Ellis, R. 2004. Individual differences in second language learning. In *The Handbook of Applied Linguistics*, A. Davies & C. Elder (eds), 525–551. Oxford: Blackwell.

Ellis, R. 2008. *The Study of Second Language Acquisition* (2nd ed.). Oxford: OUP.

Farrar, M. J. 1990. Discourse and the acquisition of grammatical morphemes. *Journal of Child Language* 17: 607–624.

Farrar, M. J. 1992. Negative evidence and grammatical morpheme acquisition. *Developmental Psychology* 28(1): 90–98.

Flege, J. 1999. Age of learning and second language speech. In *Second Language Acquisition and the Critical Period Hypothesis*, D. Birdsong (ed.), 101–132. Mahwah NJ: Lawrence Erlbaum Associates.

Foster-Cohen, S. 1999. SLA and first language acquisition. *Annual Review of Applied Linguistics* 19: 3–21.

Furman, W. & Buhrmester, D. 1985. Children's perceptions of the personal relationships in their social networks. *Developmental Psychology* 21: 1016–24.

Gibbons, P. 2006. *Bridging Discourses in the ESL Classroom*. London: Continuum.

Goldschneider, J. & DeKeyser, R. 2001. Explaining the 'natural order of L2 morpheme acquisition' in English: A meta-analysis of multiple determinants. *Language Learning* 51(1): 1–50.

Goldstein, B. 2004. Phonological development and disorders. In *Bilingual Language Development and Disorders in Spanish-English Speakers*, B. Goldstein (ed.), 259–286. Baltimore MD: Brookes.

Grosjean, F. 1998. Studying bilinguals: Methodological and conceptual issues. *Bilingualim: Language and Cognition* 1: 131–149.

Harley, B. 1998. Issues in designing form-focused L2 tasks for children. In *Focus on Form in Classroom Language Acquisition*, C. Doughty & J. Williams (Eds.), 156–174. Cambridge: CUP.

Harley, B. & Hart, D. 2002. Age, aptitude, and second language learning on a bilingual exchange. In *Individual Differences and Instructed Language Learning*, P. Robinson (ed.), 301–330. Amsterdam: John Benjamins.

Hakuta, K. 1976. A case study of a Japanese child learning English. *Language Learning* 26: 321–351.

Hartup, W. 1989. Social relationships and their developmental significance. *American Psychologist* 44: 120–126.

Hyltenstam, K. & Abrahamsson, N. 2003. Maturational constraints in SLA. In *The Handbook of Second Language Acquisition*, C.J. Doughty & M.H. Long (eds), 539–587. Malden MA: Blackwell.

Ioup, G. 2005. Age in second language development. In *The Handbook of Research in Second Language Teaching and Learning*, E. Hinkel (ed.), 419–436. Mahwah NJ: Lawrence Erlbaum Associates.

Jia, G. 2003. The acquisition of the English plural morpheme by native Mandarin Chinese speaking children. *Journal of Speech, Language, and Hearing Research* 46: 1297–1311.

Jia, G. & Aaronson, D. 2003. A longitudinal study of Chinese children and adolescents learning English in the United States. *Applied Psycholinguistics* 24: 131–161.

King, K. A. 2006. Child language acquisition. In *An Introduction to Language and Linguistics*, R. Fasold & J. Connor-Linton (eds), 205–234. Cambridge: CUP.

Krause, K. D., Bochner, S. & S. Duchesne. 2003. *Educational Psychology for Learning and Teaching*. Southbank, Victoria: Thompson.

Lakshmanan, U. 1994. *Universal Grammar in Child Second Language Acquisition.* Amsterdam: John Benjamins.

Laursen, B. & Hartup, W. 2002. The origins of reciprocity and social exchange in friendships. In *Social Exchange in Development,* B. Laursen & W. Graziano (eds), 27–40. San Francisco CA: Jossey-Bass.

Lightbown, P., Halter, R., White, J. & Horst, M. 2002. Comprehension-based learning: The limits of "do it yourself". *Canadian Modern Language Review* 58(3): 427–464.

Lightbown, P. & Spada, N. 1990. Focus-on-form and corrective feedback in communicative language teaching: Effects on second language learning. *Studies in Second Language Acquisition* 12(4): 429–448.

Long, M. 2007. *Problems in Second Language Acquisition.* Mahwah NJ: Lawrence Erlbaum Associates.

Lyster, R. & Ranta, L. 1997. Corrective feedback and learner uptake: Negotiation of form in communicative classrooms. *Studies in Second Language Acquisition* 19(1): 37–61.

Mackey, A. & Oliver, R. 2002. Interactional feedback and children's L2 development. *System* 30(4): 1–19.

Mackey, A., Oliver, R. & Leeman, J. 2003. Interactional input and the incorporation of feedback: An exploration of NS-NNS and NNS-NNS adult and child dyads. *Language Learning* 53: 35–66.

MacWhinney, B. 2005. A unified model of language acquisition. In *The Handbook of Bilingualism: Psycholinguistic Approaches,* J. Kroll & A. de Groot (eds), 49–67. Oxford: OUP.

Marinova-Todd, S. H., Marshall, D. B. & Snow, C. E. 2000. Three misconceptions about age and second language acquisition. *TESOL Quarterly* 34: 9–34.

McKay, P. 2006. *Assessing Young Language Learners.* Cambridge: CUP.

McLaughlin, B. 1984. *Second-Language Acquisition in Childhood,* Vol. 1. *Preschool Children* (2nd ed.). Hillsdale NJ: Lawrence Erlbaum Associates.

McLaughlin, B. 1985. *Second-Language Acquisition in Childhood.* Vol. 2. *School-Age Children.* Hillsdale NJ: Lawrence Erlbaum Associates.

Mercer, N. 1995. *The Guided Construction of Knowledge.* Clevedon: Multilingual Matters.

Miller, J. 2000. Language use, identity and social interaction: Migrant students in Australia. *Research on Language and Social Interaction* 33: 69–100.

Moon, J. 2000. *Children Learning English.* Oxford: Macmillan Education.

Muñoz, C. 2007. Age-related differences and second language learning practice. In *Practice in a Second Language,* R. M. DeKeyser (ed.), 229–255. Cambridge: CUP.

Nelson, K. E. 1987. Some observations from the perspective of the rare event cognitive comparison theory of language acquisition. In *Children's Language,* Vol. 6, K.E. Nelson (ed.), 289–331. Mahwah NJ: Lawrence Erlbaum Associates.

Oliver, R. 1995. Negative feedback in child NS-NNS conversation. *Studies in Second Language Acquisition* 17: 459–481.

Oliver, R. 1998. Negotiation of meaning in child interactions. *Modern Language Journal* 82: 372–386.

Oliver, R. 2000. Age differences in negotiation and feedback in classroom and pair work. *Language Learning* 50: 119–151.

Oliver, R. 2002. The patterns of negotiation for meaning in child interactions. *Modern Language Journal* 86: 97–111.

Oliver, R. in press. How young is too young? Investigating negotiation of meaning and feedback in children aged five to seven years. In *Multiple Perspectives on Interaction in SLA,* A. Mackey & C. Polio (eds). Mahwah NJ: Lawrence Erlbaum Associates.

Oliver, R., Haig, Y. & Rochecouste, J. 2005. *Tackling Talk: Teaching and Assessing Oral Language*. Perth WA: CALLR, Edith Cowan University.

Oliver, R. & Mackey, A. 2003. Interactional context and feedback in child ESL classrooms. *Modern Language Journal* 87: 519–533.

Paradis, J. 2005. Grammatical morphology in children learning English as a second language: Implications of similarities with specific language impairment. *Language, Speech, Language and Hearing Services in Schools* 36: 172–187.

Paradis, J. 2007. Second language acquisition in childhood. In *Blackwell Handbook of Language Development*, E. Hoff & M. Shatz (eds), 387–406. Malden MA: Blackwell.

Perera, N. 2001. The role of prefabricated language in young children's second language acquisition. *Bilingual Research Journal* 25: 327–356.

Philp, J., Oliver, R. & Mackey, A. 2006. The impact of planning time on children's task-based interactions. *System* 34(4): 54–565.

Pienemann, M. 1984. Psychological constraints on the teachability of languages. *Studies in Second Language Acquisition* 6: 186–214.

Pienemann, M. 1998. *Language Processing and Second-Language Development: Processibility Theory*. Amsterdam: John Benjamins.

Pienemann, M. & Mackey, A. 1993. An empirical study of children's ESL development. In *ESL development*, Vol.2: *Language and Literacy in Schools*, P. McKay (ed.), 115–259. Commonwealth of Australia and NLLIA.

Rydland, V. & Aukrust, V. G. 2005. Lexical repetition in second language learners' peer play interaction. *Language Learning* 55(2): 229–274.

Sato, C. 1986. The Syntax of Conversation in Interlanguage Development. PhD dissertation, University of California.

Sato, C. 1990. *The Syntax of Conversation in Interlanguage Development*. Tübingen: Narr.

Schneider, B. H. 2000. *Friends and Enemies: Peer Relations in Childhood*. London: Arnold.

Schwartz, B. D. 1998. The second language instinct. *Lingua* 106: 133–160.

Schwartz, B. D. 2004. Why child L2 acquisition? In *Proceedings of GALA 2003*, J. van Kampen & S. Baauw (eds) Utrecht: LOT. (Retrieved 13 December 2007, from http://www-rcf.usc.edu/~ionin/SLAgroup/Ling527papers/SchwartzChildL2.pdf).

Skehan, P. 1989. *Individual Differences in Second Language Learning*. London: Arnold.

Slattery, M. & Willis, J. 2001. *Teaching English for Primary Teachers*. Oxford: OUP.

Spada, N. & Lightbown, P. 1993. Instruction and the development of questions in L2 classrooms. *Studies in Second Language Acquisition* 15(2): 205–224.

Swain, M. 1995. The function of output in second language learning. In *Principle and Practice in Applied Linguistics: Studies in Honour of H. G. Widdowson*, G. Cook & B. Seidlhofer, 125–144. Oxford: OUP.

Swain, M. 2000. The output hypothesis and beyond: Mediating acquisition through collaborative dialogue. In *Sociocultural Theory and Second Language Learning*, J. P. Lantolf (ed.), 97–115. Oxford: OUP.

Sullivan, P. 2000. Language play and communicative language teaching in a Vietnamese classroom. In *Sociocultural Theory and Second Language Learning*, J. Lantolf (ed.), 115–131, Oxford: OUP.

Tomasello, M. 1995. Language is not an instinct. Review of Pinker's (1994) The language instinct: How the mind creates language (New York: William Morrow). *Cognitive Development* 10: 131–156.

Tomasello, M. 1998. *The New Psychology of Language: Cognitive and Functional Approaches to Language Structure*. Mahwah NJ: Lawrence Erlbaum Associates.

Tarone, E. in press. A variationist perspective on the interaction approach to SLA. In *Multiple Perspectives on Interaction in SLA*, A. Mackey & C. Polio (eds). New York NY: Routledge.

Tarone, E. & Liu, G. 1995. Situational context, variation and second language acquisition theory. In *Principles and Practice in Applied Linguistics: Studies in honour of H.G. Widdowson*, G. Cook & B. Seidhofer (eds), 107–124. Oxford: OUP.

Toohey, K. 2000. *Learning English at School.* Clevedon: Multilingual Matters.

Toohey, K. 2002. Guided participation and second language learning. *Special Research Symposium* 28(2): 77–83. Association of Teachers of English as a Second Language of Ontario.

Unsworth, S. 2005. Child L1, child L2 and adult L2 acquisition: Differences and similarities. In *Proceedings of the 28th Annual Boston University Conference on Language Development*, A. Brugos, L. Micciulla, L. & C. E. Smith (eds), 633–644. Somerville MA: Cascadilla.

Vihman, M. & McLaughlin, B. 1982. Bilingualism and second language acquisition in preschool children. In *Progress in Cognitive Development Research: Verbal Processes in Children*, C. J. Brainerd & M. Pressley (eds), 35–58. Berlin: Springer.

Wagner-Gough, K. & Hatch, E. 1975. The importance of input in second language acquisition studies. *Language Learning* 25: 297–308.

White, L, Spada, N., Lightbown, P. & Ranta, L. 1991. Input enhancement and syntactic accuracy in L2 acquisition. *Applied Linguistics* 12(4): 416–432.

Willett, J. 1995. Becoming first graders in an L2: An ethnographic study of L2 socialization. *TESOL Quarterly* 29: 473–503.

Wode, H. 1981. *Learning a Second Language: An Integrated View of Language Acquisition.* Tübingen: Narr.

Wong-Fillmore, L. 1976. The Second Time Around: Cognitive and Social Strategies in Second Language Acquisition. PhD dissertation, Stanford University.

Wong-Fillmore, L. 1983. The language learners as an individual. In *Pacific Perspectives on Language Learning and Teaching*, M. Clarke & J. Handscombe (eds), 181–209. Washington DC: TESOL.

SECTION I

Characteristics of child SLA

Defining child second language acquisition, defining roles for L2 instruction

Howard Nicholas and Patsy M. Lightbown
La Trobe University / Concordia University

In this chapter, 'child' second language acquisition is defined as distinct from both 'adult' second language acquisition and from either monolingual or simultaneous bilingual development in childhood. We argue that 'second language acquisition' begins at a very early age (certainly before age 3) and suggest that there is a gradual development of features that become recognised as 'adult second language acquisition' after approximately age 7.

Using this definition, we explore both grammatical and pragmatic features of child second language development, observing how children behave in formal instructional settings where the 'second' language is either that of the surrounding community or of a distant community. We then explore what second language acquisition research can (not) teach us about second language instruction, especially the facilitating role that teachers can play in supporting child second language development.

Introduction

A question that has often been debated in the child language literature is the age at which it can be said of a child that he or she is acquiring a *second* language rather than acquiring two primary languages simultaneously (see, e.g., McLaughlin 1984). Although this issue has been raised frequently, there is no current consensus. Consequently, there is sometimes an unfortunate equation of 'second' language development with 'adult' language development. Our purpose here is to explore second language acquisition in younger learners and to suggest a way of recognising second language acquisition in young children – to ask how early second language acquisition can begin and to ask what the fundamental insights into *Language* are that a learner must have in order for their acquisition of an additional language to be deemed 'second' language acquisition.

Understanding what we mean by 'second' and, therefore, who can be deemed to be learning a 'second' rather than a 'first' language, has consequences for the approaches that teachers take with the students in their classes. If there is no real difference between a second and a first language, there is no need to distinguish teaching approaches for students who are continuing to develop the first and only language they have been exposed to from those teaching approaches for students whose education depends on the development of an additional language. However, if the processes of learning a second language are different from those of learning a first language, some aspects of pedagogy will probably need to be differentiated if they are to meet the needs of all students.

As observers and researchers have reported for a long time, the process of second language development is fragile. It cannot be assumed that it will automatically be successful. And even when a language appears to have been mastered, it can be lost without sustained support. For example, Burling (1959) reported on the acquisition and loss of Garo by his son, Stephen. Stephen, whose primary language was English, was first exposed to Garo at the age of about 16 months. At 21 months, the absence of his English-speaking mother (due to illness) led to his being cared for mainly by Garo speakers. Even after his mother returned home, his father reported his observation that Stephen continued to make "steady progress in the Garo language, which I believe he learned in much the same way as any Garo child." (Burling 1959, reprinted in Bar-Adon & Leopold 1971, p. 171). By the age of two and a half, Stephen's preferred language was Garo, but when the family left India (when Stephen was three years old), he stopped speaking Garo and, within a few months, seemed to have lost even the ability to understand it.

A child's first language can also be fragile (Nicoladis & Grabois 2002) – sometimes with deeply negative consequences. Wong-Fillmore (1991) reported on the ways in which immigrant children's loss of their family language sometimes had negative effects on the relationships between them and their parents and grandparents. Terms such as "subtractive bilingualism" (Lambert 1980) and "semilingualism" (Skutnabb-Kangas 1981) reflect the observed fact that children with multilingual experiences can partially or totally lose or insufficiently develop their first language, even though they do not fully master the second. More recent research has demonstrated that children who commenced their exposure to a second language before age 8 but lost contact with their first language appear to have language-related brain functions that very closely resemble those of monolinguals who grew up with the second language. There appeared to be no difference in the location of the speech processing operations as recorded by magnetic resonance imaging between the two groups of speakers (Pallier et al. 2003). It is possible to speculate that all traces of the first language had been lost, which implies that mechanisms involved in language acquisition are only hard-wired to a very limited extent – perhaps as little as being only a very broad 'capacity' for Language development (O'Grady 2003; Ellis 2002). If this is the case, differences between first and second language development may depend more on context than on abstract cognitive mechanisms.

So second languages can be lost and first languages (largely) replaced. This conclusion suggests that the boundaries between first and second language development (at least in young children) are not rigidly defined by age. Sundara, Polka and Genesee (2006) found that children learning English only could distinguish /d-ð/ by age 4, but that in French-English simultaneous bilinguals this capacity did not reach native-like performance until later. Further evidence for the inter-relationship between first and second language development can be found in Mayberry and Lock's (2003) comparative study of the age-related, first and second language experiences of deaf and hearing individuals. Among the deaf participants in that study, some had not been exposed to sign language at home and their families' spoken languages were not 'accessible' to them. Thus, they had essentially learned no language before they entered pre-school programs. In contrast, other deaf participants had been exposed to sign language from very early childhood, and had begun to learn an additional language – spoken or signed English – when they entered school. Among the hearing participants, some had learned one language (English) from birth through early schooling, while others had learned a range of languages (mainly Urdu) at home and learned English only when they went to school. The findings of the study suggested a profoundly different experience of later (delayed) language learning according to whether that later language was a second language or being learned as a 'first' language. That is, those deaf individuals who had had no previous language were always disadvantaged with regard to Language development. Other participants, whether deaf or hearing, who had acquired a language system early in life, were more likely to be successful not only in mastering the first language they learned but also in the learning of subsequent languages. This suggests that the issue is not so much the age at which a particular language is acquired as the importance of acquiring Language at a very early age:

> ... early language experience helps create the ability to learn language throughout life, independent of sensory-motor modality. Conversely, a lack of language experience in early life seriously compromises development of the ability to learn any language throughout life.   (Mayberry & Lock 2003: 382)

A related conclusion was reached by Fulkerson and Waxman (2007: 224), who argued that infants' sensitivity to the relationship between words and concepts "is tied specifically to words, rather than to general attention-engaging properties associated with sound". In this chapter, we first address the definition of child second language acquisition and then explore the implications of this definition for approaches to teaching second languages to children. We will also explore ways in which teaching second languages to young children may differ from teaching second languages to older second language learners.

When can we say that a child is learning a second language?

Despite our argument above, that it is the general development of Language that is the critical feature shaping language acquisition processes, very young children clearly pay attention to the features of the specific language(s) that they are acquiring. Very young children, including those who learn two languages from birth, show clear evidence of their ability to distinguish different languages in their environment. Gerken (2004) provided evidence that there is some ability to do this already established by nine months of age. Although there is considerable debate about whether bilingual children distinguish their two languages from the beginning (e.g., Goodz 1994; Möhring & Meisel 2003) or only come to do so gradually (e.g., Volterra & Taeschner 1978), there is ample evidence that, by age 3, children raised bilingually distinguish not only the languages but also have beliefs about who is expected to speak each language.

(1)   ATL (3 years, 1 month) and his grandmother are at the park. Although she is bilingual in French and English, she usually speaks only English to ATL and he normally replies only in French (the language he speaks with his mother). Responding to the other children and parents at the park who are speaking French, ATL's grandmother speaks French as well, not only to them, but also to ATL himself. After several minutes, ATL grasps the sides of the climbing frame, looks down sternly at his grandmother and says, "Grandmaman. Parle comme il faut!" [Grandma. Speak properly.] In the following days, he sometimes 'allows' her to speak French to his babysitter and other adults, but as soon as they are alone again, he says to her, "Parle anglais." [Speak English.]
(Lightbown, unpublished data)

As Harris (2006) has argued, very early in children's lives, languages are a central realisation of the "relationship" system that "collects data on individuals" (p. 164). But as they mature (and this can be seen in ATL already by age 3), those languages are also used for the "socialization" system that helps a child "learn how to behave in a way that is acceptable to the other members of his or her society" (p. 183). As Harris also points out, and as ATL demonstrates, society is not singular and each child is socialized into multiple, sometimes conflicting, groups. In eventually developing their own personality, children also make use of a third system, the "status" system, which allows them "to compete successfully" (p. 209). Again, we can see ATL not only accepting multiple groupings but also asserting his individual status. He does this by not insisting exclusively on maintaining the usual rules of his relationship with his grandmother when others are present, but asserting his relationship with her and his place in the hierarchy in his insistence that when alone with her, English is the language that she is to use. However, these sophisticated, socially-and culturally-embedded uses of languages do not constitute the starting point of language development. Rather, they reflect an understanding that has evolved quite rapidly of how language is embedded in a complex web of so- cial and cultural relations that develops while children work to gain command of the motor and linguistic aspects of the language(s) they are developing (McCune & Vihman 2001). Even if the child cannot make a 'rule' explicit, a child such as ATL is perfectly capable of insisting on behaviour that is consistent with a 'rule'. He has observed and lived by a complex set of behaviours, on the basis of which he has developed a pattern of interactions that he expects to be honoured by those around him while also being open to the possibility that the pattern can change with time or circumstance. ATL has come to understand that Language is part of the way that life is negotiated.

One of the features of acquiring a first language is that this process is simulta- neously the process of acquiring Language. Since they have no prior experience to guide them as to what to look for in the stream of sounds and other sym- bols around them, children acquire their first language without expectations either about what they are looking for or what is possible. On the face of it, such a claim might be seen to be at odds with UG views of the processes of language development and their enabling capacities, e.g., White (2003). However, as we will argue below, the claim is less a functionalist versus UG perspective than a wider recognition of the nature of language (see also Hulk & Cornips 2005; Sorace 2005).

Slobin (2001) makes the following claim, in relation to the nativist position:

> Regardless of theoretical position ... everyone agrees that grammaticalizable no- tions are "special". ... I will propose, however, that such theorists – including myself – have erred in attributing the origins of structures to the mind of the child, rather than to the interpersonal communicative and cognitive processes that everywhere and always shape language in its peculiar expression of content and relations. (p. 406)

An interestingly related point, but from a different perspective has been made by O'Grady. He argues:

> ... there is agreement that we should seek out the most general constructs that are consistent with a viable account of the properties of language and the facts of development. What remains to be determined is whether some of these con- structs have the status necessary to justify continued adherence to the traditional conception of Universal Grammar.   (O'Grady 2003: 54)

Consistent with a weakened emphasis on an innate faculty that is language- specific, it has been observed that in the earliest stages of acquiring their first language, children produce combinations of sounds that have variable and some- times even no apparent relationship to sounds in the adult variety of the language of their environment. And although children respond differentially to the sounds of the language(s) spoken in their environment within the first year of life (Kuhl et al. 2005; Werker & Tees 2002), the manner in which sounds or sound patterns are produced by children in their early vocalisations does not necessarily directly reflect their linguistic environment. That is, even though there is some evidence of social influences (Goldstein, King & West 2003), early productions do not provide reliable associations with the ambient language (Engstrand, Williams & Lacerda 2003).

As they begin to develop some control over the vocal sounds they make, children appear to use sound patterns to make meanings that may not be discretely encoded in single words or sound patterns in the adult language. Halliday (1975) referred to these "content-expression pairs" (p. 12) as a protolanguage (p. 30) in which sound and meaning are related without an intervening level of (lexico)grammar. His examples, from the vocalisations of his own son, include the first contrast that he identified as systematic, occurring at 9 months (p. 148): a "mid or mid-low falling tone" was used to express a meaning of "let's be together" which was contrasted with the same sound but sustained for longer to mean "look, it's moving". He points out (p. 46) how this system had evolved by about 19 months into one in which "instrumental and regulatory [pragmatic] meanings" were always expressed with a rising tone whereas "personal-heuristic [mathetic] meanings" were expressed with a falling tone. This latter category involves such functions as expressing personal feelings of pleasure/disgust and seeking the names of items.

Reflecting the fact that children acquiring a second language have had experiences that have taught them some key aspects of what Language is, one of the most obvious features that distinguishes second language acquisition from first language acquisition is the absence of the protolanguage stage in second language acquisition. Second language learners (regardless of age) use units such as words, formulae/routines or utterance fragments that can be recognisably traced to the language spoken around them (Peters 1983) and they do this from their earliest attempts at using the language. As Nicholas (1986) argued, this fundamental distinction arises from the general learning about the nature of Language that has occurred in the course of first language development. During the first eighteen months or so of life, children learn that Language is a three level system involving relations between sound and meaning as mediated by lexicogrammar. It is this fundamental insight into the three level nature of the Language system that differentiates second from first language acquisition. Extrapolating from this observation, Nicholas (1986, 1992) argued that child second language acquisition can begin much younger than the age of three provisionally suggested by McLaughlin (1984). Given this claim, it will also be necessary to consider how to differentiate between the language acquisition of younger and older children in order to clarify whether there is a distinction between (older) child and adult second language acquisition.

This minimalist approach to defining second language acquisition permits other features to be used to potentially distinguish between first and second language acquisition by various age groups. These features include accent, interactional patterns, the content of conversations and the presence of specific grammatical features in the interlanguage. We will argue that these combinations of features can be used to identify three frames for second language acquisition as follows: younger children, older children and adolescents/adults. We will suggest some approximate ages that are associated with the transition from one frame to the next, but do not claim that these transitions occur at precisely these ages.

As has been recognised in research into the critical period phenomenon, 'accent' as a feature of second language development emerges increasingly (though not universally) after approximately age seven (Hyltenstam & Abrahamsson 2003)[1] and there are also language processing differences that correlate with this age boundary (Weber-Fox & Neville 2001; Silverberg & Samuel 2004). However, earlier, Weber-Fox & Neville (1996) had argued that some processing effects could be observed for syntactic features in second language acquisition beginning between ages 4 and 6, reinforcing the view that the approximate ages we are identifying are not definitive markers of changes. Nicholas (1986) argued that the emergence of 'accent' (in alliance with a range of other aspects of social and cognitive maturation) could be seen as marking the beginning of 'adult' language acquisition (see also Nicholas 1992).

Not only do features such as 'accent' increasingly emerge from age seven, but a variety of interactional patterns that are typical of both first and second language acquisition in earliest childhood diminish or disappear. For example some types of language play are rare or absent in the interaction of older children (Bongartz & Schneider 2003; Cook 2000). These changes in interactional patterns reflect the re-defining of possible relationships between learners and their interlocutors that occurs as individuals mature and are socialised into their surrounding communities (whether 'naturalistic' or 'instructed'). Children and adults are given different degrees of freedom for their behaviour. Part of being an 'adult' is knowing what (not) to do in various settings. Part of being a child is *not knowing* how to 'behave' in various settings. Nicholas (1986) identified a range of behaviours such as re-duplication, topic nomination and particular uses of 'inverted' structures in the child L2 German of a three-year old English-speaking girl (Cindy) that could not be found in the L2 German of older children and adults. Cindy's use of these patterns was consistent with her 'childishness' and what that implied for how she could relate to her interlocutors and how they would interact with her.

---

1.   Some intriguing suggestions of much earlier influences have been suggested more recently (Stölten 2006).

For instance, a young child telling an adult that the object the adult is holding is 'a watch' is usually accepted as a normal conversational act. If an adult or an older child or adolescent does the same thing, it is regarded as unusual, perhaps even threatening. What these and similar findings indicate is that all processes of second language development are shaped by the contexts in which they occur and, therefore, by the relationships between the people who are involved. These features shape what is said, how it is said and how participants interpret both the content and style of what is said.

Another way in which first and second language acquisition may be seen to differ is the range of things that learners [are able to] talk *about*. In considering whether L1 and L2 acquisition are "parallel" or distinct processes Clyne commented, "...[some] claim that second language acquisition is a different kind of process to first language acquisition. This is because basic concepts are already known in the first language; they only need to be transferred from one code to another." (Clyne 1986; see also Hakuta 1974, 1976). In contrast, first language acquisition is normally closely tied to cognitive development. Language emerges as young children develop their knowledge and understanding of the world and the objects and actors in it (Bloom, Lightbown & Hood 1975; Brown 1973). In contrast, young second language learners have already acquired cognitive concepts and semantic relations such as the roles of agents and patients, and attributes such as shape, size and colour. Young second language learners need to acquire the particular features of the new language that express these concepts. Even when their second language knowledge is very limited, they find ways to express them, creatively using the words, syntax and communicative strategies they already know. Instead of emerging gradually, these different semantic relations seem to emerge all at once (Lightbown 1977a, b). When they lack the language to say something, young second language learners may recruit words and patterns and use them *as if they meant* what the children wanted them to mean. In the speech of two 5-year old children acquiring French as a second language, Lightbown (1977a, b) recorded multiple instances of questions that looked like simple copula constructions. However, analysis of the context revealed that the intention was somewhat different. "For example, *où est ça* (where is that?) was used in a context where its meaning could only be *where does this go?* or *where shall I put this?* since the child was holding the object referred to or pointing to it" (Lightbown 1977a: 206). Similarly, Wagner-Gough and Hatch (1975) reported that the young boy whose L2 acquisition Wagner-Gough studied used "what is it tunnel!" with the meaning of "stop pushing sand in my tunnel!" Felix records a similar example when a young girl aged approximately five and a half and acquiring German as her second language announces that lunch is ready by saying *das ist mittagessen* (that is lunch) (Felix 1978: 53).

The young second language learners not only make non-standard use of second language structures to convey novel meanings, they also make repeated use of selected features that manage conversations in non-standard ways. Hatch (1978) observed that young second language learners used copula structures to nominate topics of conversation. Similarly, Nicholas (1984, 1986) documented various ways in which Cindy manipulated her uses of equational structures (variably) containing copulas to identify topics of conversations into which she succeeded in drawing adult interlocutors. On one occasion, she tried to distract her adult interlocutor from asking why she liked eating lemon with salt, by suddenly creating a new topic of conversation by asking in reference to a tape recorder *was ist das?* (what is that?). This process, as Hatch (1978) also noted, is an interactive one in which both the child and the native interlocutor take complementary roles. Clarke (1996) observed 4- and 5-year old children in bilingual kindergarten settings. She did not find frequent examples of children using copula structures to nominate topics in their use of second language English, perhaps because of the control of the interaction by the teacher. In this more formal setting, the teacher took a greater role in directing the flow of the interaction and, therefore, there was less space for the children to nominate topics of conversation.

The contrast between Clarke's findings and the patterns of use of copula structures by younger second language learners outside school settings indicates that it is not linguistic insight alone that governs the features of child SLA, but the social/interactive context in which the second language is being learned. Influential features of these contexts include the age of the interlocutors, the extent of independence that the learner has in shaping interactions, which is also connected with the number of interlocutors and their age and status. Liu (1991) recorded Bob, a five year old Chinese-background boy's variable uses in a pre-school and later in a primary school of English structures that responded to and shaped the potential for feedback from interlocutors according to features of the environment. Among these features were the perceived role and status of the interlocutors as authorities (adults) or playmates (children). These perceived roles intersected with the status of adults as 'teachers' (who in this context were native speakers of English) and 'friends' (who in this context were native speakers of Chinese who interacted in English). In an early conversation between Bob and his school teacher, the caution in Bob was obvious, presumably reflecting a concern to not make a mistake, which may have also reflected his prior experiences of 'kindergarten' in China, but also a reaction to the domination of the interaction by the teacher:

(2)   Liu (1991:125)
        Teacher: Bob you borrowed the book?
        Bob: Yeah. (While nodding his head)
        Teacher: You bring it here?
        Bob: (Shaking his head)
        Teacher: Home?
        Bob: (Nodding his head)
        Teacher: Where?
        Bob: Home (Very softly)
        Teacher: Home?
        Bob: Home.
        Teacher: Where's the book?
        Bob: Home.
        Teacher: All right.

In contrast, only one month later in conversation with another five year old in the class, the following occurred:

(3)   Liu (1991:158)
        (Bob looks at what Ray had drawn)
        Bob: What? That's not book. That's my book. That's mine. Look look mine.
                Look. Look mine book. Look this is my book. This not book.
        (Bob points at Ray's drawing)
        Bob: This my book.
        Ray: This is my picture. Ha funny.
        Bob: No. Look my black book.
        (Bob starts to draw)
        Bob: Look.
        Ray: Let me do one.
        Bob: You do.
        Ray: Now can I do one?
        Bob: No.
        Ray: Book.
        Bob: Not book. This one this one this one. Look mine. This one this one.
                No no no not this.
        (Bob looks at how Ray is drawing)
        Bob: Look my book. Look my book.
        Ray: I can do that Bob.
        Bob: Book. This book. I colour colour. Look my book book. This my book.
                Yours not book. Look my book.

At the same time as Bob was duelling with Ray about his drawing, he had the following conversation with the researcher, who also knew Bob in the context of his family and had been working with Bob for approximately one year:

(4)   Liu (1991:177)
      (The researcher knocks on the table as if knocking at the door)
      Bob: Come in.
      Researcher: You're Bob?
      Bob: Bye bye.
      Researcher: Are you Bob?
      Bob: No.
      Researcher: Who are you?
      Bob: My? Your daddy.

And three months later in interaction with two other five year old boys:

(5)   Liu (1991:149)
      (Shayne, Ben and Bob are flipping pencils. Ben hits the table)
      Ben: Ouch! Fucking!
      (Bob knocks Ben's pencil onto the floor and has to pick it up)
      Bob: Oh you fucking. Fucking Ben.
      Ben: No. Just go high. (Telling Shayne to flip the pencil higher)
      Bob: High.
      Ben: Fucking.
      Bob: Oh fucking. (Picks up pencil for Shayne) Oh fuckin fucking you folks.
              (Ben laughs)
      Bob: It's not funny. Fucking it.

Liu makes the point that Bob engaged with the different interlocutors in different
ways and learned different things from those interactions. With the teacher, appropriate, target-like forms were modelled and Bob worked to approximate to them
in a compliant manner. With the researcher, he could play language games and
take some risks, but the English he heard modelled, engaged with and used in this
context was generally target-like. With his peers he communicated in quite uncon-
ventional ways and explored more risky behaviours. All three sources of English
were important in his ultimate success in acquiring English. Across these diverse
interactions, Bob learned not only about the grammatical form of English, but also
the social constraints on what was possible to do in English. His interactions show
that he was already quite sophisticated in his understanding of what the various
differently constructed social settings would permit him to do and could offer him
as examples of English.

    Cultural shaping is clearly a feature of first language development (see Har-
ris' (2006) arguments for the 'socialization' system or Ochs & Schieffelin (1995)).
The consequence of the argument in the previous paragraph is that early first and
(child) second languages are fundamentally similar in the psycholinguistic processes that are applied. A parallel argument is made by N. Ellis (2002:323). The
difference between early first and young child second language acquisition is the

base level of understanding of what Language is as well as the range of notions –
cognitive and social – that the child wants, needs and desires to encode. The application of the same broad processes to a different knowledge base in different
sociocultural contexts is what leads to second language acquisition in young children *looking* different from both first language acquisition and second language
acquisition by older children, adolescents and adults (Achiba 2003). It also follows that children acquiring their first language(s), children acquiring a second
language and adults acquiring a second language will be attempting to achieve
different goals and interact with their interlocutors in different ways. Thus both
what they say and how they attempt to say it will be different, even though the
underlying principles of how the language signal is analysed may be similar. The
baseline for learning a second language is different from that of learning a first
language since the second language baseline contains *both* understandings about
Language and understandings about a specific language. We have indicated above
various ways in which children's understanding of what Language is shape the
approach that they take to the second language. The additional, but embedded,
experience of having learned a specific language is also used by children in their approach to the additional language. While the understanding of Language appears
categorical (i.e. children do or do not have it), the nature of the understanding
of a specific language will vary gradually with age. This results in a sequence of
(1) monolingual or simultaneous bi(multi)lingual development; (2) child second
language acquisition; (3) 'adolescent adult' second language acquisition. These developmental changes in language acquisition are associated with developments in
an individual's cognitive, social, identity and educational experiences as well.

These indicators suggest that some features distinguishing child from adult
second language acquisition represent a slow evolution across age. This evolution reflects the progressive changes in cognition and socialisation that accompany
maturation. As such, the features that distinguish child from adolescent and adult
second language acquisition are variable combinations of phonology, morphosyntax and pragmatics. There is a period of some four to five years between age 2
and age 7 when there is clear evidence of second language acquisition that usually
culminates in the attainment of native-like proficiency. There follows a period of
five to six years during which the proportion of native-like proficiency outcomes
progressively decreases until such results gradually come to be relatively rare after
approximately age 13 (Hyltenstam & Abrahamsson 2003; White & Genesee 1996).
In terms of the above sequence, we can talk of 'child second language acquisition'
being divided into a younger child period (prior to approximately age seven) and
an older child period that is characterised by the gradual incorporation of adult-
like features after that, with very little that 'linguistically' distinguishes adolescents
from adults in their second language acquisition processes.

Given the above, it seems reasonable to argue that child *second* language acquisition begins very early (perhaps even as young as age two). The period between
about 2 and 7 years of age is a time during which children's knowledge about Language and about the language(s) that they hear around them develops rapidly and,
to a very large extent, without instruction or intention.[2] Judging from the 'ultimate
attainment studies', we may infer that SLA begins to become more 'adult-like' from
about age seven. In exploring child SLA, it is important to recognise the inclusion
of the 'under-seven' age group and to be cautious about assuming that data from
learners over age seven is 'child-like' in the same way as data from younger learners.

An important development that seems to become influential from about the
age of seven for many of the learners who have so far been systematically studied
is the emergence of literacy.[3] Literacy entails the development of metalinguistic
awareness, including the knowledge that language can be divided into bits such as
words and sentences. Learning to read also brings the discovery that – for most
writing systems, at least – the pronunciation of words is related to the written
form. Another result of literacy is the increasing awareness that there are 'right'
and 'wrong' ways to say things. It seems likely that these discoveries represent a
pivotal change in the potential for language acquisition as well as in the strategies
that learners use in approaching a new language (see, e.g., August & Shanahan
2006). On the one hand, literacy provides many substantial benefits for instructed
learning, for example, allowing access to multiple kinds of input or providing a
means for recording new vocabulary to be learned and practised. First language
literacy certainly appears to be the best foundation upon which to build the kind
of second language skills that are needed for academic settings (e.g., Cummins
1991). On the other hand, literacy, and the cognitive development that results in
more sophisticated problem-solving and reasoning may create some limitations
on the ways in which learners perceive language and their expectations regarding
how it will function. For example, in some cases, literacy may lead learners to rely
on the written form of the language as a guide to pronunciation rather than relying
on aural input. It seems likely that such literacy-related differences in how learners
approach language acquisition represent a qualitative change in both processes and
outcomes of second language development.

Since it is the younger age group that has been least systematically acknowledged in the literature, we now attempt to draw together findings that can be
used to characterise young child second language development. We have already

---

2.   It is, therefore, imperative that theories of the relationship between first and second language
development (see Clahsen & Felser 2006a, b) incorporate learners who are younger than age 7.

3.   Tarone & Bigelow (2005) point out the extent to which populations without first language
literacy have been overlooked in the second language acquisition research literature.

documented the general effect of the understanding of Language and so we will not re-visit that claim. A range of studies has looked at other aspects of second language development in children under age 7. Some of the findings of these studies are illustrated in the following examples.

The selective transfer of word order patterns

Young children learning a second language can draw on specific features of their first language to achieve particular purposes. One feature that children sometimes carry into the L2 is the dominant word order of their L1. For example, in L2 questions formulated by 5- to 6-year old learners of French, Lightbown (1980) observed word order patterns that appeared to come directly from English, the children's L1. Such questions were also longer and more complex than those that were more clearly matched to the L2 input. The children whose language development was followed in this longitudinal study also used declarative word order in asking questions. This is both typical of early L2 acquisition and consistent with the L2 input, which, in spoken French consists mainly of questions without subject-[auxiliary] verb inversion. At the same time that most of their questions had SVO order, however, some questions showed clear L1 influence. For example, one of the children called to his mother, "Maman, peux-tu faire Kathy arrêter de pleurer?" (Mom, can you make Kathy stop crying."). On another occasion, he asked, "Quelle couleur était l'avion?" (What colour was the airplane?) Both sentences are essentially word for word translations of English questions and are more consistent with spoken English than with either the spoken French these two children were exposed to or the interlanguage questions that were typical of their speech at the time. This suggests that their English word order patterns were being used to allow them to produce these more complex questions in the absence of any other guide as to how to achieve this more complex task. This finding was echoed in older second language writers described in Elliott (1991). She observed some adolescents (of Lebanese-Arabic background), who selectively opted for a 'translation' or a 'begin-again' approach in their second language writing according to whether their goals were respectively matching the complexity of their first language writing ability or presenting their writing as 'English'. These two findings suggest that transfer is not a general mechanism, but rather a specific resource that is drawn on when a specific (more complex or more formal) challenge needs to be met.

Substantial silent periods

Extended periods of silence during which children show comprehension but little production of the second language have been reported in many studies (e.g., Ervin-Tripp 1974; Tabors & Snow 1994). Both Clarke (1996) and Liu (1991) observed silent periods in the second language development of the children they were studying. In each case, the silence can be seen to be strategic. Liu (2000: 148–149) records a stretch of discourse in which an unfamiliar adult (Howard) and a five year-old L2 learner (Bob) interacted with Howard speaking English and Bob speaking Chinese, a language that Howard did not understand. In the context of playing with Lego, the communication functioned effectively for some time:

(6) Bob: *Ang -. Dierge. You chu lai yi ge.*
               [The second one. Another one has turned up.]
     Howard: Good. Another door.
     Bob: *Ge na?*
               [Where to put it?]
     Howard: Where do we put it? In front of the driver? That's good.
     Bob: *Ha* (smiling).

A little later in the play, Bob gradually began to respond in English:

(7) Howard: Have you got a head somewhere?
     Bob: Yeah (and hands Howard the right Lego piece)
     Howard: A cup.
     Bob: A cup. *Wo yihuir zhao gangzi.*
                   [I'm going to find a cup]
               (Bob goes to the other side of the table to look for a Lego cup.)
               Thank you.
               Gei.
               [Here you are.]

Liu reported on how over the course of the subsequent two years and through interaction with a wide range of interlocutors, particularly in school, Bob progressed to high levels of fluency and command of English, after having spent nearly five months in extended silence (Liu 2000: 113), including periods where his total interaction in English amounted to less than a minute of speech in an hour of observation.

Clarke (1996) records a similarly extended period of even greater silence. She documents the case of Quoc, a Vietnamese-speaking child who spent almost the entirety of a pre-school year in silence – before breaking into extended, spontaneous direction of a child-play activity having given no previous indication of a willingness to speak. However, Clarke (1996: 165) also documented the extended and sustained efforts by the English-speaking teacher (Judy) to involve a group of children (deliberately designed to include Quoc) in English speaking activities in the bilingual pre-school that her informants attended.

(8) Dialogue

Context

Judy: Quoc/ hey/ where's the apple?/   Judy is playing a game using familiar objects with Quoc and Quang, a
Vietnamese-speaking friend of Quoc.

Quang: here/
Judy: no don't tell him/ where's the apple Quoc?/

Quoc points to the apple

Judy: good boy/ where's the man Quang?/
Quang: here/
Judy: right/ where's the block Quoc?/ where's the block?

Quoc points to the block

Judy: good boy/

This extended period of deliberate and engaging 'peripheral interaction', designed by the teacher to involve the children closely with English seems to have provided the input that was required for the children to progress. The four children began 'speaking' at different times and in each case appeared to carefully choose who they would begin talking to.

Clarke (1996: 150) documented the following example. After some ten months of virtual silence in English, Quoc, produced his first sustained conversation in English with an English-speaking peer, Vincent, when they were playing outside with water and containers that they filled and emptied as they spoke:

(9) Vincent: what you make?/ something?/ take this out?/
Quoc: take out/ me have this one/
Vincent: put here/
Quoc: no/ now me/ take it out/
Vincent: here/ over here/ fall down/ see/ see/
Quoc: dis mine/
Vincent: put water here/
Quoc: I not get one/ this one/ ... hey you give one/ ... that one here/ ...
Vincent: be careful!
Quoc: a big one/

These observations imply that the silence in their early learning was not a with-drawal from 'learning', but rather a choice about how to go about that learning. One of the resources that (some) young children have is the contextual support for learning during periods of silence. This resource distinguishes their contexts from those of older learners. In Clarke's case, the learners were actively supported through this phase, but in Liu's case, the pre-school teacher was less certain of how to respond and more frequently left Bob on his own in his silence. Consequently, his sources of English came from outside the pre-school.

Code switching/code mixing

Code switching and code mixing are typical of bilingual interaction. Children being brought up as bilingual from infancy learn at a very early age how this is done in their discourse communities (Goodz 1994; Paradis & Nicoladis 2007), and child second language learners must also learn when it is appropriate to use words or phrases from more than one language in the same conversation, or even in the same sentence.

Fernandez (1992: 114) recorded the following examples of English being used in German matrix discourse by children (aged approximately 6) in a bilingual program where the children's first language was English and German was their second language:

(10)   Meine Vater (my [feminine] father) und meine Mutti (my [feminine] mummy) went out last night and meine Tante (my [feminine] aunt) came over to look after us ...

but slightly later, the English items become integrated into the German pronunciation and grammatical system:

(11)   Heidi   helfen   die   Vater   get   dressen
       (Heide   help [infinitive]   the [feminine]   father   get   dress [infinitive])

These code-switching features can occur even if children are not sure that their interlocutors will understand them. In the contexts documented above, the children assumed that they would be understood by their teachers, since their behaviour was also the result of signals being given by their teachers that these kinds of combinations of linguistic systems would be taken as meaningful.

What is crucial here is how the teachers respond to these contributions (see also Nap-Kolhoff & Van Steensel 2005) so that over time the children can move to a system of language use that systematically distinguishes between contexts in which code-switching is appropriate and the other contexts in which a monolingual norm needs to be used.

Language play

In the course of second language development, children will draw on whatever resources are available to them while attempting to accommodate to their perceptions of the norms of their interlocutors. Teachers need to find the balance between being sufficiently supportive in accepting the children's intentions and sufficiently challenging in consistently pushing them into more complex material that requires both more complex and more precise uses of the new language. Otherwise, it can be easy for classroom varieties to emerge that systematically differ from those of the surrounding community (Lightbown & Spada 1990). As we have argued above, taking account of both the formal and the functional, the grammatical and the pragmatic is an essential – but also essentially negotiated – activity in child second language learning. How this is done will be different for pre-school and school-aged second language learners and will need to take account of the gradually developing socio-cultural identities and cognitive abilities of the children.

One aspect of this negotiation is 'play', a phenomenon that builds on a complex combination of social and linguistic information and relies on the delicate negotiation of relations between participants. Sociopragmatic space needs to be provided that permits children to play with language. Within that space, sufficient input in the new language will allow the children to discover the regularities of the linguistic features with which they can play. The potential for play as an aspect of child second language acquisition is one that needs thoughtful exploration so that its place is defined clearly for both learners and teachers. Too much play can distract from the need for the child to be supported/challenged to move on to language forms and functions that are more consistent with the repertoire of school registers. On the other hand, play can sometimes provide a vital means of exploring, in a 'safe' environment, exactly those more difficult aspects of the language, e.g., the use of tongue twisters to explore pronunciation or the use of poetry or song to rehearse grammatical patterns.

Instructed second language development

As we have indicated above, instructed second language development reflects its particular circumstances and the (cultural) shaping(s) of the expectations of the participants. Age and the cultural definition of the role of the teacher are part of this mix of factors that intersect with ways in which learners of all ages will process diverse aspects of the new language. Ways in which second languages can be developed depend on learners' relationships with others, on how they can interact with them and on how they balance the sometimes competing needs of participation and cognitive engagement and extension (Rydland & Aukrust 2005). Rydland and Aukrust demonstrated how 4 and 5 year-old Turkish background learners of Norwegian differentiated their use of repetition strategies according to whether the uses were associated with participation in the interaction or part of a more sophisticated cognitive challenge. They showed how the children could deploy limited linguistic resources to sustain quite extensive interactions with peers.

Tabors and Snow (1994) outlined the kinds of instructional strategies that they observed to be effective in preschool classes. In order for children to have the necessary opportunities for second language development in the preschool classroom, Tabors and Snow emphasize the importance of a consistent and predictable organizational structure, a language-rich environment in which teachers encourage both comprehension and production, and the involvement of children in the classroom who already speak the target language, ensuring that children have access to input and interaction with 'socially appropriate language partners' (p. 123; see also Wong-Fillmore 1985; Pinter 2006). Muñoz (2007) reviewed age-related differences in second language learning. In light of these differences, she suggested 'adequate L2 learning practice activities' for younger and older learners. For young children, the emphasis is on language that is associated with doing things and using language that is clearly contextualized and involves simple cognitive operations or actions. In contrast, older children are able to benefit from activities that separate language from the activities of the 'here and now' and require more complex cognitive operations (see our earlier discussion of the significance of the development of literacy).

For some young learners, instructed second language learning consists primarily of playful activities in which a few words, songs, and games are engaged in for a few minutes a day. For others, the second language is the medium through which all their subsequent education will be delivered, and for these children, the demands and expectations are considerably different. In these submersion contexts, it is noteworthy that some of the characteristics of appropriate second language instruction are often absent as learners are expected to learn the language and the school subject matter at the same time – more or less by 'osmosis'. Toohey (1998, 2000), for example, reports on kindergarten classes in which second language learners were discouraged from imitating their peers, from interacting with them during instructional activities on the principle that they needed to do their own work. They were even physically separated from other students in the classroom, on the assumption that they needed to be nearer the teacher where they could get extra supervision and assistance. Such separation deprived students of valuable opportunities to learn from their peers to use learning behaviours that are completely appropriate for child second language learners.

Muñoz (2007) reported on an unpublished survey in which she and her colleagues asked teachers to characterize various pedagogical activities according to their suitability for learners of different ages. Activities that involve listening, repetition, chanting, and singing were considered suitable for both 'preschool' and 'primary' learners. There were some differences between the two groups of young learners, however. Teachers emphasized the value to younger learners of activities that focus on aural-oral practice, while those deemed most 'suitable' for children of primary age included a literacy-based component, reflecting once again the likelihood that the age at which there is a qualitative change in children's ultimate success in learning a second language may be tied to literacy. Research suggests that reading is the most important contributor to vocabulary growth for both first and second language learners (Nation 2001), but literacy should not be restricted to just a focus on vocabulary expansion. Literacy also provides a vital insight into how the world is 'read' within various cultures and the more cognitively challenging acts of thinking that are required in schools.

Conclusion

For young learners, language acquisition involves cognitive, social, and physical engagement over long periods during which many changes take place in the developing child. In learning a first language, a child discovers both the power of Language and the characteristics of a particular language at the same time. The second language learner, even at a very early age, already knows the importance of Language as a tool and has some idea about how it works. L1 and L2 learning contexts may appear to be similar and the long term outcomes of L1 and early L2 acquisition may also be difficult to distinguish, but the child acquiring a second language has different expectations and exhibits different behaviours from the child who is discovering Language for the first time.

In this paper, we have reported on a number of observations in which children provide insights into the processes at work in their acquisition of a second language. These processes appear to indicate the existence of a distinct entity – 'young child second language acquisition' – that can be seen in children from approximately age 2 until approximately age 7. This approach shares some of the characteristics of first (monolingual or bilingual) language development and the second language acquisition of older children. However, the evidence suggests that young child second language acquisition needs to be distinguished from both first and older child second language development as well as from second language acquisition by adolescents and adults.

The distinctive nature of young child second language acquisition also means that a distinctive child second language pedagogy is required. This pedagogy can take account of the proclivity of young children to play with the forms and meaning of language, but must also be sensitive to the need to progressively move children toward control of the features of the new language. This requires consistent attention to both focus on form and focus on meaning. In both 'natural' and instructed second language development, signals about what is meant and how others are to respond are ambiguous or highly-contextualised (see Nicholas, Lightbown, & Spada 2001). On their own, young children may read the signals in ways that have the potential to mislead them about what they need to do with the new language. However, if teachers are misled by their students' misreadings to assume that what the children are doing in their second language is categorically different from what they are doing in their first language, they will miss opportunities to build on the children's general understanding of Language to foster control of the second language.

Young child second language learners are both like and unlike first language learners. They bring with them experience-related insights into the nature of Language, but the application of these insights to the learning of the additional language results in distinct processes of language development. Young children come to instructed second language development settings with sophisticated (even if implicit) understandings of the nature of Language and the relationships between Language and social context. It is precisely because they already have these insights that the way in which they go about dealing with a new language is different from the process that age-equivalent peers will be using as they continue to develop their first language. Child second language learners (both younger and older) also bring with them a willingness to innovate and go beyond models immediately surrounding them. The challenge is to recognise and build on the knowledge that children already have about Language in order to expand to its maximum their potential for productive bilingualism.

References

Achiba, M. 2003. *Learning to Request in a Second Language: A Study of Child Interlanguage Pragmatics*. Clevedon: Multilingual Matters.

August, D. & Shanahan, T. (eds). 2006. *Developing Literacy in Second-Language Learners: Report of the National Literacy Panel on Language-Minority Children and Youth*. Mahwah NJ: Lawrence Erlbaum Associates and Center for Applied Linguistics.

Bar-Adon, A. & Leopold, W. F. 1971. *Child Language: A Book of Readings*. Englewood Cliffs NJ: Prentice Hall.

Bloom, L., Lightbown, P. & Hood, L. 1975. *Structure and Variation in Child Language* [Monographs of the Society for Research in Child Development 40]. Chicago IL: University of Chicago Press.

Bongartz, C. & Schneider, M. 2003. Linguistic development in social contexts: A study of two brothers learning German. *The Modern Language Journal* 87: 13–37.

Brown, R. 1973. *A First Language: The Early Stages*. Cambridge MA: Harvard University Press.

Burling, R. 1959. Language development of a Garo and English speaking child. *Word* 15: 45–68.

Clahsen, H. & Felser, C. 2006a. Grammatical processing in language learning. *Applied Psycho-linguistics* 27: 3–42.

Clahsen, H. & Felser, C. 2006b. Continuity and shallow structures in language processing: A reply to our commentators. *Applied Psycholinguistics* 27: 107–126.

Clarke, P. 1996. Investigating Second Language Acquisition in Preschools: A Longitudinal Study of Four Vietnamese-Speaking Children's Acquisition of English in a Bilingual Preschool. PhD dissertation, La Trobe University, Melbourne.

Clyne, M. (ed). 1986. *An Early Start: Second Language at the Primary School*. Melbourne: River Seine.

Cook, G. 2000. *Language Play, Language Learning*. Oxford: OUP.

Cummins, J. 1991. Interdependence of first-and second-language proficiency in bilingual children. In *Language Processing in Bilingual Children*, E. Bialystok (ed.), 70–89. Cambridge: CUP.

Elliott, M. 1991. Case Studies of Students Learning to Write in English as a Second Language. PhD dissertation, La Trobe University, Melbourne.

Ellis, N. 2002. Reflections on frequency effects in language processing. *Studies in Second Language Acquisition* 24: 297–339.

Engstrand, O., Williams, K. & Lacerda, F. 2003. Does babbling sound native? Listener responses to vocalizations produced by Swedish and American 12–18-month-olds. *Phonetica* 60(1): 17–44.

Ervin-Tripp, S. 1974. Is second language learning like the first? *TESOL Quarterly* 8: 111–127.

Felix, S. W. 1978. *Linguistische Untersuchungen zum natürlichen Zweitsprachenerwerb*. Munich: Wilhelm Fink Verlag.

Fulkerson, A. L. & Waxman, S. R. 2007. Words (but not tones) facilitate object categorization: Evidence from 6- and 12-month-olds. *Cognition* 105: 218–228.

Gerken, L. 2004. Nine-month-olds extract structural principles required for natural language. *Cognition* 93: B89–B96.

Goldstein, M. H., King, A. P. & West, M.J. 2003. Social interaction shapes babbling: Testing parallels between birdsong and speech. (Electronic Version). *Proceedings of the National Academy of Sciences of the United States of America*, 100, 8030–8035. (Retrieved 19.3.07 from http://www.pnas.org/cgi/reprint/100/13/8030.pdf).

Goodz, N. 1994. Interactions between parents and children in bilingual families. In *Educating Second Language Children: The Whole Child, the Whole Curriculum, the Whole Community*, F. Genesee (ed.), 61–81. Cambridge: CUP.

Hakuta, K. 1974. Prefabricated patterns and the emergence of structure in second language acquisition. *Language Learning* 24: 287–298.

Hakuta, K. 1976. A case study of a Japanese child learning English as a second language. *Language Learning* 26: 321–351.

Halliday, M. A. K. 1975. *Learning How to Mean*. London: Edward Arnold.

Harris, J. R. 2006. *No Two Alike: Human Nature and Human Individuality*. New York NY: W.W. Norton & Company.

Hatch, E. 1978. Discourse analysis and second language acquisition. In *Second Language Acquisition: A Book of Readings*, E.M. Hatch (ed.), 401–435. Rowley MA: Newbury House.

Hulk, A. & Cornips, L. 2005. Neuter gender and interface vulnerability in child L2/L1 Dutch. *Language Acquisition and Language Disorders* 39: 107–134.

Hyltenstam, K. & Abrahamsson, N. 2003. Maturational constraints in SLA. In *The Handbook of Second Language Acquisition*, C. J. Doughty & M. H. Long (eds), 539–588. Oxford: Blackwell.

Kuhl, P. K., Conboy, B. T., Padden, D., Nelson, T. & Pruitt, J. 2005. Early speech perception and later language development: Implications for the "critical period". *Language Learning and Development* 1(3/4): 237–264.

Lambert, W. 1980. The two faces of bilingual education. *Focus* 3: 1–4.

Lightbown, P. 1977a. Consistency and Variation in the Acquisition of French: A Study of First and Secondn-Language Development. PhD dissertation, Columbia University, New York.

Lightbown, P. M. 1977b. French L2 learners: What they're talking about. *Language Learning* 27: 371–381.

Lightbown, P. M. 1980. The acquisition and use of questions by French L2 learners. In *Second Language Acquisition: Trends and Issues,* S. Felix (ed.), 151–175. Tübingen: Narr.

Lightbown, P. M. & Spada, N. 1990. Focus-on-form and corrective feedback in communicative language teaching: Effects on second language learning. *Studies in Second Language Acquisition* 12: 429–448.

Liu, G.-q. 1991. Interaction and Second Language Acquisition: A Case Study of a Chinese Child's Acquisition of English as a Second Language. PhD dissertation, La Trobe University, Melbourne.

Mayberry, R. I. & Lock, E. 2003. Age constraints on first versus second language acquisition: Evidence for linguistic plasticity and epigenesis. *Brain and Language* 87: 369–384.

McLaughlin, B. 1984. *Second Language Acquisition in Childhood,* Vol. 1: *Preschool Children* (2nd ed.). Hillsdale NJ: Lawrence Erlbaum Associates.

Möhring, A. & Meisel, J. M. 2003. The verb-object parameter in simultaneous and successive acquisition of bilingualism. In *(In)vulnerable Domains in Multilingualism*, N. Müller (ed.), 295–334. Amsterdam: John Benjamins.

Muñoz, C. 2007. Age-related differences and second language learning practice. In *Practice in a Second Language,* R. M. DeKeyser (ed.), 229–255. Cambridge: CUP.

Nap-Kolhoff, E. & Van Steensel, R. 2005. Second language acquisition in pre-school playgroups and its relation to later school success. *European Educational Research Journal* 4: 243–255.

Nation, I. S. P. 2001. *Learning Vocabulary in Another Language*. Cambridge: CUP.

Nicholas, H. 1984. 'To Be' or 'Not to Be': Is that really the question? Developmental sequences and the role of the corpula in the acquisition of German as a second language. In *Second Languages: A Cross-linguistic Perspective*, R.W. Andersen (ed.), 299–317. Rowley MA: Newbury House.

Nicholas, H. 1986. The Acquisition of German as a First and as a Second Language. PhD dissertation, Monash University, Melbourne.

Nicholas, H. 1992. Language awareness and second language acquisition. In *Language Awareness in the Classroom*, C. James & P. Garrett (eds), 78–95. London: Longman.

Nicholas, H., Lightbown, P. M. & Spada, N. 2001. Recasts as feedback to language learners. *Language Learning* 51: 719–758.

Nicoladis, E. & Grabois, H. 2002. Learning English and losing Chinese: A case study of a child adopted from China. *The International Journal of Bilingualism* 16: 441–454.

O'Grady, W. 2003. The radical middle: Nativism without Universal Grammar. In *The Handbook of Second Language Acquisition,* C. J. Doughty & M. H. Long (eds), 43–62. Oxford: Blackwell.

Ochs, E. & Schieffelin, B. 1995. The impact of language socialization on grammatical development. In *The Handbook of Child Language,* P. Fletcher & B. MacWhinney (eds), 73–94. Oxford: Blackwell.

Pallier, C., Dehaene, S., Poline, J.-B., LeBihan, D., Argenti, A.-M., Dupoux, E., et al. 2003. Brain imaging of language plasticity in adopted adults: Can a second language replace the first? *Cerebral Cortex* 13: 155–161.

Paradis, J. & Nicoladis, E. 2007. The influence of dominance and sociolinguistic context on bilingual preschoolers' language choice. *International Journal of Bilingual Education and Bilingualism* 10: 277–297.

Peters, A. 1983. *The Units of Language Acquisition.* Cambridge: CUP.

Pinter, A. 2006. *Teaching Young Language Learners.* Oxford: OUP.

Rydland, V. & Aukrust, V.G. 2005. Lexical repetition in second language learners' peer play interaction. *Language Learning* 55: 229–274.

Silverberg, S. & Samuel, A. G. 2004. The effect of age of second language acquisition on the representation and processing of second language words. *Journal of Memory and Language* 51: 381–398.

Skutnabb-Kangas, T. 1981. *Bilingualism or Not: The Education of Minorities.* Clevedon: Multilingual Matters.

Slobin, D. I. 2001. Form-function relations: How do children find out what they are? In *Language Acquisition and Conceptual Development,* M. Bowerman & S.C. Levinson (eds), 406–449. Cambridge: CUP.

Sorace, A. 2005. Selective optionality in language development. In *Syntax and Variation: Reconciling the Biological and the Social,* L. Cornips & K. P. Corrigan (eds), 55–80. Amsterdam: John Benjamins.

Stölten, K. 2006. Effects of age on VOT: Categorical perception of Swedish stops by near-native L2 speakers. *Lund University, Centre for Languages and Literature, Department of Linguistics and Phonetics Working Papers* 52: 125–128.

Sundara, M., Polka, L. & Genesee, F. 2006. Language experience facilitates discrimination of /d-ð/ in monolingual and bilingual acquisition of English. *Cognition* 100: 369–388.

Tabors, P. O. & Snow, C. E. 1994. English as a second language in preschool programs. In *Educating Second Language Children: The Whole Child, the Whole Curriculum, the Whole Community,* F. Genesee (ed.), 103–125. Cambridge: CUP.

Tarone, E. & Bigelow, M. 2005. Impact of literacy on oral language processing: Implications for second language acquisition research. *Annual Review of Applied Linguistics* 25: 77–97.

Toohey, K. 1998. Breaking them up, taking them away: ESL students in grade 1. *TESOL Quarterly* 32: 61–84.

Toohey, K. 2000. *Learning English at School: Identity, Social Relations and Classroom Practice.* Clevedon: Multilingual Matters.

Volterra, V. & Taeschner, T. 1978. The acquisition and development of language by bilingual children. *Journal of Child Language* 5: 311–326.

Wagner-Gough, K. & Hatch, E. M. 1975. The importance of input in second language acquisition studies. *Language Learning* 25: 297–308.

Weber-Fox, C. & Neville, H. J. 1996. Maturational constraints on functional specializations for language processing: ERP and behavioral evidence in bilingual speakers. *Journal of Cognitive Neuroscience* 8: 231–256.

Weber-Fox, C. & Neville, H. J. 2001. Sensitive periods differentiate processing of open- and closed-class words: An ERP study of bilinguals. *Journal of Speech, Language, and Hearing Research* 44: 1338–1353.

Werker, J. F. & Tees, R. C. 2002. Cross-language speech perception: Evidence for perceptual reorganization during the first year of life. *Infant Behavior and Development* 25: 121–133.

White, L. 2003. *Second Language Acquisition and Universal Grammar.* Cambridge: CUP.

White, L. & Genesee, F. 1996. How native is near-native?: The issue of ultimate attainment in adult second language acquisition. *Second Language Research* 12: 238–265.

Wong-Fillmore, L. 1985. When does teacher talk work as input? In *Input in Second Language Acquisition*, S. M. Gass & C.G. Madden (eds), 17–50. Rowley MA: Newbury House.

Wong-Fillmore, L. 1991. Second language learning in children: A model of language learning in social context. In *Language Processing in Bilingual Children*, E. Bialystok (ed.), 49–69. Cambridge: CUP.

Perspectives on second language acquisition at different ages

Christine Dimroth
Max-Planck Institut für Psycholinguistik

Empirical studies addressing the age factor in second language acquisition have mainly been concerned with a comparison of end state data (from learners before and after the closure of a putative Critical Period for language acquisition) to the native speaker norm. Based on longitudinal corpus data, this paper investigates the affect of age on end state, rate and the process of acquisition and addresses the question of whether different grammatical domains are equally affected. To this end, the paper presents summarized findings from the acquisition of word order and inflectional morphology in L2 German by Russian learners of different ages and discusses theoretical implications that can be drawn from this evidence.

Introduction

It has often been taken for granted in research on age effects on language acquisition that success in child second language acquisition is as robust as in L1 acquisition. We have become only slowly aware of the fact that child L2 acquisition is not always easy and successful (see e.g., Kaltenbacher & Klages 2006). As a consequence, comparably little research has been devoted to the study of child second language acquisition in its own right, investigating for example the minimal conditions (e.g., regarding the necessary amount of input) that child L2 learners need in order to reach native-like proficiency.

This paper is concerned with the acquisition of morpho-syntactic properties of L2 German by a very successful child learner and her slightly less successful older sister. The findings conform to the rule of thumb "The younger the better" (see e.g., Singleton & Ryan 2004). Most researchers, who are concerned with the relation between a learner's age at the onset of second language acquisition and his or her eventual success, would probably subscribe to this generalization.[1] This can

---

1.   This holds at least for acquisition in immersion situations. As Muñoz (1999) shows, young classroom learners do not seem to profit from the same advantage.

be seen as just another example of children outperforming adults in the acquisition of skilled activities: "It is usually very easy to identify in a group of skiers or tennis players or piano players those who began learning their skill in early childhood and those who are adult learners – and language is no exception." (Tomasello 2003: 287). In this paper I would like to maintain, however, that language is a learning target with some distinctive properties that distinguish it from tennis or piano playing, and make the age question in this domain a particularly interesting one.

Reasons for the observation that children are generally much more successful than adults in language acquisition have been hotly debated in the last few decades. The debate has centered on the question of how much certain age-related factors contribute to the explanation of age effects, i.e., observed differences in L2 development and ultimate attainment. The relative impact of the following "age-related learner properties" as I shall call them most neutrally, has been focus of the literature and will be addressed in this paper: neurobiology, motivation, cognitive development, and prior linguistic knowledge/experience.[2] Which age-related learner properties are conceived of as the most relevant ones, differs as a function of

1. different conceptualizations of the structure of language and consequently different views on the kind of knowledge and learning mechanisms needed for successful acquisition, and
2. the level of analysis (e.g., properties of learner grammars vs. automaticity of processing)

Since the interpretation of age effects depends to a large degree on basic assumptions about the structure of language and the related question of what it means to acquire a language, Section 2 addresses these theoretical underpinnings in more detail. Regarding the level of analysis, the results of the longitudinal case study on the untutored L2 acquisition of German by the two young Russian sisters that will be reported in Section 3 is concerned with morpho-syntactic properties of learner grammars as evidenced in oral language production. Section 4 presents and discusses some conclusions.

---

2.   Other learning circumstances that often correlate with age (e.g., type and amount of input) are also important, but will not be considered here in detail.

Different approaches to age effects in second language learning

Maturational approaches

Maturational approaches to language acquisition (see Birdsong 2005a for an overview) assume that the observed age effects in second language acquisition are temporally aligned with maturation and therefore most likely due to biological changes affecting the human language acquisition capacity. The idea that there is such a critical period for language acquisition goes back to Penfield and Roberts (1959). Advocates of this view (e.g., Long 1990, 2005; Meisel 2007) assume that there is a biological 'window of opportunity' for attaining native-like levels of competence in a (second) language that closes during or after (brain) maturation, leading to a sharp decline in success around the end of the critical period and making native-like attainment thereafter impossible. The exact temporal boundaries of the critical period are very much under discussion (Singleton 2005), as are the neurobiological processes causing the decrement in language learning potential (e.g., the loss of cerebral plasticity affecting language processing circuits (Penfields & Roberts 1959), the lateralization of language functions (Lenneberg 1967), or a process called myelination (Pulvermüller & Schumann 1994)).

A common version of the hypothesis pairs the assumption that age effects in (second) language learning are determined by neurobiological maturation with a modular view on grammar and grammar acquisition. According to the generative view, the human language faculty is not comparable to any other kind of cognitive achievement. Grammar is seen as a system of abstract rules, underdetermined in the input and therefore not learnable from it, the consequence being that successful language acquisition is impossible without innate knowledge about basic structural principles of human language (UG). The relevant variant of the Critical Period Hypothesis rests on the idea that it is innate language specific knowledge that makes early language acquisition uniformly successful, and that maturation somehow goes hand in hand with a loss of (full) access to this helpful knowledge.[3] Adult learners therefore have to approach the task by relying on domain general problem solving strategies that are less well suited to language acquisition (compare the "Fundamental Difference Hypothesis", Bley-Vroman 1989). The predictions of this assumption relate not only to the end state of second language acquisition but also to the shape of intermediate learner grammars. A broad range of empirical data is therefore taken into consideration (e.g., Schwartz 1992, calling for the comparison of acquisition sequences observed in child and adult second language acquisition).

---

3.   It is important to stress that the Critical Period Hypothesis has also been applied to domains of analysis beyond those covered by UG.

Recently, a growing body of evidence, challenging the Critical Period Hypothesis, comes from both data sources (end state and process data). There are currently three main counterarguments under discussion:

1. The slope of the age function (ultimate attainment in relation to different ages of onset (AoAs)) suggests a rather continuous decrement, decreasing at AoAs both before and after maturation where no decline is predicted by the Critical Period Hypothesis (Bialystok 2002; Birdsong 2005a).

2. The predictions of the Critical Period Hypothesis for L2A are most directly addressed by ultimate attainment data from early and late L2 learners and their comparison to native speakers. This comparison is not always a straightforward one, however. There are basically two problems. (i) 'Reaching the native speaker norm' can mean different things. It can mean that a learners' language is indistinguishable from that of native speakers in that no deviations in comprehension or production can be detected in everyday language use. Some researchers maintain, however, that 'real' native-likeness can only be tested in challenging judgment tests in experimental situations where speakers cannot hide subtle traits of non-native behavior through the avoidance of certain features (e.g., Hyltenstam & Abrahamsson 2003).[4] (ii) There is the more fundamental problem that comparing second language speakers to whichever conceptualization of the native speaker norm always means comparing bilingual to monolingual speakers, a situation in which monolingual nativelikeness is not to be expected (Grosjean 1992; Cook 2002) – particularly when it comes to online measures of speech processing (Birdsong 2005b).

3. Claims supporting maturational accounts are mostly based on group comparisons. It has been possible, however, to identify individual adult learners whose ultimate attainment in one or many domains falls into the native speaker range (e.g., Bongaerts 1999; Marinova-Todd 2003; VanBoxtel 2005). Although some researchers maintain that nativelike proficiency is never attested across the board (Hyltenstam & Abrahamsson 2003; Long 2005), every target language property investigated to date has been found to be learnable by at least some adult learners, which has led Birdsong to propose the Universal Learnability Hypothesis, stating that "there is no task which all sampled subjects fail to perform at native levels" (Birdsong 2005b: 182).

None of these counterarguments disavows the existence of age effects. Taken together, however, they indicate that we are not dealing with a sharply bounded interval in human development that is followed by a biologically determined in-

---

4.   See Birdsong (2005c) for a critical discussion of the nativelikeness criterion.

capacity to attain native like levels of proficiency in a second language. Other age-related factors must be at work.

In addition or as an alternative to maturational constraints, the following learner properties have been claimed to be responsible for the observed differences in ultimate attainment: age-related types of motivation, general cognitive development, and the amount of prior language knowledge and use (L1 entrenchment), (see e.g., Singleton 2005). The idea of L1 entrenchment continuously increasing with age has played a particularly important role in work concerning the acquisition of phonology (Flege *et al.* 1995) and does so also in usage based approaches to the acquisition of morpho-syntactic properties of language (Tomasello 2003; Ellis 2008) which will be addressed in the following section.

Usage based approaches

In sharp contrast to the generative perspective, advocates of a usage-based theory of language acquisition (e.g., Tomasello 2003) start with the view that linguistic rules are meaningful constructions which have emerged through language use and are grammaticalized, or abstract, to varying degrees. "As opposed to conceiving linguistic rules as algebraic procedures for combining words and morphemes that do not themselves contribute to meaning, this approach conceives linguistic constructions as themselves meaningful linguistic symbols – since they are nothing other than the patterns in which meaningful linguistic symbols are used in communication" (Tomasello 2003:5). Domain general learning principles, such as associative learning, are sufficient to develop a knowledge system that is fine tuned in order to cope with the properties of L1.

The reason that many second language learners do not reach native-likeness in their second language lies in the observation that it is almost impossible to reorganize the system, such that it can cope equally economically with the properties of another language. Form-function mappings established during L1 acquisition and use bias the way in which speakers attend to new linguistic stimuli (MacWhinney 2001; Flege et al. 1995). Interference occurs because patterns and relations that were encoded earlier in time, inhibit the storage of new mappings. Based on a general learning theory, Ellis (2008) distinguishes between overshadowing ("the more a cue is already associated with an outcome, the less additional association that outcome can induce") and blocking ("learned inattention"). In this approach, the time course of learning is seen as an important factor. Overshadowing and blocking do not occur in simultaneous bilingual first language acquisition. In the case of two typologically different first languages cues are simultaneously associated with different outcomes, and no inattention is learned towards features that are important in either one of the two languages involved.

Evidence suggests that these principles do indeed play an important role in determining what is learned and what is typically not learned in untutored second language acquisition (see contributions in Hulstijn & Ellis 2005). But some questions remain, and they become particularly worrisome in relation to age effects. If "human statistical reasoning is bound by selective attention effects whereby informative cues are ignored as a result of overshadowing or blocking" (Ellis 2008:387) – then why are relatively competent L1 users in later childhood typically so good at second language acquisition in immersion situations?

In a recent case study involving three six to nine year old children Dimroth and Haberzettl (to appear) show that these learners are faster at acquiring verbal inflectional morphology in their second language German than young monolingual children acquiring the same language as their L1. These findings point to the possibility that L1 influence can be compensated by other factors, such as advanced general cognitive development, or experience in language acquisition. Unlike L1 learners, L2 learners can perform an experience guided search, and manage to analyze target categories without a detour via proto-grammatical categories,[5] e.g., when acquiring verbal morphology. On some level, L2 learners must "know" how to perform a distributional analysis, for example.

An explanation that relies on associative learning alone not only runs into problems when older L2 learning children outperform younger L1 learning children. It is also unclear how it can deal with the asymmetric patterns of acquisition typically attested in older learners. Unquestionably, L1 entrenchment increases over time, and the later in life an L2 is acquired, the more difficult it might be to overcome the L1 shaped processing mechanisms. Associative mechanisms, however, cannot explain why different features with similar surface properties and a similar distribution in the input are often acquired with varying success by one and the same learner. Older learners, in particular, seem to make choices that are not determined by statistical distribution of features in the input alone (see Section 3 below). This has to do with the fact that language acquisition is not an additive procedure, but involves a constant reorganization of smaller or larger parts of the learner language that is under construction. The selection of features that can be integrated at a given point in time depends on the specific interplay of forms and functions in the input *and* on the current structure of the communicative system the learner is developing (Benazzo 2003). These and similar points are taken to be essential by the Learner Varieties approach, which I will present next.

---

5.   Compare the proto-grammatical categories proposed by Bittner (2003) for L1 acquisition.

The learner varieties approach

Advocates of a learner variety approach (e.g., the contributions in Perdue 2000; Dimroth & Starren 2003; Hendriks 2005) maintain that the 'learning choices' made by untutored adult L2 learners are informed by principles specific to language and communication. This conclusion is based on the finding that learner languages[6] partly deviate from source *and* target language in systematic ways. Early untutored adult L2 learners have been found to develop a so-called Basic Variety (Klein & Perdue 1997), a learner language characterized by the absence of functional inflectional morphology and by a word order that is mainly based on semantic principles and principles of information structure.[7]

It is unlikely that this kind of learner language has emerged as a result of across the board application of learning principles based on probability distributions. The conceptualization of the language acquisition task that these adult learners entertained must have included the activation of principles of information linearization for communication (Levelt 1981; Perdue 2006), the finding and learning of items from the input that would be of maximal communicative use in simple but systematically structured utterance frames, and assumptions about the most functional integration in given discourse contexts. The passage through a learner variety with similar structures has not been reported for child L2 learners. Are there age-related learner properties explaining the capacity to construct a communication system that is dramatically reduced in complexity?

The choices that learners make not only allow for successful communication (within certain limits), they are also mainly systematic in nature. In other words, the question then is, how do adult learners decide what to learn if their 'mature' communicative needs push them to create simplified versions of their target language? Given that these learner languages partly exhibit properties that are not found in the input language, the adult capacity to construct simple but systematic communication systems must be intact. Klein (to appear) proposes distinguishing the following abilities or faculties that play a role in language acquisition:

A. The faculty to construct linguistic systems by pairing sounds with meanings and the ability to form complex expressions ("Construction Faculty")
B. The faculty to integrate this knowledge into the flow of ongoing information ("Communication Faculty")

---

6.   Such findings are mainly based on production data, but see Verhagen 2005 for a recent study involving comprehension measures.

7.   Learner varieties of the type described above are not necessarily permanent. For many adult L2 learners, the Basic Variety cannot be equated with the end state (about two thirds of the 40 adult immigrant learners studied by Klein & Perdue (1997) went beyond the Basic Variety during the observation period).

C.   The faculty to organize linguistic knowledge in such a way that the output is a
     perfect copy of the target language ("Copying Faculty")

Klein points out that age does not affect these language capacities in a uniform way.
"Adult second language learners maintain the ability to pair sounds or gestures
with meanings, and they maintain the ability to form complex expressions – at
least for a long time. But their ability – and perhaps their willingness – to do this
in exactly the same way as is done in the input, diminishes over time. (...) Age
appears to affect the Copying Faculty much more than the Construction Faculty."

     Nothing is said here about the Communication Faculty, but it is likely that
it is affected by age as well. As was discussed earlier, adults differ from children
in the amount of prior linguistic knowledge available. Depending on when exactly first contact to the L2 takes place, certain language properties might in fact
still be under development. One such property that is known to develop late in
L1 is pragmatic knowledge (Hendriks 2000; Watorek 2004), affecting the ability
to express how utterances are integrated into the flow of discourse. "The fact that
adults, in contrast with children, get the discourse functions right from the start
..." (Hendriks 2000: 394) points to a domain in which the amount of prior knowledge is still growing at an age when child L2 learners encounter a new system of
form-function mappings, whereas adults can rely on this knowledge, and appar-
ently do so when building basic learner varieties in an L2. I will come back to this
and related points in the final discussion (Section 4).

     The aim of this discussion was to show that the interpretation of age effects
and their relation to one or more of the age-related learner properties crucially
depend on how we conceptualize the task of untutored language acquisition. Only
three different views on the properties of the task were presented, furthermore in
a somewhat schematic way. Statistical learning and utterance construction based
on language specific principles (be they of the presumably grammar-specific or
more of the functional type) are not mutually exclusive, of course, it is rather a
question of relative weight. This presentation of the extreme ends might, however,
be a fruitful starting point for the description of potential age-related differences
between the learners of the empirical case study to which we will turn now.

The DaZ-AF[8] case study

In the DaZ-AF study, the untutored acquisition of German as a second language by two learners with Russian as a first language was documented for a period of one and a half years. This study is interesting in the current context for three reasons: (i) there is not only information on the end state but also on the process of L2A, since language development was longitudinally documented from early on in weekly intervals; (ii) the two learners who participated in the study were sisters whose overall learning circumstances were relatively comparable (given that we are dealing with a real-life situation), and (iii) there was a relatively small age difference, allowing insights of a more gradual type than comparisons of the more extreme ends (e.g., young children vs. adult learners).

Upon arrival in Germany the child learner NASTJA was 8,7 and the adolescent learner DASCHA 14;2 years old. Apart from three private lessons before leaving, neither of them had had contact with German before. Both lived with their Russian speaking mother, a scientist invited to the University of Cologne, and the family language, also for interactions between the siblings, continued to be Russian. Their acquisition of German was entirely untutored. German input was mainly provided through interactions at schools, and, to a lesser degree, with German speaking friends and playmates in the afternoons. The younger learner attended the 2nd grade of a German primary school and the older learner the 9th grade of a German comprehensive secondary school. The younger learner had had no prior contact with languages other than Russian, whereas the older learner had learned English for six years in a relatively formal setting in her Russian school, and instruction continued in her German school.

The participants' oral speech production was audio-recorded on a weekly basis (for approximately one hour/week), mainly in free conversation with adult or age-matched native interlocutors. The recordings started in the third week of the sisters' residence in Germany. They were transcribed in the CHAT format by a native speaker of German, and double-checked by another native speaker. Transcripts were then coded for selected morpho-syntactic properties, and analyzed using the CLAN tools (MacWhinney 2000). The resulting corpus consists of roughly 130 hours of transcribed and annotated speech and has been investigated with the help of the CLAN tools in a number of studies on the acquisition of different morpho-syntactic properties (Bast 2003; Dimroth 2008; Dimroth and Haberzettl, to appear; Pagonis 2007).

---

8. *Deutsch als Zweitsprache – Altersfaktor*; a study under the direction of Christine Dimroth and Ursula Stephany that was funded by the German Science Foundation (DFG) between 2000 and 2002. See Bast (2003) and Dimroth (2008) for details.

The learners' age-related properties

In Section 1 and 2 above, age-related learner properties that different approaches consider in addition or as an alternative to neurobiological changes were introduced. These are prior linguistic knowledge, motivation, and general cognitive development. I will briefly take them up in turn, and ask how they might be manifested in relation to the participants of the DaZ-AF study.

When discussing the impact of *prior linguistic knowledge* on second language acquisition, existing L1 knowledge is often treated as a monolith. During childhood, however, it is obvious that L1 knowledge is under development itself. This is reflected in the difficulty of distinguishing bilingual first language acquisition from successive second language acquisition (see Thoma & Tracy 2006). There is no consensus on when first language acquisition should be regarded as completed. The answer depends at least partly on the selection of target language properties that are viewed as crucial (reflected in notions such as "core grammar").[9] It is quite likely that differences would be found in the participants' L1 lexicon and probably also in any complex and non-frequent syntactic construction. The greatest differences between L1 users of that age range are, however, to be expected in the late-learned domain of information structure and context integration. A large-scale cross-linguistic project on L1 development found clear differences between 7- and 10 year olds in this respect (Watorek 2004), and other authors point out that even 14 year olds have often not yet fully acquired adult-like ways of information organization in L1 discourse (Carroll 2002). The more advanced the acquisition of these language-specific organizational principles is in L1, the harder it becomes to reorganize them according to the preferences of an L2 (Carroll & Lambert 2003).

A learner can also have prior linguistic knowledge of a language other than the native language. The likelihood of there being knowledge of more than just one prior language also increases with age. The 14-year old learner in our study had learned English at school before coming to Germany and continued to do so later on. Whether this has positive or negative effects on the acquisition of another L2 is in principle as difficult to answer as when there is only one prior language.[10] As with all transfer phenomena it also depends on the (perceived) typological differences between the languages (Kellerman 1983). However, a general advantage might lie in the fact that speakers of more than one prior language know that sound-to-meaning mappings are arbitrary in most cases.

---

9.   It is even more difficult to quantify L1 entrenchment i.e., to independently assess how deep-rooted certain L1 related processing routines are, when comparing an 8 year old to a 14 year old learner.

10.   Work on L3 acquisition explicitly taking the role of the L2 into account is still in its infancy; but see Cenoz et al. 2001.

Concerning *motivation*, anecdotal remarks aside, there is no independent evidence about the young learners in the DaZ-AF study. Based on a thorough literature review, Pagonis (2007) shows, however, that the need for social *and* linguistic integration is intrinsically linked to the process of identity construction during childhood and therefore more than accidentally related to age. Whereas children seek to develop linguistic identification alongside social identification, this typically ceases to be the case in older learners with more complete identity formation (Erikson 1980; Schumann 1997). It has even been proposed that adult learners may maintain certain deviant properties in order to protect an identity that has been developed in a different linguistic environment (Schumann 1975). We can therefore assume that the adolescent learner in our case study is more advanced in the construction of a stable identity than the child learner, and that the necessity and the disposition to social and linguistic assimilation and identification with a new group has decreased as a consequence. From occasional comments of both learners during data collection it is also clear that the older learner was much more aware of the fact that the family's residence in the target language community was most likely restricted to one and a half years.

Another critical parameter that changes during the development from toddler to adult is the state of *cognitive development*. Newport (1990) assumes that age-related differences in perception and memory capacity have consequences for language processing and the representations of input properties. In particular, while adult learners are able to store complex forms from the input, children's internal data base will rather consist of smaller pieces. Interestingly, this is not seen as a disadvantage for language acquisition. Newport (1990, 1991) proposes the *Less-is-More* Hypothesis which assumes that the contrary is actually the case: "the cognitive limitations of the young child during the time of language learning may (…) provide a computational advantage for the acquisition of language, and (…) the less limited cognitive abilities of the older child and the adult may provide a computational disadvantage for the acquisition of language" (Newport 1991: 125).

Dimroth and Haberzettl (to appear) show, however, that 6–8 year old second language learners of German (with L1 Russian) are faster in acquiring verbal inflectional morphology than young monolingual children acquiring the same language. Given that the *Less-is-More* Hypothesis explicitly targets the acquisition of inflectional morphology, it is unlikely that a bigger memory capacity is a hindrance for successful language acquisition. Small children are very conservative language learners (Tomasello 2003), and it is plausible that older learners with more developed cognitive capacities need less time to assemble a stock of stored exemplars on the basis of which they can generalize. The problem is that the advanced cognitive development of older learners is not easily distinguished from their greater linguistic experience. This is true for memory development in general: "…development of basic memory abilities is a result of the dynamic interaction between biological and experiential factors that vary over time" (Schneider 2002: 242).

Summing up, the most important age-related differences between the two learners in that study concern:

i.   the amount of prior L1 knowledge (in particular in the in late-learned domain of information structure and context integration; less clear with respect to possible effects of L1 entrenchment);
ii. presence vs. absence of an earlier L2; and
iii. a child- vs. adolescent-type of motivation for linguistic integration and adaptation.

Research questions

When discussing the question of which age-related properties of learners are most responsible for non-native outcomes in second language acquisition, researchers do not necessarily assume that all linguistic subsystems are equally affected by age. It is generally assumed, for example, that there is no age-related decrease in the capacity of lexical acquisition. But also within grammar, more fine-grained distinctions have been proposed. Schwartz (2003: 46) hypothesizes that "...children and adults can both acquire (certain) aspects of L2 syntax, but it is generally the children who have an easier task of acquiring inflectional morphology." Within the domain of inflectional morphology, Birdsong and Flege (2001: 124) assume that "the Rule-based or regular items (...) are less affected by increasing age of arrival than are the irregular items (Lexicals)."

In order to address the hypotheses, that (a) age-related differences affect inflectional morphology more than syntax, and (b) irregular items are more strongly affected than regular ones, the following target language properties[11] have been selected from the available results on the DaZ-AF project (see work by Bast 2003; Dimroth 2008; Dimroth & Haberzettl to appear; and Pagonis 2007):

–   Syntax: word order in declarative main clauses (verb raising over negation and verb second / inversion)
–   Inflectional morphology: Subject-verb agreement, tense, noun plural, adjective-noun agreement.

In the following, I will briefly describe the relevant target language properties, try to characterize the corresponding learning tasks in terms of formal complexity and

---

11.   These represent but a subset of domains investigated on the basis of the DaZ-AF data. See for example the findings on the acquisition of gender and case in Bast (2003), or the findings on lexical development in Pagonis (2007).

functional value, and summarize the findings in a very scetchy way. For a complete demonstration of the empirical evidence, including exact indications of the data sample underlying a given investigation and the results of quantitative data analysis, the reader is referred to the original studies indicated at the beginning of every section. A detailed description of the relevant properties of the learners' L1 (Russian) can also be found there.

Findings

Word order[12]

Whereas Russian is considered a free word order language, in German declarative main clauses, finite verbs appear in second position ('verb second', V2) whereas nonfinite verbs (infinitives, participles) appear at the end. If the sentence initial position is filled by an adverbial, subject and finite verb are inverted (1). Negation follows the finite verb and precedes the non-finite verb as in (2) or stays behind if the lexical verb is finite and thus is raised to second position (3).

(1)   *Heute habe ich Marianne getroffen.*
      Today have-1st-sg I Marianne met
      'Today I met M.'

(2)   *Heute habe ich Marianne nicht getroffen*
      Today have I M. not met
      'Today I didn't meet M.'

(3)   *Heute treffe ich Marianne nicht.*
      Today meet-1st-sg I M. not
      'Today I won't meet M.'

Both learners start out with a basic word order that is similar to the one that was also attested in the early productions of untutored adult learners ('Basic Variety'; see Klein & Perdue 1997): SVO with as many topical constituents preceding the verb as context integration requires (4), (5). As in the Basic Variety, negation precedes it's domain of application, i.e., either precedes lexical verbs (6) or follows lexically empty finite verbs (7), when they first appear.

(4)   *morgen wir habt sechs stunde* (D-01)[13] tomorrow we have six lessons

(5)   *in winter mama in russland kaufen äpfel* (N-03) in winter mummy in Russia buy apples

---

12.   See Dimroth (2008) and Pagonis (2007) for details.

13.   The indications in brackets refer to the months of target language contact, e.g. 'D-01' = 'dascha, 1st month'.

(6)   *er nicht kauf steine* (N-01) he not buy stones

(7)   *ich bin nicht evangelisch* (D-01) I am not protestant

The younger learner NASTJA quickly gives up preverbal negation (like (6)), and only produces target like structures (8), (9). Her older sister on the other hand uses post verbal negation only in copular constructions like (7) or in combination with other light verbs (e.g. modals). This strategy might be influenced by her prior knowledge of English (see Dimroth 2008, for discussion). In the next step, she acquires the 'Perfekt', an analytic construction involving the auxiliary *haben* (have) and a past participle (10). Post verbal negation with lexical verbs (11) occurs only after the acquisition of 'Perfekt'. This corresponds to the order of acquisition found in adult learners where productive verb raising over negation occurs only after the acquisition of non-modal auxiliaries (Becker 2005; Parodi 2000; Verhagen 2005). These isolated carriers of finiteness seem to be particularly well suited to help learners understand the relation between both verbal positions (Jordens & Dimroth 2006). It is the more perplexing that the younger learner shows a different order of acquisition and produces post-finite negation before using auxiliaries (8), (9).

(8)   *heute ich geht nicht* (N-02)
today I go not
'today I don't go'

(9)   *sie kauft nicht torte* (N-02)
she buys not torte
'she doesn't buy tortes'

(10) *in landhaus sie hat mäuse und auch frosch gefresst* (D-05)
in cottage she has mice and also frogs eaten

(11) *er spricht nicht (...) richtig wie deutscher* (D-05)
he speaks not (...) really like German
'he doesn't really speak like a German'

A short time later, both learners start to use target-like subject-verb inversion (12), (13) in free variation with the earlier V3 structures (14), (15). During the second half of the observation period the younger learner NASTJA restricts the use of the ungrammatical V3 structures to occurrences of the adverbial *dann* (then) in first position (14), and then ceases to use them all together. The older learner DASCHA continues to use both, inversion and V3 until the end of the observation period, with a tendency to use inversion with auxiliaries (13) and V3 with lexical verbs (15).

(12) *jetzt müssen wir ein bisschen platz   haben* (N-06)
now must we a bit   place have
'now we must have a little more room'

(13) *alle juli habe wir viel   geschwimmen* (D-09)
      all july have we much swum
      'during the entire month of July we were swimming a lot'

(14) *dann die frau R. nehmt den bären* (N-09)
      then Mrs. R.   takes the bear

(15) *in Russland ich habe einen couputer mit   spiele* (D-11)
      in Russia   I · have a   computer with games

Summing up, we have attested different orders of acquisition with verb raising, where the younger learner seems to have skipped logical intermediate steps
towards the acquisition of syntactic finiteness that adult learners, and also her
older sister, pass through with great regularity (Dimroth 2008, see also Haberzettl
2005: 125).[14] These differences in the acquisition process did not have consequences for the end state at which both learners' verb raising is indistinguishable
from the target language. At the same time there is a clear difference in the use of
inversion/V3 in that the younger learner used only the target adequate V2 order
at the end state, whereas there is a lot of variation in the learner language of her
older sister.

It is unclear, however, if we are dealing with differences in rate or ultimate
attainment which is normally operationalized as length of residence of at least
five years (Birdsong 2004). It is not excluded that DASHA would have acquired the
relevant structures had she had more time. However we do not even observe a re-
striction to certain (short) adverbials. Ungrammatical V3 utterances are used with
heavy prepositional phrases (15) up to the end. Inversion and V3 occur in free
variation, sometimes even with the same adverbial (Pagonis 2007).

What can we conclude with respect to the claim that there are only relatively
mild effects of age on syntax (Schwartz 2003)? There are similarities but also telling
differences in the acquisition of word order. With both learners, word order is
used at the outset for a one-to-one signaling of information structure and scope
relations. Both learners are reluctant to place negation to the right of lexical verbs,
i.e., in a position where it does not precede the elements in its scope. Whereas the
younger learner switches to post verbal negation very early on, the older learner
overcomes this problem only after the acquisition of auxiliaries has contributed to
the establishment of the relation between finite and nonfinite verb positions. The
order of acquisition of verb raising and auxiliaries differs, but ultimate attainment
in this domain does not, which is predicted by the hypothesis.

This is different for the acquisition of verb second (V2). As with verb raising, both learners are oscillating for a while between target language syntax and

---

14. Most authors seem to assume that child and adult L2 learners do not show different orders
of acquisition (Hyltenstam & Abrahamson 2003; Singleton & Ryan 2004).

the straightforward signaling of information structure. Topical elements tend to occur in initial position, which results in ungrammatical V3 or V4 structures whenever there is more than one of them. Whereas target language syntax wins in the younger learner, the V2 property of German does not become obligatory in the learner language of the older learner, even though it is a frequently instantiated core property of German word order.

As we have just seen, word order at the outset was quite similar to what has been found for untutored adult learners' Basic Variety. This is different in the domain of inflectional morphology. Whereas nouns, verbs, and adjectives are not systematically inflected in the Basic Variety (Klein & Perdue 1997), the young learners investigated in the present study are concerned with inflectional morphology from early on. This does of course not mean that the forms they use always correspond to the target like use, but in the majority of investigated domains, there is no phase in which inflection was totally ignored.

Inflectional Morphology

In the domain of inflectional morphology, findings for the acquisition of the following phenomena will be reported: subject-verb agreement, tense, noun plural, and adjective declension. According to the hypotheses introduced in 3.2 we are not only interested in finding out if the differences between the learners in the domain of inflectional morphology are greater than in syntax – we also want to know if irregular items are affected in a particular way.

Subject-verg agreement and tense:[15] From the first recordings onwards, both learners exploit the target language repertoire of finite present tense forms (one out of four suffixes covering the six person/number constellations) – these however do not always occur in the right contexts. Vowel changes are not always realized (e.g., **esst* instead of *isst* (eats)). Both learners learn to systematically distinguish between different person and number markings, and later tense forms, in the same order (1. and 3. singular > 2. singular > 1. and 3. plural). After a short phase of confusion in which the 3rd person singular suffix -*t* is used as a past tense marker for all person-number contexts, the preterit of a few (mainly irregular) light verbs occurs (*haben* (have), *sein* (be), *wollen* (want)), then the 'Perfekt' (auxiliary plus past participle) is acquired, and then the preterit is used with all sorts of lexical verbs (more frequently by the younger than by the older learner). Overgeneralizations of the regular (weak) inflections occur in both learners, too. At the end of the observation period, both learners use regular inflections in a target-like manner.

---

15.   See Dimroth (2008) and Pagonis (2007) for detailed studies on the acquisition of verbal inflection by the DaZ-AF learners.

In the younger learner, however, the lexical exceptions are target-like as well – this is not the case for her older sister who continues to regularize strong verbs in the present tense paradigm (*schlaft (sleeps), *fahrt (drives)), the preterit (*beginnte (began), *schreibte (wrote)), or the past participle (*gesitzt (sat), *gelest (read)).

Noun plural:[16] The plural is marked in the target language with one out of five allomorphs most of which can be combined with a vowel change (Umlaut): *Haus – Häus-er* (house – houses) as opposed to *Bild – Bild-er* (picture – pictures). The frequency and productivity of these plural suffixes differ dramatically. The assignment is to a certain degree arbitrary (*Tor – Tor-e* (gate-gates), but *Ohr – Ohr-en* (ear-ears)). Several sets of rules have been proposed (based on gender and morphophonology of the singular nouns) that cover the majority of basic nouns (see Wegener 1994, for a discussion), but rely on other nominal properties (e.g., gender) that are still under development in learner language.[17]

Both learners use different plural suffixes from early on. After three months of residence nearly all target language plural suffixes are attested – many more than were found in Spanish and Italian adult immigrants after several years (HDP, 1977), as Bast (2003) points out. Whenever a plural target form is unknown, the younger learner tends to replace it with the singular, whereas the older learner creates new plural forms through overgeneralization of the most frequent suffixes (Bast 2003:68). In the course of further development, both learners holistically store low frequent forms and overgeneralize the frequent endings. The older learner also relies on knowledge from English (overextension of -s plural on German-English cognates, e.g., *schuh-s, *kanal-s) and presumably Russian (Bast 2003) and tends to leave out plural marking where it is maximally redundant, e.g., following quantifying expressions (e.g., *viele Oktave (many octave)). At the end of the observation period the younger learner's plural marking does not differ from the target language, whereas the older learner still overgeneralizes frequent allomorphs to some extent.

Declension of attributive adjectives:[18] Adjectival inflection in German is totally regular. Adjectives agree with number, gender, and case of the head noun. In addition, the presence and type of the accompanying determiner leads to the choice of one out of three declension types. The relevant inflectional paradigms are furthermore characterized by a high amount of syncretism (5 suffixes cover 72 constellations: gender (3) × case (4) × number (2) × declension type (3)).

---

16.   See Bast (2003) for details.

17.   See Köpcke (1998) for a proposal that is based on abstract schemas instead of rules.

18.   See Pagonis (2007) for details.

Given the complexity of the learning task, it is clear that the learners are in a hopeless position – at least at the beginning of the acquisition process. But adjectives are communicatively important and both learners start using them early, albeit choosing radically different strategies with respect to inflection. The younger learner produces many different inflected forms in free variation (*ein groß-en klavier* (a big piano), *eine weiß-es ring* (a white ring), *ein braun-e ring* (a brown ring)), thereby employing four out of five target suffixes. The older learner on the other hand uses only stem forms[19] which precede the nouns without a determiner (*schwarz haar* (black hair), *groß pause* (long break), *klein straße* (small street), *gut foto* (nice foto), *gelb zähne* (yellow teeth)). Shortly after, this strategy is replaced by the tendency to have all attributive adjectives end in -e which is used in up to 90% of all cases (Pagonis 2007) and continues up to the end of the observation period.[20]

After the first stage that was characterized by a rich variety of forms without functions, the younger learner soon reaches a stage of systematic use during which stable, but sometimes target deviant form-function mappings evolve. In the last months of recordings all adjectives are inflected in a target-like manner. Whereas the younger learner starts with unconstrained imitation of forms and ends up with target like command of the complex but regular inflection paradigms, the older learner leaves out suffixes with inscrutable functions altogether and finally goes for a phonologically adapted minimal version (bysyllabic with *schwa*-ending).

In comparison with adult learners, both learners are relatively successful in the acquisition of inflectional morphology. However, overall we can maintain that the younger learner's end state is clearly more target-like. Her strategy to imitate unanalyzed input forms from early on seems to be more promising than her older sister's tendency to create new forms where needed or leave out unanalyzed material. Given the older learners problems with basic syntactic rules, it is however, hard to judge in an overall fashion if inflectional morphology is more affected by age than syntax (Schwartz 2003). The distinction proposed by Birdsong and Flege (2001) is clearly confirmed for the regularization of lexical exceptions (strong verbs) by the older learner. This is similar for the noun plurals, even though it is somewhat difficult to distinguish between regular and irregular in this domain. Adjective declension on the other hand, is totally regular and is still not acquired by the older learner.

Summing up, we can conclude that the generalization quoted in the beginning of this paper "the younger – the better" is confirmed by the learners whose

---

19.   These forms occur in the input in the function of predicative adjectives.

20.   The older learner's difficulties concerning the acquisition of adjectival inflection have to be seen in connection to her very limited knowledge of the German gender system (Bast 2003).

language acquisition was investigated in the present case study. The results of the younger learner clearly point in the direction of a total assimilation to the target language, whereas this is not the case for the older learner. However, the findings for the older learner do not correspond to the Basic Variety attested in beginning adult learners either. Even in the early stages of acquisition we did not observe a radical reduction to the minimally necessary, neither in syntax nor in inflectional morphology. This is an interesting finding as such – it is however unclear how much of this difference is due to the fact that the adult learners who developed the Basic Variety had typically much less access to the target language than the child and the adolescent learner presented above.

Conclusions

Given the multitude of factors influencing natural language acquisition, it is impossible to establish a causal link between the different processes and end states that were found for the L2 learners of our case study and the age-related factors discussed in the beginning of this paper. However, in order to foster a discussion of what the most likely candidates are, it seems promising to ask what the differences are, on a more general level, between those target language properties that both learners acquired, and those that only the younger learner acquired. Without postulating a direct causal relation, we will at least see how these relate to the age-related differences between the two learners that were established in Section 3.1. These are:

i.   the amount of prior L1 knowledge (in particular in the in late-learned domain of information structure and context integration; less clear with respect to possible effects of L1 entrenchment);
ii. presence vs. absence of an earlier L2; and
iii. a child- vs. adolescent-type of motivation for linguistic integration and adaptation.

With respect to the acquisition of the word order regularities of German, the findings of the DaZ-AF study have revealed a number of similarities but also some telling differences between the two learners. Concerning verb placement, both learners start out with the same (SVO) word order, but then show different orders of acquisition of verb raising over negation (first in the younger learner) and auxiliaries (first in the older learner, which conforms to the order attested in adult learners). Whereas both finally reach the same target-like end state in that finite verbs are always raised over negation, only the younger learner also acquires the V2 rule. Development and entrenchment of prior L1 knowledge do not seem to be likely candidates for the explanation of these differences. The older learner's frequent use of light verbs in negation contexts could be due to an influence of the older learners earlier L2 (the English *do*-support). This need not be the case, however, since a similar strategy (only light verbs raise over negation, lexical verbs stay in base position) has also been attested in adult learners with a variety of first languages, including romance languages (Parodi 2000) that do not have properties similar to the English *do*-support.

Overall it seems as if the older learner sticks to a 1:1 mapping between word order and information structure for a longer time than the younger learner (verb raising) or even until the end of the observation period (frequent V3 instead of V2 structures). Regarding the functional side of the latter phenomenon, it becomes clear that the learner prefers to avoid misunderstandings by fronting as many (topical) constituents as information structure requires. Whereas V1 would signal a question, V3 is not associated with grammatical meaning in the target language and is therefore readily interpreted by native speakers as a learner variant of the target-adequate V2 pattern. The older learner thus opts for a target-deviant but communicatively valid strategy. This is at least compatible with the assumptions of a more instrumental type of motivation aiming at the development of a functioning communication system rather than at linguistic adaptation to target language properties with less communicative value.

Broadly summing up the differences found in inflectional morphology, we can maintain that the acquisitional tasks that were investigated fall into two distinct groups. The acquisition of verb morphology (tense as well as S-V agreement) and noun plurals is characterized by the early occurrence of inflected forms, which do however not always occur in the target contexts. In the course of further development their use approaches the target language, whereby the older learner seems to make stronger use of prior linguistic knowledge (L1 Russian and L2 English), in particular for plural formation. There are differences at the end state, in particular concerning irregular forms (strong verbs, infrequent noun plurals) which the older learner tends to regularize. It is nevertheless true for verb inflection as well as noun plural that the similarities in the development of both learners clearly outweigh the differences. This becomes particularly clear when comparing the learners with what is known from the early stages of untutored second language acquisition in adults: none of the learners investigated here develop a Basic Variety (Klein & Perdue 1997).

Big differences between the learners are only found in the acquisition of adjective declension, which is characterized by a high degree of syncretism and a complex dependency of presence and type of different determiners. Whereas the younger learner masters this target language property at the end of the observation period, the older learner continues to radically simplify it.

Can the age-related differences between the two learners explain some of these findings? Differences in prior language knowledge (see (i) and (ii) above) might account for the fact that transfer from Russian (more entrenchment?) and English seems to have played a more important role in the older than in the younger learner's development.[21]

In order to discuss the possible impact of an age-related type of motivation for linguistic integration and adaptation, we must take the formal complexity and the functional value of the properties studied into account. Only the communicatively relevant properties would also be predicted to be acquired by an older learner with a presumably more instrumental motivation. This accounts quite well for the findings that group verb morphology and noun plural together (only small differences between the learners), as opposed to adjective-noun agreement (acquired only by the younger learner). In comparison to verbal inflection and noun plural the communicative usefulness of the latter feature is relatively limited, since the relation between adjective and modified noun is marked through adjacency in all cases occurring in the corpus. The early phases of the acquisition process are of particular interest here. The older learner seems to have concluded from early on that the attempt to copy these formal markings is not worthwhile, while the younger learner copies forms from the input that do not yet have a discernable function in her learner variety.

The difficulty of this approach lies in the fact that both cognitive costs and communicative benefits have to be taken into account. When considered as a learning target in relation to the system as a whole, each of the four morphological inflection systems studied here has a very specific mixture of properties. Subject-verb (S-V) agreement and the declension of attributive adjectives mainly signal grammatical relations, tense and noun plural signal semantic categories, both of which can however be replaced by more informative lexical means (temporal adverbials and quantifiers). While it is relatively simple to figure out that finite verbs agree with person and number of the subject, it is much harder to understand what determines adjectival inflection. Whereas the assignment of plural marking suffixes (one out of eight allomorphemic variants) is partly arbitrary, adjectival inflection is totally regular but characterized by a high amount of syncretism (with 5 suffixes covering 72 constellations). Inflection paradigms in S-V agreement and tense are regular, but there is an important number of lexical exceptions (so-called strong verbs) with irregular inflection and/or vowel changes.

The idea that second language learners are to some extent performing a cost-benefit analysis on the basis of measures such as complexity and communicative value is also suggested by some formulations in Ellis (2008), for instance when

---

21. Concerning the acquisition of subject-verb agreement, where a detailed comparison between L2-learning children and young first language learners of German was carried out (see Dimroth & Haberzettl, to appear), the findings indicate, however, that the presence of prior linguistic knowledge as such did not hamper, but rather speed up the acquisition process.

it is claimed about the acquisition of the article system that "the fuzziness and complexity of these mappings surely goes a long way to making ESL article acquisition so difficult" (p. 377) or when it is stated that "…low salience cues whose redundancy denies them any more than low outcome importance (…) may never become integrated into a consolidated construction" (p. 379).[22]

Ellis presents these problems in an age neutral fashion as applying to L2 but not to L1 learners. I think however that there might be an age factor right here in that older learners differ from children in their ability to judge complexity and usefulness and make informed choices. This kind of cost-benefit calculation requires more than Bates and MacWhinney's (1989) computation of "cue cost" which rather relates to the amount of energy needed for speech processing under different conditions (e.g., computing subject-verb agreement in adjacent as opposed to distant positions). Making informed choices as to what can be neglected to reduce the acquisition burden – and most older learners do not make random, but clever choices – requires a deeper understanding of the functioning of language and communication than younger children seem to have.

Properties of the target language grammar which are frequent, salient and communicatively relevant, but at the same time not too complex and not redundant are going to be acquired at all ages. However, with respect to properties which are non-frequent, difficult to perceive, complex on the form side and which at the same time encode redundant or communicatively irrelevant information, even small age differences can have consequences for successful acquisition. Possibilities for non-target like acquisition range from the omission of certain features to their regularization or their target-deviant interpretation. Which of these possibilities applies depends again to a large degree on the structure of the target language and the functioning of the relevant learner variety at any given point in time.

In untutored adult beginners, highly informative though less frequent cues (e.g., temporal adverbials) regularly win out against frequent but less informative cues (e.g., verbal inflections). Their prior linguistic knowledge allows adults to make an informed choice between the two competing target language forms: in contrast to small children, adult learners know that temporal adverbials are much more precise and unambiguous in signaling temporal relations than verbal morphology, and they also know how to build adverbials into their learner variety such that they can best exploit their communicative potential. Starren (2001) shows how the scope of temporal adverbials changes as a consequence of the way they are integrated in learner utterances at different stages of grammaticalization. But nobody has told those adult learners that they can manipulate two different tem-

---

22. 'Outcome importance' is a measure of the degree to which the interpretation of a construction contributes to the interpretation of a message (Ellis 2008).

poral parameters by using temporal adverbials in different positions. Where does this knowledge come from?

It has been argued that adult second language learners can rely on an over-all simplified version of L1 (Corder 1978) and transfer what they find to be most language-neutral: "Now language neutral then represents what is shared by the most languages, and our learners showed a remarkable degree of agreement in this respect." (Perdue 2006: 860). If that is true, the age question is whether adult L2 learners differ from – at least younger – children in the availability of intuitions about such language neutral organizing principles. What is at issue here are very general principles of utterance structure, relating for example to the organization of information primitives such as topic and comment and their relation to seman-tic scope. This is what the learners investigated by Starren (2001) exploit for the integration of temporal adverbials and this is also why native speakers tend to un-derstand what learners mean. The idea that older learners seem to be more capable of exploiting such language neutral linguistic knowledge might again be connected with their more fully-fledged communication faculty, understood as the capacity to integrate utterances in context that develops over time (see the discussion in 2.3 above).

Knowledge about language and communication changes radically during the development from young children up to young adults, i.e., from the time when hu-mans begin to be first language learners to when they are competent first language users in all domains. During this time a stock of L1 specific knowledge about words and principles guiding their combination is built up. Learners are increasingly able to adapt the form of their utterances to the larger context, be it in conversation with interlocutors or when organizing larger amounts of information according to the regularities and characteristics of certain discourse types.

In the course of this development, learners gain experience with the kinds of analyses that are important for language learning and experience with general principles of information organization. Both can be very useful in the early stages of second language learning and use. Further acquisition is not directly hindered by the application of language neutral principles, but it may be less strongly pur-sued, as long as learners find confirmation for the operation of such principles in the input and as long as they are – at least relatively – communicatively successful with such a strategy.

References

Bast, C. 2003. Der Altersfaktor im Zweitspracherwerb. Die Entwicklung der grammatischen Kategorien Numerus, Genus und Kasus in der Nominalphrase im ungesteuerten Zweitspracherwerb des Deutschen bei russischen Lernerinnen. PhD dissertation, University of Cologne. (http://kups.ub.uni-koeln.de).

Bates, E. & MacWhinney, B. 1989. Functionalism and the Competition Model. In *The Crosslinguistic Study of Sentence Processing*, E. Bates & B. MacWhinney (eds), 3–73. Cambridge: CUP.

Becker, A. 2005. The semantic knowledge base for the acquisition of negation and the acquisition of finiteness. In *The Structure of Learner Varieties*, H. Hendriks (ed.), 263–314. Berlin: De Gruyter.

Benazzo, S. 2003. The interaction between verb morphology and temporal adverbs of contrast. In *Information Structure and the Dynamics of Language Acquisition*, C. Dimroth & M. Starren (eds), 187–210. Amsterdam: John Benjamins.

Bialystok, E. 2002. On the reliability of robustness: A reply to DeKeyser. *Studies in Second Language Acquisition* 24: 481–488.

Birdsong, D. 2004. Second language acquisition and ultimate attainment. In *The Handbook of Applied Linguistics*, A. Davies & C. Elder (eds), 82–105. London: Blackwell.

Birdsong, D. 2005a. Interpreting age effects in second language acquisition. In *The Handbook of Bilingualism: Psycholinguistic Perspectives*, J. Kroll & A. de Groot (eds), 109–127. Oxford: OUP.

Birdsong, D. 2005b. Why not fossilization. In *Studies of Fossilization in Second Language Acquisition*, Z. H. Hahn & T. Odlin (eds), 173–188. Clevedon: Multilingual Matters.

Birdsong, D. 2005c. Nativelikeness and non-nativelikeness in L2A research. *International Review of Applied Linguistics* 43: 319–328.

Birdsong, D. & Flege, J. E. 2001. Regular-irregular dissociations in L2 acquisition of English morphology. In *Proceedings of the Boston University Conference on Language Development 25*, A. H.-J. Do, L. Domínguez & A. Johansen (eds), 123–132. Somerville MA: Cascadilla.

Bittner, D. 2003. The Emergence of verb inflection in two German-speaking children. In *Development of Verb Inflection in First Language Acquisition. A Cross-linguistic Perspective*, D. Bittner, W.U. Dressler & M. Kilani-Schoch (eds), 53–88. Berlin: De Gruyter.

Bley-Vroman, R. 1989. What is the logical problem of foreign language learning? In *Linguistic Perspectives on Second Language Acquisition*, S. Gass & J. Schachter (eds), 41–68. Cambridge: CUP.

Bongaerts, T. 1999. Ultimate attainment in foreign language pronunciation: The case of very advanced late foreign language learners. In *Second Language Acquisition and the Critical Period Hypothesis*, D. Birdsong (ed.), 133–159. Mahwah NJ: Lawrence Erlbaum Associates.

Carroll, M. & Lambert, M. 2003. Information structure in narratives and the role of grammaticised knowledge. A study of adult French and German learners of English. In *Information Structure and the Dynamics of Language Acquisition*, C. Dimroth & M. Starren (eds), 267–288. Amsterdam: John Benjamins.

Carroll, M. 2002. Information structure and the concept of a critical period in language acquisition. Paper presented at the Annual Meeting of the German Linguistics Society (Deutsche Gesellschaft für Sprachwissenschaft), Mannheim.

Cenoz, J., Hufeisen, B. & Jessner, U. (eds). 2001. *Cross-linguistic Influence in Third Language Acquisition*. Clevedon: Multilingual Matters.

Cook, V. 2002. Background to the L2 User. In *Portraits of the L2 User*, V. Cook (ed.), 1–29. Clevedon: Multilingual Matters.

Corder, S. P. 1978. 'Simple codes' and the source of the second language learner's initial heuristic hypothesis. *Studies in Second Language Acquisition* 1: 1–10.

Dimroth, C. & Starren, M. (eds). 2003. *Information Structure and the Dynamics of Language Acquisition*. Amsterdam: John Benjamins.

Dimroth, C. 2008. Age effects on the process of L2 acquisition? Evidence from the acquisition of negation and finiteness in L2 German. *Language Learning* 58: 117–150.

Dimroth, C. & Haberzettl, S. To appear. The older the better, or more is more: Language acquisition in children. In *The Age Factor and the End State of Language Acquisition*, S. Haberzettl (ed.). Berlin: De Gruyter.

Ellis, N. 2008. Usage-based and form-focused language acquisition: The associative learning of constructions, learned-attention, and the limited L2 end state. In *Handbook of Cognitive Linguistics and Second Language Acquisition*, P. Robinson & N. Ellis (eds), 372–405. New York NY: Routledge.

Erikson, E. H. 1980 [1959]. *Identity and the Life Cycle*. New York NY: Norton.

Flege, J. E., Munro, M. J. & MacKay, R. A. 1995. Effects of age of second-language learning on the production of English consonants. *Speech Communication* 16: 1–26.

Grosjean, F. 1992. *Life with Two Languages*. Cambridge MA: Harvard University Press.

Haberzettl, S. 2005. *Der Erwerb der Verbstellungsregeln in der Zweitsprache Deutsch durch Kinder mit russischer und türkischer Muttersprache*. Tübingen: Niemeyer.

Hendriks, H. 2000. The acquisition of topic marking in L1 Chinese and L1 and L2 French. *Studies in Second Language Acquisition* 22: 69–397.

Hendriks, H. (ed.). 2005. *The Structure of Learner Varieties*. Berlin: De Gruyter.

Hulstijn, J. H., & Ellis, R. (eds). 2005. Implicit and explicit second-language learning. *Studies in Second Language Acquisition* 27.

Hyltenstam, K. & Abrahamson, N. 2003. Maturational Constraints in SLA. In *The Handbook of Second Language Acquisition*, C. J. Doughty & M. Long (eds), 539–588. Oxford: Blackwell.

Jordens, P. & Dimroth, C. 2006. Finiteness in children and adults learning Dutch. In *The Acquisition of Verb Grammar and Verb Arguments*, D. Bittner & N. Gagarina (eds), 173–200. Dordrecht: Kluwer.

Kaltenbacher, E. & Klages, H. 2006. Sprachprofil und Sprachförderung bei Vorschulkindern mit Migrationshintergrund. In *Kinder mit Migrationshintergrund. Spracherwerb und Fördermöglichkeiten*, B. Ahrenholz (ed.), 80–97. Freiburg: Fillibach.

Kellerman, E. 1983. Now you see it, now you don't. In *Language Transfer in Language Learning*, S. Gass & L. Selinker (eds), 112–134. Rowley MA: Newbury House.

Klein, W. To appear. Finiteness, Universal Grammar and the Language Faculty. In *Crosslinguistic Approaches to the Study of Language: Research in the Tradition of Dan Isaac Slobin*, J. Guo, E. Lieven, S. Ervin-Tripp, N. Budwig, S. Özçaliskan & K. Nakamura (eds). New York NY: Routledge.

Klein, W. & Perdue, C. 1997. The basic variety. Or: Couldn't natural languages be much simpler? *Second Language Research* 13: 310–347.

Köpcke, K.-M. 1998. The acquisition of plural marking in English and German revisited: Schemata versus rules. *Journal of Child Language* 25: 293–319.

Lenneberg, E. 1967. *Biological Foundations of Language*. New York NY: Wiley.

Levelt, W. J. M. 1981. The speaker's linearization problem. *Philosophical Transactions of the Royal Society, London* [Series B], 295: 305–315.

Long, M. H. 1990. Maturational constraints on language development. *Studies in Second Language Acquisition* 12: 251–285.

Long, M. H. 2005. Problems with the supposed counter-evidence to the Critical Period Hypothesis. *International Review of Applied Linguistics* 43: 287–317.

MacWhinney, B. 2000. *The CHILDES Project: Tools for Analyzing Talk* (3rd ed.). Mahwah NJ: Lawrence Erlbaum Association.

MacWhinney, B. 2001. The Competition Model: The input, the context, and the brain. In *Cognition and Second Language Instruction*, P. Robinson (ed.), 69–91. Cambridge: CUP.

Marinova-Todd, S. H. 2003. Comprehensive Analysis of Ultimate Attainment in Adult Second Language Acquisition. PhD dissertation, Harvard University.

Meisel, J. 2007. Mehrsprachigkeit in der frühen Kindheit: Zur Rolle des Alters bei Erwerbsbeginn. In *Mehrsprachigkeit bei Kindern und Erwachsenen*, T. Anstatt (ed.), 93–114. Tübingen: Narr-Francke.

Muñoz, C. 1999. The effects of age on instructed foreign language acquisition. In *Essays in English Language Teaching*, S. Gonzales & Fernández-Corugedo (eds), 1–21. Oviedo: Universidad de Oviedo.

Newport, E. 1990. Maturational constraints on language learning. *Cognitive Science* 14: 11–28.

Newport, E. 1991. Contrasting conceptions of the Critical Period for Language. In *The Epigenesis of Mind*, S. Carey & R. Gelman (eds), 111–130. Hillsdale NJ: Lawrence Erlbaum Associates.

Pagonis, G. 2007. Der Einfluss des Alters auf den Spracherwerb. Eine empirische Fallstudie zum ungsteuerten Zweitspracherwerb des Deutschen durch russische Lerner unterschiedlichen Alters. PhD dissertation, Universität Heidelberg.

Parodi, T. 2000. Finiteness and verb placement in second language acquisition. *Second Language Research* 16: 355–381.

Penfield, W. & Roberts, L. 1959. *Speech and Brain Mechanisms*. Princeton NJ: Princeton University Press.

Perdue, C. 2006. 'Creating language anew': Some remarks on an idea of Bernard Comrie's. *Linguistics* 44: 853–871.

Perdue, C. (ed.), 2000. *The structure of learner varieties*. Special Issue: *Studies in Second Language Acquisition* 22(3).

Pulvermüller, F. & Schumann, J. 1994. Neurobiological mechanisms of language acquisition. *Language Learning* 44: 681–734.

Schneider, W. 2002. Memory development in childhood. In *Blackwell Handbook of Childhood Cognitive Development*, U. Goswami (ed.), 236–256. London: Blackwell.

Schumann, J. 1975. Affective factors and the problem of age in second language acquisition. *Language Learning* 25: 209–35.

Schumann, J. 1997. *The Neurobiology of Affect in Language*. Oxford: Blackwell.

Schwartz, B. D. 1992. Testing between UG-based and problem-solving models of L2A: Developmental sequence data. *Language Acquisition* 2: 1–19.

Schwartz, B. D. 2003. Child L2 acquisition: Paving the way. In *Proceedings of the Boston University Conference on Language Development* 27, B. Beachley, A. Brown & F. Conlin (eds), 26–50. Somerville MA: Cascadilla.

Singleton, D. 2005. The Critical Period Hypothesis. A coat of many colors. *International Review of Applied Linguistics* 43: 269–285.

Singleton, D. & Ryan, L. 2004. *Language Acquisition: The Age Factor*. Clevedon: Multilingual Matters.

Starren, M. 2001. *The Second Time: The Acquisition of Temporality in Dutch and French as a Second Language*. Utrecht: LOT.

Thoma, D. & Tracy, R. 2006. Deutsch als frühe Zweitsprache: zweite Erstsprache? In *Kinder mit Migrationshintergrund. Spracherwerb und Fördermöglichkeiten*, B. Ahrenholz (ed.), 58–79. Freiburg: Fillibach.

Tomasello, M. 2003. *Constructing a Language. A Usage-Based Theory of Language Acquisition.* Cambridge MA: Harvard University Press.

VanBoxtel, S. 2005. *Can the Late Bird Catch the Worm? Ultimate Attainment in L2 Syntax.* Utrecht: LOT.

Verhagen, J. 2005. The role of the auxiliary 'hebben' in Dutch as a second language. *Zeitschrift fuer Literaturwissenschift und Linguistik* 140: 99–127.

Watorek, M. (ed.). 2004. Construction du discours par des enfants et des apprenants adultes. Special Issue: *Languages* 155.

Wegener, H. 1994. Variations in the acquisition of German plural morphology by second language learners. In *How Tolerant is Universal Grammar?*, R. Tracy & E. Lattey (eds), 267–294. Tübingen: Niemeyer.

Instructed language learning in the early years of education

When the gate opens

The interaction between social and linguistic goals
in child second language development

Jenefer Philp and Susan Duchesne
University of Auckland / University of Wollongong

This study offers a cross disciplinary approach to exploring the potential benefits
of peer interaction for the second language development of a six year old child,
based on a qualitative analysis of interactions between the child and her peers over
6 weeks in a mainstream grade 1 classroom. We argue that the young learner's
second language development in school can only be understood in the context
of her relationships with others. Her social goals of affiliation and participation
impact her interactions and these interactions in turn have consequences for
language use and language development. The findings point to the importance of
peer relationships, and the recognition that other children are a resource for the
young language learner in the classroom.

Literature review

What can children learn from other children (Hartup 2005)? What is the contribution of peer interaction to the L2 development of children in mainstream
classrooms? These questions need to be explored both in terms of linguistic and
social benefits, as the two are inextricably linked.

As noted in the introduction to this volume, research carried out in a variety of language classrooms suggests that children can benefit linguistically from
interaction with their peers, be their interlocutors native speakers or L2 learners themselves. Peer interaction can foster opportunities for negotiation, feedback
and modified output (Oliver 1995, 2000; Oliver & Mackey 2003; Van den Branden
1997) and offers a source of L2 input that children may assimilate as formulaic sequences and gradually build on (Cekaite this volume; Philp 2007; Wong-Fillmore
1976; Wray 2002). At the same time, peers' influence is not universally positive:
peers can act as gatekeepers, preventing opportunities for interaction (Miller 2000;
Toohey 2001; Willett 1995).

Studies of children in their early years of schooling attest to the complex interactions between the linguistic, social and cognitive needs of students; peers are more than just a source of linguistic input, they provide the social context in which language is learnt and practiced. This resonates with research that has recognized identity as a factor influencing the language learning experiences of adults (Norton 2000; Pavlenko 2002; Sayahi 2005), and children (Day 2002; Dagenais, Day & Toohey 2006). Whether their influence is positive or negative, the roles peers play go beyond their linguistic input.

In researching the benefits and constraints of peer interaction for language acquisition, we argue that it is important to view the child's linguistic, social and cognitive needs and development as interconnected. This is in keeping with recent calls for L2 acquisition research to take a more holistic approach to understanding the benefits and hindrances of interaction with others, and to draw on perspectives from other disciplines (Batstone 2002; Block 2003; Mackey in press). Hence, we explore parallels between research on peer interaction from developmental psychology literature and research in second language acquisition.

Social goals direct language choices

Research that focuses on linguistic interaction can contain unspoken assumptions that the learner is primarily a willing recipient of input and feedback, without goals that affect learning, or that the learner's linguistic goals are uppermost. However, for children in and out of classrooms (and probably for many adult learners as well) social and participatory goals are paramount, with linguistic goals subordinate to them. For example, in the early years of school, establishing friendships and desirable social positioning within the class group are important social goals. Language is used as one means to achieve these social goals.

Accordingly, in this paper we focus on two interrelated social goals that are sought through peer interaction; affiliation (friendship), and social positioning. Associated with these, and contributing to them, are goals of equality and reciprocity. We argue that these goals shape children's interaction with their peers and thereby impact on their language development.

Social goals: Affiliation and social positioning

Hartup (1992) suggests that in early childhood, friendships centre around affiliation and reciprocity. If the social goal of making friends affects language, we might expect this to be reflected in children's language use, with mimicry, play and negotiation emerging as features of children's language, and there is some evidence from child studies of both L1 acquisition (McLaughlin 1984, 1985; Mercer 1995; Wells 1985) and SLA (Bongartz & Schneider 2003; Cekaite & Aronsson

2005; Wong-Fillmore 1976) that this is the case. Wray (2002), for example, noted the use of formulaic sequences, including mimicry, by children; both to engage in interaction, and to align themselves with peers.

A second goal of establishing position within the peer group is similarly attained in part through language. Willett (1995), reporting on a year long study of four ESL children in a mainstream first-grade classroom, described the way in which the children's social integration developed through interaction with others. Willett noted the children's increasing participation in class, and their particular use of formulaic sequences for social purposes, "to enact a socially significant event in order to construct identities as competent students (...) and construct collaborative relations with one another' (p. 490). Similarly Perera (2001) in a study of four Japanese preschoolers in a bilingual program, reflected on how the children appropriated language gleaned from teachers and peers in the classroom "thereby [becoming] not only linguistically, but also socially, connected to the community in which the language is used" (p. 11). Thus the goals of being accepted by peers and of attaining kudos in the class contribute to second language acquisition by motivating children to take on the language of their peers as a means of gaining affiliation.

In Willett's study, the desire for perceived competence contributed to the extent to which the ESL children were accepted by their peers and included in normal classroom discourse. All four children quickly learned "how to look like they were participating appropriately" (p. 486), through use of formulaic utterances gleaned from standard classroom routinized interaction. Willett notes that, while the abilities of the four children were not dissimilar, the girls, by working together, could jointly construct competence. The boy, however, isolated from his peers by classroom structural practices, was not perceived as a competent 'independent learner'. The position of the children was not solely within their power to create, it arose from the particular classroom management practices of the teacher, and from the social structure of the group. However, 'looking like they were participating appropriately' was a goal pursued by the children. In this sense it represented their sought identity. Toohey (2000) similarly observes the differential success of children according to their access to help from more experienced peers through whom they are able to appropriate the means to participate in the classroom community. She also notes that establishing classroom identity is a social goal for children, particularly as they enter school or a new class. We can hypothesise that children, like adults, will seek particular identities, may accept or resist others' positioning of them, and use language to establish their chosen position in the class.

These two social goals of establishing friendships and desirable social positioning are both enacted through language, and shape a context for the development of language. There is a synergistic relationship between social goals and peer interaction, such that social goals shape peer interaction, while peer interaction is

Figure 1. Social goals and peer interaction

a means of achieving those goals. In the process, L2 acquisition can be advanced through the peer interaction, with social goals acting to sustain and shape these interactions. This is illustrated in Figure 1.

In his work on children's friendship relations, Hartup (1992) suggested several ways in which friendship contributes to development. Peer interactions, when they represent potential friendships, can serve similar functions in L2 development. Firstly, peer interaction provides a context for learning of language skills, and secondly, peer interaction helps the child to become a more effective language partner.

Peer interaction as a context for learning language skills

Developmental researchers (e.g., Hartup 1996; Newcomb, Bukowski, & Bagwell 1999) describe peers, not just as contributors to development, but as a context for development, in the same way that the family and the school can be described as contexts, to which the child contributes as much as s/he is influenced by them. The relationships and their outcomes are co-determined by the individual and his/her peers. These outcomes may be variably positive or negative for development. Just as relationships are contexts for socialisation, in which children can take on social norms, and find models for future relationships (Hartup 1996), peers can be a context for language socialisation, providing children with linguistic 'norms' and models for participation.

This process of language socialisation is illustrated by Wong-Fillmore (1976) in the peer interaction of five Spanish-speaking children, each paired with an English-speaking friend from an ESL immersion class over one year. Wong-Fillmore pointed to the importance of interaction with peers as a key source of input and meaning construction in the L2. Equally significant is the use of peers' sayings as a source of gaining peer acceptance. She suggests that "children ... acquire expressions in the context of social situations *which are important to them*, figure out patterns on the basis of these expressions they know how to use and pick up vocabulary items by freeing them from formulaic expressions" (1976: 728–729 Our emphasis). That is, interaction with peers fosters L2 development partly as a consequence of the social and emotional importance peers hold. Once again the interaction between social, linguistic and developmental goals is highlighted. Wong-Fillmore's study suggests that the relationship between competence and acceptance is bi-directional, a principle reiterated by Willett.

Learning to be a language partner

Interaction with peers is instrumental in the development of social competence. Developmental researchers have proposed that informal peer play activities are an important context for young children's learning of interpersonal as well as relationship-management skills (Ladd & Hart 1992; Ladd 1999). In particular, one model of social competence argues that peer acceptance allows children access to opportunities for positive social interaction, in which they learn the social skills necessary for future acceptance by peers. Children who are rejected by their peers may associate with other rejected children who have poor social skills, and so have limited opportunity to learn the positive social skills necessary for peer acceptance (Bagwell, Newcomb & Bukowski 1998). Similarly, in L2 acquisition, peer acceptance can allow children access to opportunities for interaction in which they further their language acquisition, while peer rejection denies these opportunities.

Peer acceptance as a means for providing opportunities for interaction is so important, in fact, that peers have been described as 'gatekeepers' to interactional opportunities (Pavlenko 2002). For example, in Willett's study described above (1995), differences in young children's peer acceptance impacted on their ability to gain access to the classroom peer network. Miller's (2000) study of ESL students in an Australian high school found students tended to group themselves along language and racial lines, with little interaction between the groups outside of class, and, consequently, few opportunities for interaction in English for L2 learners. Similarly, Toohey's (2001) exploration of disputes among young children in Canadian public school classes demonstrates subordination and exclusion of some children and consequent regulation of their access to opportunites for learning English. Such work suggests the social significance of peers and the potentially positive or negative consequences for language learning. Toohey (2000) (see also Day 2002; Norton & Toohey 2001) points out that it is not just what learners do, but the opportunities their communities offer them that influence their success. Both peer positioning and the perceived responsiveness of the child, including sociability and willingness to communicate, affect the children's opportunities for interaction in their new language and hence overall SLA potential (Wong-Fillmore 1976).

Much of the work describing peers as gatekeepers has looked at how peers limit the opportunities for L2 learners. Fewer studies have shown what results when that gate is opened and peers seek to interact with the L2 learner. In summary, social goals such as affiliation, mutuality and reciprocity, which are associated with friendship, could provide opportunities for children's language development, performing similar functions to those friendships are argued to perform in development generally.

Peer interaction and adult-child interaction

As noted in the introduction to this volume, adult-child and child-child relationships tend to serve different but complementary and interrelated functions in L2 development. While adults, particularly teachers, may provide more scaffolding and recasting of the child learner's language, and work harder to negotiate language, the child's peers appear to provide contexts for practice. Further, children are active in their own development; they choose roles for themselves, for their peers and for those adults with whom they have a relationship (Azmitia & Hesser 1993, cited in Schneider 2000; Furman & Buhrmester 1985; see also Mitchell & Lee, this volume). This needs to be taken into account when investigating the influence of peers and adults in an individual's development.

This study examines the effect of the learner's social goals on her peer interaction and L2 development. It focuses on the interaction between one young L2 learner and her peers in a school context. We expect, from research reviewed above, that the child's interaction will be shaped by her social goals of: developing friendships, demonstrated in seeking affiliation through language use, equality, language play and reciprocity; and social positioning, demonstrated in shared language and intersubjectivity.

We evaluate how one child's L2 development is supported in the context of her interactions with her peers, and how she is enabled through those interactions, to take on new roles and relationships within the classroom.

We also hypothesise that there will be differences in the nature of her interactions with adults and peers, reflecting their differing roles as teachers and friends or playmates.

Two general questions underpin analysis of the data, reflecting the broad aim of investigating the relationships between peer interaction, social relationships and language development.

Research questions

1. What are the characteristics of peer interaction?
2. How do social goals shape peer interaction and language acquisition?

Method

Participants

This research involves one child, 27 peers and three adults present in the classroom at various stages of the data collection. Yessara is a 6 year old child adopted from Ethiopia eight weeks prior to the commencement of the data collection, by an Australian family with four children aged 8 to 23. She began school in Grade 1 with minimal English. The primary school of 425 children sits in the heart of a small rural Australian community of approximately 2000 residents.

Yessara is the only non-Anglo-Saxon child among the 28 children in the class. Her peers, with one exception, are monolingual L1 English speakers, unused to L2 speakers. Scholastically, the children range from having poor pre-literacy skills to being independent readers. The children's parents' socio-economic status ranges from semi-skilled and skilled workers to professionals. The teacher prepared the class for Yessara's arrival; they looked at pictures of Ethiopia, discussed the difficulties she might face in coming to a new country, and how they might help her. As a result, the children were eager to meet Yessara and to become her friend.

The three adults that appear in the transcripts are all native speakers of English. Mrs. T., their experienced teacher, has lived and worked in the community for over twenty years. Mrs. A, an additional teacher, teaches Yessara one on one for 30 to 60 minutes 3–4 days a week. She is often in the class for short periods. Par., the first author, is the mother of one of Yessara's classmates and provides weekly "parent-help" support.

Data collection procedures

The data collection began in the third week of the final term of the school year. This was Yessara's fourth full formal week of school. Data were recorded with the use of a small tape recorder and tie-pin microphone, carried in a shoulder bag by Yessara or one of her friends, allowing mobility and independence. Table 1 provides a summary of the time and content of each of the seven recorded sessions of 20 to 40 minutes duration; three before school, in the playground or class, and four in class time, during morning group activities. Morning group work involved either literacy or numeracy activities. Yessara was grouped with children who had sufficient literacy skills to work independently (i.e., they could write the alphabet with confidence, read high frequency words by guesswork and could write phonetically).

During group work, children were encouraged to be independent workers, allowing the teacher to work with particular groups or individuals. The children were expected not to seek teacher approval and to use resources such as charts, or large format story books which were the focus of the lesson. One or two parent

Table 1. Recorded sessions*

Session	Context	Activity	Content	Participants
1:1	Before school	Drawing at the table	Zoo pictures	Y, E, T, A, R, Researcher
1:2	Morning group work	Literacy – write about a pet	Pets	Y, R, S, G,
				Mrs A
				Researcher
2	Late morning group work	Maths task	Addition	Y, S, J
		Constructing sums with blocks		Researcher
3				
4:1	Before school	Puzzles	Alphabet puzzle	Y, J, S, S, Researcher
4:2	Late Morning group work	Maths task	Shapes	Y, R, S, Researcher
		Making shapes with tiles		
5	Morning group work	Writing	Friends	Y, R, S, Mrs A
6	Morning group work	Drawing	Christmas	Y, R, S
				Mrs T
				Researcher

*Sessions are numbered according to the week of data collection.
Participants: Y = Yessara   S = unidentified student   E = Elsa   T = Tina
          Mrs A = ESL Teacher   Mrs T = Classroom teacher   R = Roberta   J = Jack

helpers also assisted by ensuring children remained on task, giving encouragement or help where needed, such as spelling words, listening to a story being read, assisting in cleaning up or replenishing supplies. It was in the capacity of parent-help that the first author was present for all taping sessions and made observational notes following each session. These observational notes provided contextual descriptions for the recorded data and were of particular use in the absence of video data. Audio recordings precluded the inclusion of non-verbal information.

Data analysis

The first author transcribed all the data. A research assistant rechecked these two months later and completed second transcriptions of the first and penultimate transcripts. IRR, calculated as percentage agreement on these transcriptions was 83% and 93%. IRR for identification of Yessara in the transcripts was 96% and 97%. The first author and the research assistant double coded interaction between peers and between an adult and children, in which Yessara was a participant, for instances of 1) scaffolding, and 2) interactional modifications in the form of recasts

Table 2. Operationalisation of interactional modifications and scaffolding

	Definition	Example	
Scaffolding	"temporary support or assistance, provided by someone more capable, that permits a learner to perform a complex task or process that he or she would be unable to do alone." (Peregoy 1999: 138)	Y	me me me me me play
		Mrs A	you play with her
		Y	today
		Mrs A	at lunchtime
Recast	Reformulation of a non target-like utterance in the subsequent turn, the central meaning is retained while linguistic form is changed. Recasts may be made in response to single or multiple errors.	Y	ele::phant
		E	yeah elephant
Negotiated interaction	Conversational adjustments are made in an effort to make language more comprhehensible. The speaker repeats, paraphrases, segments and restates their utterance in response to a signal of communication difficulty.	Y	I don't know my name little baby arm broken (.) little baby
		Mrs A	when you were a little baby you had=
		Y	no no no I don't know so so someone someone baby braken arm =they did

and negotiation of meaning. These are operationalised in Table 2. IRR reliability, calculated on percentage agreement was 96%. A grounded analysis was then used to evaluate the connections between language and social development. This analysis was carried out independently by the two researchers and cross checked.

Results and Discussion

Research Question 1: What are the characteristics of peer interaction?

The children's language is characterized by short turns, and fluctuates according to activity. Although Yessara begins by using very short turns compared to her peers (means of 2.9 and 5.4 words per turn respectively in week 1), the length of these increases in later weeks while conversely, peers' turns are reduced, so they are similar in length by week 6 (4.6 compared to 4.2 respectively). In contrast, teachers produce consistently higher numbers of words per turn. This is illustrated in Figure 2 and summarized in Table 3.

There is little evidence of provision of feedback or scaffolding by peers, as seen in Figure 3; they provide 5 instances, compared to 17 by adults, over the 7 recorded sessions. Both instances of negotiated interaction with peers involved the

Table 3. Comparison of words per turn

Session	Words/Turn (mean)		
	Adults	Peers	Yessara
1.1	271/43 (6.3)	150/28 (5.4)	58/20 (2.9)
1.2	140/14 (10)	700/89 (7.9)	114/48 (2.4)
2	1199/144 (8.3)	379/75 (5.1)	343/118 (2.9)
4.1	474/66 (7.2)	378/79 (4.8)	173/42 (4.1)
4.2	271/38 (7.1)	137/52 (2.6)	112/26 (4.3)
5	152/30 (5.1)	32/8 (4)	140/48 (2.9)
6	701/82 (8.5)	482/115 (4.2)	289/63 (4.6)

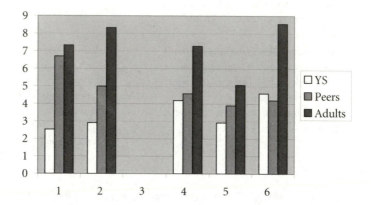

Figure 2. Mean words per turn over time

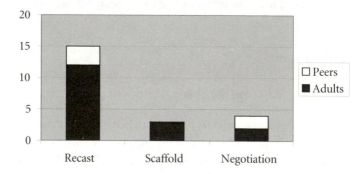

Figure 3. Feedback on Yessara's L2 production

peer's repetition of incomprehensible input, while both those with adults involved negotiation of the child's production, and resulted in successful modified output.

The children in Yessara's class provide her with much of her L2 input in school, yet this input is highly variable as a model of the target language. Compared with

Yessara's interactions with adults, her conversations with peers appear less optimal for language acquisition in terms of providing target-like models, scaffolding and providing feedback on her production. Peer interaction is nonetheless the context of Yessara's early language learning, and appears to perform other important functions, as we discuss later. Peers provide both target like and nontarget like input including phonologically, syntactically and lexically illformed utterances, as they mimic IL forms, simplify wildly and use high pitched intonation patterns while interacting with their L2 language peer. This is illustrated in Examples (1) & (2) below.

In Example (1) below, the children are working together in a group, writing about their pets. Yessara is copying Roberta's work as her means of participating in the task. Initially, Roberta addresses Yessara using exaggerated intonation, pitch and enunciation (marked in the transcription by double brackets) (lines 1, 2, 3). She fragments language and at times uses ungrammatical "baby talk" (lines 1, 4, 8, 10). Roberta explicitly directed the other children to use "baby talk" for Yessara, because "otherwise she won't understand".[1] Roberta, without intended malevolence, mimics Yessara's accent, as do the other children. These traits are more evident in the earlier transcripts than later, changing as Yessara establishes herself in the class and as she becomes more proficient in English, so that the children treat her less patronizingly and more as a language partner.

(1) 1. R Yessara Yessara do you need a book? <<Yessara need book? >> Book? Book?
     2. R <<Yessara sit down sit down sit down>>
     3. R <<now Yessara you go and write the long story>>
     4. R sit down Yessara you right?
     5. Y yep
     6. R you right?
     7.   [later turn]
     8. R <<me go up canteen and get me me go up canteen and get you XX>>
     9. S hey rub hey rub later later
    10. R hey Yessara lo:ok its oka:y [high sing song intonation] << hey me go to canteen>> at big lunch and you come with me and me buy some frogs for you [rising intonation] for you?
    11. Y yes ok don't anymore

---

1.   By week two of the study, the teachers had all commented on the children's use of baby talk to Yessara, to the extent that the class teacher expressly spoke to the class about their use of baby talk, encouraging them to talk to Yessara "normally" (Personal communication with the teacher).

Example (2) demonstrates the ways in which other children's speech can provide chunks which then scaffold Yessara's own production (see Philp 2007). Emy and Yessara are drawing together before school. After Emy describes Yessara's picture in line 3, once again adopting exaggerated intonation and enunciation, Yessara then appropriates the same description in line 6 to attract her friend Roberta's attention.

(2) 1. Em that's blu:e. Whats this? Zebra?
     2. YS yeah
     3. Em <<Very colourful zebra>> [baby talk]

[several turns later]

     4. Em [Roberta arrives] oh hello Roberta I thought you were sick.
     5. R   no mum XX
     6. YS [excitedly] look at the zebra very colourful zebra isn't it? Very very colourful

While speech directed specifically to Yessara is often modified, equally she receives unmodified input, particularly when she is part of group interaction, as seen in Example (3) below. The children are physically constructing a pattern together on the floor, using flat shaped blocks. As they do so they organise their activity through language (line 2, 11) hypothesising and evaluating (line 2, 11), at times with complex language. Interestingly, Yessara is as engaged as the other children, and also directs activities (line 6, 7) and evaluates their efforts (line 4, 12) through language, albeit in a greatly simplified way. Here, peers provide both a model for language and a context for using language. Language accompanies and is scaffolded by the activity itself; the blocks provide the scaffold for what Yessara is doing, so that her minimal language here is sufficient.

(3) 1. Y   one big one
     2. R   wait on I reckon we'll use all the blocks and we'll see what we can make
             [inaudible]
     3. S   yes the biggest one in the whole wide world
     4. Y   big!
     5. S   da da da da da da da
[later turn]
     6. Y   thi:s one [adding to blocks with Roberta]
     7. Y   too long Roberta
     8. R   we're nearly finished
     9. Y   oh
     10. R   this is gonna be excellent
     11. S   wonder if we'll be able to use all these blocks. That'd be fun if we could use all these blocks wouldn't it?
     12. Y   XX lot block (..) bi:g one block

In summary then, peer interaction is characterized by variable TL input, with little feedback on Yessara's own production. Her language tends to be scaffolded by the activity itself, including material objects, rather than linguistically. Nevertheless, peer interaction performs important functions in Yessara's language acquisition by helping her to learn to be a language partner and to take her place in the classroom. This is explored further in the next research question.

Research Question 2: How do social goals shape peer interaction and language acquisition?

We expect, from research reviewed above, that the children's interaction will be shaped by their social goals of developing friendships, equality and reciprocity. These social goals are promoted in different ways by peer interaction, as the children seek affiliation through shared language use and language play. Peer interaction provides the context in which friendship and solidarity are negotiated and expressed.

Affiliation and reciprocity
A salient feature of the children's language is repetition for language play, found in the speech of both Yessara and her peers. In Example (4) below, the peers, including Yessara, enjoy imitating one another, as they share the rubber ("eraser" in U.S. English), and they repeat it over and over, enjoying the sound of the word, trying it out with a rolled /r/. Yessara, in particular, enjoys writing copious amounts in her book and then rubbing it all out again, necessitating the frequent sharing of the eraser.

(4) 1. R I've got a sticker
    2. S I've got a sticker
    3. Y hey Roberta
    4. S hey Roberta I'll tell you something
    5. Y rubber rubber
    6. S rubber rubber rubber [imitating rolled /r/ of Yessara]
    7. R rub rub rubber
    8. S rubber rubber rubber [attempting rolled /r/ without success]

For this group of children, mimicry, shared ideolects and repetition function to cement friendships and are a mark of solidarity, as seen again in Example (5) below. For Yessara the potential benefits are both social and linguistic; it is a shared language she can appropriate and it is a practice which can provide valuable repetition of input and articulatory practice (Wray 1999). Cekaite and Aronsson (2005) note a similar phenomenon in their study of 9 children aged 7–10 years in a Swedish immersion classroom.

> When the present children jokingly played with their second language, they were
> thus involved in a twofold process, that of practicing language and of qualify-
> ing as participants in the classroom community, thereby securing occasions for
> practicing L2. (p. 118)

Copying one another as a sign of friendship is bi-directional. Yessara is one of
the participants: her language is appropriated by her peers (lines 8, 9), just as
she appropriates that of her friends. In this excerpt, the friends delight in copying one another in more ways than one as they write out identical lunch orders on
paper bags.

(5)   1. S   I'm lunch ordering
      2. R   so am I
      3. B   Is Yessara?
      4. R   I dunno ask her
      5. B   Yessara are you lunch ordering?
      6. Y   yes
      7. B   oh all three of us are! [delighted]
      8. Y   Yessara my name is [single contour]
      9. R   Roberta my name is [copying] too and chicken nugget
     10. Y   chicken=
     11. B   =two chicken nuggets

Examples of successful negotiation of meaning are rare in the data, perhaps because as a social act the meaning is less important to the children than the interaction itself. As Dunn (1999: 270) has observed: "What is in common across so many
child-child interactions – and especially those between friends – is that they *matter*
to the children; their emotional salience is unquestionable."

Equality and social positioning

One of the distinctive features of child-child rather than adult-child relationships
is relative equality (Hartup 1989; Laursen & Hartup 2002; Philp, Oliver, Mackey
this volume). This is not to say that there are not power differentials in children's
relations (Toohey 2001). Indeed, it is the establishment of equality that becomes
a focus for Yessara in her relations with her peers. Yessara's goal of establishing
herself as a peer (of equal status with the other children in the class) is seen in
her quite different treatment of adult and peer input. Striving for equality with
her peers, as time progresses she comes to accept help only from adults, as is seen
during a maths task in Example (6) below. The equality of relationship between
Roberta and Yessara is reflected in their interaction. Although Roberta is directed
to help Yessara by the parent helper (who is busy attending to other children),
Yessara won't accept this help (lines 7, 17, 25, 27, 31), but insists on the adult input

(lines 9, 29).Yessara doesn't play the passive learner and when cast in the student role with another peer as teacher, she tends to maintain a measure of control.

(6) 1. PAR [to Jeremy] right two more to go [to R+Y] Roberta XX do it to-
              gether
     2. R   which right what's 8 plus [assuming authoritative teacher tone]
     3. Y   = here? One
     4. R   no ah what's 1 plus
     5. Y   =see?
     6. R   **yep what's 1 plus ah I'll do it**
     7. Y   **no**
     8. R   ok
     9. [later, after Yessara has called over the parent to help her]
    10. PAR there you are 7 plus 3
    11. Y   which
    12. R   equals
    13. PAR you already added that up didn't you how many are there?
    14. Y   oh 1 2 3 4 5 6 7 8 9 10 10 [counting blocks]
    15. PAR 10! Yes! So write 10
    16. R   **do you want me to show you?**
    17. Y   **no a 1 and a zero**
    18. Reb this one and this one [pointing to chart]
    19. PAR 10 [claps] good girl Yessara
    20. Y   finish?
    21. PAR mm last one 8: =1 2 3 4 5 6 7 8=
    22. Ss   =1 2 3 4 5 6 7 8= [chorus]
    23. PAR no w Roberta you choose a number for Yessara to add to that [turns
              to help a different group]
    24. R   **I'm going to use 3**
    25. Y   **no Roberta**
    26. R   **3 Yessara**
    27. Y   **no 8**
    28. R   8
    29. Y   1 2 3 4 5 67 8 9 10 10? Which?
    30. PAR what number did you choose Roberta?
    31. R   **she won't let me**
    32. PAR oh she's going to choose have you got another activity you're sup-
              posed to do now?

The above example suggests that Yessara chooses the roles she will play. Her so-cial goal of positioning herself as an equal with her peers directs her language behaviour: She does this by not asking for help from her peers, instead asking adults, and by insisting on choosing rather than having topics, numbers etc., chosen for her.

Yessara's language use with adults is typically more adventurous than that she uses with her peers. It is also interesting to note that there is more negotiation of meaning in this situation. Yessara tells stories when an adult is there to scaffold, but doesn't rely upon peers in the same way. In the first weeks of the data collection, Yessara would sit next to Roberta and copy out what she had written as this allowed her to participate in the perceived task at hand: writing and drawing. However, by the end of the six weeks Yessara preferred the help of a willing adult when she needed assistance with her writing. Asking adults for help aligns her with the other students.

When talking to her peers Yessara tends to limit her talk to what she is confident communicating. Hence her social goals are at cross-purposes with her linguistic goals, and take precedence. This limits the language input Yessara receives, and, as a consequence, her development. Thus the primacy of social goals does not necessarily have a beneficial effect in terms of opportunities for modified output and feedback.

In Example (7), two other children, Yessara and Mrs A. are looking through their writing books for the term. In Yessara's book, they find a page illustrating her broken arm. Mrs. A assists Yessara in her attempts to participate in their conversation. Yessara builds up a story using formulaic phrases "I don't know" "my name is" "little baby" (lines 7–11), which is initially misunderstood by Mrs. A. The ensuing negotiation pushes Yessara to modify her language (from "I don't know" to "someone"; from "arm broken" to "braken arm"; and the addition of "they did" as a time marker). Besides illustrating ways in which the adult assists the learner's production through recasting, this example demonstrates the type of support offered by adults, in contrast to that offered by peers in interaction.

(7) 1. R   where's your name Yessara has= [reading]
2. Mrs A =a broken arm [reading] o:h
3. R   =o;h
4. Mrs A your arms all better now isn't it? Strong again
5. R   I hope I get a broken arm and so does XX
6. Mrs A yeah [daughter's name] wants a broken arm too so she can have some plaster
7. Y   I don't know I don't know I don't know yeah I I don't know my name little baby arm broken (.) little baby
8. Mrs A when you were a little baby you had=
9. Y   no no no I don't know so so someone someone baby braken arm =they did
10. Mrs A oh someone had a baby who had a broken arm?
11. Y   yeah
12. Mrs A yeah that can happen. OK well I'll see you tomorrow

Peer interaction as a support for L2 production and development
It is in the context of Yessara's interaction with her peers that she develops her skills as a participant in classroom interaction. Turn-taking, interruption, and some collaborative discourse are all evident. Peers provide Yessara with opportunities to talk, to work with them, and to be part of the group, as seen in the examples provided above. Yessara herself is active in this process, shaping the context for her language use by choosing roles for herself and others. Yessara also contributes to the language of the classroom in that the other children's speech is modified – they copy her accent and phrasing, and adapt their speech to suit her.

Generally, peer interaction is a context of L2 learning for children in schools. This context can be supportive, as in the present case; or obstructive, as other research has found (Toohey 2001). The extent to which this context is supportive depends on the child themselves, on their peers – and the interaction of personalities. Yessara's confidence, determination and outgoing nature mean she is able to use the welcoming class to advantage. She actively participates, making the most of her limited English, getting mileage out of prefabricated chunks and single words (Philp 2007). The data suggests a recursive/synergistic relationship between communicative and social skill competence. In other words, her social skills help her to maintain relationships that contribute to her language acquisition, which gives her further resources to maintain and develop social skills.

It may be that peer interactions are supportive when they are most like friendships (offering affiliation, mutuality, reciprocity, acceptance and equal desire to communicate). Wray (2002: 148), in a review of studies of L2 learners of primary school age suggests,

> the degree of success in L2 learning seems to depend in part on their social alliances with peers. Most helpful will be if their friends do not speak the learner's L1, are talkative, are committed to mutual social integration, and engage in patterns of play which naturally incorporate (second) language use.

All these features are true for Yessara. Similarly, other researchers (Barnard 2005; Wong-Fillmore 1976; Willett 1995), tracking the interlanguage development of L2 child learners, note the benefits of interaction for those who are accepted by their peers. They reflect on how personality factors and perceived competence affect children's opportunities to receive input and try out their own language.

We have argued that the potential of peer interaction for language development extends beyond it being a source of input and feedback. This aspect may be something more consistently provided by adults, and there are clearly particular benefits of adult-child interaction. However, when peers are supportive and accepting, then peer interaction models ways of using language and, crucially, affords opportunities or contexts in which to use language. Future research could compare the nature and contribution of a number of different kinds of interaction with child L2 learners.

Summary of findings

This data points to the importance of peer input and interaction to the young learner's social and L2 development. Peer interaction is seen here as a context in which roles and relationships are played out, including relationships of friendship (who plays with who, who sits next to who) and roles of competence (Thornborrow 2003: 30–31). These roles and relationships direct the language that is used and, for this second language learner, are themselves the context of her acquisition. We have argued that the social goals associated with friendship of affiliation, equality, and social positioning direct this learner's interaction with others and so shape the context of her language acquisition. In this we recognize that the learner is an agent actively involved in the process of L2 acquisition, just as she is in her social development. Yessara is selective in whom she gets help from and in doing so, constructs an identity of competence which delivers her equality with her peers. Peer interaction performs important functions in the learner's language acquisition, by providing a context for learning language skills, and by helping her to become a language participant through formulaic sequences and language play, and through the children's willingness to include and interact with Yessara which overrides other (linguistic) considerations.

Limitations, implications and future directions

One of the limitations of this study was the selectivity of data collection. This study focused only on group work, which afforded less opportunity to investigate adult interaction with the children. Additionally, the length of the data collection precluded the opportunity to determine language development. Nevertheless, the study suggests interesting directions for future research, ideally investigating the interaction between social and linguistic development over a longer time frame.

This small study underlines the importance of context in understanding language acquisition (Batstone 2002; Firth & Wagner 1997; Kanagy 1999; Lantolf 2000; Oliver & Mackey 2003; Willett 1995). Without a consideration of their social function, Yessara's peer interactions appear less than helpful to her language acquisition. However, peer input and interaction crucially contributed to this learner's acceptance within social networks and therefore to her continued access to input/output opportunities.

There are implications in the study for classrooms in which L2 learners are working alongside L1 speaking peers, suggesting the benefit of informal interaction for SLA (Ellis 2005). Other studies have reported the effect of a teacher's classroom management practices on peer acceptance (Barnard 2005; Toohey 2001), and consequently, on L2 development. Teachers may need to pay as much attention to supporting informal peer interactions, as they do to developing formal situations for language practice. Future research could further explore the benefits teachers' support can offer to students' peer interactions. Work in similar classroom contexts with longitudinal data could delve deeper into the relationships between: peer interaction and acquisition, in particular the role the language learner plays; and between L2 acquisition, interaction and friendship. Taking account of the social powers of language use is an obvious area for future research on interaction and L2 development.

References

Bagwell, C. L., Newcomb, A. F. & Bukowski, W. M. 1998. Preadolescent friendship and peer rejection as predictors of adult adjustment. *Child Development* 69: 140–153.

Barnard, R. 2005. Isolated learners from diverse language backgrounds in the mainstream primary classroom: A sociocultural perspective. In *Refereed Conference Proceedings of the 1st International Conference on Language, Education and Diversity*, S. May, M. Franken & R. Barnard (eds), *LED2003*. Hamilton: Wilf Malcolm Institute of Educational Research, University of Waikato.

Batstone, R. 2002. Contexts of engagement: A discourse perspective of 'intake' and 'pushed output'. *System* 30: 1–14.

Block, D. 2003. *The Social Turn in Second Language Acquisition*. Washington DC: Georgetown University Press.

Bongartz, C. & Schneider, M. L. 2003. Linguistic development in social contexts: A study of two brothers learning German. *The Modern Language Journal* 87: 13–37

Cekaite, A. & Aronsson, K. 2005. Language play, a collaborative resource in children's L2 learning. *Applied Linguistics* 26: 169–191.

Dagenais, D., Day, E. & Toohey, K. 2006. A multilingual child's literacy practices and contrasting identities in the figured worlds of French immersion classrooms. *International Journal of Bilingual Education and Bilingualism* 9: 205–218.

Day, E. 2002. *Identity and the Young English Language Learner*. Clevedon: Multilingual Matters.

Dunn, J. 1999. Siblings, friends, and the development of social understanding. In *Relationships as Social Contexts*, W. A. Collins & B. Laursen (eds), 263–279. Mahwah NJ: Lawrence Erlbaum Associates.

Ellis, R. 2005. Instructed second language acquisition: A literature review. Report to the Ministry of Education. Wellington: Ministry of Education, New Zealand.

Firth, A. & Wagner, J. 1997. On discourse, communication, and (some) fundamental concepts in SLA research. *The Modern Language Journal* 81: 286–300.

Furman, W. & Buhrmester, D. 1985. Children's perceptions of the personal relationships in their social networks. *Developmental Psychology* 21: 1016–1024.

Hartup, W. W. 1989. Social relationships and their developmental significance. *American Psychologist* 44: 120–126.

Hartup, W. W. 1992. Having friends, making friends and keeping friends: Relationships as educational contexts. *ERIC Digest.* ED345854.

Hartup, W. W. 1996. The company they keep: Friendships and their developmental significance. *Child Development* 67: 1–13.

Hartup, W. W. 2005. Peer interaction: What causes what? *Journal of Abnormal Child Psychology* 33: 387–394.

Kanagy, R. 1999. Interactional routines as a mechanism for L2 acquisition and socialization in an immersion context. *Journal of Pragmatics* 31: 1467–1492.

Ladd, G. 1999. Peer relationships and social competence during early and middle childhood. *Annual Review of Psychology* 50: 333–59.

Ladd, G. W. & Hart, C. H. 1992. Creating informal play opportunities: Are parents' and preschoolers' initiations related to childrens' competence with peers? *Developmental Psychology* 28: 1179–1187.

Lantolf, J. (ed.) 2000. *Sociocultural Theory and Second Language Learning.* Oxford: OUP.

Laursen, B. & Hartup, W. W. 2002. The origins of reciprocity and social exchange in friendships. In *Social Exchange in Development* [New Directions for Child and Adolescent Development 95], B. Laursen & W. G. Graziano (eds), 27–39. San Francisco CA: Wiley Periodicals.

Mackey, A. In press. *Input, Interaction and Corrective Feedback in L2 Learning.* Oxford: OUP.

McLaughlin, B. 1984. *Second-Language Acquisition in Childhood,* Vol. 1: *Preschool Children* (2nd ed.). Hillsdale NJ: Lawrence Erlbaum Associates.

McLaughlin, B. 1985. *Second-Language Acquisition in Childhood,* Vol. 2: *School-Age Children.* Hillsdale NJ: Lawrence Erlbaum Associates.

Mercer, N. 1995. *The Guided Construction of Knowledge.* Clevedon: Multilingual Matters.

Miller, J. 2000. Language use, identity and social interaction: Migrant students in Australia. *Research on Language and Social Interaction* 33: 69–100.

Newcomb, A. F., Bukowski, W. M. & Bagwell, C. L. 1999. Knowing the sounds: Friendship as a developmental context. In *Relationships as Developmental Context,* W. A. Collins & B. Laursen (eds), 63–84. Mahwah NJ: Lawrence Erlbaum Associates.

Norton, B. 2000. *Identity and Language Learning.* Harlow: Pearson Education.

Norton, B. & Toohey, K. 2001. Changing perspectives on good language learners. *TESOL Quarterly* 35: 307–322.

Oliver, R. 1995. Negative feedback in child NS/NNS conversation. *Studies in Second Language Acquisition* 18: 459–481.

Oliver, R. 2000. Age differences in negotiation and feedback in classroom and pair work. *Language Learning* 50: 119–151.

Oliver, R. & Mackey, A. 2003. Interactional context and feedback in child ESL classrooms. *The Modern Language Journal* 87: 519–533.

Pavlenko, A. 2002. Postcultural approaches to the study of social factors in second language learning and use. In *Portraits of the L2 User,* V. Cook (ed.), 275–302. Clevedon: Multilingual Matters.

Perera, N. 2001. The role of prefabricated language in young children's second language acquisition. *Bilingual Research Journal* 25: 327–356.

Philp, J. 2007. Sounding the same, being the same: The role of formulaic sequences in the second language classroom production of a six year old. Ms, University of Auckland.

Sayahi, L. 2005. Language and identity among speakers of Spanish in northern Morocco: Between ethnolinguistic vitality and acculturation. *Journal of Sociolinguistics* 9: 95–107.

Schneider, B. H. 2000. *Friends and Enemies: Peer Relations in Childhood.* London: Arnold.

Thornborrow, J. 2003. The organization of primary school children's on-task and off-task talk in a small group setting. *Research on Language and Social Interaction* 36: 7–32.

Toohey, K. 2000. *Learning English at School.* Clevedon: Multilingual Matters.

Toohey, K. 2001. Disputes in child L2 learning. *TESOL Quarterly* 35: 257–278.

Van den Branden, K. 1997. Effects of negotiation on language learners' output. *Language Learning* 47: 589–636.

Wells, C. 1985. *Language Development in the Pre-School Years.* Cambridge: CUP.

Willett, J. 1995. Becoming first graders in an L2: An ethnographic study of L2 socialization. *TESOL Quarterly* 29: 473–503.

Wong-Fillmore, L. 1976. The Second Time Around: Cognitive and Social Strategies in Second Language Acquisition. PhD dissertation, Stanford University.

Wray, A. 1999. Formulaic language in learners and native speakers. *Language Teaching* 32: 213–21.

Wray, A. 2002. *Formulaic Language and the Lexicon.* Cambridge: CUP.

Appendix

Transcription conventions

Participant codes

R	Roberta
Y	Yessara
Em	Emy
E	Elsa
S	unidentified student
J	Jack
A	Ashley
T	Tiffany
Mrs A	A teacher aide
P	Parent-help (researcher)
T1	Teacher

XX	unintelligible word
<< >>	double brackets indicate high pitch, slowed speech and exaggerated pronunciation.
underline	one phonemic unit e.g., <u>my name is</u>
[ ]	square brackets around transcriber's comments
:	elongated vowel e.g., oka:y

Developing conversational skills in a second language

Language learning affordances in a multiparty classroom setting

Asta Cekaite

Linköping University

From a longitudinal perspective, the present study explores L2 novices' development of conversational skills in a primary school immersion classroom. Securing the teacher's conversational involvement in a multiparty classroom setting usually involves a considerable amount of interactional work. The present study focuses on changes in the lexical and interactional design of the utterances aimed at initiating exchange with the teacher. The design of the novices' initiating moves changed over the course of the year, moving from simple attention getters (vocatives) to lexically elaborate moves. It is argued that the interactional task of securing the teacher's uptake provides a powerful language-learning context in which success or failure to recruit a conversational partner results in modified strategies for solving interactional problems.

Introduction

Viewed from a learner perspective, the classroom is a multiparty setting that structures the learner's participation in certain ways. It is not restricted to the teacher-student dyad, but also involves the peer group, multiple interactional partners and the overwhelmingly present audience. When participating in classroom activities, children need to be attentive to the surrounding talk, including other students' talk with the teacher. According to Hatch's early statement, language evolves out of learning how "to do conversations" and "to interact verbally" in the social context of interactions (1978:404). Attention to multiple participation frameworks of the classroom setting is, thus, a fundamental aspect of school-based language acquisition (e.g., Leather & van Dam 2002). As yet, few studies have specifically explored how the multiparty setting constitutes particular language learning affordances (but see Cekaite 2007; Ohta 2001; Pallotti 1996, 2001; van Dam 2002).

From within a longitudinal perspective, the present study explores L2 novices' development of conversational skills in the multiparty interactional context of a primary school classroom. More specifically, it focuses on changes in the lexical and interactional design of children's utterances aimed at initiating a conversational exchange with the teacher. As demonstrated by ethnographic L2 classroom studies, teacher's differential treatment of L2 learners' verbal initiatives may augment or curtail learners' space for conversational participation, and consequently, language learning (Toohey 2000; Willet 1995). Securing the teacher's conversational involvement is a basic communicative challenge that the novice faces in the context of the multiple voices of a classroom (Cathcart 1986; Merritt 1982). Analyses of children's *initiating moves*, therefore, may provide insights into how the language novices actively seek out and establish opportunities for (sustained) interactions.

The present study draws on the theory of *situated learning*, which argues that learning is evident in novices' moves from initially limited peripheral involvement to increasingly active participation in the communicative practice (Lave & Wenger 1991). Language learning thereby is related to students' socialization into institutionally "ratified" ways of participating in the classroom community (Watson-Gegeo 2004). With a focus on child novices' changing participation in individual seatwork over the school year, this study highlights the ways in which the multiparty interactional setting configures specific learning affordances (i.e., opportunities) (Gibson 1979).

Several discourse-oriented studies have explored in detail the ways in which the multiparty setting may provide a context conducive to L2 beginners' linguistic and interactional development. In a longitudinal study of language learning processes in adult Japanese beginner classrooms, Ohta (2001) demonstrated that learners made use of linguistic information available in the interactional contexts of the classroom. As they participated in the classroom, the students took on a variety of interactional roles: They not only acted as "addressees who interact with the teacher", but also as overhearers, that is, "auditors who are privy to the interaction of the teacher with others" (2001:xvi). These multiple interactional floors enabled the learners to use the overheard information (from teachers and peers) in constructing their own answers. Ohta's study, however, concerns adult learners.

Related aspects of affordances provided by the multiparty framework of participation were explored in Pallotti's (2001) longitudinal case study of a 5-year-old Moroccan girl's language socialization during her first year in an Italian kindergarten classroom. Linguistic information available in the interactional setting during multiparty unstructured conversational activities was systematically employed by the novice as a conversational strategy to gain access to the ongoing interaction. The novice employed other-repetitions ("external appropriations") of the ongoing conversations to launch her own conversational initiatives.

A number of studies have demonstrated that peer group interactions constitute a fruitful site for recycling and appropriating instructional teacher talk (Björk-Willén, in press; Kanagy 1999). In classroom settings, peer interactions provide a support for L2 development by creating contexts for language use providing opportunities to talk, and to "be a part of the group" (Philp and Duchesne this volume). At an early stage of L2 acquisition, creative recycling of teaching routines in peer group language play affords collaborative attention to language form and learning through collaborative pushed output (Broner & Tarone 2001; Cekaite & Aronsson 2005; Cook 2000; Swain 2000).

A full appreciation of what early language learning is, requires that we recognize that nonverbal aspects, gestures, artifacts and body movements "all blend with language in the communicative context" (van Lier 2000: 256) and are an inextricable part of a learner's relation to the learning environment. Early language learning is largely "indicational", directly focusing on the task at hand, relying on deictic expressions and nonverbal actions (Olmedo 2003; van Lier 2000). The beginner learner's participation in classroom life, therefore, can be facilitated in instrumental classroom activities (e.g., individual work on assignments) where talk is just one means of participating (see Cekaite 2007; Goffman 1963).

During individual seatwork, students are involved in work on assignments (e.g., writing, aesthetic activities), while the teacher walks around the classroom assisting students. In a participation framework of such activities, the "incipient state of talk" is established and participants may begin new segments of conversation at every moment (Schegloff & Sacks 1973: 325). The students summon the teacher's help as needed. Because the teacher is "multitasking" when assisting the group of the students, her/his conversational involvement is fragile and the teacher often withdraws to assist other students. Therefore, in order to secure the teacher's conversational involvement the students need to issue numerous (re)initiating moves. For instance, in her study of Spanish children's interactions in a bilingual English-Spanish class, Cathcart (1986) demonstrated that novices' initiating moves soliciting the teacher's attention ('Mrs P.'; 'Lookit') constituted a substantial proportion of their language use during classroom seatwork. Several studies demonstrated that verbally elaborate initiating moves indicate (young) children's growing L1 conversational skills and their ability to design such moves in relation to the recipient's state of knowledge (Keenan Ochs et al. 1978; McTear 1985). In L1 primary classrooms, interactional moves soliciting the recipient's response involve numerous lexical repetitions and reformulations accompanied by nonverbal actions (Merritt 1982). Students verbally indicate their reason for wanting the teacher's assistance (e.g., 'Ms. C. I haven't done this yet'). These discursive strategies, however, are not explicitly taught by L2 teachers, and need to be appropriated and developed through (initially peripheral) participation in the communicative practice.

Previous child SLA studies suggest that different classroom activities appear to result in different patterns of feedback, modifications, and learning (e.g., Oliver & Mackey 2003). However, what is not clear is the effect of interactional (pragmatic) and language competencies when learners attempt to get conversational access to classroom activities. By examining these aspects our understanding of socialization into classroom norms of language use may be better understood (e.g., Watson-Gegeo 2004).

Within a longitudinal framework, the present study explores how beginner L2 learners develop language and interactional skills that are required when they initiate a conversational exchange with the teacher during individual seatwork. The lexical and syntactic shape of initiating moves will be examined in conjunction with other semiotic systems employed by the participants: paralinguistic (prosody, voice quality, pitch), nonverbal (gestures, body posture) and classroom artifacts (e.g., Goodwin 2000; Pennycook 1985). In line with a discourse-oriented approach to L2 learning (Hatch 1978), the present study will explore the ways in which the interactional task of securing the teacher's conversational involvement can contribute to the learners' development of L2 in terms of increased L2 vocabulary and increased grammaticalization. I will argue that this development is intimately related to the classroom setting as a multiparty framework for participation.

Method

Setting

The data consists of video- and audio-recordings of everyday interactions in a Swedish immersion class for refugee and immigrant children in a *mottagningsklass* (literally: "reception classroom"). The present group included children in grades 1 to 3 (7–10 years old). All children in this class of 9 students (4 girls and 5 boys) were beginning learners who had recently arrived in Sweden. Time spent in Sweden and in this class varied and the children also differed in their L2 proficiency. The main teacher, Vera, was a native speaker of Swedish. A teacher's aid, Fare (Swedish–Arabic bilingual), assisted Vera.

The present study concerns two 7-year-olds, Fusi, a Kurdish girl from Iraq and Nok, a girl from Thailand. They were the youngest children in the group and the latest arrivals in the class. They were also the least proficient in Swedish.

Classroom activities
Vera and Fare employed teaching techniques that were centered on active student participation. The activities ranged from teacher-led book reading, language drills and singing to individual work on tasks such as writing, mathematics and aes-

thetic activities (e.g., drawing). The aesthetic activities were intended to introduce new Swedish vocabulary in the context of the project work (e.g., building cartoon houses, cutting paper, and drawing). During the early stage of L2 acquisition the novices' participation was limited to individual seatwork activities.

Recordings and data

The children's classroom interactions were video-recorded during three periods, covering an early (autumn), middle (winter) and late phase (late spring) of the school year (90 hours of recordings). The data for this study are recordings of individual work on assignments. The translations were done by a native speaker of English. Our ambition has been to preserve the children's original style of speaking to the greatest possible extent, including errors (e.g., omitted verb copulas as in *jag klar* 'I ready', pre-verb negations *jag inte skriva här* 'I not write here' and word order *så måla* 'like this paint'.

The analytic unit of the present study is comprised of children's interactional moves designed to initiate (or re-initiate) an exchange with the teacher. They have been analysed in relation to the children's *communicative projects* (Linell 1998). The term communicative project is meant to include not only the verbally invoked topic, but also a range of visible displays (e.g., of classroom artefacts) that invoked the reason for the initiating move. A communicative project is defined "in terms of the task it is designed to solve, and/or in fact actually solves" (Linell 1998:220). In the present classroom, communicative projects frequently encompass getting feedback, evaluation, instructions, or asking for permission for some action.

Methodological considerations

Methodologically, the choice of longitudinal naturalistic data was inspired by studies within language socialization paradigms (Ochs 1996; Watson-Gegeo 2004). Longitudinal data collection, combined with a microanalytical approach, allowed for explorations of the novices' performances over time as well as documenting the genesis of novices' language and interactional skills within the situated activity context (Kasper & Rose 2002; Ochs 1996).

First phase: Establishing the teacher's visual attention

In order to outline a more complete picture of the interactional ecology of the present classroom, I will briefly comment on the methods that advanced students in the classroom relied upon when soliciting the teacher's response. At the time, these students displayed a broad range of interactional repertoires and L2 skills. When soliciting the teacher's assistance, they recurrently introduced their communicative project verbally, as a request for action on the teacher's part. In the following example (see Appendix for transcription conventions), Abdi, an advanced learner, is finishing his work with modeling clay and calls the teacher.

(1)

→   1 Abdi: JAG KLAR. ((puts modelling clay inside his desk))
                I READY. ((puts modelling clay inside his desk))
     2 Vera: ((occupied with another child))

((several turns omitted))

→   5 Abdi: Vera jag ska gå ut. Hejdå! ((smiles, leaves his place))
                Vera I'm going out. Goodbye! ((smiles, leaves his place))
     6 Vera: (20) ((occupied with another child))
→   7 Abdi: Vera: Vera jag ska gå på rasten?
                Vera: Vera I'm going out for the break?
     8 Vera: Ah (.) Det kan du göra.
                Yeah (.) you can do that.

Abdi calls the teacher several times before he finally secures her involvement. Noticeably, his initiating moves entail both verbal and nonverbal features. Abdi solicits her reply with an announcement of his work progress *jag klar* 'I ready' (line 1). The formula 'I ready' was a widely used method for engaging in exchanges with the teacher, when calling for evaluation or help with a new task.

Later, he uses an attention-getting device (a vocative) and specifies his communicative project, *Vera jag ska gå ut* 'Vera I'm going out'. His farewell 'Goodbye' (line 5) is accompanied by an embodied performance of "leaving", in his moving toward the classroom door. Abdi gains the teacher's involvement by summoning her by her name and spelling out his communicative project: *Jag ska gå på rasten* 'I'm going out for the break' (line 7).

Some of the important maxims of children's (appropriate) participation in interaction are "being persistent" (Cathcart 1986) and "being relevant" to the conversational activity at hand (Grice 1975; Sacks 1992). In educational settings, children have restricted rights to initiate talk and to choose topics. In the present classroom, one way of "being relevant" was to indicate that one's initiating move was related to classroom work. When previous attempts to obtain the teacher's response failed, Abdi, the advanced learner, was persistent in pursuing the teacher's response (Ex.1). He shaped his soliciting moves by verbally introducing and reformulating his communicative project. Thereby, he appealed to the teacher's responsibility to assist the children. Being persistent and being informative about the communicative project constituted important interactional devices for securing the teacher's conversational uptake.

Novices' initiating moves: vocatives, deictic and one-word directives

At the outset of the school year, that is, during their early phase of the immersion classroom, the girls, Nok and Fusi, were speakers of a basic variety of Swedish (Klein & Perdue 1997). The girls were rather silent and their interactional participation was limited to the individual work on the given assignment. The girls' L2 resources were very limited and included a deictic *här* 'here', proper names, a handful of nouns and verbs, numerals (one to ten), and several formulaic phrases (greeting and leave-taking routines). However, the beginners', similar to the more advanced learners', initiating moves were also, at least to some extent, informative about the communicative project. A detailed analysis of the multiple semiotic modalities employed by the novices indicates the intricate work that they undertake to achieve the communicatively loaded content of initiating moves.

Resources the novices relied on included: visual displays of classroom artifacts, gestures, verbal attention-getters (proper names at the turn-initial position, Keenan Ochs *et al.* 1978; McTear 1985) and rudimentary lexical information on the communicative project. The novices employed (one-word) directives *titta*, *kom*, a deictic *här*. Occasionally they nominated some action *klippa* 'cut' or the object or person to look at *titta Layla* 'look Layla'; *Vera bad titta* 'Vera bath look' (e.g., "attention directing devices", McTear 1985). By directing the teacher's gaze to a certain assignment-related object, such actions solicited evaluation or instructions on classroom work. In Example 2, the children are doing writing exercises.

(2)

→   1 Fusi: Vera titta
              Vera look
     2 Vera: ((turns to Fusi))
→   3 Fusi: Här ((points at the book))
              Here ((points at the book))
     4 Vera: Va fint du har skrivit. ((in a positive voice))
              How nicely you have written. ((in a positive voice))
     5 Vera: Va duktig du är Fusi!
              How clever you are Fusi!

Upon finishing her task, Fusi solicits the teacher's attention using a vocative and a directive to look at something (line 1). When Vera turns toward Fusi, Fusi issues a deictic *här* and points to her book (line 3). Thereby, Fusi invokes the topic of the exchange and indicates why the teacher's assistance is needed. Vera looks at her writing assignment and positively evaluates her work (line 4; 5). She, thus, makes an adequate interpretation of the visual display of the classroom artifact.

Such lexical items (attention getters, directive 'titta' and deictic 'här') did not provide specific verbal information about the child's progress on the task. Rather, the children and the teachers had to rely primarily on cues in the domain of the mutually acknowledged classroom activity and expressive nonverbal behavior (e.g., gestures, classroom artifacts and the specifics of the current classroom assignment) (see also Olmedo 2003). Instead of directly telling the teacher why they needed the teacher's assistance, the girls first had to establish the teacher's visual attention.

Upgrading initiating moves

Because the classroom constituted a multiparty framework of participation, the teacher's immediate uptake could not be taken for granted. The novices employed a range of methods for handling competition for the teacher's attention and assistance. For instance, they sometimes simply left their desk and approached the teacher with their books. They also upgraded the visibility of their initiating moves by calling the teacher while standing, or simultaneously visually displaying the relevant classroom artifact. In the following episode, the children are working with Ikea catalogues. They have to find pictures of different pieces of furniture. Before Fusi starts her work, she raises her magazine toward Vera.

(3)

→	1	Fusi:	Här Vera? ((catalogue raised toward Vera))
			Here Vera?
	2	Vera:	((assists Ahmed))
	3	Fusi:	((holds the catalogue (1 minute), then puts it down))
→	4	Fusi:	Vera här? ((raises the catalogue toward Vera))
			Vera here? ((raises the catalogue toward Vera))
	5	Vera:	((steps toward Fusi, but again stops at Ahmed))
	6	Fusi:	((puts down the catalogue))
	7	Vera:	((approaches Fusi))
→	8	Fusi:	Här? ((points at her catalogue))
			Here? ((points at her catalogue))
	9	Vera:	Ah. Titta vilket du vill ha? ((turns the pages of the catalogue))
			Yeah. Look which one do you want?((turns the pages of the catalogue))
	10	Fusi:	((points at a picture))
	11	Vera:	((goes to another student))

In her initiating move, Fusi draws the teacher's visual attention to the catalogue *här Vera*. She highlights her talk by raising the catalogue toward the teacher. Moreover, she holds the catalogue for a considerable time (lines 1; 3). The teacher, however, is busy assisting Ahmed, and Fusi repeats her summons (line 4). When Vera finally approaches Fusi's desk, she provides further instructions on the task (line 9).

Hence, the visual display of the catalogue (relevant to the current classroom assignment) served as a device in securing the teacher's uptake.

The girls also highlighted their initiating moves by indexing them as affectively charged action. Affective stance refers to a "mood, attitude, feeling, and disposition, as well as degrees of emotional intensity vis-à-vis some focus of concern" (Ochs 1996:410) and can be indexed using verbal and nonverbal devices. When indexing affective stances, the girls primarily relied on paralinguistic resources, laughter, interjections ('ojojoj') and playful "enactments" (acting "smelling something disgusting", showing "too much glue on the paper"). In this example, the children are pulling out letters from the plastic sheet.

(4)

→   1 Nok: ha ha titta Vera titta: ((acts out 'difficulty of pulling out the letters'))
                 ha ha look Vera loo:k ((acts out 'difficulty of pulling out the letters'))
    2 Vera: Ah. Man får vara försiktig. ((turns to Nok))
               Yeah. One needs to be careful. ((turns to Nok))

Nok frames her initiating move as entertaining and playful: when summoning Vera, she laughs and "acts" that pulling out the letters is difficult (line 1). As demonstrated by Vera's response, such playful "enactments" made relevant the teacher's (affective) alignment and a co-assessment of some aspect of the classroom work.

Rudimentary lexical design: Nominating assignment-relevant objects and actions
On several occasions, the novices provided rudimentary lexical information on the communicative project. The novices nominated some (assignment-relevant) object or action. These resources were limited to a handful of vocabulary items taught during aesthetic activities. Such labelings were, however, comprehensible only in the context of the classroom activity at hand.

In the following episode, the children have got pictures of different pieces of furniture that have to be cut from paper. Fusi has a picture of a toilet.

(5) a.

    1 Sawan: ha ha ha FUSI HAR EN TOALETT. FUSI TOALETT. ((to Nok))
                  ha ha ha FUSI HAS A TOILET. FUSI TOILET. ((to Nok))
→   2 Fusi: Nok toalett ((calls Nok, shows her picture))
                 Nok toilet ((calls Nok, shows her picture))

Upon seeing that Fusi gets a picture of a toilet, Sawan playfully addresses Nok and laughs at Fusi *Fusi toalett* (line 1). Fusi then calls Nok, shows her the picture and nominates the object to look at (line 2). Noticeably, she appropriates the lexical item *toalett* from Sawan's utterance.

Some time later, the teacher Fare gives a new assignment. He asks the children to write from the whiteboard new Swedish words (different pieces of furniture that the children were working with).

(5) b.

→ 1 Fusi: TOALETT ((standing, to Fare))
              TOILET ((standing, to Fare))
   2 Fare: ((leaves the whiteboard and approaches Fusi))
   3 Fare: Du skriver här ((points at Fusi's paper))
              You write here ((points at Fusi's paper))
   4 Fusi: ((writes)

Fusi rises from her seat and solicits the teacher's response by nominating an assignment-relevant object (in a markedly high volume). Her actions direct the teacher's attention to her work on the current assignment: Fare approaches her and provides detailed instructions (lines 2, 3).

The next extract (Ex. 6a, b) presents another example of how a novice recycles a lexical item indicating an assignment-relevant object. The children have to cut out a picture of a bathtub. Nok does not know which of the several pictures (of a bathtub) she has to cut out and calls the teacher.

(6) a.

   1 Nok: Vera bad titta ((shows the action of cutting paper))
              Vera bath look ((shows the action of cutting paper))
   2 Vera: Är badet klippt? ((turns to Nok)) (.) Får jag se?
              Have you cut out the bath? ((turns to Nok)) (.) *May I see?*
   3 Nok: ((slowly displays the paper))
   4 Vera: ((turns to another student))
→ 5 Nok: Vera det klippa
              Vera it cut
   6 Vera: Badkaret ja (.) där ((points)) ska du klippa. ((goes away))
              The bathtub yeah (.) there ((points)) *you should cut.* ((goes away))

Nok addresses the teacher and nominates the object to look at *bad* (line 1). She also displays the sheet of paper from the journal. The teacher, however, misunderstands Nok's actions: she asks whether Nok has already finished her task and offers an evaluation (*är badet klippt? får jag se*, line 2). While Nok displays her cutting, the teacher turns to another student. Nok then summons the teacher again. She directs the teacher to the trouble source by displaying the paper and nominating the assignment-related object and action *det klippa* (verb appropriated from the teacher's turn, line 5). Noticeably, whereas the teacher uses a participle form 'klippt' (line 2), in her appropriation (line 5). Nok relies on a generalized uninflected verb form 'klippa' (characteristic for the basic variety of Swedish, Klein &

Perdue 1997: 320).[1] Vera identifies Nok's difficulties with the assignment – Nok was looking at the wrong side of the paper – and instructs her about the assignment (line 6). As part of a vocabulary practice, Vera repeats (emphatically marking) the gloss *badkaret* and points to the image of the bathtub (line 6).

Studies of child L2 learners' encounters in informal settings have demonstrated that participation in conversational exchanges (e.g., attention-getting, topic nominations and expansions) may facilitate L2 acquisition (e.g., through vertical and horizontal constructions) (Hatch 1978; Pallotti 2001; on L1 see Corrin *et al.* 2001; Scollon 1979). Once the participants' mutual focus of attention on a relevant artifact is established, the competent speakers (adults) expand the indicated topic in collaboration with the child. The adult assists the child in building up various language constructions (which may consist of a set of such relationships as object identification, agent-action, or attribute description) (Hatch 1978).

In the present classroom, the teachers did not always have time to get involved in sustained interactions and lengthy development of the topic. They primarily engaged in instructional talk about the assignment. Their responses to the learners ranged from minimal acknowledgements (e.g., a head nod, *mh*, *bra* 'good'), assessments and evaluations of work on assignment (*va duktig du är* 'how clever you are'), confirmation questions (*är du klar?* 'have you finished'?), to further instructions on assignment (*där ska du klippa* 'there you should cut'). Importantly, however, novices appropriated and recycled parts of the teacher's instructional talk (e.g., object or action labels, agent-action) when designing their initiating moves. The following example is an immediate continuation of the previous episode (Ex. 6a). It demonstrates how such rudimentary and lexicalized initiating moves are employed for soliciting a classmate's response.

(6) b.

→	1 Nok:	Titta jag ((to Fusi, shows the action of cutting paper))
		Look I ((to Fusi, shows the action of cutting paper))
	2 Fusi:	((turned away from Nok))
→	3 Nok:	Titta jag klippa
		Look I cut
	4 Fusi:	((turns to Nok, looks smiling))

When Nok's initial attempt (*titta jag*) to draw Fusi's attention to her visual display of the cutting paper is unsuccessful, she rearranges her utterance by adding additional information: she nominates the assignment-relevant action (line 3). She

---

1. In Ex. (6a), Nok can be seen not being able to identify and repeat the participle form employed by the teacher. Both novices relied on generalized uninflected verb forms (e.g.,'klippa') during the early and the middle period of the year.

incorporates verbal resources from her previous encounter with Vera *jag klippa* 'I cut' (that can be seen as an agent-action construction) and finally secures Fusi's involvement (line 3). Silently smiling, Fusi observes Nok's actions.

In sum, although the L2 novices could not make initiating moves that provided elaborate semantic information about their communicative projects, their initiating moves were still informative about the upcoming topic, primarily through their use of nonverbal resources. A thorough analysis of these activities also demonstrates some of the initial steps toward development of the language and interactional skills, in that the novices configured the L2 resources available so as to create incentive for the teacher to respond.

Middle phase: Changing conditions for participation

By the middle of the year, during the second phase, the girls displayed increasing L2 skills. Their lexical repertoires covered a broader range of semantic domains, and they produced simple utterances with a few constituents organized around the verb. The lexical items, however, usually occurred in one invariant form (e.g., verbs, nouns were in base form), and the negative form was predominantly located in the pre-verb position (e.g., typical of Swedish basic variety). Their verbal contributions were largely based on conventionalized phrases and recyclings of Swedish children's songs or parts of language drills.

Conventionalized phrases

The girls' participation in individual seatwork activities changed. They had developed a broader range of methods to solicit the teacher's conversational involvement. Along with simple vocatives and imperatives (e.g., attention-getters, 'look', 'come'), they could indicate the communicative project using more elaborate lexical means. They employed a limited set of assignment-related conventionalized expressions that covered the lexical domain of their progress on on-task work and task-related objects: boundary markers *klar* 'ready', *jag klar* 'I ready', *alla klar* 'all ready', *kom klar jag* 'come I ready', complaints ('competence disclaimers') *jag inte kan* 'I not can', *jag inte skriva här* 'I not write here'; *nej skriv* 'no write', directives to look at a specific object *titta på min bok* 'look at my book', and reading aloud the mathematical operation they were about to solve (*plus fem?* 'plus five?'). Such initiating moves constituted a first pair part of an adjacency pair (statement-comment, request for assistance-reply) and made relevant a response: the teacher's comment, evaluation or further instructions (e.g., Sacks 1992). In the following example, Fusi is working on a math exercise.

(7)

→ 1 Fusi: Klar ((looks at Fare))
              Ready ((looks at Fare))
   2 Fare: ((talks to Sawan, turned from Fusi))
→ 3 Fusi: Fare jag klar
              Fare I ready
   4 Fare: ((talks to Sawan))
→ 5 Fusi: Kom jag klar ((to Martin, pointing at her book))
              Come I ready ((to Martin, pointing at her book))
   6 Martin: ((moves toward Fusi))
→ 7 Fusi: ((points at her exercise))
   8 Martin: ((checks Fusi's exercise)) va bra
              ((checks Fusi's exercise)) *good*

In her initiating utterance, Fusi announces the completion of her task (*klar* line 1) and looks at Fare. She is persistent and solicits the teacher's response through several repetitions and transformations of the initial utterance (providing lexical information on the status of her work on the exercise, lines 3; 5). Initially, this conventionalized phrase *jag klar* 'I ready' was employed by more advanced learners (Ex. 1). As can be seen, the novices "overhear" these utterances as peripheral participants in the advanced students' interactions with the teacher and recycle them in their own initiating moves (e.g., Ohta 2001).

When the teacher, Fare, does not respond, Fusi changes the addressee and calls Martin, a temporary substitute teacher. Simultaneously, she is pointing to the exercise (line 5). Martin's response ('good') indicates that he adequately interprets Fusi's soliciting move as a request for evaluation.

Socialization into appropriate pragmatic action
In the middle of the year, the girls were participating more actively in classroom activities. They were asserting their participation rights, for instance, by demanding the teacher's assistance. However, as the time the girls spent in the classroom accumulated, norms for their participation in classroom activities were changing. Some of these changes involved a prohibition against leaving the desk during the lesson. Such moves were tolerated when the girls were still newcomers, but during the second phase, they were usually negatively sanctioned. Lexically more elaborate turns provided a resource for eliciting the teacher's response in a socially appropriate and informative manner.

In the following example, both girls, Fusi and Nok, had been calling the teacher Fare, for a considerable time, but without success. After some time, the girls engaged in an open competition for Fare's assistance. Just before this episode,

Fusi had left her desk and tried to drag the teacher to her desk. However, Fare refused to comply.

(8)

   1   Fare: JAG HJÄLPER Layla. Du skall sitta där! ((to Fusi))
                I'M HELPING Layla. You must sit there! ((to Fusi))

→ 2   Nok: Fare jag klar ((demanding, points with a pencil at her book))
                 Fare I ready ((demanding, points with a pencil at her book))

   3   Fare: Gå ditt (0.5) gå ditt! ((to Fusi))
                 Go there (0.5) go there! ((to Fusi))

→ 4   Fusi: x **taali** ((in Arabic))
                 x come ((in Arabic))

   5   Fare: Sitt där och vänta din tur! ((pushes her gently to her desk))
                 Sit there and wait your turn! ((pushes her gently to her desk))

→ 6   Fusi: xxx! ((angry, goes back to her desk))

   7   Fare: Nej nej! [Vänta på din tur!
                 No no! Wait for your turn!

→ 8   Nok: [Ett två tre] Fare ((points at her book))
                      One two three Fare ((points at her book))

   9   Fare: ((talks with Layla))

→ 10 Nok: Titta på min bok ((to Fare, 'smiley' voice, displays her book))
                 Look at my book ((to Fare, 'smiley' voice, displays her book))

  11 Fare: ((talks with Layla))

→ 12 Nok: Titta (.) titta på min bok. Ett två tre ((pointing, to Sawan))
                 Look (.) look at my book. One two three ((pointing, to Sawan))

  13 Sawan: Jag skall titta på Nok! ((smiles))
                 I'll look at Nok! ((smiles))

Some minutes later Fare finishes assisting Layla and approaches Nok:

  23 Fare: Vad vill du fråga om? ((to Nok, looks at her book))
                 What do you want to ask? ((to Nok, looks at her book))

Although Fusi tries to argue (in Arabic) that Fare must come to help her, he refuses and disciplines her, ordering her to go back and sit at her place (lines 1–7). Nok also tries to secure the teacher's response with the use of a vocative, an announcement about the progress of her work (conventionalized request for evaluation *jag klar*), and a pointing gesture (line 2). Nok upgrades her actions: She indicates what exercises the teacher must look at by counting them and pointing at the book (*ett två tre* 'one two three', line 8). She even explicitly directs the teacher to scrutinize her book *titta på min bok* 'look at my book' (line 10). Compared to Nok's similar soliciting move *Vera bad titta* 'Vera bath look' (Example 6a) at the outset of the school year, her soliciting move here demonstrates her emergent language and interactional skills: Her utterance is more grammaticalized (she uses the preposition *på* 'at' and the possessive pronoun *min* 'mine'). Moreover, by employing the possessive 'mine', Nok specifically draws the teacher's attention to her book.

However, Fare is busy with Layla and Nok turns to the boy Sawan instead. She employs a similar phrase (line 12). Sawan announces that he will look at Nok, and the children (Nok and Sawan) establish a publicly visible playful alignment (line 13).

When Fare finishes assisting Layla, he directly approaches Nok (line 23). His question *vad vill du fråga om* 'what do you want to ask?' indicates that he has heard Nok's earlier attempts to secure his response (although the reason for Nok's soliciting attempts is not specified in detail).

Fare's different responses to Nok and Fusi provide evidence of socialization into "appropriate" classroom behavior. Fare insists that Fusi modify her actions, while his positive response to Nok indicates that verbalized initiating moves are appropriate interactional resources for recruiting the teacher's uptake. By employing an "appropriate" pragmatic turn design with modulated affective displays, Nok achieved participation in classroom discourse and brought about both the classmate's and the teacher's attention (i.e, she "won" the competition). Lexicalized initiating moves thereby created qualitatively different opportunities for the novices' participation in classroom discourse.

At the time, the girls were acquiring L2 linguistic means for expressing affect. Along with the extensive use of prosodic means for affective indexing of the initiating moves, some of the (emerging) linguistic means used were: intensifiers *lilla* 'little', *mycket* 'a lot', and affectively charged discursive actions of complaining (competence disclaimers *jag inte* + *x* 'I not + x' or *jag inte kan* + *verb/noun/deictic* 'I not can + verb/noun/deictic'). When prosodically indexed with a moaning voice, markedly elongated last vowels, or "pretend crying", they were employed to indicate the student's inability to continue work on the assignment. In the following example, Nok has a problem with her math assignment and she has been calling Fare for some time.

(9)

	1	Fare:	Var är din mattebok? ((to Hiwa))
			Where is your math book? ((to Hiwa))
→	2	Nok:	Fare: ((lies on desk)) ne ((erases something in her book))
			Fare: ((lies on desk)) no ((erases something in her book))
	3	Fare:	((talks to Hiwa))
→	4	Nok:	Fare:: ((lying on the desk, monotonously))

→   5   Nok: Jag inte skriva här här ((croaky voice, points to her book))
                I not write here here ((croaky voice, points to her book))
→   6   Nok: a:: Fare::: ((moaning))
    7   Fare: ((talks with Hiwa, then turns to Nok))

Nok summons Fare (line 2). She indexes her turn with a "resigned" affective stance prosodically (croaky voice, markedly elongated final vowel) and through her body posture (half-lying on her desk, indicating "not working"). She elaborates her subsequent attempt with a complaint *jag inte skriva här här* that serves as a request for the teacher's assistance, and an interjection 'a::' (a nonlexicalized affect marker, pretend "crying", lines 4–6). Although her utterance is grammatically incorrect (the modal auxiliary *kan* is left out, and negation *inte* is located prior to the verb), the multimodal resources invoke the "resigned" affective stance of a student who is not able to continue her current assignment.

In sum, the girls' L2 repertoires were still limited and they primarily relied on simple attention-getting devices (vocatives) and a set of conventionalized phrases, elaborating their actions with paralinguistic and nonverbal resources. Compared with their affectively marked contributions (indexed by playfulness and laughter) at the beginning of the school year, the girls broadened their interactional repertoires with displays of "needy" and "demanding" affective stances. By displaying the emotions "needy", "irritated", "demanding", "frustrated", "resigned", the students acted upon the teacher's responsibility to supervise classroom work, thereby making her/him accountable for responding. Importantly, such initiating moves needed to be finely-tuned according to the local norms of classroom behavior (see the teacher's disciplining of Fusi, Ex. 8).

The late phase: Verbally informative initiating moves

By the third period (at the end of the year), the girls become active members of the classroom community. They participated in a wide range of classroom activities. However, they were still speakers of a basic variety of Swedish. They relied primarily on pragmatic principles of discourse organization and they still used rather uncomplicated syntax. On the other hand, their utterances were longer and entailed more creative constructions emerging from gradual analysis, break up and recombination of formulas (initially found in teacher and peer talk on various assignments).

There were also significant changes in how they organized their interactional participation in individual work on task, and in the ways in which they solicited the teacher's conversational involvement. The girls' initiating utterances clearly exceeded in length and complexity those made earlier (e.g., in the middle of

the year). They employed a broad range of semantically, syntactically, and prag-
matically more complex actions: wh-questions (*Vera vad jag skriva?* 'Vera what
I write?') and Y-No questions (*Fare här åtta fel?* 'Fare here eight wrong?', *Vera
ta den papper?* 'Vera take this paper?') that invited the teacher to answer; evaluation; further instructions; or, permission. The ongoing elaboration of vocabulary
and inflectional morphology provides evidence of further linguistic development
(e.g., emerging copula and tense markers). The modal system has been developing
(primarily including modal verbs that expressed volition). The girls formulated
requests by specifying their wishes with respect to some aspect of the classroom
work (*jag vill också Olles bok* 'I want also Olle's book'). They were thereby able
to bring about the teacher's response by verbally indicating their communicative
projects.

Specifying the trouble source
The learners were able to produce utterances that verbally specified the source of
trouble, thus indicating why the teacher's assistance was needed. The conversational features available in classroom discourse provided patterns for such interactional moves. Recurrently, they were modeled on the teacher's assignment-related
talk. In the following example, Fusi is working on math.

(10)   a.

→   1   Fusi: FARE här åtta fel? ((book raised)) Ojdå ((eraser falls down))
                FARE here eight wrong? ((book raised)) *Oops* ((eraser falls down))

→   2   Fusi: Kom här åtta fel?
                Come here eight wrong?

    3   Fare: Nej det är rätt. ((looks))
                No it's right ((looks))

→   4   Fusi: Jag gör rätt! ((gladly))
                I do it right! ((gladly))

Fusi's initiating moves (lines 1–2) entail both verbal and nonverbal features: She
summons Fare with an emphatically marked vocative, raises her book toward him,
and verbally specifies why the teacher's assistance is needed. She asks whether her
math results are wrong (*här åtta fel?* 'here eight wrong?'). Fusi's questions (lines
1–2) are formed as statements with interrogative intonation (they do not follow
the inverted verb-subject word order, as required in Swedish). Fare turns to Fusi
and looks at her book. His response (*nej det är rätt* 'no it's right') demonstrates
that he orients not only to Fusi's display of the classroom artifact, but also to the
verbal content of her turn (line 3). Upon receiving a positive evaluation, Fusi announces her "academic competence" in a celebratory manner by appropriating

the key word *rätt* ('right') from Fare's evaluation turn (line 4). Some minutes later, Fusi calls Vera, who is talking to another student.

(10) b.

→   1   Fusi: Här är rätt Vera? ((points to the exercise)) Här är-
                    This is right Vera? ((points to the exercise)) This is-

     2   Vera: Det här är rätt ((turns to Fusi, marks her exercise))
                    This one is right ((turns to Fusi, marks her exercise))

Fusi's soliciting move *'här är rätt Vera?'* 'this is right?' specifically invites an evaluation. Her question is formulated as a statement with interrogative intonation (with non-inverted word order). She also points to the exercise (line 1). Vera turns to her and evaluates her assignment using a similar construction *det här är rätt* 'this one is right' (line 2).

Analysis of teacher talk provides some of the situational cues as to where these forms are used and how they are acquired (e.g., Cathcart 1986). Fusi's question *här är rätt?* 'this is right?' resembles the lexical and syntactic shape of the teacher's routine evaluation statements (e.g., adj. *fel* 'right', *rätt* 'wrong'; the non-inverted word order in a partial recycling of copula and predicate construction). Noticeably, both Vera and Fare employed this evaluative statement (*det här är rätt*) in their talk with Fusi (Examples 9a, b).

Furthermore, even with more complex linguistic resources available, the interactional design of Fusi's initiating moves involved both verbal and nonverbal resources. The nonverbal actions (including use of the classroom artifacts) were, thus, an inextricable part of the learners' interactional repertoire and "efficient" means for securing the teacher's uptake in this instrumental classroom activity (see Leather & van Dam 2002).

Increased participation: Nominating different steps in work on assignment
The novices displayed their emergent interactional skills and creative language use in other domains as well. They adjusted their lexical choices when nominating the topic from general, conventionalized utterances to more specific vocabulary. The communicative projects became more varied and they included different domains of work on the assignment. In the following example, the children are cutting different shapes (a flower, a heart).

(11) a.

→   1   Fusi: JAG HAR OCKSÅ PLUPPAR VERA JAG ÄR KLAR
                    I ALSO HAVE STARS VERA I'M READY

     2   Vera: Har du sex stycken nu? ((cutting paper))
                    Do you have six now? ((cutting paper))

→   3   Fusi: A jag har alla jag har alla
                        Yeah I have them all I have them all

     4   Vera: Då kan du faktisk börja måla lite då.
                        Then you can start painting a little.

     5   Abdi: VERA: =

     6   Miran: =JAG ÄR KLAR=
                        =I'M READY=

→   7   Fusi: =OKEY JAG MÅLAR.
                        =OK I'M PAINTING.

In her initiating move (line 1), Fusi asks for positive feedback to her work (*jag har också pluppar* 'I have also stars'[2]). She also provides an account concerning why she deserves it: *Vera jag är klar* 'Vera I'm ready'. Vera then specifically inquires about Fusi's assignment (line 2). Fusi accounts for her work results *a jag har alla* 'yeah I have all' (line 3). Upon receiving Vera's instructions, Fusi verbalizes her next action *Okey jag målar*, thereby loudly ratifying the teacher's instructions (line 7).

A short time later, Fusi calls the teacher again. This time she asks for permission to color a paper heart.

(11) b.

→   1   Fusi: VERA (.) jag vill måla den ((raises the paper heart))
                        VERA (.) I want to paint this ((raises the paper heart))

     2   Vera: Ah du kan börja göra det ((looks at Fusi))
                        Yeah you can start doing it ((looks at Fusi))

     3   Fusi: O:key: ((starts coloring))

→   4   Fusi: SÅ MÅLA VERA? ((turns to Vera, raises the paper heart))
                        LIKE THIS PAINT VERA? ((turns to Vera, raises the paper heart))

→   5   Fusi: VERA SÅ MÅLA också? (.) VERA så måla? ((moves the heart))
                        VERA LIKE THIS PAINT too? (.) VERA like this paint? ((moves the heart))

     6   Vera: Ah du målar så. ((comes to Fusi, demonstrates how to color))
                        Yeah you paint like this. ((comes to Fusi, demonstrates how to color))

Fusi arranges her turn to indicate its noteworthiness: She specifies the recipient, Vera, and verbally introduces her request *jag vill måla den* 'I want to paint this'. Fusi also uses embodied action: She raises the paper heart (line 1). Vera turns to Fusi and provides further instructions *du kan börja göra det* 'yeah you can start doing it' (line 2). Fusi then asks for more specific instructions *så måla också?* (lines 4–5).

---

2.   Usually, when the children finished their assignments, Vera rewarded them with 'pluppar': She drew small stars on the whiteboard beside the child's name. Fusi is referring to this procedure.

Vera, however, has turned to other students, and Fusi recycles her soliciting move several times before she finally brings about Vera's involvement (lines 4–5).

Although Fusi's utterances (Ex. 10a, line 7; Ex. 10b, lines 1; 4–5) involve repetitive use of a single verb *måla*, she is able to accomplish a range of inter-actional moves (i.e., questions, requests, ratifications, and a simple argumentative sequence). With her verbally and nonverbally elaborated soliciting moves, Fusi skillfully manages to re-establish the teacher's uptake several times, and is able to achieve instructions on different stages of her work on task, thereby demonstrating her fuller management of the activity.

Affect-loaded terms of address

At the end of the year, the girls have broadened their L2 repertoires and have acquired a range of affect-carrying linguistic devices (e.g., verbs, adjectives denot-ing emotions). When calling the teacher, they employed the affect-loaded term of address *snälla* 'dear'. The address term *snälla* is usually employed in informal con-versations and mitigates a request, indexing it as an appeal (by literally portraying the addressee as a 'dear', 'kind' person[3]). In the present institutional setting, the affect marked address routine "snälla + the child's name" was initially used by the teachers when requesting something from the children. In the following example, Nok calls the teacher while she is working on a math assignment.

(12)

→   1   Nok: FARE SNÄLLA: KOM du:: (('pleading' voice))
                FARE DEA:R COME you:: (('pleading' voice))
    2   Fare: ((approaches Nok))
    3   Nok: Jag vet titta titta ((browses in her book))
                I know look look ((browses her in book))
    4   Fare: mh

Nok summons Fare by indexing her turn as an affectively charged action: She em-ploys prosodic resources (elongated vowels, "pleading" voice, in a markedly loud volume) and the affect-loaded term of address *snälla* (line 1). Fare approaches Nok, and she shows him her exercise book.

When calling the teacher, the more advanced learners employed *snälla* already during the second period, in the middle of the year. Nok and Fusi (the less ad-vanced learners) appropriated and employed *snälla* by the end of the school year. The interactional task of gaining participation in a competitive multiparty setting may thus contribute to the learner's development of L2 affective vocabulary (see

---

3.   'Snälla' can also be translated as 'sweet', 'kind'.

also studies on children's L2 socialization Pallotti 1996, 2001; Willet 1995, on L1 see Ochs 1988).[4]

Concluding discussion

Some of the crucial tasks the children face in the classroom are related to gaining access to classroom activities and to interactions in general. In the present immersion class, the children produced a range of different kinds of initiating moves, some of which were successful, but most of which were not. Gaining the recipient's attention and securing conversational involvement in the multiple chorus of a classroom usually involved a considerable amount of interactional work. Successful achievement of involvement depended on the children's knowledge of the social ecological demands of the classroom.

The present longitudinal study highlights the ways in which the multiparty interactional context shaped learning affordances in classroom interactions. Participation in the communicative practices of the present classroom community involved crucial learning of how to handle interactional competition. From a longitudinal perspective, these local interactional constraints shaped the novices' development of interactional repertoires. Over the course of the year, the children's initiating moves show us both the learners' developing L2 in terms of increased grammaticalization, and increased L2 vocabulary. The girls' developmental trajectory from simple (one word) to lexically more complex and informative initiating moves can be partly attributed to the need to assert oneself in order to bring about the teacher's involvement.

In the present immersion setting, the learners shaped their initiating moves in a number of ways. From the outset of the school year, the advanced learners frequently employed lexicalized, verbally elaborate initiating moves (Ex. 1). They presented and verbally spelled out the communicative project (e.g., requests for evaluation, further instructions on classroom work) orienting to the teacher's duties and obligations to supervise and help the children.

At an early stage of L2 acquisition, the beginning learners, Fusi and Nok, were mainly dependent on nonverbal resources, attention-getting devices (proper names) and imperatives such as 'look', 'come'. These resources, however, were not

4.   In the present classroom, the novices appropriated the affect-loaded address terms relatively late (at the end of the school year), whereas Pallotti's (1996) study, conducted in a kindergarten setting, demonstrates that the five-year old novice acquired similar linguistic devices (affective affixes in address terms) rather early. This difference in the rate of acquisition might be accounted for by the more formal character of interactions in school as compared to the kindergarten setting.

loaded with semantic information about the upcoming topic of exchange. A detailed analysis of the multiple modalities invoked by participants demonstrates the intricate work that L2 novices engage in to achieve the communicatively loaded content of initiating moves. They indicated their communicative project nonverbally (e.g., through book displays, playful enactments) (Ex. 2 and Ex. 3).

During the second period (in the middle of the year), when calling the teacher, the girls relied to a great extent on deictics, directives and a set of local conventionalized expressions. They covered a limited range of semantic domains concerning work on assignments. Phrases such as 'Fare I ready', 'look I ready', 'I not write' served as requests for the teacher's assistance (Ex.7). The girls also employed verbal and nonverbal devices for highlighting their soliciting attempts through (finely-tuned) affective stances. By displaying "resigned", "unhappy", they appealed to the teacher's institutional responsibilities for the children's classroom work and their conduct (Ex. 9).

By the end of the year, the girls had mastered a more elaborate Swedish repertoire and interactional skills allowing them to produce lexically more complex and informative initiating moves. They recurrently employed parts of the teacher's assignment talk (e.g., evaluative comments, formulated as questions, Ex. 10a; b). They were also able to nominate different steps in their classroom work, thereby demonstrating their fuller management of the classroom activity and their increased participation (Ex. 11a, b) (see Lave & Wenger 1991). The nonverbal resources, however, were not replaced by the emergent language skills. Instead, talk, gestures and paralinguistic features mutually elaborated each other, providing the children with rhetorical means for competent and interactionally "efficient" participation during individual seatwork (Ex. 12).

The multiparty, flexible participation structure of the classroom provided a context within which language and interactional skills could emerge and grow. The need for gaining the teacher's attention and securing uptake pushed the students to try certain strategies, some they found didn't work or were prohibited, and this led them to use the models provided by other children, and to build on their own repertoire. As demonstrated, the girls took advantage of and appropriated linguistic information available on the multiple interactional floors of the classroom (see also Ohta 2001). When soliciting the teacher's response, the girls produced parts of assignment-related talk. The students recurrently experienced these conversational features when the teacher addressed them and when other students called the teacher (Ex. 1). The girls also employed similar methods when addressing their peers (Ex. 6b; Ex. 8). Thereby, multiple interactional floors of the classroom allowed for different participant constellations (including peer interactions) and created opportunities for language use, where lexical and interactional resources from the various classroom interactions could be recycled and developed. Through participation in social interaction, the discourse features that were initially used by others became part of the language learners' linguistic and interactional repertoires, allowing them to participate as full-fledged members of the classroom community (Lave & Wenger 1991; Ohta 2001).

The present in-depth longitudinal analysis of seemingly mundane classroom interactions adds to our knowledge of L2 learners' informal learning and provides some insights into how learning affordances are co-constructed through classroom interaction. As demonstrated, getting the teacher's attention and securing conversational uptake in the context of the multiple voices of a classroom usually involves a considerable amount of interactional work. In so far as language is seen to evolve from learning how to "do" conversations, how to solve interactional problems and how to "interact verbally" (Hatch 1978: 404), the interactional task of securing the teacher's uptake may provide a powerful language-learning context in which success or failure to recruit a conversational partner may result in modified strategies for solving interactional problems.

References

Björk-Willén, P. in press. Multilingual preschool routines and interactional trouble: How preschool children participate in multilingual education. *Applied Linguistics*.

Broner, M. & Tarone, E. 2001. Is it fun? Language play in a fifth-grade Spanish immersion classroom. *Modern Language Journal* 85: 363–379.

Cathcart, R. 1986. Situational differences and the sampling of young children's school language. In *Talking to Learn: Conversation in Second Language Acquisition*, R. Day (ed.), 118–140. Rowley MA: Newbury House.

Cekaite, A. 2007. A child's development of interactional competence in a Swedish L2 classroom. *Modern Language Journal* 91: 45–62.

Cekaite, A. & Aronsson, K. 2005. Language play, a collaborative resource in children's L2 learning. *Applied Linguistics* 26: 169–191.

Corrin, J., Tarplee, C. & Wells, B. 2001. Interactional linguistics and language development: A conversation analytic perspective on emergent syntax. In *Studies in Interactional Linguistics*, M. Selting & E. Couper-Kuhlen (eds), 199–225. Amsterdam: John Benjamins.

Cook, G. 2000. *Language Play, Language Learning*. Oxford: OUP.

Gibson, J. J. 1979. *The Ecological Approach to Visual Perception*. Boston MA: Houghton Mifflin.

Goffman, E. 1963. *Behavior in Public Places. Notes on the Social Behaviour of Gatherings*. New York NY: Free Press.

Goodwin, C. 2000. Action and embodiment within situated human interaction. *Journal of Pragmatics* 32: 1489–1522.

Grice, H. P. 1975. Logic and conversation. In *Syntax and Semantics*, Vol. 3: *Speech Acts*, P. Cole & J. Morgan (eds), 41–58. New York NY: Academic Press.

Hatch, E. 1978. Discourse analysis and second language acquisition. In *Second Language Acquisition. A Book of Readings*, E. Hatch (ed.). 402–435. Rowley MA: Newbury House.

Kanagy, R. 1999. Interactional routines as a mechanism for L2 acquisition and socialization in an immersion context. *Journal of Pragmatics* 31: 1467–1492.

Kasper, G. & Rose, K. R. 2002. *Pragmatic Development in a Second Language*. A supplement to *Language Learning*. Volume 52, supplement 1.

Keenan Ochs, E., Schieffelin, B. & Platt, M. 1978. Questions of immediate concern. In *Questions and Politeness*, E. Goody (ed.), 44–55. Cambridge: CUP.

Klein, W. & Perdue, C. 1997. The basic variety. *Second Language Research* 13: 301–347.

Lave, J. & Wenger, E. 1991. *Situated Learning: Legitimate Peripheral Participation*. Cambridge: CUP.

Leather, J. & van Dam, J. (eds). 2002. *Ecology of Language Acquisition*. Dordrecht: Kluwer.

Linell, P. 1998. *Approaching Dialogue: Talk, Interaction and Contexts in Dialogical Perspectives*. Amsterdam: John Benjamins.

McTear, M. 1985. *Children's Conversations*. Oxford: Blackwell.

Merritt, M. 1982. Repeats and reformulations in primary classrooms as windows of the nature of talk engagement. *Discourse Processes* 5: 127–145.

Ochs, E. 1988. *Language and Language Development. Language Acquisition and Language Socialization in a Samoan Village*. Cambridge: CUP.

Ochs, E. 1996. Linguistic resources for socializing humanity. In *Rethinking Linguistic Relativity*, J. Gumperz & S. Levinson (eds), 407–437. Cambridge: CUP.

Ohta, A. 2001. *Second Language Acquisition Processes in the Classroom*. Mahwah NJ: Lawrence Erlbaum Associates.

Oliver, R. & Mackey, A. 2003. Interactional context and feedback in child ESL classrooms. *Modern Language Journal* 87: 519–533.

Olmedo, I. M. 2003. Language mediation among emergent bilingual children. *Linguistics and Education* 14: 143–162.

Pallotti, G. 1996. Towards an ecology of second language acquisition: SLA as a socialization process. In *Proceedings of EUROSLA 6* [Toegepaste Taalwetenschap in Artikelen 55], E. Kellerman, B. Weltens & T. Bongaerts (eds). Nijmegen: University of Nijmegen.

Pallotti, G. 2001. External appropriations as a strategy for participating in intercultural multiparty conversations. In *Culture in Communication*, A. Di Luzio, S. Günthner & F. Orletti (eds), 295–334. Amsterdam: John Benjamins.

Pennycook, A. 1985. Actions speak louder than words: Paralanguage, communication, and education. *TESOL Quarterly* 19: 259–282.

Sacks, H. 1992. *Lectures on Conversation*. Vols I & II, G. Jefferson (ed.). Oxford: Blackwell.

Schegloff, E. A. & Sacks, H. 1973. Opening up closings. *Semiotica* 8: 289–327.

Scollon, R. 1979. A real unzippered condensation of a dissertation on child language. In *Developmental Pragmatics*, E. Ochs & B. Shieffelin (eds), 215–227. London: Academic Press.

Swain, M. 2000. The output hypothesis and beyond: Mediating acquisition through collaborative dialogue. In *Sociocultural Theory and Second Language Learning*, J. P. Lantolf (ed.), 97–114. Oxford: OUP.

Toohey, K. 2000. *Learning English at School*. Clevedon: Multilingual Matters.

van Dam, J. 2002. Ritual, face, and play in a first English lesson: Bootstrapping a classroom culture. In *Language Acquisition and Language Socialization*, C. Kramsch (ed.), 237–265. London: Continuum.

van Lier, L. 2000. From input to affordance: Social-interactive learning from an ecological perspective. In *Sociocultural Theory and Second Language Learning*, J. P. Lantolf (ed.), 245–259. Oxford: OUP.

Watson-Gegeo, K. A. 2004. Mind, language and epistemology: Toward a language socialization paradigm for SLA. *Modern Language Journal* 88: 331–350.

Willett, J. 1995. Becoming first graders in an L2: An ethnographic study of L2 socialization. *TESOL Quarterly* 29: 473–503.

Appendix: Transcription key

:	prolonged syllable
[ ]	demarcates overlapping utterances
(.)	micropause, i.e. shorter than (0.5)
(2)	numbers in single parentheses represent pauses in seconds
YES	relatively high amplitude
x	inaudible word
jala	word in Arabic
(( ))	further comments of the transcriber
?	denotes rising terminal intonation
.	indicates falling terminal intonation
=	denotes latching between utterances
Fare	sounds marked by emphatic stress are underlined

The impact of teacher input, guidance and feedback on ESL children's task-based interactions

Rhonda Oliver, Jenefer Philp and Alison Mackey

Edith Cowan University / University of Auckland / Georgetown University

In this chapter we examine children's interaction during authentic lessons involving tasks in L2 classrooms, comparing the effects of teacher guidance for 5–7
year olds (n = 22) and 11–12 year olds (n = 20). Three experimental conditions
representing a continuum of teacher guidance were examined: task instructions
alone, task instructions with examples, and task instructions followed by on-task
guidance and feedback. In all conditions, regardless of age, children interacted
in ways deemed facilitative of language learning, although older children seemed
to benefit most from on-task guidance. We discuss these findings in terms of the
potential benefits of tasks for L2 production and interaction in children's ESL
classrooms, as well as the under-researched but important role of the teacher's
input and guidance.

Introduction

What are task-based interactions and why are they helpful for L2 learning?

A task is generally defined as an activity in which language is used meaningfully
to achieve the goal of the activity, which is generally non-linguistic. For example, communicative games like 'information gap' activities are popular classroom
tasks in schools. Tasks can provide the motivation and the reason for learners to
communicate with each other, to produce the L2 and to work to understand their
interlocutors. With their focus on content and communication, tasks are attractive
for children's classrooms, where teachers often seek to provide a range of different
types of interesting and engaging activities. The basis tenets of task-based language
teaching have been described by Ellis (2003), Nunan (2006) and Van den Branden
(2006) among others.

Many researchers have advocated tasks for use in language classrooms as
a means of promoting interaction facilitative of second language learning (for

review see Ellis 2003). With its focus on communication, task-based interaction integrates many of the processes claimed to be important to second language learning, including input, output, attention, feedback and noticing. By participating in tasks, learners can engage in meaningful interaction with interlocutors. Tasks provide opportunities for learners to develop both production and comprehension skills. When tasks involve learners through the need for mutual comprehension, they provide a context for feedback on L2 production. Through feedback, such interaction indicates difficulties in communication or accuracy, and may draw learners' attention to particular features in the input by increasing the saliency and comprehension of language features (Bygate, Skehan & Swain 2001; Long 1996; Mackey 2007). In turn, learners may respond to feedback through modifying their output towards more targetlike forms, and in this way develop through language practice, proceduralizing knowledge, and experimenting with form. Feedback and modified output are demonstrated in Example 1, where two girls are spotting different activities in a picture. Student B's response encourages student K to try to modify her output (data from this study).

(1)   K: one. How many girls can you see feeling [flying]?
       B: What?
       K: how many girls you can see feeling fly fling [flying]?

Research into tasks and language learning

Research has explored a range of factors that impact on the potential benefits of tasks. Specifically, studies have investigated relationships between variables such as task type, the nature and weight of the cognitive load different tasks present; time on task (communicative pressure); type of planning (attentional resources); amount of planning (attentional resources) and guidance in planning (for overviews, see Ellis 2005; Bygate, Skehan & Swain 2001) and their effects on output in terms of constructs such as fluency, accuracy, and complexity. Research to date also suggests that the linguistic outcomes of tasks may vary according to a range of factors, including the setting, the presentation and the type of instructions provided. Despite general agreement that setting and the teacher's contribution can influence tasks and interactional processes (e.g., Lyster & Mori 2006; Mackey, Oliver, & Leeman 2003; Oliver & Mackey 2003; Samuda 2001; Van Avermaet, Colpin, Van Gorp, Bogaert, & Van den Branden 2006; Nassaji & Swain 2000), there is little published research on the impact of teachers' input on effectiveness of tasks for second language production. There is little consideration, for example, of teachers' provision of language models during task-based interaction. This lack of research is particularly pertinent to the instructional context for children, who researchers have suggested require and are sensitive to greater external regulation than adult learners (Yamaguchi & Miki 2003). For this reason the impact of teachers' input may have greater consequences for younger rather than older child learners (Philp, Oliver & Mackey 2006).

L1 research on teachers and tasks

In L1 research the role of the teacher's input in tasks in relation to younger and older school-aged children has been explored in a number of ways, with findings suggesting different outcomes depending on the level of guidance or direction by the teacher. For example, Hogan, Nastasi and Pressley (1999) compared teacher-guided and peer-guided discussion in grade 8 science classrooms and found that weak or incomplete ideas improved as children attained higher levels of reasoning through interaction in each context, but that this occurred in different ways. When teachers acted as catalysts, discussion was more efficient. However, when peers instructed each other, the discussion involved greater exploration of ideas and was more generative. In a study of 51 much younger learners, aged 3 to 6 years, Gmitrová and Gmitrov (2003) compared children's cognitive performance during teacher-directed pretend play and child-directed pretend play. The teacher-directed play involved joint activity between the children and the adult: The teacher organized and monitored activity, ensuring that all children participated in the interaction. The child-directed play involved free play in groups, without any external intervention. Group sizes ranged from 11 to 19. Based on a qualitative analysis of children's behavior over 26 lessons, the authors found more benefits for child-directed play, concluding that "children think more, learn more, remember more, spend more time on task, and are more productive in well-implemented cooperative groups rather than directive, competitive structures of the frontal organization of the playing process" (p. 246). In other words, young children can benefit cognitively and socially by interacting in group activities without teacher direction.

At the same time, however, others contend that teachers can direct their students in ways that promote their students' use of exploratory and collaborative talk (e.g., Barnes 1976; Mercer 1995, and also Naassaji & Wells 2000) which in turn enhances not only their content learning, but also their cognitive and linguistic development. From a pedagogic point of view, therefore, there is a need to consider desired outcomes and balance these with a careful scrutiny of how they might be achieved when considering the role of the teacher's directions and models in relation to a task.

In addition, and as indicated above, such considerations may also be mediated by the age of the learners. Specifically, research from L1 content-based classrooms suggests differential benefits for teacher-directed and peer-directed interaction in problem-solving and discussion activities for both older and younger children, but also that the nature of these benefits may differ according to age.

L2 research on teachers and tasks

To our knowledge there is relatively little research on the effects of teacher guidance on task-based interaction in L2 instructional contexts. Johnson & Jackson (2006) compare guidance by trainers in non-linguistic skill areas, and note the detailed nature of pre-task instructions compared to that provided to adult language class-rooms, but say little on effects of on-task feedback and guidance. As they point out, on-task guidance may be a neglected but important area for teachers: " [in group or pair work], the teacher is either unable for logistical reasons to moni-tor performance, or indeed may not feel this important, considering that the real value of performance is that learners 'learn by doing'. Perhaps 'learning by feed-back on doing' plays an equally important role" (p. 541). In a discussion of the role of the teacher in task-based language teaching, Van Avermaet, Colpin, van Gorp, Bogaert, and Van den Branden (2006) identify different ways in which teachers promote effective learning during task-based interaction with children. They sug-gest teachers assist through motivation and affective support; for example, gaining the interest of the children at the beginning of a lesson, stimulating persistence with the task in the face of difficulty, and providing encouragement. Provision of linguistic and cognitive support is also important, for instance; the teacher may facilitate children's performance through scaffolding. Such support may take the form of preemptive and reactive focus on form, including implicit feedback and modeling. However, the researchers also note that a teacher's intervention can be detrimental, by being overly directive in problem solving tasks rather than allow-ing children time to work it out. Similarly, teachers may focus on accuracy at the expense of encouraging meaningful interaction. Van den Branden's research (this volume) on negotiation work during a reading task similarly demonstrates the potential benefits of a responsive teacher's guidance, while cautioning against too much control.

We are interested in the sorts of input that teachers provide to guide learners, in particular, the instructions and models teachers provide to help learners carry out a task. In classrooms, such directing input is typically provided prior to the task being undertaken and often also when tasks do not go quite according to plan. This is particularly the case in children's classrooms, where it is typical for not everyone to be listening at the beginning of a task. It is important to note that things may not go according to plan procedurally, when learners are not sure what to do to complete the task, or linguistically, when they do not seem to have the linguistic resources necessary. In both cases, teachers often solve the problem through instructions and by modeling the linguistic forms necessary to do the task. This is explained further with examples below.

We designed the current study to investigate the effects of teachers' guidance by looking at the instructions and examples they provide in relation to the task-based interactions of both younger and older children. We devised three conditions, which formed a continuum from less directed to more directed: (a) Pre-task instructions (b) Pre-task instructions plus examples, and (c) Pre-task instructions plus on-task feedback and examples. These conditions are explained in more detail below together with examples of each type.

Research Questions

1. What are the relationships among instructions, examples, and children's task-based interactions?
2. Do these relationships differ for younger and older children?

Methodology

Participants

Four teachers working in Australia and their intact ESL classrooms, consisting of a total of 42 child ESL learners from a range of L1 backgrounds (see Table 1) participated in this study. Two of the classrooms were junior primary classes (children aged 5–7) and two were senior primary classes (children aged 10–12 years).

Table 1. L1 of participants

Background	Age	
	5–7 years	11–12 years
African (language unspecified)	6	9
Arabic (language unspecified)		1
Chinese	1	1
French	1	
Indian (language unspecified)	1	
Russian	3	
Serbo-Croatian	6	5
Vietnamese	4	4
Total	22	20

Materials

To maintain as much ecological validity as possible, we developed the materials used in this study in collaboration with the teachers from the four classes. The tasks were based on activities that the teachers reported were typical of the children's daily classroom routines. The development process involved group discussions with the teachers followed by full-day classroom observations, which also examined how teachers provided pre-task guidance in classes. Prototype tasks were developed based on the program of thematic work planned by the teachers and on the language in use in the curriculum at that time. For example, at the time of the study there was a forthcoming sports carnival. Work was planned by the teachers to cover the verbs and lexical items related to sporting activities and so a task was developed around this theme. Follow-up meetings with the teachers were held to elicit feedback on the materials, and these were then fine-tuned until they met the satisfaction of all. These tasks were pilot tested to ensure comparability in terms of the language they elicited from each age group.

The five tasks were two-way, information gap activities and were typical of tasks used every day by the teachers. Each child saw a series of pictures of objects with which they were familiar (since they were topics connected to class events and themes, such as the school athletics carnival and a trip to the zoo). The learners were required to describe these pictures in detail to their partner in order to fill in an information grid together.

As noted above, three experimental conditions were examined: (1) Pre-task instructions, where the students commenced the task after the teacher provided nothing more than a simple description of what it was and how to do it, but without providing specific language examples; (2) Pre-task instructions plus examples, where the teacher first provided the simple description of the task and how to do it, then elicited and provided examples of language useful for doing it; and (3) Pre-task instructions plus on-task feedback and examples, where the teacher first provided the simple description of the task and how to do it, then provided more examples to learners as they undertook the task. These experimental conditions were typical of the teacher behaviors that were found to occur during the class observations. For purposes of ecological validity, the planned conditions were discussed and developed with the teachers prior to finalizing the project, and as a group they concurred that the conditions outlined captured the behavior they engaged in when using tasks in their classroom. Next, we provide examples from these three conditions:

1. Pre-task instructions

    (2)   Teacher: Have I got everybody looking this way and listening carefully because you're all going to do this activity. You know we've been

learning about some zoo animals, I'm going to give you a paper like this with some animals on it and I want you to say which things the animals have. And you take it in turns. So, one of you will ask a question and the other one's going to give the answer.

After these instructions were given the students commenced work and no further instructions, direction or feedback was given.

2. Pre-task instructions plus examples:
In this condition, after the task instructions were given as above, the teacher provided examples of how to do the task for the children by interactively discussing how they would perform the task, eliciting and modeling the language relevant to the task, sometimes also providing feedback if warranted, as shown in Example 3.

(3)   T: Now what do you think a question would be about the jungle?
      S: Are there some snakes?
      T: What a good question to ask. What would be another good question?
      S: (indecipherable)
      T: Right, does it live in the jungle? So when you get to that one you could say does it live in the jungle? Then your partner would say no, it lives on a farm.

3. Pre-task instructions plus on-task feedback and examples
In this condition, after the task instructions were provided as above, the class started working on the task and the teacher walked around providing examples for the learners, and feedback on their production while they were engaged with the task. This meant that the teacher monitored the children as they performed their tasks and often commented on what they were doing while eliciting and providing more examples, sometimes also providing corrective feedback (see Example 4).

(4)   S2:   Square. Like – like this?
      S1:   No. Go – not circle, square. Go here. Here!
      S2:   This?
      S1:   Go there. Under square.
      T: Very good, but now you have to ask "where are they?"
      S1:   Where are they?
      T: And you have to say what? When she says where are they you have to draw a picture of the tree, okay a little one.
            Alright? This is where you do your writing or your drawing. Okay? Good.
      S1:   Okay=
      S2:   =okay=
            [teacher walks away]

Table 2 depicts the experimental procedure.

Table 2. Experimental design for age, group and task

Age group	A. Picture description	B. Picture description	C. Picture description
6–7 yrs	Pre-task instructions	Pre-task instructions and pre-task examples	Pre-task instructions and on-task feedback and examples
(11 dyads)		Pre-task instructions and on-task feedback and examples	Pre-task instructions and pre-task examples
11–12 yrs	Pre-task instructions	Pre-task instructions and pre-task examples	Pre-task instructions and on-task feedback and examples
(10 dyads)		Pre-task instructions and on-task feedback and examples	Pre-task instructions and pre-task examples

Procedure

Data collection

Data were collected from 21 dyads, 5 dyads ($n = 10$) from each of the four classes, with one additional dyad of 5–7 year olds (due simply to uneven sizes of the classes). The pairs of children carried out the tasks, working with the same partner for each task, as part of their regular classroom instruction and daily activities over two weeks. The tasks were counter-balanced in relation to conditions two and three, but not for condition one because there the teachers followed a lock-step route that they deemed to be most appropriate and feasible for their classes. Although this is discussed further in the limitations section below, a post hoc analysis (the Friedman non-parametric test) of amount and type of speech revealed no significant differences according to task type.

Coding

Our first step was to see what the impact of instructions and examples might be on the interaction. We devised our coding schemes based on constructs in general use in the task and interaction based research paradigms, as discussed in Philp, Oliver and Mackey (2006). (See also Ellis & Barkhuizen 2005 and Mackey & Gass 2005 for discussion of coding schemes for these sorts of data). To summarize, the data were coded following a system used in a number of earlier interaction studies including Oliver (2000), Mackey, Oliver and Leeman (2003), and, Braidi (2002). Specifically the data were coded in the following manner:

1. Each participant's turn was coded as target-like or non-targetlike;
2. If non-targetlike, these turns were then coded based on whether feedback was provided in response by the leaner's conversational partner. This feed-

back included recasts, clarification requests, confirmation checks, and explicit correction;

3. If feedback was provided, then the original learner's next turn was coded according to whether or not there was an opportunity to use it. For instance, if one of the conversational partners produced an error to which the other provided a recast (i.e., reformulating the erroneous utterance in a more targetlike way, whilst maintaining the original meaning) but then continued speaking without allowing the first partner to respond, then this was coded as 'no opportunity';

4. Finally, turns that followed the feedback were coded as either modified output or non modified output. For this research the stringent criteria of successful uptake was applied.

This coding is based on the premise that feedback can only be given when the initial production is non-targetlike, and that the modified output resulting from this feedback can only be produced when there is an opportunity to do so. Hence, the coding excludes any interactional moves that are not concerned with non-targetlike language. Results were calculated as percentage scores, and because of the categorical nature of the data, chi-square tests were used for the purpose of analysis.

Inter-rater reliability was obtained by training two other raters to undertake the coding. First they were provided with input about the category definitions, and then they worked through a number of examples independently. Differences in coding these examples were carefully discussed and any remaining discrepancies resolved. These raters then coded one-third of the interaction data set, representing approximately 18 hours of recording. The inter-rater reliability measure, calculated using simple percentage agreement in each category was in all cases >95%.

Results

The research questions sought to explore the relationship between instructions and examples in respect to younger and older child learners. In order to do this, a comparison was made between the interaction of younger and older child learners in the three experimental conditions: pre-task instructions, pre-task instructions with examples, and pre-task instructions plus on-task feedback and examples.

Table 3 presents a summary of the percentage results for the different types of interaction in the three conditions.

None of the results for 1) non-targetlike turns, 2) the opportunity to use feedback or 3) the provision of feedback were statistically significant for the two age

Table 3. Percentage results for the provision and use of feedback under three conditions

Feedback use	Pre-task instructions		Pre-task instructions and examples		Pre-task instructions and on-task feedback and examples	
	Younger n = 22	Older n = 20	Younger n = 22	Older n = 20	Younger n = 22	Older n = 20
Non-targetlike turns	45	50	30	15	28	31
Feedback[a]	13	21	11	31	9	14
Opportunities to use feedback	83	92	91	85	66	81
Use of feedback (Modified output)[b]	13	11	17	13	3	21

Note [a]Feedback in response to non-targetlike turns
[b]Use of feedback when opportunity for use is provided

groups of learners. However, some caution needs to be used when interpreting this result. It may be that large differences within the groups may have contributed to this null result.

Modified output

The criteria applied to coding modified output in this study were quite stringent. To be coded as modified output, successful uptake was required. That is, in response to feedback, modification of the initial non target-like utterance into a target like form had to occur. This contrasts to previous coding that simply required production of forms that were more targetlike (as per Mackey, Oliver & Leeman 2003; Oliver & Mackey 2003). Even with these stringent criteria, the production of modified output was considerable in some conditions and comparable in most conditions to a number of other studies (e.g., Oliver 1995).

The patterns of use for the three conditions differed between the two age groups with significant difference being present for age (χ^2 (df = 2) = 12.65, p <. 001). What this means is that younger learners modified their output least when they received "the most" from teachers, pre-task instructions, pre-task examples and on-task examples (3%). The statistical difference between the age groups can be attributed to the considerable proportional difference according to the pair-work condition, with on-task examples (older learners, 21%, versus 3% for younger children); older learners produced a great deal of modified output when receiving on-task examples, but the younger learners were hampered by the on-task examples.

Discussion

So, whether teachers provided instructions only, or instructions with examples before and during the task did not result in significant differences in the children's
interaction as measured by non-targetlike turns, the opportunity for, or the provision of feedback. However, in terms of the production of modified output, the
teacher's input had an effect according to age. Since output during interaction has
been found by several researchers to be facilitative of acquisition, the impact of
teacher input, specifically with respect to instructions and examples, clearly needs
to be considered in classroom task-based pedagogy. In particular, while on-task
examples were not helpful for the production of modified output for younger
children, they were very helpful for older children.

In terms of the differences that occured in the on-task examples condition,
it could be that the greater cognitive maturity of the older children means that
they are more inclined to hear, notice, and make use of this fine-tuned interaction,
that is, utterances directed at them specifically, rather than at the whole class, and
usually following something they had just said, hence relevant to their immediate
communicative needs. It may also be that the production of older children enables
teachers to provide helpful examples, whereas younger learners were less able to
produce the type of output to which teachers can helpfully respond by providing
examples. This can be seen in the following excerpt, Example 5, where the teacher
provides an example for a pair of older learners in the form of a new vocabulary
item [line 2] and she also recasts their production [lines 4, 6] into a more targetlike form. In this example, both learners appear to benefit from this input –
although they mispronounce it [lines 8, 9] they do recall the word "desert" and
use it appropriately.

(5) 1. S2: Does does what's this?
     2. T: It's called a desert.
     3. S2: Does horse live in cosert [desert]?
     4. T: desert
     5. S2: //desert//
     6. T: //desert//

[10 turns later, teacher is not present]

     7. S1: Yes does cow live in Jungle?
     8. S2: jungle> no does cow live disert [desert]?
     9. S1: disert dusert [desert] no does cow live in a farm?
     10. S2: No>

In contrast, younger learners tended to modify their output more when the teacher
only provided pre-task examples for the whole class, than when they received

on-task examples. It may be that pre-task examples are more helpful because of the young children's stage of development. It is possible that it enabled them to begin the task and to focus, without interruption, on the procedures and language required. Younger children, when working under this condition and left to their own devices, appear to have taken on more responsibility for their own production. In Example 6 below, the learners provide each other with positive feedback (modeling the teacher's example) [lines 5, 12] and take care that the task is successfully executed [line 7]. While there are many inaccuracies in their production, they are able to communicate well together. Variation in their output is also seen throughout the task: L1 self corrects her pronunciation of "bear" [line 3], only for them both to subsequently revert to "bay" [lines 17, 18]. Conversely, the two learners' incorrect production of "ship" for sheep is correctly modified in a later turn [lines 19, 20].

(6)   1.   S1: How many bay legs?
      2.   S2: How many legs.
      3.   S1: Bay – How many BEAR legs?
      4.   S2: Is four.
      5.   S1: Good job. Good job.
      6.   S2: Four. Four.
      7.   S2: You forgot the (?)
      8.   S1: How- how many?
      9.   S2: Shhipp
     10.   S1: How many ship legs?
     11.   S2: Four.
     12.   S2: Good. Good girl.
           [later turn]
     13.   S1: How many =
     14.   S2: =giraffe=
     15.   S1: =How many giraffe bottom?
     16.   S2: One. One.
     17.   S1: How many – how many bay bottom?
     18.   S2: Bays nos have bottom.
     19.   S1: Thank you. How many sheep bottom?
     20.   S2: Sheep have bottom.
     21.   S1: How – how many?
     22.   S2: One.

When younger children received on-task examples, they appeared to be more of an intrusion than an aid to their interaction. In these data, when the teachers interact with younger learners they tended to be more controlling and tended to provide pre-emptive examples rather than responsive ones, in the form of recasts. This is

clear in the excerpt below (Example 7), collected from the on-task examples condition with younger children, when the teacher shifts the focus of the interaction
according to his own intentions (finding shapes in the picture in an ordered fashion) [line 10], and when he explicitly provides the learners with examples of what
they are to say [line 14]. Interestingly, once the teacher leaves, these examples are
abandoned.

(7) 1. S2: Circle. And this is square.
    2. S1: Ummh>
    3. S2: 1 2 3 (...) rubber rubber
    4. S1: It's not mine. Who's this?
    5. S2: A bill
    6. S1: Ah?
    7. S2: A bill
    8. S1: A bill>
    9. S2: No this is not bill, it's a XX
    10. T: These squares are excellent. That's right. They are all squares. Have
            a look, can you see all the other pictures have got squares, where are
            the squares?
    11. S2: XX no
    12. T: No a square is this. Look at the square, see the square? A pic-
            ture that has a shape like that. Probably you can say building, this
            building, say it
    13. S2: This building
    14. T: This building has squares.
    15. S1: 1 2 3
    16. S2: 1 2 yes

The examples provided by these teachers for younger children tended to be more
directive than collaborative. In other words, rather than starting from the child's
own meanings and ways of expressing themselves, the teachers tended to provide
their own examples and expect the children to play along.

There are of course other factors to consider when evaluating the effectiveness of teacher guidance. The provision of teacher guidance can diffuse potential
difficulties pairs experience in carrying out a task together. Frustration between
pairs sometimes followed a lack of guidance, as shown in Example 8 below, from
the pre-task instruction condition. The two children differ in how they want to resolve the difficulty of the task: S1 seeks to look at S2's picture, obviating the need to
use language to complete the missing information in his grid; S2 is torn between
the difficulty of providing the missing information and the improper resolution
of simply allowing S1 to see the information himself. Although such negotiation is not without potential benefits, it presents obvious problems for classroom

management, and could have been more positively resolved through teacher guidance. This is a consideration for task design and implementation, particularly important for child L2 classrooms.

(8) 1. S1: Do you have any kangaroos on your paper?
     2. S2: You looking
     3. S1: No I didn't
     4. S2: Not doing like that... see... you know it... because you look my one
     5. S1: No
     6. S2: I don't know what to do... stupid thing... [This one] is stupid
     7. S1: xx xx
     8. S2: Not doing like that... just put it out... not doing like that
     9. S1: xx xx
    10. S2: Don't look
    11. S1: I'm not looking... I'm looking=
    12. S2: Just look there then
    13. S1: OK
    14. S2: I don't know what to do
    15. S1: I'm not looking
    16. S2: I don't know what to do
    17. S1: Yeah what ... See you want to do like... and you want to look like that
    18. S2: I don't
    19. S1: Ok... I look your one too... you can look my one
    20. S2: (Makes frustrated, growl noise.) Not good

Limitations

Like much classroom research of this type, this study is limited in important ways. First, we examined only one type of task, albeit one commonly employed in ESL classes. It was a task that made fewer cognitive demands than problem based tasks, for example. Further research with a wider range of tasks, also varying in levels of complexity (Robinson 2006) would add to our understanding of the effects of guidance on task-based interaction and language production. Next, this study involved a small sample of four intact classes and their teachers. Variation inevitably occurred between the teachers in the nature and quantity of the guidance and feedback they provided. Replication with larger numbers would be helpful. Also, it would be interesting to carry out this study with additional comparable children of different age groups, different proficiency levels, and different sorts of teachers (i.e., with NNS teachers as well as NSs), and with adults as well as children.

The effects of instructions, guidance and feedback in other contexts, such as foreign language contexts should also be investigated. As mentioned earlier, the tasks in two of the conditions were administered in a similar counter-balanced way by the teacher, with one not being counter-balanced, which might have affected the validity of results. Since this study only spanned two weeks, a longitudinal study which examines the effects of different forms of instructions and examples might be helpful in clarifying the impact of guidance on learner development. And finally, effects of guidance in this study were investigated in terms of provision and use of feedback and production of modified output. Future research which includes measures of linguistic development over time, could consider the impact of instructions and examples on learning.

Conclusion

This paper explored the relationship between teacher input, guidance and feedback, and linguistic outcomes, on task-based interaction. Age combined with conditions related to the teacher's contribution in dynamic ways to impact the patterns of interaction that occur while children are carrying out tasks. This seems intuitive. While one type of teacher input, guidance or feedback might favor older learners, for example in this study, receiving instructions and both pre-task and on-task examples resulted in significantly more modified output for older children than it did for younger children, another condition might privilege younger learners. The teacher, the relationships between peer participants and the task itself are all considerations in learning outcomes, working in concert with how the task is introduced, explained and facilitated in real time by the teacher. Our research suggests that it would be helpful to make decisions about these aspects of teacher interaction during tasks in the context of considerations of the age of the children. As others have argued (Samuda 2001; Van Avermaet et al. 2006), aside from the task itself, teachers play a crucial role in the effectiveness of task-based learning through the kind of input they provide. Further, while previous research on outcomes of task-based interaction has often included proficiency as a variable, age is clearly another.

Acknowledgements

This research was supported by a research grant (3605316) from the University of Auckland to Jenefer Philp, and by a senior faculty research leave from Georgetown University to Alison Mackey. We are indebted to the teachers and children in Perth, Western Australia, who participated in this project. We thank external reviewers for their insightful comments. We gratefully acknowledge the research assistance of Yiqian Cao, Jaemyung Goo, Mika Hama, Sue McKenna, Bo Ram Suh, Samantha Vanderford and Jamie Lepore Wright and thank them for their hard work and consistent attention to detail. All errors are of course our own.

References

Barnes, D. 1976. *From Communication to Curriculum*. Harmondsworth: Penguin Education.
Braidi, S. M. 2002. Reexamining the role of recasts in native-speaker/nonnative-speaker inter-actions. *Language Learning* 52: 1–42.
Bygate, M., Skehan, P. & Swain, M. (eds). 2001. *Researching Pedagogical Tasks: Second Language Learning, Teaching and Testing*. Harlow: Pearson Education.
Ellis, R. 2003. *Task-based Language Teaching and Learning*. Oxford: OUP.
Ellis, R. 2005. *Planning and Task Performance in a Second Language*. Amsterdam: John Benjamins.
Ellis, R. & Barkhuizen, G. 2005. *Analysing Learner Language*. Oxford: OUP.
Gmitrová, V. & Gmitrov, J. 2003. The impact of teacher-directed and child-directed pretend play on cognitive competence in kindergarten children. *Early Childhood Education Journal* 30(4): 241–246.
Hogan, K., Nastasi, B. & Pressley, M. 1999. Discourse patterns and collaborative reasoning in peer and teacher-guided discussions. *Cognition and Instruction* 17(4): 379–432.
Johnson, K. & Jackson, S. 2006. Comparing language teaching and other-skill teaching: Has the language teacher anything to learn? *System* 34: 532–546.
Long, M. H. 1996. The role of the linguistic environment in second language acquisition. In *Handbook of Second Language Acquisition*, W. C. Ritchie & T. K. Bhatia (eds), 413–468. New York NY: Academic Press.
Lyster, R. & Mori, H. 2006. Interactional feedback and instructional counterbalance. *Studies in Second Language Acquisition* 28: 321–341.
Mackey, A. 2007. Interaction as practice. In *Practice in a Second Language*, R. M. DeKeyser (ed.), 85–110. Cambridge: CUP.
Mackey, A. and Gass, S. M. 2005. *Second Language Research: Methodology and Design*. Mahwah NJ: Lawrence Erlbaum Associates.
Mackey, A., Oliver, R. & Leeman, J. 2003. Interactional input and the incorporation of feedback: An exploration of NS-NNS and NNS-NNS adult and child dyads. *Language Learning* 53: 35–66.
Mercer, N. 1995. *The Guided Construction of Knowledge*. Clevedon: Multilingual Matters.
Nassaji, H. & Swain, M. 2000. A Vygotskian perspective on corrective feedback: The effect of random versus negotiated help on the learning of English articles. *Language Awareness* 9: 34–51.
Nassaji, H. & Wells, G. 2000. What's the use of "triadic dialogue"? An investigation of teacher-student interaction. *Applied Linguistics* 21(3): 376–406.
Nunan, D. 2006. *Task-based Language Teaching*. Cambridge: CUP.
Oliver, R. 1995. Negative feedback in child NS-NNS conversation. *Studies in Second Language Acquisition* 17: 459–481.

Oliver, R. 2000. Age differences in negotiation and feedback in classroom and pair work. *Language Learning* 50: 119–151.

Oliver, R. & Mackey, A. 2003. Interactional context and feedback in child ESL classrooms. *Modern Language Journal* 87(4): 519–533.

Philp, J., Oliver, R. & Mackey, R. 2006. The impact of planning time on children's task-based interactions. *System* 34: 547–565.

Robinson, P. 2006. Cognitive complexity and task sequencing: Studies in a componential framework for second language task design. *International Review of Applied Linguistics* 43: 1–32.

Samuda, V. 2001. Guiding relationships between form and meaning during task performance: The role of the teacher. In *Researching Pedagogic Tasks: Second Language Learning, Teaching and Testing*, M. Bygate, P. Skehan & M. Swain (eds), 119–140. Harlow: Pearson Education.

Van Avermaet, P., Colpin, M., van Gorp, K., Bogaert, N. & Van den Branden, K. 2006. The role of the teacher in task-based language teaching. In *Task-Based Language Education*, K. Van den Branden (ed.), 175–196. Cambridge: CUP.

van den Branden, K. (ed.) 2006. *Task-Based Language Education: From Theory to Practice*. Cambridge: CUP.

Yamaguchi, H. & Miki, K. 2003. Longitudinal analysis of the relations between perceived learning environment, achievement goal orientation, and learning strategies: Intrinsic-extrinsic regulation as a mediator. *Psychologia* 46(1): 1–18.

Negotiation of meaning in the classroom

Does it enhance reading comprehension?

Kris Van den Branden
Katholieke Universiteit Leuven

This study focuses on young children's negotiation behaviour in the classroom. Through negotiating for meaning, children may unravel the meaning of difficult input or be pushed to produce more adequate and correct output. Previous research has shown that young children, while reading for comprehension, are able and willing to negotiate the meaning of words and phrases they do not understand. However, in the classroom, many variables prevent children from displaying their non-understanding, producing spontaneous output or negotiating meaning while doing so. Among the variables that determine the quantity and quality of negotiation routines during reading comprehension activities in primary school, the role of the teacher is a crucial one. On the basis of the reported classroom observation study, this chapter lists a number of recommendations as to how the quantity and quality of negotiation of meaning in primary school classes can be enhanced.

Introduction

This chapter reports on a study into the quantity and quality of negotiation of meaning during reading comprehension activities in primary school. The study was conducted with a view to the many studies that have empirically substantiated the positive impact of negotiation of meaning on the comprehension of input and the production of output in a second language. However, most of this research has been conducted in tightly controlled laboratory conditions and has involved adult students. In general, there is a lack of research that studies (a) whether children are willing and able to negotiate meaning with their teachers and/or peers in the second language classroom, and (b) whether these negotiation sequences have the same positive impact on second language acquisition as negotiation does among adults.

In the first part of this chapter, I will define the term 'negotiation of meaning' and discuss its potential value for language learning from the perspective of Long's

Interaction Hypothesis. Next, I will review the research that is currently available on the impact of negotiation of meaning on young children's input comprehension and output production. I will then move into the classroom and discuss an empirical study into the quantity and quality of negotiation of meaning that spontaneously occurs during reading comprehension activities. The discussion of the results of this study will allow me to draw a number of conclusions and formulate some recommendations in view of enhancing the occurrence of negotiation of meaning during reading activities in the primary school.

Negotiation of meaning defined

In current theories of second language acquisition, negotiation of meaning is a crucial concept. The notion is linked with Long's Interaction Hypothesis (Long 1985, 1996; also see Gass 2003). The Interaction Hypothesis starts from the basic idea that conversation is not merely a forum for practice of linguistic forms that a language learner has already acquired, but also the means by which learning takes place. Stretches of conversation during which problems of message comprehensibility occur may be particularly facilitative for language learning. These conversational stretches are believed to give rise to all kinds of interactional modifications through which the learner's attentional resources may be oriented to (a) a particular discrepancy between what she or he knows about the second language and what the target language feature she or he is confronted with actually looks like, or (b) particular features of the second language about which the learner has little or no information (Gass 2003). This is illustrated in the following examples:

(1)   English native speaker: Okay, with a big chimney.
      English L2 learner: What is chimney?
      English native speaker: Chimney is where the smoke comes out of.
      (taken from Pica, Holliday, Lewis, Berducci, & Newman 1991:345)

(2)   NS: there's there's a pair of reading glasses above the plant
      NNS: a what?
      NS: glasses reading glasses to see the newspaper
      NNS: glassi?
      NS: you wear them to see with, if you can't see. Reading glasses
      NNS: ahh ahh glass to read you say reading glasses
      NS: yeah
      (from Mackey 1999:558–559)

The two examples contain stretches of negotiation of meaning, i.e., particular conversational side-sequences in which interlocutors, directly or indirectly, signal comprehension difficulties and try to overcome them (Gass & Varonis 1985; Long 1996; Mackey 1999; Oliver 2002). Pica (1994) defined negotiation of meaning as:

> ... the modification and restructuring of interaction that occurs when learners and their interlocutors anticipate, perceive, or experience difficulties in message comprehensibility. As they negotiate, they work linguistically to achieve the needed comprehensibility, whether repeating a message verbatim, adjusting its syntax, changing its words, or modifying its form and meaning in a host of other ways. (p. 494)

Negotiation of meaning has been claimed to strongly facilitate language acquisition. It does this by solving temporary communication breakdowns through joint negotiation work, and as such, language learners may gain access to language items that they have not acquired yet and so elaborate their linguistic repertoire (Long 1985; Pica 1994). In addition, Swain has argued that negotiation of meaning does not only support language learners in comprehending new L2 input but also in producing more complex, accurate and/or adequate output. Second language learners will often fail to produce what they intend to say in adequate or correct terms. By signalling incomprehension or by helping the language learner solve the resulting communication breakdown, interlocutors may 'push' the learner's output, either by alerting the language learner to the fact that his/her output was not fully comprehensible, accurate or appropriate (as in Example 3) or by integrating a more adequate or accurate target language formulation into their reply (as in Example 4):

(3)   NNS 1 Where is the-the, where is the [life] go?
      NNS 2 (Pause)
      NNS 2 What you say?
      NNS 1 The [life]
      NNS 2 The life?
      NNS 1 The b[r]ead knife
      (Oliver 1998:378)

(4)   NNS There's this thing in the wall, uhm ... a ...
      NS   A thing? You mean a safe?
      NNS Yeah a safe, and the thief opens the safe
      (Van den Branden 1997:596)

Thus by working their way towards mutual understanding, language learners can be alerted by their interlocutors' negative feedback to certain gaps or inadequacies in their current interlanguage system. Moreover, as the examples show, in these short side-sequences of meaning negotiation the target language form and the interlanguage form are often confronted with each other in adjacent turns, allowing the learner to make a cognitive comparison between the two forms and potentially 'notice the gap' (Long 1996; Long & Robinson 1998; Mackey, Gass & McDonough

2000). Following this line of reasoning, the Interaction Hypothesis claims that environmental contributions to language acquisition are mediated by selective attention and the learner's developing L2 processing capacity, and these resources are brought together most usefully, although not exclusively, during negotiation of meaning:

> ...*negotiation for meaning*, and especially negotiation work that triggers *interactional* adjustments by the NS or the more competent interlocutor, facilitates acquisition because it connects input, internal learner capacities, particularly selective attention, and output in productive ways.
>
> (Long 1996:451–452, original emphasis)

In view of this wide potential for language learning, much empirical research in the 1980s and 1990s, mainly conducted in laboratory settings rather than in real classrooms, has been concerned with finding out which particular language tasks in second language classrooms give rise to negotiation of meaning (see Pica 1994 for an overview). This appears to be the case for tasks in which information between the interlocutors is unevenly divided (such as in one-way information gap tasks or two-way information gap tasks) and the successful exchange of information is crucial for the completion of the task. In such tasks, negotiation of meaning can be regarded as task-essential (Loshky & Bley-Vroman 1993): if language learners do not understand the interlocutor's (or text) input, they will not be able to perform the task successfully and thus will be motivated to look for solutions to the comprehension problems that arise. Besides task type, other factors, such as the proficiency levels of the interlocutors and their gender, have been shown to impact on the quantity of negotiation of meaning that occurs during task performance.

A number of authors have pointed out some problems involved with identifying, coding and hence, quantifying sequences of negotiation of meaning (Ellis 1999; Polio & Gass 1997). The most restrictive definition of negotiation of meaning is based upon purely formal criteria, i.e., on the occurrence of typical interactional devices used by interlocutors during the negotiation of meaning. These include comprehension checks (any expression designed to establish whether the speaker's preceding utterance was understood by the interlocutor), a confirmation check (any expression immediately following an utterance by the interlocutor and repeating all or part of it, designed to check whether the utterance was correctly understood or heard) or a clarification request (any expression designed to elicit clarification of the interlocutor's preceding utterance). A slightly less restrictive definition would be based on a more functional interpretation of the presence/absence of negotiation of meaning: this would include any side-sequence in the conversation in which the interlocutors temporarily move away from the main flow of the conversation in order to make sure that mutual understanding is still maintained, and in the case that this is not, try to repair this. Contrary to the first, this definition would also include negotiation sequences in which the interlocutors signal non-understanding in non-verbal ways (e.g., by frowning or not following up an instruction that was given). The least restrictive definition actually regards all human verbal interaction as negotiation of meaning (Wells 1986): conversation, then, is an ongoing negotiation process during which interlocutors try to establish and exchange meaning and find common ground while doing so. The term 'negotiation' then refers to the fact that people enter interactional settings with their own perspectives, values, concepts, and so on, and that, for communication to run smoothly, people will continuously have to make sure that they establish 'shared' meaning.

Ultimately, what all these definitions have in common is that they view language learning as an essentially social phenomenon: what learners comprehend and produce today in interaction and negotiation with their interlocutors, they will internalize and comprehend independently tomorrow.

Negotiation of meaning and reading instruction in primary schools

Most of the available studies focussing on the occurrence and effects on negotiation of meaning on input comprehension and/or output production have involved adults or adolescents. The question, however, may be raised whether young children are equally willing, and able, to negotiate meaning with their peers or with an adult interlocutor during the performance of language tasks. In other words, do children (a) monitor their own and their interlocutors' understanding and (b) engage in the explicit signalling and repair work that adults appear to do when making conversation?

The number of studies that have explored this question is quite limited (Ellis & Heimbach 1997; Foster 1998; Oliver 1998; Oliver 2002; Van den Branden 1997; Van den Branden 2000), but those that have clearly show that the above-mentioned question can be answered in the affirmative. From her study, in which children of 8 to 13 years old were involved, Oliver (1998:379) concludes that primary school children:

> ... can, and indeed do, negotiate for meaning with age-matched peers when working on communication tasks. Also like adults, they employ a variety of negotiation strategies when they undertake this process. The results suggest that even children of this age are aware of their conversational responsibility and attempt to work towards mutual understanding.

Just like in adult communication, negotiation of meaning provides child learners with comprehensible input, the opportunity to manipulate comprehensible output, and feedback about their attempts to make successful conversation. Van den

Branden (1997) found that 10-year old children who are asked to describe pictures to an age-matched partner who could not see the picture but who needed the information in the picture in order to solve a mystery, were strongly pushed by their partner's negotiation moves to make their output more comprehensible, complete or coherent. Moreover, in his pretest-posttest design, Van den Branden found that children very eagerly picked up words and idioms they had been offered by their partner during negotiation work and recycled them during later performances of a similar task.

Nevertheless, Oliver found that, compared to adults, children engage in a proportionally smaller amount of negotiation sequences and that children tend to focus more on their own conversational needs than on their interlocutors':

> Possibly because of their level of development and their purported egocentric nature, primary school children tend to focus on constructing their own meaning, and less on facilitating their partner's construction of meaning. Thus, they are more likely to use clarification requests, confirmation checks and repetition, but tend not to use comprehension checks. (ibid.)

There is almost no research on child negotiation of meaning during reading comprehension activities. Most of the above-mentioned studies on children's negotiation of meaning involved oral communication tasks. Quite typically, these studies invite language learners to orally exchange information that is unequally divided among interlocutors, for instance in information gap tasks, where children are asked to describe pictures or graphs to each other (e.g., spot-the-differences tasks or map descriptions).

Van den Branden's study (2000) is one of the few exceptions that specifically focussed on the impact of negotiation of meaning on reading comprehension in primary schools. In that study, 157 pupils, aged 11 to 12, were invited to read the different chapters of a motivating detective story and after each story to answer comprehension questions. Four reading conditions were distinguished in the study, two of which involved some form of negotiation of meaning, while the other two did not. The results of the comprehension tests revealed a consistent picture. All classes, irrespective of the order in which they worked through the conditions, showed significantly higher mean comprehension scores in the negotiation conditions than in the two conditions in which the children were not allowed to negotiate meaning. Comparing the two conditions involving negotiation of meaning, the 'collective negotiation condition' in which the class negotiated the meaning of difficult words together with a teacher (who was specifically trained to engage in negotiation sequences with young children) yielded statistically significantly higher comprehension scores than the pair negotiation condition, in which the children were allowed to negotiate meaning with one other pupil. Van den Branden's study, then, not only provided empirical evidence for the fact that primary school children do negotiate for meaning when this is considered relevant (or even necessary) to the performance of a reading comprehension task, but also that the negotiation of meaning they were involved in enhanced their reading comprehension.

The question, however, can be raised whether negotiation of meaning also occurs in ordinary classrooms, i.e., when the pupils are working under the guidance of their regular teacher, who may not have received any specific training on task-based negotiation strategies or who may be working with syllabuses that do not contain the kind of motivating reading tasks that were used in the above-mentioned quasi-experimental study.

Starting from these observations, a research study was devised aiming to answer the following research questions:

a. What is the quantity of negotiation of meaning that spontaneously occurs during reading comprehension activities in primary school?
b. What is the basic structure of these negotiation sequences in terms of (1) who is involved, (2) who takes the initiative to open the negotiation sequence, and (3) how the comprehension problem is resolved?
c. What is the quality of these sequences of negotiation of meaning in terms of enhancing reading comprehension?
d. What variables have an impact on the quantity and quality of negotiation of meaning in primary school classes?

Data collection

This study was conducted in eight grade 5 classes in Flemish primary schools. The eight classes belonged to eight different schools. In Flemish primary schools, the official medium of instruction is Dutch.

The children involved in the study were 11–12 years old. As Table 1 shows, the number of pupils in the eight classes ranged from 19 to 26. Each of the eight classes included both native speakers of Dutch and non-native speakers. The percentage of NNS pupils varied between 17 percent and 66 percent.

Table 1. Number of pupils in the eight classes

Class	1	2	3	4	5	6	7	8	Total
No. of pupils	25	19	12	21	21	23	26	26	173
NS-pupils	15	12	4	8	10	19	16	20	104
NNS-pupils	10	7	8	13	11	4	10	6	69
% NNS	40	37	66	62	52	17	38	23	41

In all eight classes, observations were carried out during one entire school day. In Table 2, the total amount of time observed in each of the classes is reported. In order to avoid an observer's paradox, the teachers were not explicitly told that the main focus of the observations was on negotiation of meaning during reading comprehension activities. The researcher introduced himself as an applied linguist doing research into interaction in the classroom, but no further details were added. During the observed school day, the teachers took care that 'language-poor' activities such as gymnastics, music and handicraft were restricted to a minimum. The observed activities included maths lessons, language lessons and science activities.

The analysis of the data focused on the reading comprehension activities that occurred. A reading comprehension activity was defined as any educational activity in which the comprehension of written text was asked of the children. So, both activities that the teacher explicitly labelled as 'reading comprehension lessons' and activities that mainly consisted of oral communication but in which the comprehension of a short written text was inserted, were included in the analyses. In Table 2, the total amount of time that was devoted to reading comprehension activities is summarized. Eighty percent of this total amount of time was realized during language activities, primarily during activities that were explicitly labelled 'reading comprehension lessons' by the teachers. The other 20 percent of the reading activities mainly occurred during science activities.

A standardised framework for describing and coding meaning negotiation in the classroom was used (see appendix). This was largely based on the framework developed by Varonis and Gass (1985) and further elaborated by Pica, Holiday, Lewis and Morgenthaler (1989). Following Pica (1994), negotiation of meaning was defined as any modification and restructuring of interaction that occurred when the pupils and/or their teacher anticipated, perceived, or experienced difficulties in message comprehensibility. Clearly, the occurrence of explicit comprehension checks, clarification requests and confirmation requests were regarded as strong indicators of negotiation work, however, when these were not realised but there were other convincing clues that the interaction was being modified in view of maintaining or repairing understanding, a negotiation sequence was counted.

The framework that was used for coding the negotiation sequences divides the process of a meaning negotiation into its main constituent parts:

a. *the trigger*: the utterance (or part of the utterance) that gives rise to negotiation of meaning (i.e., that triggers off a particular side-sequence in the conversation aimed to signal and resolve non-understanding);

b. *the indicator*: the verbal or non-verbal signal making clear to the interlocutor that some form of non-understanding has occurred. Typical indicators are clarification requests, confirmation requests and non-verbal indicators (such as frowning). In the framework, also 'indirect indicators' were included: this category included all kinds of indicators that implicitly indicate that understanding may not have been complete, for instance, when a listener fails to perform some action (that was asked for in an instruction) or when the listener gives an incorrect or inappropriate response to a question. Only the instances that elicited a response from the interlocutor that unambiguously revealed his/her non-understanding were coded as indirect indicators.

c. *The response*: the verbal utterance following the indicator of non-understanding. The subcategories of responses that were distinguished in the framework primarily referred to the extent to which (part of) the indicator or trigger were repeated or modified.

d. *The reaction to the response*: this could be realised as an utterance signalling that understanding is now complete (so the problem of non-understanding has been resolved) or not yet. In the latter case, the reaction to the response was coded as a new indicator, and so the negotiation sequence 'loops back'.

e. *Comprehension check*: in the framework, a separate category for comprehension checks was distinguished. This category refers to any utterance that explicitly aims to check whether the interlocutors have understood (part of) a particular utterance. In some cases comprehension checks may function as triggers, yet they also may be inserted later in the sequence, for instance as part of the response.

Example 5 below illustrates a negotiation sequence containing a non-verbal indicator. The primary school teacher interrupts a grammar exercise for a short time because he strongly suspects that many of the pupils have forgotten what the concept 'adjective' stands for (original in Dutch; English translation by the author):

(5) T OK, dus de opdracht is... onderstreep het bijvoeglijk naamwoord in de zin. (....) Ik zie het al... (lacht naar onderzoeker). (tot de leerlingen) Wat is een bijvoeglijk naamwoord ook al weer?

T (*Okay, so the task is... underline the adjective in the sentence (...) I can tell from your faces... (laughs at the researcher sitting in the back of the class). Let's repeat this once more: What is an adjective?*)

P (roept) Lelijk, mooi

P (*shouts) Ugly, pretty*

T Ja, heel goed, een woordje dat iets zegt over een ander woord, over een ding bijvoorbeeld

T (*Yes, very good, a word that tells you more about another word, about an object for instance*)

In terms of the framework, the utterance containing the word 'adjective' is the trigger, the children's frowning is the non-verbal indicator, which then is followed by a comprehension check ('What is an adjective?'), a response (a pupil's answer) and a reaction to the response ('very good...').

Results

In Table 2, the quantity of negotiation sequences that were observed in each of the 8 classes during reading activities is summarized:

Table 2. Number of negotiation routines in 8 observed classrooms during reading activities

School	Total time observed	Time devoted to reading activities	No. of negotiation routines
1	152 minutes	35 minutes	7
2	196	55	9
3	172	44	6
4	107	15	6
5	148	48	9
6	138	25	2
7	170	55	6
8	140	21	4
Total	1223 minutes	298 minutes	49 routines

The total number of negotiation routines that occurred during all the observed reading comprehension lessons was 49, which equates to one negotiation routine every 6.1 minutes. As can be inferred from Table 2, there were differences in the amount of negotiation of meaning that were observed in the different classrooms. However, these differences were not linked to the pupils' linguistic background, i.e., to the percentage of non-native versus native speakers in the classes.

Impact of methodological format

The methodological format that the teachers used during their reading instruction did not appear to make much difference to the negotiation that occurred. This may be due to the fact that there was very little variation between the different classes in these terms. In almost all reading activities that were observed, the pupils were confronted with a text they were asked to read in silence individually, after which they were invited to, again individually, solve questions about the text. After some individual preparation time, the answers to the questions were discussed collectively. During the latter phase of the activity, the teachers tightly focussed on correcting the pupils' answers to the questions. No explicit training of reading strategies or discussion of text features could be observed.

Only during one reading activity that was observed was group work set up in which small groups of about four pupils worked with a text. However, this activity had little to do with reading comprehension, because the group members were merely asked to take turns at reading parts of the text aloud to each other. When giving the instructions for this group work, the teacher briefly mentioned that the children were permitted to ask each other about the meaning of difficult words. The group work yielded only one meaning negotiation routine. The main reason for this was probably that the teacher in his instructions so strongly, and repeatedly, stressed the importance of the reading aloud task, and only once mentioned the possibility of negotiating meaning in very vague terms, that the pupils treated this lesson as a reading aloud session, rather than as a reading comprehension activity.

Seven of the forty-nine negotiation routines occurred while the pupils were individually reading in silence. In each of these seven cases, the teacher was walking around and was called upon by a pupil who started a private conversation with the teacher by asking about the meaning of a difficult word (i.e., producing an indicator of non-understanding). In 6 of these 7 cases, the teacher started negotiating about the meaning of the signalled word with the pupil; in the 7th case (which is quoted below), the teacher involved the whole class into the negotiation routine by producing a comprehension check (T = teacher; P = pupil):

(6)　P　(pointing to a word he does not understand) Comes about
　　　T　Yes, comes about, who knows the meaning of that expression, guys?
　　　　　(no response)
　　　T　Tom, what does it mean?
　　　　　(no response)
　　　T　To come about means to happen. (to first pupil) Any more words?
　　　P　(nodding 'no')

The negotiation routines that did not occur during the group work or silent, individual reading all occurred during collective moments, when the teacher set up interaction with all the pupils. The fact that neither the pupils' background variables, nor the methodological formats could explain much of the variation between the classes in terms of the number of negotiation routines suggests that the teachers' personal interactional style may have been a decisive factor in this respect.

Quality of negotiation routines

The great majority of the observed negotiation routines (46 out of 49) were triggered by a teacher's utterance or by input that the teacher confronted the pupils with rather than by a pupil's utterance. This is not surprising in reading comprehensions lessons, since these activities focus on the comprehension of language

Table 3. Initiation of negotiation routines in the observed classrooms

Spontaneous indicator produced by pupil	8
Indirect indicator produced by pupil	5
Comprehension check	36
Total	49

that does not come from the pupils themselves. These 46 negotiation routines began in one of three ways:

a. A pupil spontaneously takes the initiative to produce an indicator of non-understanding (a clarification request, a confirmation request or a non-verbal signal);
b. The teacher infers from an indirect indicator of non-understanding (e.g., a pupil fails to read a word aloud or fails to provide the answer to a reading comprehension question) that a pupil does not comprehend particular input;
c. The teacher aims at eliciting an indicator of non-comprehension by producing a comprehension check.

As Table 3 shows, only 8 negotiation routines were spontaneously initiated by a pupil. Most of these occurred during the above-mentioned individual reading phases of the lesson. The great majority of the negotiation routines (35) were initiated by a teacher's comprehension check.

Most of the indirect indicators occurred when a pupil showed some difficulty in reading a word aloud and the teacher speculated that this was the case because the pupil did not comprehend its meaning. This is illustrated in example 7 below (T = Teacher; P = pupil):

(7)   P   (luidop lezend) .... Dame (...) d.... (...) sachtig?
          (reading aloud) .... Lady (...) L... (...) like?
       T   Damesachtig. Dat betekent zoals een dame.
          (Ladylike. That means like a lady.)

That the pupils produced so few spontaneous indicators of non-comprehension was surprising in view of the fact that in some classes the number of non-native speakers of Dutch was relatively high (even up to 66%) and the complexity of many of the texts they were confronted with was well above their current level of Dutch language proficiency (this was mainly so because the texts were full of abstract, decontextualised academic language).

To compensate for the lack of pupils' spontaneous indicators of non-understanding, the teachers tapped into a number of sources. In a way, one could regard the whole methodological format of all the reading lessons that were observed (i.e., asking pupils to read a text and have them answer questions about it) as one continuously ongoing comprehension check, and thus the whole lesson

Table 4. Comprehension checks opening a negotiation routine

Type	Addressee	Number of checks indicator
General whole class	12	3
General one pupil	2	1
Specific whole class	11	6
Specific one pupil	9	7
Total	36	17

could be regarded as one extended episode of negotiation of meaning. That would bring us close to the broad definition of negotiation of meaning that was discussed above. However, narrowing the concept down again, Table 4 shows that the teachers also produced many comprehension checks (i.e., speaking turns that explicitly asked the pupils whether they understood certain input), more so, that this constituted the most 'visible' feature of the negotiation routines that were observed in these classrooms. However, as Table 4 below shows, half of the teacher's comprehension checks were not followed by a signal of non-understanding produced by a pupil.

Typical instances of a general comprehension check addressed to the whole class were "Are there any words that you don't understand?" or "Everything's clear?". To the latter question, the pupils' answer was often "yes" or an affirmative nodding, to the former question a negative nodding or a "no". Specific comprehension checks asked about the meaning of a specific word, such as "Does everybody know what a scale is?" (= whole class, specific), or "Danny, do you know what a cuckoo is?" (= one pupil, specific). As Table 4 clearly shows, comprehension checks addressed to individual pupils were more effective in eliciting an indicator of non-understanding than checks addressed to the whole class. When the teacher singled out one particular pupil, the latter was left with little choice but to make a contribution to the ongoing negotiation.

In most of the cases when one of the pupils actually signalled non-understanding, the teacher was found to strongly dominate the rest of the negotiation routine. Rarely did the teacher refer back to the class regarding the indicator of non-understanding, and it was not usual for him to invite the other pupils to produce a response by making explicit what they believed the word or phrase might mean. The teacher very often just provided a synonym or a brief explanation of the signalled word or phrase and then moved on. Even in the cases where the teacher did repeat the indicator (of non-understanding), the pupils did not appear particularly keen to make explicit their hypotheses, nor did they wildly speculate about the meaning. For instance, in the example already mentioned (treating the meaning of 'to come about'), the teacher provided a synonym after two quick attempts to elicit a response from the pupils. The first one of these was addressed to the whole class, the second one to one particular pupil. Waiting time in both of these cases was very short; the teacher actually appeared to be very keen to solve the problem himself.

In sum, the quantity and quality of negotiation of meaning occurring in the eight classrooms that were observed may be summarized as relatively poor, especially in view of the fact that the observations were of reading comprehension activities. Ultimately, reading comprehension activities are about enhancing (written) input comprehension, which, according to the Interactional Hypothesis, contains great potential for elaborating (young) language learners' linguistic repertoires through the negotiation of meaning.

Discussion

On the whole, the behaviour that the pupils display during the reading activities in the eight Flemish classrooms suggests that by the age of 11 children have a clear idea of what it takes to play the role of a pupil. The pupils in the study appeared to know very well what was expected of them in terms of linguistic and non-linguistic behaviour, and what was not expected of them. They also seemed to know what they should expect of the teacher. For example, spontaneously signalling their non-understanding of teacher's utterances or input in reading texts did not appear to belong to typical or expected pupil behaviour. Thus the findings of this study support previous research that highlights the archetypal patterns of classroom negotiation (e.g., Musumeci 1996). However, if the comprehension of unfamiliar target language input is essential for building up linguistic proficiency, and negotiation of meaning constitutes an effective way of enhancing comprehension, then the pupils' lack of spontaneous non-understanding signals might actually work to their own disadvantage (in terms of language learning and building up reading comprehension skills).

One of the main questions resulting from this research is to what extent the observed lack of negotiation of meaning is typical for primary education in general or should merely be attributed to the particular research context and personality features of the eight Flemish primary school teachers who were involved in the study. Since there is very little other empirical research available that specifically focuses on the negotiation of meaning during reading instruction in primary schools, we have to turn to other, more general observation studies of classroom interaction and studies of negotiation of meaning occurring in the classroom during speaking/listening tasks (e.g., Doughty & Pica 1986; Foster 1998; Foster & Ohta 2005; Musumeci 1996; Pica 1994; Rulon & McCreary 1986).

These studies suggest that in primary schools around the world, a number of factors may actually inhibit pupils from signalling their non-understanding. First, in education in general, the pupils' main task is often to provide correct answers rather than to ask questions. Pupils failing to give the elicited answer or asking for an explanation of difficult input may raise the impression that they have been inattentive, have not been entirely devoted to comprehending the assigned text or cannot cope with the subject-matter at hand. This can be linked to Aston's (1986) and Foster's (1998) suggestion that negotiation of meaning can be face-threatening for language learners. In a classroom, the face-threatening nature of signalling incomprehension may be further aggravated by the audience effect (Barnes 1973). Any pupil displaying his non-understanding does not only do so for the teacher, but in front of the whole class. Rather than losing face, many pupils prefer to remain quiet and either feign understanding (Aston 1986) or signal their incomprehension in non-verbal and more implicit ways. One probable reason for the fact that in the current study conducted in the Flemish classrooms nearly all spontaneous indicators of non-comprehension occurred during the individual reading phase is that the audience effect ebbs away. The same explanation may be applied to research findings showing that negotiation of meaning is more likely to occur in group work than in teacher-led interactions (Rulon & McCreary 1986; Doughty & Pica 1986). In this respect, Musumeci (1996), analyzing interaction during content-based classroom activities, suggests that there may be an "intimacy requirement" for negotiation of meaning to arise. For many students, small groups and one-to-one exchanges will fulfil this requirement more easily than whole-class activities.

Besides attempting to avoid losing face, language learners may also be disinclined to negotiate for meaning because interrupting the flow of the conversation each time a comprehension problem occurs may slow down task performance in a frustrating way. Thus, in order to keep up the pace of the interaction, language learners help each other in other ways than explicitly signalling non-understanding. It might be for this reason that Foster and Ohta (2005) found in their study that learners were more likely to co-construct and prompt each other than to engage in negotiation.

Similarly it seems that teachers are more concerned with keeping the classroom interaction going, than engaging in protracted negotiation for meaning (Musumeci 1996; Van den Branden 2006). The teachers in Musumeci's study, for instance, insisted that it is their responsibility to ensure that communication in the classroom is successful. So, if they did not understand what a pupil was saying, rather than setting up a negotiation routine and explicitly telling the students they did not understand, they tried to infer what the pupil was saying in order to avoid having to put the pupil on the spot. In this way, the teacher may at the same time maintain control over what happens in the classroom and over the specific path the discourse takes. In fact, data drawn from Musumeci's and Van den Branden's teacher interviews show that many teachers regard unexpected, spontaneous pupil initiatives as disrupting the educational process they have in mind, as time-consuming and as leading to unwanted diversions from the main focus of the lesson. Instead they attempt to maintain learner comprehension and avoid communication breakdown, often by simplifying the nature of their language.

The latter approach, however, may in the long term be counterproductive for second language acquisition: if teachers avoid producing oral or written input that they expect will cause non-understanding problems, the language learning potential of the input may strongly diminish. This is the case in many simplified reading materials that are presented to second language learners because genuine, authentic reading materials are considered too difficult for the learners to understand. As an alternative for simplified texts, Doughty and Long (2003) propose the use of elaborated text. This kind of text is created by integrating the kind of interactional modifications that native speakers make in order to enhance input comprehensibility (such as adding redundancy, paraphrase, and highlighting important concepts). Elaborated texts have been empirically shown to be superior to simplified text by yielding comparable levels of input comprehension, while retaining the new vocabulary and grammatical items in the input that second language learners need to encounter in order to further develop target language proficiency (Long & Ross 1993; Yano, Long, & Ross 1994; Van den Branden 2000). Obviously, elaborated input can be provided in advance (e.g., by skilfully manipulating reading materials), but also during classroom discourse, more particularly during classroom negotiation of meaning.

Thirdly, pupils may be less likely to signal their non-comprehension in the classroom if they are not interested in the input or the reading task they are confronted with. One of the guiding principles of modern language teaching methodologies, such as task-based language learning, is that language learners should be intrinsically motivated to perform tasks in the classroom and use language in meaningful ways while doing so. Intrinsic motivation launches language learners into action, for example, into reading for comprehension (Day & Bamford 1998; Dörnyei 2001; Matthewson 1994), and makes them persist in investing mental energy in task performance, even when obstacles such as reading comprehension problems arise. Even more so, intrinsic motivation to perform a task successfully may drive learners to actually try and solve comprehension problems, for instance through the negotiation of meaning. In Van den Branden's (2000) quasi-experimental study into the effect of negotiation of meaning on reading comprehension, a detective story was chosen because of its motivational power. The pupils had to comprehend the text in order to solve a fascinating mystery, which may have pushed them into setting up negotiation with the teacher or their partner. In the pair negotiation condition, pupils who had a relatively low level of language proficiency profited significantly more from the negotiation if they were teamed up with a pupil with a relatively higher level of proficiency than with a partner with equally low language proficiency. Van den Branden partly explains this result by referring to motivational factors, especially when it comes to explaining the enhanced input comprehension by the higher proficient partner of mixed-ability pairs. Besides profiting from the fact that trying to explain a difficult word or sentence to another may be a way of narrowing down its meaning for themselves, the expectation of having to explain something to another may have had a positive impact in the pair negotiation condition for the higher proficient partner. It might be argued that in heterogeneous dyads the members with the superior language skills felt more motivated to comprehend the written input with which they were confronted just because there was a less proficient partner who depended on them. In the observed reading activities with the regular teachers, however, almost no group work was organized.

Conclusions and recommendations

From this chapter it is clear that we need more empirical studies of the interaction and negotiation of meaning that occurs in intact primary school classrooms. It is also clear that children appear to be able to negotiate for meaning. Further, the negotiation work that they engage in appears to have the same potential for enhancing second language acquisition as it does with adults. More specifically it creates opportunities for noticing gaps; for comprehending input that second language learners are unfamiliar with and, in turn, this enables the elaboration of their linguistic repertoire; for pushing output and receiving feedback; and, for making cognitive comparisons between interlanguage and target language utterances. In addition, integrating negotiation of meaning into reading activities appears to have the same potential as it does with adults, namely providing language learners with new and comprehensible input.

However, the dearth of available research suggests that in regular classrooms the basic conditions that enable negotiation of meaning to become a natural component of powerful learning environments are often not fulfilled. At the same time, the available research points towards a number of aspects of reading activities which may enhance the natural occurrence of negotiation of meaning. These are formulated below in the form of recommendations:

a. *Work with interesting texts and motivating reading comprehension tasks*: this will enhance pupils' willingness to read the text for comprehension, and to invest energy in solving non-understanding problems if these arise.

b. *Work with texts that are slightly above the pupils' current level of language proficiency:* texts that are so much simplified that they are at, or even under, the pupils' current level of language proficiency may work for comprehension, but not for language learning. They will elicit little negotiation work, since the learners will not be challenged by new vocabulary or grammatical items, and will hardly be involved in the kind of interactional modification that negotiation of meaning gives rise to.

c. *Work in small groups*: Reading activities built up around motivating, challenging comprehension tasks that have to be performed in small groups create the intimacy condition required for many learners to signal their incomprehension to each other and to negotiate meaning. Equally, for many pupils, individual reading comprehension tasks or small group works will create a safer environment to signal their incomprehension to their teacher than whole-group activities.

d. *Work with mixed-ability groups*: these groups, consisting of a more highly proficient pupil and less highly proficient pupil have been shown to lead to higher quantity and quality of negotiation work than same-ability groups.

e. *Train teachers to develop the necessary interactional skills to negotiate meaning in an efficient way*: In the classroom, the teacher will often be the most crucial interlocutor of the pupil in terms of promoting language learning. If the Interaction Hypothesis holds true, teachers should develop the basic skills to efficiently elicit negotiation of meaning and to do the negotiation work together with the pupils in a way that (a) protects the pupil's face, (b) allows pupils and teachers together to solve comprehension problems efficiently in terms of time invested, (c) generates the children's active contribution to the negotiation work, (d) maintains children's motivation to further invest mental energy in the reading comprehension task and future negotiation sequences.

f. *Sensitize the teacher to develop a basically positive attitude towards negotiation of meaning*: Much of the above is founded on the premise that pupils can learn much from the communication problems they face and the errors they make. Rather than constantly trying to make sure that classroom communication is running smoothly and is completely under control, teachers should allow ample space for the learners' initiatives, for their questions, worries and problems, and for their particular reactions to the tasks they are confronted with.

References

Aston, G. 1986. Troubleshooting interaction with learners: The more the merrier? *Applied Linguistics* 7: 128–143.

Barnes, D. 1973. *Language in the Classroom*. Bletchley: Open University Press.

Day, R. & Bamford, J. 1998. *Extensive Reading in the Second Language Classroom*. Cambridge: CUP.

Dornyei, Z. 2001. *Motivation Strategies in the Language Classroom*. Cambridge: CUP.

Doughty, C. & Long, M. 2003. Optimal psycholinguistic environments for distance foreign language learning. *Language Learning & Technology* 7: 50–80.

Doughty, C. & Pica, T. 1986. 'Information-gap' tasks: Do they facilitate second language acquisition? *TESOL Quarterly* 20(2): 305–326.

Ellis, R. 1999. *Learning a Second Language through Interaction.* Amsterdam: John Benjamins.

Ellis, R. & Heimbach, R. 1997. Bugs and birds: Children's acquisition of second language vocabulary through interaction. *System* 2: 247–259.

Foster, P. 1998. A classroom perspective on the negotiation of meaning. *Applied Linguistics* 19: 19–23.

Foster, P. & Ohta, A. 2005. Negotiation for meaning and peer assistance in second language classrooms. *Applied Linguistics* 26: 402–430.

Gass, S. 2003. Input and interaction. In *The Handbook of Second Language Acquisition*, C. Doughty & M. Long (eds), 224–255. Malden MA: Blackwell.

Gass, S. & Varonis, E. 1985. Task variation and nonnative/nonnative negotiation of meaning. In *Input in Second Language Acquisition*, S. Gass & C. Madden (eds). Rowley MA: Newbury House.

Long, M. 1985. Input and second language acquisition theory. In *Input in Second Language Acquisition*, S. Gass & C. Madden (eds.), 377–393. Rowley MA: Newbury House.

Long, M. 1996. The role of the linguistic environment in second language acquisition. In *Handbook of Second Language Acquisition*, W. Ritchie & T. Bathia (eds), 413–468. New York NY: Academic Press.

Long, M. & Robinson, P. 1998. Focus on form: Theory, research and practice. In *Focus on Form in Classroom SLA*, C. Doughty & J. Williams (eds), 15–41. Cambridge: CUP.

Long, M. & Ross, S. 1993. Modifications that preserve language and content. In *Simplification: Theory and Application*, M. Tickoo (ed.), 29–52. Singapore: SEAMEO Regional Language Centre.

Loshky, L. & Bley-Vroman, R. 1993. Grammar and task-based methodology. In *Tasks and Language Learning: Integrating Theory and Practice*, G. Crookes & S. Gass (eds), 123–167. Clevedon: Multilingual Matters.

Mackey, A. 1999. Input, interaction and second language development: An empirical study of question formation in ESL. *Studies in Second Language Acquisition* 21: 557–587.

Mackey, A., Gass, S. & McDonough, K. 2000. Do learners recognize implicit negative feedback as feedback? *Studies in Second Language Acquisition* 22: 471–497.

Matthewson, G. 1994. Model of Attitude influence upon reading and learning to read. In *Theoretical Models and Processes of Reading*, R. Ruddell, M. Ruddell & H. Singer (eds), 1131–1161. Newark NJ: International Reading Association.

Musumeci, D. 1996. Teacher-learner negotiation in content-based instruction: Communication at cross-purposes? *Applied Linguistics* 17: 286–325.

Oliver, R. 1998. Negotiation of meaning in child interactions. *Modern Language Journal* 82: 372–386.

Oliver, R. 2002. The patterns of negotiation for meaning in child interactions. *Modern Language Journal* 86: 97–111.

Oliver, R. & Mackey, A. 2003. Interactional context and feedback in child ESL classrooms. *Modern Language Journal* 87: 519–543.

Pica, T. 1994. Research on negotiation: What does it reveal about second language learning conditions, processes and outcomes? *Language Learning* 44: 493–527.

Pica, T., Holliday, L., Lewis, N. & Morgenthaler, L. 1989. Comprehensible output as an outcome of linguistic demands on the learner. *Studies in Second Language Acquisition* 11(1): 63–90.

Pica, T., Holliday, L., Lewis, N., Berducci, D. & Newman, J. 1991. Language learning through interaction: What role does gender play? *Studies in Second Language Acquisition* 13: 343–376.

Polio, C. & Gass, S. 1997. Replication and reporting: A commentary. *Studies in Second Language Acquisition* 19: 499–508.

Rulon, K. & McCreary, J. 1986. Negotiation of content: Teacher-fronted and small group interaction. In *Talking to Learn: Conversation in Second Language Acquisition*, R. Day (ed.), 182–199. Rowley MA: Newbury House.

Van den Branden, K. 1997. Effects of negotiation on language learners' output. *Language Learning* 47: 589–636.

Van den Branden, K. 2000. Does negotiation of meaning promote reading comprehension? A study of primary school classes. *Reading Research Quarterly* 35: 426–443.

Van den Branden, K. 2006. Training teachers: Task-based as well? In *Task-based Language Education: From Theory to Practice*, K. Van den Branden (ed.), 217–248. Cambridge: CUP.

Varonis, E. & Gass, S. 1985. Non-native/non-native conversations: A model for negotiation of meaning. *Applied Linguistics* 6(1): 71–90.

Wells, G. 1986. *The Meaning Makers. Children Learning Language and Using Language to Learn.* Portsmouth: Heinemann.

Yano, Y., Long, M. & Ross, S. 1994. The effects of simplified and elaborated texts on foreign language reading comprehension. *Language Learning* 44: 189–219.

Appendix: Framework for negotiation of meaning

1. Trigger

2. Indicator
2a. Clarification request
2b. Confirmation request
    2b1. non-modifying confirmation request
    2b2. modifying confirmation request
2c. non-verbal indicator
2d. Indirect indicator

3. Response
3a. Switch to a new topic
3b. Repetition of trigger
3c. Modification of trigger
    3c1. morpho-syntactic modification only
    3c2. semantic modification included
3d. Repetition of indicator
3e. Modification of indicator
    3d1. morpho-syntactic modification only
    3d2. semantic modification included
3f. Acknowledgement/negation of indicator only
3g. Inability to respond

4. Reaction to the response
4a. Explicit comprehension signal
    4a1. explicit formula
    4a2. repetition of trigger/response
    4a3. modification of trigger/response
4b. Implicit comprehensions signal

5. Comprehension check
5a. General check
    5a1. addressed to many hearers
    5a2. addressed to one hearer
5b. Specific check
    5b1. addressed to many hearers
    5b2. addressed to one hearer

Instructed language learning in the later years of education

Incidental focus on form and learning outcomes with young foreign language classroom learners

Eva Alcón Soler and María del Pilar García Mayo

Universitat Jaume I / Universidad del País Vasco (UPV/EHU)

This chapter addresses the issue of how unplanned focus on form is accomplished in an English as a foreign language (EFL) classroom and its effect on adolescents' learning outcomes. The findings support previous research indicating that adolescents benefit from interaction in foreign language classrooms as well as claims that for adolescents, as with adults, focus on form is an effective means of raising awareness of lexical items. Findings also suggest that the relationship between noticing, uptake and longer-term learning requires more research with this population in order to better understand the processes.

Introduction

Second language acquisition (SLA) research has provided evidence that interaction creates opportunities for language learning. Learners' participation in conversations can draw their attention to form-meaning relationships and help them to notice mismatches between the input received and their own interlanguage (García Mayo & Alcón 2002; Gass 1997, 2003; Gass & Mackey 2006; Gass, Mackey & Pica 1998; Long 1983a, 1983b, 1996; Mackey 2007; Pica 1994). Also, both the linguistic information learners receive as feedback during interaction and the learners' own modified output have been shown to be associated with L2 learning (Mackey & Gass 2006; Swain 1985, 1995). In short, SLA research based on the interaction hypothesis has provided evidence about the opportunity that negotiation during interaction offers language learners for connecting input, internal learners' capacities, particularly selective attention and output, in productive ways (Long 1996: 451–452).

SLA research has also shown that communicative activities with an exclusive focus on meaning are not adequate for language learning and there is also a need for a focus on form (Alegría de la Colina & García Mayo 2007; Doughty & Williams 1998; García Mayo 2002a, 2002b, 2005; García Mayo & Pica 2000a, 2000b). Long

(1996: 40) defines focus on form as interactional moves directed at raising learner awareness of forms by "briefly drawing students' attention to linguistic elements (words, collocations, grammatical structures, pragmatic patterns, and so on), in context, as they arise incidentally in lessons whose overriding focus is on meaning, or communication." Research on focus on form instruction has been undertaken to conceptualize and describe the procedures for teaching form in the context of a communicative activity. Ellis (2001) and Ellis, Basturkmen and Loewen (2002) distinguish between *planned* versus *incidental* focus on form. Planned focus on form involves the use of communicative tasks designed to elicit forms which have been pre-selected by the teacher. In incidental focus on form, tasks are designed to elicit and use language without any specific attention to form, although the role of participants in performing the task will determine the accomplishing of a reactive or pre-emptive focus on form, as will be seen in the current study. Descriptive studies on focus on form instruction also show that reactive focus on form can be realized as explicit or implicit feedback. On the one hand, explicit feedback provides metalinguistic information, indicating directly that an error has been committed or elicits the correct form (Lyster 1998, 2001; Lyster & Ranta 1997; Williams 1999, 2001). On the other hand, implicit feedback may be provided by means of recasts, which have been shown to be the most frequent type of feedback in different classroom settings (Doughty 1994; Lyster & Ranta 1997; Tsang 2004). Aditionally, descriptive studies on pre-emptive focus on form (Ellis, Basturkmen & Loewen 2001a, 2001b) illustrate that the teacher or a student may choose to make a specific form the topic of the discourse, even though no error has been committed. In this case, an explicit focus on form is achieved either by students' questions about linguistic forms or by teachers' display questions and information about the linguistic code (Loewen 2004, 2006).

The question in many investigations of attention to form has been the extent to which corrective feedback should be implicit or whether it should involve overt intervention or even explicit metalinguistic instruction. Another important issue is whether these types of corrective feedback are present in different settings (see Sheen 2004 for a comparison of teachers' feedback and learners' uptake in ESL and EFL classrooms) and whether or not they vary according to the age of the learners (Philp, Mackey and Oliver, this volume). To date most studies have dealt with adults, initially in experimental settings, more recently in adult language classrooms. Current research has moved to investigate the effect of different variables on the amount of negotiation and the relationship between the salience of interactional exchanges and learning outcomes with young learners. Thus, studies by Oliver (2000) – with children ages 6–12- and Mackey, Oliver and Leeman (2003) – with children aged 8–12- have shown that differences in the provision and use of negative feedback vary according to the age of the learners and the context of the exchanges, suggesting that patterns of interaction and immediate outcomes may be different for children and adults.

Research dealing with middle childhood (7–11 years) and adolescent (12–17 years) learners has examined the role of classroom interaction in language learning and the relationship between type of form-focused feedback and L2 learning. For instance, Alcón (1994, 2007) examines the effectiveness of focus on form in intact foreign language classrooms with adolescent learners (14–15 years old). Alcón (1994) focuses on the relationship between learners' verbal behaviour and learning outcomes and shows that negotiation, independently of the learners' proficiency level or active involvement in classroom interaction, functions as a language awareness device for vocabulary items. The occurrence of teacher incidental focus on form and its effectiveness on noticing and vocabulary learning is examined in Alcón (2007). In line with previous research, the author claims that most interactional feedback in these contexts seems to be triggered by lexical problems and teacher reactive feedback by means of recasts is the most frequent type of feedback. In addition, Alcón reports that, although there is no significant difference between teacher pre-emptive and reactive feedback, teachers' pre-emptive focus on form seems to direct learners' selective attention to vocabulary items, resulting in learners' noticing. However, while teacher reactive feedback in Alcón's study was not associated with higher levels of noticing, as measured by learners' reporting of learned items, it did positively impact subsequent written production of vocabulary items.

Lyster and his colleagues (Lyster 1998, 2001; Lyster & Ranta 1997) studied French immersion classroom learners aged 9–11 and indicated that young L2 learners may not notice target-non target mismatches by means of recasts. They suggest that other forms of feedback such as elicitations, metalinguistic clues and clarification questions (more recently referred to as prompts in Lyster 2004) may lead to immediate repair and seem to be more effective for drawing children's attention to language. In a similar vein, Van den Branden (1997) investigated the effect of various types of negotiation on the acquisition of Dutch by 11 to 12 year-old learners in a Flemish primary school. The results showed that participants' output was determined by the type of negative feedback they received: learners who had been pushed in preceding negotiation produced a significantly greater quantity of output. However, those negotiations did not have significant effects on the syntactic complexity or on the grammatical accuracy of the learners' output in the post-test.

Doughty and Varela (1998) operationalized an implicit focus on form approach in a content-based ESL class in the United States. The subjects in their study were 34 middle school students ranging in age from 11–14 and the focus of the 6-week study was past-time reference in written and oral science reports. The learners in the control group were audio-taped and the treatment group was taught by one of the researchers in order to ensure that corrective feedback was the distinguishing feature between the two groups. The findings show that there were significant gains for the group who had received corrective feedback (intonational focus and corrective recasting) regularly, while the control group did not progress. This study also shows that corrective feedback that draws the learners' attention to linguistic form can facilitate learning.

Researchers in foreign language contexts have questioned whether the absence of learner responses limits the effectiveness of recasts. Thus, Havranek (2002) and Havranek and Cesnik (2001) present findings from a comprehensive study on oral corrective feedback involving 207 EFL learners (first language, German) at different ages, from 10-year-old beginners to mature university students specializing in English. Although the researchers do not organize the results considering the different age groups, the general finding is that the most successful format of correction, both for the learners receiving the feedback and for their peers, is feedback successfully eliciting self-correction in practice situations. Among the least successful formats are recasts without further comment or repetition by the corrected learner.

Tsang (2004) analyzed 18 non-native English lessons on teacher feedback and learner uptake at secondary level in Hong Kong with 481 learners of grades 7–11 (aged 12–17). The results of the study indicate that recasts and explicit correction were the most frequent types of feedback but the former may give way to more effective types of feedback such as elicitation, clarification, request, metalinguistic feedback and repetition, which – the author claims- may be more effective than explicit correction. The author also concludes that recasts and explicit correction may be more appropriate for phonological errors, whereas negotiation moves facilitate grammatical repairs.

The above-mentioned studies have produced findings suggesting that different types of feedback may be more or less effective with learners of different age ranges. As this brief review has shown, the research is divided, with some studies suggesting benefits for a more explicit type of corrective feedback which brings the form into the learner's focal attention, and others suggesting benefits for more unobstrusive and indirect forms of feedback that allow the form-meaning mapping process to continue uninterrupted. Current research in SLA places great emphasis on the study of cognitive processes and in particular the study of attention and awareness and L2 development through interaction (Long 1996; Robinson 1995, 2001, 2003; Schmidt 1995, 2001). Attention allows learners to notice the gap between their production and the production of the native speaker of the target language. In Schmidt's (1993) Noticing Hypothesis he argues that learners must consciously notice the input in order for it to become intake. He suggests that since many features of the L2 input are likely to be non-salient, intentionally focusing attention on them is a necessity for successful language learning. While a number of studies are addressing Schmidt's claims with adults, a logical question is whether corrective feedback provides younger learners with opportunities to pay attention to target language forms.

In the studies reviewed so far, the interactional context and the feedback-learning relationship have been noted as areas in need of further enquiry with younger learners. For example, Mackey and Silver (2005) describe the need for data driven studies to provide information about the role of interaction in new environments with younger learners at a range of different ages. The participants in the current study are 14–15 year old adolescents, an age range that falls into its own category, being neither "classic" child SLA, nor classic adult SLA. As Philp, Mackey and Oliver (in their introduction to this edited collection) point out, adolescent learners (both early and late) are distinct from middle childhood and adult learners (18 years of age and beyond). Adolescents have the advantage of a greater capacity for abstract thinking than younger learners, and are able to reflect on language issues, which could be an advantage for the use of form-focused instructional approaches. For example, one typical and interesting characteristic of adolescents is their reliance on peers, which might be of importance when considering classroom interactional patterns. A more detailed account of the linguistic behaviour of adolescents in relation to corrective feedback is critical in order to provide the field with a more complete picture of SLA in all age ranges.

Against this backdrop, the present investigation was descriptive (no control group was included) and addresses the issue of whether feedback operationalized as incidental focus on form occurs in foreign language environments with adolescents, and assesses its effects on learning outcomes in this age group. In particular, the present study addresses the following research questions:

1. To what extent does focus on form occur in adolescent meaning-focused foreign language classrooms?
2. Does focus on form have a positive impact on adolescent learners' uptake?
3. Are the forms in focus on form episodes used accurately in subsequent written production by adolescent learners?

The study

Instructional setting

The context in which this research was carried out is an English as a foreign language (EFL) classroom in Spain. Although the need for positive and negative input, as well as the need for learner production of meaningful L2 output are shared by learners in both EFL and ESL settings, there are differences in these contexts that might affect the ways in which these needs are addressed. Unlike ESL learners,

EFL learners often lack access to native speaker models for their linguistic information and to actual samples from everyday social interaction (Block 2007; Gass
1990). In the Spanish EFL context, Alcón (1994) reported that high-school learners' attention to language during meaning negotiation provided conditions for
language learning. Similarly, García Mayo and Pica (2000a, 2000b) showed that the
interaction among advanced adult EFL learners appeared to be a suitable resource
for learning, although a definite need for more attention to form was observed.
The data for the current study were obtained from one intact meaning-focused
class over a whole academic year. In some schools in Spain lessons are divided in
three-hour periods per week, two of them following a mixture of meaning-focused
and form-focused instruction, and the third session using communicative activities linked to meaning-focused instruction. Although 36 EFL learners and one
non-native English language teacher participated in the first two sessions, for the
third sessions learners were divided in three groups in order to offer them more
opportunities to use the language through communicative activities. The present
study focuses exclusively on the interaction generated during the meaning-focused
activities carried out in the third session.

Participants

The participants were 12 Spanish speakers (7 female and 5 male) learning English
as a compulsory subject. All participants had Spanish or Catalan (some of them
were bilingual) as their mother tongue, they had been studying English as a compulsory subject for six years at school, and their ages were between 14 and 15. They
were told that the aim of the study was describing interaction in a foreign language
classroom, but no information was provided about the research questions of the
study or the specific issues the researchers were interested in.

Data collection and analysis

The database for this study consisted of seventeen 45-minute lessons of audio-
recorded teacher-led conversations (from the third sessions mentioned above), 204
(17 sessions x 12 learners) diary entries reporting items noticed, that is, items the
learners identified as having learned; 204 post-test translations, and 204 delayed
post-test translations, which were created on the basis of the items reported in
learners' diaries after each lesson. The learners performed different types of communicative activities including one-way opinion tasks (in which they provided
their opinion about a specific topic they had just read in a newspaper article),
two-way opinion tasks (where they had to negotiate a solution for a problematic
situation) and debates.

Two non-native English language teachers helped in transcribing the data. Both of them had a University degree in English and an M.A in Applied Linguistics and had been teaching English for eight years. The data were then coded by the researchers. Whole class interaction as well as teacher interaction with individuals was recorded using a wireless microphone. As the study is basically descriptive, a data driven approach to identify the structure of focus on meaning and focus on form episodes was followed. However, for the present study focus on meaning episodes were excluded and our analysis was carried out on focus on form episodes (FFEs), defined as "the discourse from the point where the attention to linguistic form starts to the point where it ends, due to a change in topic back to message or sometimes another focus on form" (Ellis et al. 2001a: 294).

Before data-coding, researchers first practised together on similar data not used in this study to ensure consistency. Then, twenty per cent of the data of the present study was coded and rates of agreement were established following Cohen's (1960) procedure for the following characteristics found in FFEs: linguistic focus, type of FFE, successful uptake, and learning outcomes. The linguistic focus in each episode could be on grammar, vocabulary, pronunciation or spelling. Coding between the two researchers resulted in agreement of 96% with respect to the identification of FFEs and of 94% when determining their linguistic focus. In addition, focus on form episodes were coded as reactive or pre-emptive. Firstly, within reactive episodes we included negotiation sequences in which there seems to be some language problem and the teacher either provides the information by means of a recast or forces learners to establish the correct form by means of elicitation techniques (repetition of the word, pausing, using clarification questions, or asking students to reformulate the utterance). We eliminated reactive FFEs where an explicit correction was provided because they were very few: just 10% of the total (276 reactive FFEs) versus 60% of recasts and 30% of prompts such as clarification requests, repetitions or questions used to elicit student's production of the correct form.[1] Secondly, within pre-emptive FFE we considered negotiation sequences in which there seems to be no communication problem, but they are teacher- or learner-initiated with a clear focus on language. Negotiation sequences often appear in embedded sequences but, when coding type of FFE, we considered

---

1.   On the basis of descriptive studies of teacher-student interaction such as Lyster (2002), Lyster and Mori (2006: 271) classify feedback moves as one of three types: explicit correction, recasts and prompts. Prompts include "a variety of signals – other than alternative reformulations – that push learners to self-repair. Among those signals Lyster and Mori include (a) teacher's elicitation, (b) metalinguistic clues, (c) clarification requests and (d) repetition. Although there is a current debate about the effectiveness of recasts vs prompts (see, among others, Ellis, Loewen & Erlam 2006; Havranek 2002; Lyster 2004; Lyster & Mori 2006; McDonough & Mackey 2006), that issue is beyond the scope of this paper.

who among the participants initiated an observable episode. Thus, each FFE could be classified as follows:

1. Reactive FFE: correct form supplied by the teacher, as in (1), or by the learners with the help of the teacher,[2] as in (2):

    (1) S4. The boy do not have an alibi. He wasn't in class
         T.   *Right. He does not have an alibi and then*
         S4. And *he does not have an alibi* and is guilty

    (2) S1. Yesterday we go to the cinema, but..
         T.   *Yesterday you go?*
         S1. *Yes I went to the cinema* but it was closed

2. Pre-emptive FFE, which could be teacher-initiated, as in (3), or learner-initiated, as in (4):

    (3) T.   Today we are going to talk about custom officers. *Do you know what a custom officer means?*
         S1. Frontera? (*border*)

    (4) T.   So, all of us want a new way of testing, so let's create it. We are going to find the characteristics of a good way of testing. So you start saying things and Marta will write them on the blackboard. Finally we will present an alternative to the headmaster
         S12. *Headmaster?*
         T.   The person in charge of the school is the headmaster
         S1. *Eliminar? How do you say eliminar?*
         T.   Any?
         S6. Abolish
         S1. Abolish the exams
         S12. Ok we can tell the *headmaster* to abolish exams

The following rates of agreement were established for each FFE type: teacher supplier in reactive FFEs, 91%, student supplier in reactive FFEs, 84%, pre-emptive teacher initiated, 97%, and pre-emptive student initiated, 96%.

In order to answer our second research question, that is, in order to assess the impact of focus on form on learners' uptake, we followed Ellis et al.'s (2001a, 2001b) study where they ascertain that uptake can occur both in pre-emptive and reactive FFEs. In addition, in the current study we only considered instances of

---

2. Reactive focus on form has always been analyzed in relation to teachers' feedback in the classroom but we aimed to incorporate learners' reactive focus on form episodes by analyzing the instances in which the correct linguistic form is provided by the learner with the help of the teacher.

successful uptake, that is, learners' production of target linguistic items after provision of feedback. This production could occur immediately after the provision
of feedback (cf. (1)) or later in discourse (cf. (4)). Successful uptake was only considered as a sign of noticed input when, both in reactive or pre-emptive FFEs,
learners responded to the provision of linguistic information by incorporating the
appropriate feedback in their responses. We did not count instances of simple ac-
knowledgment on the part of the learner, as they are ambiguous (Carpenter, Jeon,
MacGregor & Mackey 2006). For instance, in (1) above the learner incorporates
the teacher's recast in the next turn and in (4) the learners' uptake of the lexical item "headmaster" appears later in discourse. There were also some instances
in which more than one learner incorporated the target linguistic form after feedback, and in those cases we calculated uptake by each individual learner. Intercoder
agreement for uptake was 80%.

Finally, following Schmidt's (1993, 2001) and Robinson's (2001, 2003) claims
about the roles of attention and awareness in language learning, our third research
question aimed at testing the relationship between focus on form instruction and
learning outcomes. Thus, we measured the impact of focus on form instruction on
learners' noticing assessing their reports about what they learned and the accuracy
of their use of these items in subsequent written production. Immediately after
the end of each lesson students were asked to write down what they thought they
had learned. Since 80% of the total items reported were lexical words, we matched
lexical items remembered with learners' participation in FFEs. In coding learners'
participation in negotiation sequences we did not distinguish between initiator
or supplier, since, as reported by Alcón (1994), negotiation in foreign language
classrooms seems to have a positive effect on those who trigger, initiate or respond
within the negotiation sequences. We measured the impact of focus on form on
accurate use by means of tailor-made written sentences created on the basis of
the lexical words reported as learned items. Learners were asked to translate the
sentences from Spanish into English, first immediately after the lesson and then
after a week. This allowed the researchers to match active involvement in lexically
oriented FFEs with learners' uptake and accurate use in the translation post-tests
and delayed post-tests.

Results and discussion

In relation to our first research question, Figure 1 describes features of a total of
459 FFEs occurring in the seventeen 45 minute-lessons that make up the database
of this study. This means that there was one episode every 0.6 minutes. Ellis et al.
(2001a, 2001b) report FFEs in second language classrooms with adult learners oc-
curing at a rate of 1 FFE every 1.6 minutes. In the instructed adolescent foreign

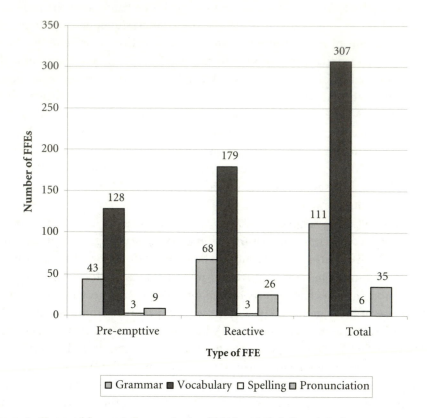

Figure 1. Types of focus on form episodes (FFEs) and their linguistic focus.

language classroom examined in the current research, focus on form occurred even more frequently. Our data also indicate that reactive and pre-emptive focus on form both featured in the foreign language classroom and that there was no statistically significant difference between the two in terms of occurrence (Fisher's test p =.335; 1df, n = 459).

In addition, out of the total FFEs, 24.2% addressed grammar, 66.9% vocabulary, 1.3% spelling and 7.6% pronunciation. Likewise, both in pre-emptive and re-active focus on form the aspects that receive more attention are vocabulary (27.9% in pre-emptive and 39.0% in reactive FFE) and grammar (9.4% in pre-emptive and 14.8% in reactive). Thus, in line with research conducted in second language contexts (Williams 1999, 2001), we can claim that in this foreign language setting the majority of linguistic items that young participants pay attention to in FFEs are largely lexical. As already pointed out by Pica (1994), this can be explained be-cause negotiation, by its very nature, is bound to revolve around lexical meaning

Table 1. Type of focus on form episode and participants' involvement

	Type FFE		Type FFE			
Supplier	Pre-emptive	%	Reactive	%	Total	%
Teacher	101	22.0%	192	41.8%	293	63.8%
Students	82	17.9%	84	18.3%	166	36.2%
Total	183	39.9%	276	60.1%	459	100.0%

in response to its focus on comprehensibility of message. Figure 1 also seems to indicate that, in spite of the importance that the Spanish primary and secondary education reform (1993) allocates to communicative language teaching, English classes in Spanish secondary schools focus mainly on vocabulary and grammar.

As mentioned above, we also examined whether pre-emptive focus on form was initiated by teacher or students. Thus, reactive FFE were classified taking into account if the correct form was established by students or it was supplied by the teacher. As illustrated in Table 1, teachers' initiation (pre-emptive FFEs) and provision of the correct form (reactive-FFEs) is higher than learners', probably because of the teacher's power and the asymmetric relationship found in several studies on classroom interaction (Alcón 2001). Learners initiate a FFE whenever they perceive a linguistic gap. Williams (1999) reports that adult learners in her study, carried out in an intensive English program with instructional emphasis on communication of meaning, initiated FFEs but neither frequently nor extensively, especially at lower proficiency levels. However, Williams (1999) also shows clear differences in frequency of FFEs across activity types and mentions that if learners perceive the activity to be a language lesson the number of FFEs goes up. This could be the reason why both in Ellis et al. (2001a, 2001b) and in our study learners perceive the need to focus on language and the number of FFEs increases. As for students' involvement in establishing the correct form, the percentage of instances where the teacher guides students to be suppliers shows that a dual focus on meaning and form can be achieved in communicative language classrooms.

So far, the data show that focus on form instruction occurs with young learners in adolescent foreign language classrooms, but what impact does it have on uptake with this age group? In order to answer this question we examined whether focus on form could benefit uptake, understood as learners' production of target linguistic items after feedback provision, and if so, whether it was influenced by type of FFE and information supplier.

As can be observed in Table 2, the level of overall successful uptake (34%) is not as high as the one reported by Ellis et al. (2001a) (72%). Our findings are similar to those in Lyster and Ranta's (1997) study of learners aged 9–11 in French immersion classrooms. They report that 55% feedback moves responding to learner errors resulted in uptake and only 27% resulted in successful uptake.

Table 2. Type of focus on form episode and supplier

Type of FFE and supplier	Total	Uptake	% Uptake
Preemptive teacher initiated	101	9	8.9%
Preemptive student initiated	82	68	82.9%
Reactive teacher supplier	192	17	8.9%
Reactive student supplier	84	63	75.0%
Total	459	157	34.2%

Table 2 also shows that the percentage of uptake is more frequent both in student initiated FFEs and when learners provide the information in reactive FFEs. Although complexity has not been considered in this study, closer examination of our data indicates that, in line with Loewen (2004), it may influence uptake in reactive FFEs when learners supply the correct form. Similarly, our results on student-initiated focus on form are in line with Ellis et al. (2001a, 2001b) who found that student-initiated FFEs were associated with higher levels of uptake. However, in order to compare results among studies, care should be taken to consider the way uptake has been operationalized in the present research. In the case of student-initiated reactive FFEs, the discourse structure features the following pattern: a learner initiates a FFE because there seems to be a need to know a word and then acknowledges the feedback. Nevertheless, the topicalized item may be incorporated as uptake immediately following the teacher's feedback (as in Loewen 2004) or after several turns. In the present study learners' uptake has been operationalized by including incorporated items after the teacher's feedback and after several turns. Having clarified this issue, it seems that once learners become aware of potential linguistic problems (as indicated by their initiation of FFEs) they take some time to incorporate the noticed items in language production.

The teacher's pre-emptive focus on form was mainly achieved by means of display questions, to which learners replied in their mother tongue. If they did not know the answer, the teacher provided the information and learners had a tendency to respond with silence or an acknowledgement. The learners' uptake is in line with the findings reported by Lyster (1998), Mackey and Philp (1998) and Oliver (1995). Mackey and Philp (1998) reported that 33% of the recasts were incorporated. In Oliver's (1995) study only 10% of the recasts were incorporated. Similarly, Lyster (1998) reports that recasts, although frequently found in child interaction, may not lead to uptake by learners and, therefore, may not turn out to be an effective learning device.[3] Our data support research suggesting that suc-

---

3.   However, as also suggested by Mackey and Philp (1998) and more recently by Loewen and Philp (2006), uptake does not necessarily equate with the potential benefits of recasts because noticing may occur without uptake. Loewen and Philp (2006) report that "whereas a relationship existed for other types of feedback between successful uptake and subsequent successful

Table 3. Matrix of Pearson correlation for reported learned items, uptake, post-test production and delayed post-test production in student-initiated FFEs

	Learning in FFEs	Uptake	Post-test	Delayed Post-test
Learning in FFEs		0.757	0.786	0.314
Uptake			0.841	0.548
Post-test				0.762
Delayed Post-test				

cessful uptake in the classroom is more likely when students perceive problems than when the teacher anticipates potential problems. Thus, it seems as if these adolescent learners did not pay so much attention to the teacher as to their own learning needs. In addition, they appear confident in asking whatever they do not know or in testing hypotheses about language use with the help of the teacher. Later on, once they obtain the information required or the correct form they need is provided, they focus on conversation incorporating such feedback.

So far we have analysed focus on form in relation to learners' successful uptake. This successful uptake in learners' initiated pre-emptive and supplied reactive focus on form sequences constitutes the database to answer our third research question. As mentioned above, since 80% of the items noticed were vocabulary items, we focused on the lexical items that appeared in pre-emptive student-initiated FFEs, indicating that there was a linguistic gap, and in reactive FFEs where learners were suppliers of the lexical items. Our aim was to establish any possible correlation between noticing, measured by means of reported learned items while learners actively participate in both student-initiated and reactive FFEs, learners' uptake, and subsequent use of the lexical items in translation post-tests and delayed post-tests created on the basis of reported learning.

Table 3 features the Pearson product-moment correlations between reported noticed items while learners participate in FFEs, uptake, and immediate and delayed language use of the items, as measured in the translation post-tests and delayed-post tests in student-initiated FFEs.

The Pearson product-moment correlation shows a positive correlation between noticing (reporting the learned item), and uptake ($r = 0.75$) and some relationship between noticing and accurate use as measured in the immediate post-test ($r = 0.78$) and between uptake and immediate post-test ($r = 0.84$). In contrast, the same statistical test shows no correlation between noticing and the delayed post-test ($r = 0.31$) or uptake and delayed production ($r = 0.54$). These results indicate that focus on form plays a role in learners' noticing, and uptake

---

recall, for recasts, successful uptake was not a significant factor" in adult English second language classrooms.

Table 4. Matrix of Pearson Correlation for reported learned items, uptake, post-test production and delayed post-test production in students' reactive FFEs.

	Learning in FFEs	Uptake	Post-test	Delayed Post-test
Learning in FFEs		0.368	0.995	0.818
Uptake			0.361	0.465
Post-test				0.858
Delayed Post-test				

bears some relationship to immediate production or short term learning. We argue this to mean that focus on form in a foreign language classroom context likely raises adolescent learners' awareness of lexical items and facilitates accurate language use. The relationship between noticing and uptake with long-term learning, as measured by delayed translation tests was not so clear.

These results should be considered with caution, though, given the small number of subjects in our study. To further understand the role of focus on form with these young learners in a classroom context, we adopted a qualitative approach to the data. Figure 2 confirms the Pearson product-moment correlations provided above. First, the number of reported learned lexical items in FFEs is higher than those of uptake and subsequent language use. Second, although learners' reported noticing of lexical items seems to influence subsequent uptake, S5, S6, S7 and S8 were able to use those lexical items independently of uptake. Third, the verbal behaviour of S9 suggests that uptake is not associated with initiated FFEs or learning outcomes. Thus, it seems likely learning style and perhaps other individual factors also play a role in understanding our participants' verbal behaviour in interaction and its effect on learning outcomes (as argued by Mackey 2006). Finally, Figure 2 shows that not all lexical items reported result in short or long term learning, as results from the post- and delayed translation tests show. However, accurate use was measured in this study by means of immediate and delayed written production tests and further research could investigate subsequent spontaneous oral production.

Focusing on reactive focus on form where learners establish the correct linguistic form, Table 4 features the Pearson product-moment correlations between reported noticed items - while learners participate in FFEs -, uptake and immediate and delayed language use of the items, as measured in the translation post-tests and delayed-post tests.

The results obtained in reactive FFEs show a high correlation between noticing and immediate ($r = 0.99$) and delayed written production ($r = 0.81$). However, there seems to be no correlation between uptake and noticing ($r = 0.36$), uptake and immediate language use ($r = 0.36$) or delayed language use ($r = 0.46$). Thus, our data suggest that in reactive focus on form the repetition of lexical items does not contribute to their noticing nor to their uptake (cf. Mackey & Philp 1998;

Learning outcomes in students' initiated preemptive FFEs

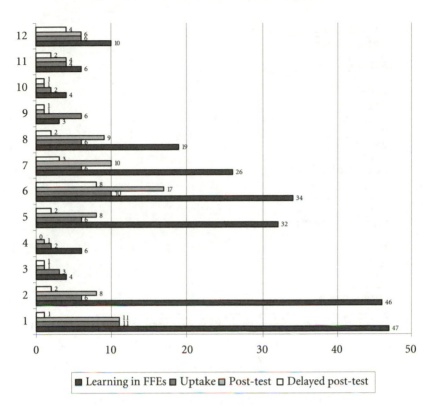

Legend: ■ Learning in FFEs ■ Uptake ◻ Post-test ◻ Delayed post-test

Figure 2. Lexical words noticed in pre-emptive FFEs, learners' uptake and learning outcomes.

Loewen & Philp 2006). However, learners' noticing occurs in FFEs, a finding that might be interpreted as follows: as learners take an active role in reactive FFEs, these might function as language awareness devices at some yet to be determined level, even if they don't influence uptake. Figure 3 features a detailed analysis of outcomes in relation to noticing and uptake and confirms the high scores of noticing associated with short term, and to a lesser extent, with long term learning outcomes.

Conclusions and lines for further inquiry

Relatively little research has been carried out empirically addressing the connection between form focus in a foreign language context and linguistic outcomes. Little research has been carried out with adolescent foreign language learners. The

Learning outcomes in students' reactive FFEs

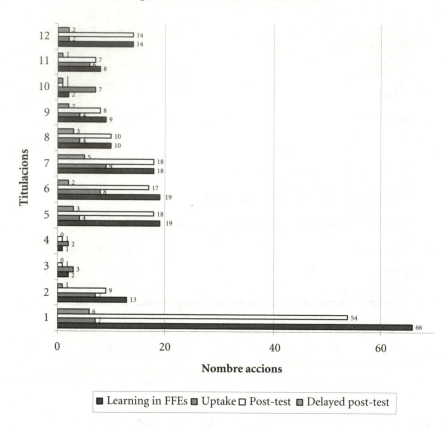

Figure 3. Lexical words noticed in reactive FFEs, learners' uptake and learning outcomes.

current study has aimed to contribute to our understanding of the type and nature of focus on form with adolescents in a foreign language setting. Findings show that:

i.   Reactive and pre-emptive FFEs occur in meaning-focused activities;
ii. Successful uptake is more likely to occur when learners themselves perceive problems in their output than when the teacher anticipates those problems. Successful uptake is higher in pre-emptive and reactive student-initiated FFEs, which goes along with the fact that these adolescents appeared confident asking about formal issues of the foreign language they are learning, and
iii. The relationship between uptake and long-term accurate use of lexical items is unclear.

This study has been exploratory and descriptive in nature and, therefore, its results should not be assumed to be generalized beyond this context. More classroom research is necessary with early and late adolescent learners in order to provide a wider picture of L2 acquisitional processes within an interactionist framework (Mackey & Silver 2005: 254) and to achieve ecological validity (Ellis, Loewen & Erlam 2006: 365). It would be useful to explore similar issues with a younger population like primary school children in a Spanish EFL context. Of particular interest would be research on subject-matter content in foreign language learning, an approach already being implemented in some Spanish primary and secondary schools. The extent to which teachers modify interaction with learners to focus attention on formal issues in this context deserves further investigation (cf. Pica 2002 for second language contexts and the lack of relevant modification that could draw the learners' attention to developmentally difficult form-meaning relationships).

This research suggests a number of avenues for further investigation. Future work in classrooms could employ delayed post tests in order to address the issue of a possible connection between uptake and long-term use of the lexical items noticed during FFEs (both pre-emptive and reactive). Learners' incorporation of the lexical items on which they focused their attention during class interaction could be assessed through the use of oral production tasks. Appropriate mechanisms should be established to check whether the learners knew the lexical items beforehand or whether they were new to them.

Authors' note

We are grateful to Jenefer Philp, Rhonda Oliver and Alison Mackey for kindly inviting us to contribute to this volume and for useful suggestions on earlier versions of this paper. Thanks also go to the reviewers for valuable comments and suggestions for improvement. We are also grateful to Sheila O'Connor for her help in coding the data and to David Singleton for the facilities he provided to one of the authors in Trinity College (Dublin). Financial support from research grants HUM2004-04435, HUM 2006-09775-C02-01/FILO and Consolider Ingenio-2010 (CSD2007-00012) from the Spanish Ministry of Science and Technology, P1 1B2004-34 from Bancaixa and IT-202-07 from the Basque Government (Departamento de Educación, Universidades e Investigación) are hereby gratefully acknowledged.

References

Alcón, E. 1994. Negotiation, foreign language awareness and acquisition in the Spanish secondary education context. *International Journal of Psycholinguistics* 10: 83–96.

Alcón, E. 2001. Interacción y aprendizaje de segundas lenguas en el contexto institucional del aula. In *Estudios de Lingüística*, S. Pastor Cesteros & V. Salazar García (eds), 271–287. Alicante: Universidad de Alicante.

Alcón, E. 2007. Incidental focus on form, noticing and vocabulary learning in the EFL classroom. *International Journal of English Studies* 7: 41–60.

Alegría de la Colina, A. & García Mayo, M. P. 2007. Attention to form across collaborative tasks by low-proficiency learners in an EFL setting. In *Investigating Tasks in Formal Language Learning*, M. P. García Mayo (ed.), 91–116. Clevedon: Multilingual Matters.

Block, D. 2007. *Second Language Identities*. London: Continuum.

Carpenter, H., Jeon, K. S., MacGregor, D. & Mackey, A. 2006. Learners' interpretation of recasts. *Studies in Second Language Acquisition* 28: 209–236.

Cohen, J. A. 1960. A coefficient of agreement for nominal scales. *Educational and Psychological Measurement* 20: 37–46.

Doughty, C. 1994. Finetuning of feedback by competent speakers to language learners. In *GURT 1993: Strategic Interaction*, J. Alatis (ed.), 96–108. Washington DC: Georgetown University Press.

Doughty, C. & Varela, E. 1998. Communicative focus on form. In *Focus on Form in Classroom Second Language Acquisition*, C. Doughty & J. Williams (eds), 114–138. Cambridge: CUP.

Doughty, C. & Williams, J. 1998. *Focus on Form in Classroom Second Language Acquisition*. Cambridge: CUP.

Ellis, R. 2001. Investigating form-focused instruction. *Language Learning* 51(1): 1–46.

Ellis, R., Basturkmen, H. & Loewen, S. 2001a. Learner uptake in communicative ESL lessons. *Language Learning* 51: 281–318.

Ellis, R., Basturkmen, H. & Loewen, S. 2001b. Preemptive focus on form in the ESL classroom. *TESOL Quarterly* 35: 407–432.

Ellis, R., Basturkmen, H. & Loewen, S. 2002. Doing focus-on-form. *System* 30: 419–432.

Ellis, R., Loewen, S. & Erlam, R. 2006. Implicit and explicit corrective feedback and the acquisition of grammar. *Studies in Second Language Acquisition* 28: 339–368.

García Mayo, M. P. 2002a. The effectiveness of two form-focused tasks in advanced EFL pedagogy. *International Journal of Applied Linguistics* 12(2): 156–175.

García Mayo, M. P. 2002b. Interaction in advanced EFL grammar pedagogy: A comparison of form-focused activities. *International Journal of Educational Research* 37(3–4): 323–341.

García Mayo, M. P. 2005. Interactional strategies for interlanguage communication: Do they provide evidence for attention to form? In *Investigations in Instructed Second Language Acquisition*, A. Housen & M. Pierrard (eds), 383–405. Berlin: Mouton de Gruyter.

García Mayo, M. P. & Alcón, E. (eds). 2002. The role of interaction in instructed language learning. *International Journal of Educational Research* 37: 3–4.

García Mayo, M. P. & Pica, T. 2000a. L2 learner interaction in a foreign language setting: Are learning needs addressed? *IRAL: International Review of Applied Linguistics* 38(1): 35–58.

García Mayo, M. P. & Pica, T. 2000b. Interaction among proficient learners: Are input, feedback and output needs addressed in a foreign language context? *Studia Linguistica: A Journal of General Linguistics* 54(2): 272–279.

Gass, S. M. 1990. Second and foreign language learning: Same, different or none of the above? In *Second Language Acquisition – Foreign Language Learning*, B. VanPatten & J. F. Lee (eds), 24–44. Clevedon: Multilingual Matters.

Gass, S. M. 1997. *Input, Interaction and the Second Language Learner*. Mahwah NJ: Lawrence Erlbaum Associates.

Gass, S. M. 2003. Input and interaction. In *The Handbook of Second Language Acquisition*, C. Doughty & M. Long (eds), 224–255. Oxford: Blackwell.

Gass, S. & Mackey, A. 2006. Input, interaction and output in second language acquisition. In *Theories in Second Language Acquisition*. B. VanPatten & J. Williams (eds), 175–199. Mahwah NJ: Lawrence Erlbaum Associates.

Gass, S. M., Mackey, A. & Pica, T. 1998. The role of input and interaction in second language acquisition. *The Modern Language Journal* 82(3): 299–307.

Havranek, G. 2002. When is corrective feedback most likely to succeed? *International Journal of Educational Research* 37: 255–270.

Havranek, G. & Cesnik, H. 2001. Factors affecting the success of corrective feedback. In *EUROSLA Yearbook* I, S. Foster-Cohen & A. Nizegorodcew (eds), 99–122. Amsterdam: John Benjamins.

Loewen, S. 2004. Uptake in incidental focus on form in meaning-focussed ESL lessons. *Language Learning* 54: 153–188.

Loewen, S. 2006. Incidental focus on form and second language learning. *Studies in Second Language Acquisition* 27: 361–386.

Loewen, S. and Philp, J. 2006. Recasts in adult English L2 classroom: Characteristics, explicitness, and effectiveness. *The Modern Language Journal* 90(4): 536–556.

Long, M. H. 1980. Input, Interaction and Second Language Acquisition. PhD dissertation, UCLA.

Long, M. H. 1983a. Linguistic and conversational adjustments to non-native speakers. *Studies in Second Language Acquisition* 5: 177–193.

Long, M. H. 1983b. Does second language instruction make a difference? A review of research. *TESOL Quarterly* 17: 359–382.

Long, M. H. 1996. The role of the linguistic environment in second language acquisition. In *Handbook of Second Language Acquisition*, W. C. Ritchie & T. K. Bathia (eds), 413–468. San Diego CA: Academic Press.

Lyster, R. 1998. Recasts, repetition and ambiguity in L2 classroom discourse. *Studies in Second Language Acquisition* 20: 51–81.

Lyster, R. 2001. Negotiation of form, recasts and explicit correction in relation to error types and learner repair in immersion classrooms. *Language Learning* 51: 265–301.

Lyster, R. 2002. Negotiation in immersion teacher-student interaction. *International Journal of Educational Research* 37: 237–253.

Lyster, R. 2004. Differential effects of prompts and recasts in form-focused instruction. *Studies in Second Language Acquisition* 26: 399–432.

Lyster, R. & Mori, H. 2006. Interactional feedback and instructional counterbalance. *Studies in Second Language Acquisition* 28: 269–300.

Lyster, R. & Ranta, L. 1997. Corrective feedback and learner uptake: Negotiation of form in communicative classrooms. *Studies in Second Language Acquisition* 19: 37–66.

Mackey, A. 2006. Feedback, noticing and instructed second language learning. *Applied Linguistics* 27: 405–477.

Mackey, A. (ed.). 2007. *Conversational Interaction in Second Language Acquisition*. Oxford: OUP.

Mackey, A. & Philp, J. 1998. Conversational interaction and second language development: Recasts, responses, and red herrings? *The Modern Language Journal* 82: 338–356.

Mackey, A. & Silver, R. E. 2005. Interactional tasks and English L2 learning by immigrant children in Singapore. *System* 33: 239–260.

Mackey, A., Oliver, R. & Leeman, J. 2003. Interactional input and the incorporation of feedback: An exploration of NS-NNS and NNS-NNS adult and child dyads. *Language Learning* 53(1): 35–66.

McDonough, K. & Mackey, A. 2006. Responses to recasts: Repetitions, primed production, and linguistic development. *Language Learning* 56(4): 693–720.

Oliver, R. 1995. Negative feedback in child NS/NNS conversation. *Studies in Second Language Acquisition* 18: 459–481.

Oliver, R. 2000. Age differences in negotiation and feedback in classroom and pairwork. *Language Learning* 50: 119–151.

Pica, T. 1994. Research on negotiation: What does it reveal about second language learning conditions, processes and outcomes? *Language Learning* 44: 493–527.

Pica, T. 2002. Subject-matter content: How does it assist the interactional and linguistic needs of classroom language learners? *The Modern Language Journal* 86(1): 1–19.

Robinson, P. 1995. Review article: Attention, memory and the "noticing" hypothesis. *Language Learning* 45: 283–331.

Robinson, P. 2001. *Cognition and Second Language Instruction*. Cambridge: CUP.

Robinson, P. 2003. Attention and memory. In *The Handbook of Second Language Acquisition*, C. Doughty & M. H. Long (eds), 631–678. Oxford: Blackwell.

Schmidt, R. 1993. Awareness and second language acquisition. *Annual Review of Applied Linguistics* 13: 206–226.

Schmidt, R. 1995. Consciousness and foreign language learning: A tutorial on the role of attention and awareness in learning. In *Attention and Awareness in Foreign Language Learning*, R. Schmidt (ed.), 1–63. Honolulu HI: University of Hawai'i, Second Language Teaching and Curriculum Center.

Schmidt, R. 2001. Attention. In *Cognition and Second language Instruction*, P. Robinson (ed.), 3–32. Cambridge: CUP.

Sheen, Y. 2004. Corrective feedback and learner uptake in communicative classrooms across instructional settings. *Language Teaching Research* 8: 263–300.

Swain, M. 1985. Communicative competence: Some roles of comprehensible input and comprehensible output in its development. In *Input and Second Language Acquisition*, S. Gass & C. Madden (eds), 235–253. Rowley MA: Newbury House.

Swain, M. 1995. Three functions of output in second language learning. In *Principles and Practice in Applied Linguistics*, G. Cook & B. Seidlhofer (eds), 125–144. Oxford: OUPs.

Tsang, W. 2004. Feedback and uptake in teacher-student interaction: An analysis of 18 English lessons in Hong Kong secondary classrooms. *Regional Language Centre Journal* 35: 187–209.

Van den Braden, K. 1997. Effects of negotiation on language learners' output. *Language Learning* 47: 589–636.

Williams, J. 1999. Learner-generated attention to form. *Language Learning* 49: 583–625.

Williams, J. 2001. The effectiveness of spontaneous attention to form. *System* 29: 325–340.

Speeding up acquisition of *his* and *her*

Explicit L1/L2 contrasts help

Joanna White
Concordia University

This paper reviews three pedagogical intervention studies that demonstrate the effectiveness of providing pre-adolescent and adolescent learners in communicatively-oriented classrooms with explicit metalinguistic information and opportunities to use it. The studies, which target the possessive determiners (PDs), *his* and *her*, follow a pretest/posttest design and were carried out in intact treatment and comparison classes. Measures consist of grammaticality judgement, metalinguistic comment, and oral picture description tasks. A number of issues are discussed in the context of older children's second language learning in a classroom setting. These include implementing age-appropriate instruction that takes into account learners' cognitive and linguistic readiness for form-focused instruction, their learning style and motivation, and the context of instruction.

Introduction

Research carried out in communicatively-oriented second language (L2) classrooms has shown convincingly that although elementary school-age learners can figure out a lot about the language they are learning on their own while engaged in meaning-focused activities, they still need help from their teachers in acquiring those linguistic features that remain troublesome, even after many hours of classroom exposure. For some first language (L1) speakers of Romance languages such as French, Spanish and Catalan, the English possessive determiners (PDs) *his* and *her* represent such a learning challenge, and it is not uncommon to hear otherwise proficient adult speakers of English use one form when the context requires the other. Since many learners will not be able to move to the most advanced stages of PD development on their own, it is important to identify age-appropriate pedagogical techniques that can be used when learners are linguistically and cognitively ready to benefit from them.

This chapter reviews three pedagogical intervention studies targeting PDs that investigated the effectiveness of different types of form-focused instruction provided within a communicative context. Two studies were conducted in intensive ESL classes in Quebec with pre-adolescent French L1 children in elementary school grade six (age 12). The third study was carried out in regular ESL programs in secondary school grade eight (age 14) classes in Quebec and Catalonia with French L1 and Catalan/Spanish bilingual learners, respectively. The studies address a number of issues that are relevant in the context of older children's L2 learning. These include implementing age-appropriate instruction that takes into account learners' cognitive and linguistic readiness for form-focused instruction, their learning style and motivation, and the instructional setting.

Children as language learners

Although pronouns emerge gradually over the early years of childhood, most children have sorted out the personal pronoun system of their L1 by the age of three, and by the time they reach school age, "confusions between different personal pronouns rarely occur" (Chiat 1986: 349). Indeed, persistent errors with third person singular pronouns are an indication of L1 language impairment (Moore 2001). Furthermore, the use of pronouns to achieve discourse cohesion, as in oral narratives, is well established by middle childhood, ages 8–9 (for discussion, see Karmiloff & Karmiloff-Smith 2001). As the acquisition of pronouns is implicit, and because these forms are not problematic, children are not taught a rule of thumb for determining the gender of third person possessive pronouns. However, they do learn the metalanguage they need to talk about aspects of their L1 that are difficult to say or write correctly (see Foster-Cohen 1999, 2001; Karmiloff-Smith 1986; Trévise 1996). Thus, by the end of elementary school, children have already had several years of explicit instruction in the grammar of their L1 and are familiar with metalinguistic terminology referring to parts of speech, word order, and agreement. By the time they reach grade eight, they have had even more experience thinking and talking about the nature and functions of their L1, and they have applied their metalinguistic knowledge to a wider variety of oral and written tasks.

In classroom SLA, we know from pedagogical intervention studies targeting several problematic linguistic features that children in the last years of elementary school are able to make use of explicit, metalinguistic information in their second language when it is contextualized in meaningful practice (Spada 1997; Spada & Lightbown 1999). The studies discussed in this chapter expand this line of research to include PDs and extend it to the early years of high school and to another L1 context.

The learning challenge: Possessive determiners

The pedagogical rule for English third person singular PDs would seem to be an easy rule according to the criteria of scope and reliability (Hulstijn 1995).[1] It covers only two forms, *his* and *her*, and has no exceptions. The rule can be stated simply in the following way: use *his* when the possessor is masculine (a man/boy) and use *her* when the possessor is feminine (a woman/girl).

In contrast, in French and Catalan the equivalents for *his* and *her* agree with the grammatical gender of the object possessed: *son* and *sa* in French and *el seu* and *la seva* in Catalan. Initially, French and Catalan learners of English may assume that gender assignment works the same way in the two languages; that is, *his* = *son/el seu* and *her* = *sa/la seva*. In reality, however, there is not a one-to-one correspondence since the equivalent of *his* can be both *son* and *sa* (or *el seu* and *la seva*), as can the equivalent of *her*. In Spanish, there is only one third person singular PD, *su*. The learning problem for Spanish learners of English is making the gender distinction between the masculine and feminine forms. In so doing, bilingual Catalan/Spanish learners of English tend to be influenced by the Catalan agreement rule.

In addition to the problems caused by the deceptive similarity between the English and L1 rules for PD agreement, the English rule may be difficult for learners to induce because *his* and *her* may be neither frequent nor phonologically salient in the classroom input. White, Collins, Trofimovich, Cardoso, and Horst (2007) analyzed the teacher talk of three intensive ESL teachers in Quebec, a total of 50 hours of classroom input at four intervals over five months, and found that the most frequently used PD was *your* (71% of all instances);[2] *his* and *her* represented only 10% of all PDs used by these teachers. When *his* and *her* did occur, they were usually in an unstressed position before a noun, making the vowel weak (i.e. lax) and the forms difficult to perceive:

(1)　She told _*er* story to the police.

Moreover, initial *h* is usually not pronounced in mid-sentence in informal, connected speech:

(2)　I asked Marc to turn around in _*is* seat. I want you to pay attention, too, Robert.

(3)　She took _*er* time with that one!

1.　See also DeKeyser (2005), Hulstijn and de Graff (1994).

2.　Most of the management of instruction involved imperatives, such as 'Open *your* books', 'Work with *your* partner'.

Indeed, the perception (and pronunciation) of *h* is a known learning problem for French L1 speakers of English (Mah, Steinhauer, & Goad 2006), and it is frequently deleted or oversupplied in their oral and written production.[3] All together, these factors add to the challenge learners face in hearing the instances of *his* and *her* that do occur in the classroom input.

One could argue that there is a strong motivation to acquire control over PDs since using the wrong form can lead to a communication breakdown. It makes a difference to the listener whether Bill took *his* sister or *her* sister to the party, and if the context does not disambiguate an error, the speaker's intention may not be communicated. It is not possible to be communicatively effective solely on the basis of memorized chunks of language. In each situation, the correct referent has to be determined. However, when all of the learners in a class share the same L1, they (and the teacher) may in fact understand each other, thereby reinforcing the hypothesis that PDs function the same in English and the learners' L1.

PD stage framework

A number of studies involving young (ages 10–12) French L1 learners of English in Quebec have documented a pattern in the emergence of third person singular PDs in oral production (Lightbown & Spada 1990; Martens 1988).[4] White (1996, 1998) fine-tuned the earlier descriptions of the interlanguage development of PDs into a framework consisting of eight stages. She found it useful for interpreting patterns in the data to group the stages into three broad categories: Pre-emergence, Emergence, and Post-emergence (see Table 1).

In the two Pre-emergence stages, there are no instances of *his* or *her* in the learner's oral production. In Stage 1, possession is not marked, and the learner uses *the*, or no determiner at all in contexts requiring a PD. In Stage 2, an over-generalized possessive form is used, typically *your*, which is unmarked for gender. In the two Emergence stages, a few instances of *his* and/or *her* emerge (Stage 3) or the learner overgeneralizes one form, either *his* or *her*, to all linguistic contexts (Stage 4). In the Post-emergence stages (5–8) the learner gradually differentiates between *his* and *her*, becoming more accurate in the application of the English PD

---

3.   Confirmation of this comes from written data reported by Lightbown, Halter, White and Horst (2002) and White (2006), in which many young learners spelled *his* as *is*.

4.   See Zobl (1985) regarding an order of difficulty based on error rates for *his* and *her* following a brief exposure to the target forms. His participants were university students whose previous (secondary level) ESL instruction had been based on an inductive (audiolingual) approach.

rule, notably in the difficult kin-different contexts. Possessive determiner errors are typical of learner language at all stages below Stage 8.

The framework describes the learners' gradual acquisition of the ability to produce *his* and *her* during an oral production task in which the primary purpose is to convey a meaningful message. Assignment to an oral stage is based on emergence

Table 1. Developmental sequence in the acquisition of the english agreement rule for *his/her* by French-speaking Learners (Adapted from Spada, Lightbown, & White 2005; White 1998; White, Muñoz, & Collins 2007)

Pre-emergence

Stage 1	**Avoidance of *his* and *her* and/or use of definite article** (no more than 3 instances of *his* and/or *her*, correct or incorrect) The little boy play with bicycle. He have band-aid on *the* arm, *the* leg, *the* stomach.
Stage 2	**Use of <u>your</u> for all persons, genders and numbers** (at least 4) This boy cry in the arm of *your* mother. There's one girl talk with *your* dad.

Emergence

Stage 3	**Emergence of either or both *his/her*** (4 correct or incorrect instances) A little boy do a cycle ride and he fall. He have a pain on back. He said the situation at *her* mom.
Stage 4	**Preference for *his* or *her*** (4 correct instances) The mother is dressing *her* little boy, and she put *her* clothes, *her* pant, *her* coat, and then she finish. The girl making *hisself* beautiful. She put the make-up on *his* hand, on *his* head, and *his* father is surprise.

Post-emergence

Stage 5	**Differentiated use of *his* and *her*, but not in kin-different contexts*** (4 correct instances each of *his* and *her*) The girl fell on *her* bicycle. She look **his* father and cry. The dad put **her* little girl on *his* shoulder, and after, on *his* back.
Stage 6	**Differentiated use of *his* and *her*; agreement rule applied to kin-different gender for <u>either</u> *his* or *her*** (4 correct instances each of *his* and *her*; of these, two correct instances in kin-different contexts for *his* <u>or</u> *her*) The mother dress *her* boy. She put *his* pants and *his* sweater. He's all dressed and he say at **her* mother he go to the bathroom.
Stage 7	**Differentiated use of *his* and *her* to criterion; agreement rule applied to kin-different gender for <u>both</u> *his* or *her*** (4 correct instances each of *his* and *her*; of these, two correct instances in kin-different contexts for *his* <u>and</u> *her*) The little girl fell the floor, and after she go see *her* father, and he pick up *his* girl in *the* arms.
Stage 8	**Error-free application of agreement rule to *his* and *her* in all contexts, including body parts** The little girl with *her* dad play together. And the dad take *his* girl on *his* arms.

criteria. That is, learners are assigned to a stage depending on the number of PDs produced and in which contexts. A criterion of 4 was used in analyzing the oral production data reported here (see Table 1 for details).[5]

The stage framework was used in the three pedagogical intervention studies discussed in this chapter, as well as in several other studies that will be cited. [6] In the studies reviewed here, instruction was varied in terms of the amount and type of information about PDs that was provided to the learners and the type of practice they had in deploying this information. In Study 1, the pedagogical interventions aimed to <u>attract</u> learners' attention to PDs without providing a rule of thumb; in Studies 2 and 3, the instruction aimed to <u>direct</u> learners' attention to the English PD rule and to contrast it with the L1 rule.[7]

Three pedagogical intervention studies: Possessive determiners

Context and participants

The learners were in intact classes assigned to different treatment conditions. They had all begun learning English in grade three (Catalonia) or four (Quebec) in regular programs of 90–120 minutes of instruction a week. All of the participant teachers were highly proficient speakers of English with many years of ESL teaching experience.

Study 1 (White 1996, 1998) and Study 2 (White & Ranta 2002) were carried out in Quebec, Canada, in French-medium schools in which English is taught intensively all day, every day, for five months of the 10-month school year (approximately 400 hours). Learners were francophone children age 12 in grade six. Despite the fact that the schools were less than an hour's drive from Montreal, the children had few opportunities to speak English outside of class, and they had no immediate need for English language academic skills. Accordingly, the teaching focused on the development of interpersonal communication skills, and there was

---

5.   The stage framework makes the following assumptions: 1) the three stage clusters are qualitatively different; 2) together they represent a developmental sequence characterized by the acquisition of additional semantic features (case, number, person, gender) and an increasing ability to differentiate between *his* and *her* in kin-different contexts; 3) stages are not discrete, rather, they overlap such that behaviour typical of lower stages can occur in higher stages so long as emergence criteria are met; 4) learners do not skip stages.

6.   The PD studies that have used the stage framework are Ammar (2003), Ammar and Spada (2006), Pahissa (2001), and Ranta (1998). In another PD study, Pacheco (2004) adapted the oral stage framework to written production data.

7.   It is important to point out that the pedagogical interventions involved PD input that represented Stage 8 as all lower stages are ungrammatical.

little explicit focus on language form other than vocabulary.[8] The two studies were conducted during the spring; learners had completed their academic program intensively in French during the fall term and were just past the mid-point in their intensive English program.[9]

The sustained instruction within one intensive ESL course offers an ideal context in which to observe language development. In this environment, learners develop from beginners at the start of their program into confident intermediate-level users of English by the end of it (Lightbown & Spada 1994), and their overall proficiency gains are large and measurable (e.g., White & Turner 2005). This growth is important for the investigation of PD development since learners must be able to understand and produce sentences beyond a single noun phrase in order to use PDs correctly in English. Most intensive program learners reach this level of proficiency after about 250 hours in the program. Furthermore, they are of an age that they may benefit from instruction targeting PDs.

Study 3 (White, Muñoz, & Collins 2007) consists of two parallel investigations that were conducted in large secondary schools in Quebec and Catalonia. The two contexts were similar in a number of ways: 1) learners were adolescents, age 14, in grade eight; 2) they were in regular ESL programs of about 150 minutes per week; 3) English was a compulsory subject; 4) the secondary schools were each located about an hour outside a large city, where there was little exposure to English beyond the English class.

Research design
The studies followed a pretest/posttest design. In each case, the learners were pretested immediately before the start of the pedagogical treatment. The experimental lessons were taught by the learners' own ESL teachers, who were trained by the research team. Immediately following the intervention, learners were posttested. A delayed posttest was administered in Study 1, but the research schedule made it impossible to do so in the other two studies. The 30-minute

---

8. In intensive programs, fluency is emphasized over accuracy, and the many oral interaction activities are organized around themes relevant to the learners' everyday lives. Pair and group work activities are common, as are rules requiring learners to speak English with the teacher and each other. See Lightbown and Spada (1994, 1997), for more information about intensive programs in Quebec.

9. French is the language of instruction in all of the Quebec schools in which the research reported here was conducted. According to the language laws of Quebec, academic instruction in French schools must be offered in French. Thus, while French immersion programs originated and continue to thrive in English school boards in Quebec, there is no English immersion equivalent for French L1 children. Intensive programs are optional, and intensive ESL learners, along with their parents, choose this alternative over the regular program of 90–120 minutes per week.

pedagogical interventions were implemented every day for two weeks in Study 1. In Studies 2 and 3, they were spread out over six weeks.

Measures

Two measures were used in all three studies: a measure of metalinguistic knowledge and a measure of oral production ability. In addition, a metalinguistic interview was conducted in Studies 2 and 3. These measures were administered in the order in which they are described below. Learners in Study 1 also took a multiple choice pronoun test that is not reported here because of a ceiling effect at the immediate posttest (for details, see White 1996).

Immediate and delayed posttest results were considered to be statistically significant at $p < .05$. However, when multiple one-way ANOVA and ANCOVA comparisons were made, the level of significance was lowered to $p < .01$ to account for the probability of a type-1 error. Pretest results were considered to be significant at $p < .10$.

Metalinguistic task: Passage correction

In the first task, learners read an illustrated story that contained both PD and distracter errors. The PD errors included *kin-different* contexts, which are essential in determining post-emergence stages. Learners were told that there was a maximum of one error per sentence, but they did not know how many errors the text contained, nor what kind they were. They were asked to read the story carefully, to put an X on each error they found, and to write the correction above it. The task was scored by counting the total number of correctly corrected PD errors for each student. Since performance on this task does not require the learners to explain their corrections, it can be completed using implicit metalinguistic knowledge (Gaux & Gombert 1999).

Oral production task: Picture description

Next, learners described a series of cartoon pictures representing family situations in which there was a child and one or more adults/parents. The cartoons offered contexts for the use of *his* and *her*, many of them kin-different, but no explicit cuing of the target forms. Learners were prompted with the following: *We're going to look at some cartoon pictures of children and their parents. Can you tell me about this little boy/girl? What's the problem?* Learners were permitted to look at each picture for as long as they wanted before beginning to speak. The task can be considered to involve "free production" since learners were free to use the target forms or not and since meaningful communication was the goal (Doughty 2003; Ellis 2002). In this sense, the forms are task natural, but not task essential (Loschky & Bley-Vroman 1993). The task was administered to learners individually, audio-recorded, and transcribed. They were assigned to a PD stage based on emergence criteria. This approach emphasized development, rather than mastery, and learners were assigned to the highest stage for which the required number of instances characteristic of a stage was produced.[10]

Meta-comment task
A stimulated recall task was carried out in Studies 2 and 3 immediately after the oral picture description task at the time of the posttest. The learners were asked to explain every correction they had (or had not) made earlier in a sub-section of the passage correction test. They were cued in the following way: "Why did you change X to Y in this sentence?" or, in the case of a PD not changed, "Why did you think X was correct?". The explanations were analyzed for evidence of the underlying rule the learner was using. The meta-comments provided qualitative information to help the researchers interpret the data on the other tasks and increased their understanding of how pre-adolescent and young adolescent learners made use of the input they received.

Study 1: *Typographical input enhancement: Pre-adolescent French L1 learners*

The intention in Study 1 (White 1996, 1998) was to increase the perceptual salience of *his* and *her* in the classroom input in a way that would not place excessive demands on the attentional resources of the learners (see VanPatten 1990). For this reason, typographical enhancement (Sharwood Smith 1981, 1991) was selected to target PDs. Although this linguistic feature is known to be problematic for French L1 learners of English of all ages, it had not been investigated in a sustained way in a pedagogical intervention study.[11] Typographical enhancement was expected to direct learners' attention to PDs more explicitly than input flooding, a sort of form-focused instruction previously investigated with comparable groups of pre-adolescent learners to enhance the salience of adverbs of frequency (Trahey 1992; Trahey & L. White 1993), and less explicitly than rule explanation, previously investigated with adverbs (L. White 1991) and question formation (L. White, Spada, Lightbown & Ranta 1991).

The research questions that were asked were the following: 1) Can pre-adolescent francophone learners benefit from typographically enhanced input in their acquisition of *his* and *her*?; 2) Is typographically enhanced input more

---

10. As noted above, the criterion used in the studies reported here is 4. The criterion could be adjusted up or down, according to the data elicited. For examples of learners' oral production at different stages, see White and Ranta (2002).

11. The pedagogical intervention carried out by Zobl (1985) lasted only 15 minutes.

effective than unenhanced input?; 3) Is typographically enhanced input more effective when combined with a "book flood"?

Methodology

To investigate these questions, three treatment conditions were provided, each assigned to a different intact class of grade six intensive ESL learners. Two groups, Group E+ (n = 27) and Group E (n = 30) received the same typographically enhanced input flood. (Note that *E* refers to *enhanced input*.) The pedagogical rule was not presented at any time to the learners, nor was there any explicit reference to the L1. Instead, learners in the two groups read stories and poems in which all third person singular pronouns and PDs were enhanced visually through combinations of enlargement, bolding, underlining, and italicizing the font. The purpose of enhancing subject (*he, she*) and object (*his, her*) pronouns along with PDs was to draw the learners' attention to the third person singular forms as a system, and to increase the salience of the gender distinctions. However, *his* and *her*, the target features of the study, were always enlarged more than subject and object pronouns, and care was taken not to make them so large they would distract the learners while they were reading.

Whenever it was possible to do so, third person pronouns and PDs were added to the texts to further increase their frequency in the input. Comprehension questions focused the learners' attention on the meanings of these forms. The enhancement activities represented ten hours of class time, and were implemented over two weeks. During the rest of the time, learners carried on with their regular communicative activities. Teachers confirmed that they had not previously taught the learners a PD rule, and they did not provide corrective feedback on pronouns or PDs during or outside of this study.

Group E+ and Group E were exposed to the same typographically enhanced texts and tasks; in addition, Group E+ engaged in extensive reading and listening activities (a *book flood*) involving unenhanced materials for thirty minutes a day over the entire five months of the intensive program. In order to ensure that the comparison group was also exposed to written input containing the target forms, Group U (n = 29) read *unenhanced* versions of the texts read by Groups E+ and E and completed tasks that provided general comprehension practice. To account for the possibly distracting effect of textual enhancement, all past-tense -ed endings were enhanced for this group. No analyses related to past-tense verb forms were carried out.

The pedagogical intervention was consistent with the beliefs held by the teachers in the school, namely that comprehensible input is essential for SLA. For this reason, they acknowledged the potential value of input flooding. Furthermore, although they felt strongly that explicit teaching of grammar rules is unnecessary, and maybe even harmful to students' enthusiasm for learning, they were open-minded about typographically enhancing language forms that they agreed were problematic for their students since it did not involve direct rule instruction. The book flood teacher was already using stories in her classroom every day and enthusiastically agreed to implement this component of the intervention.

It was predicted that learners in Groups E+ and E would significantly outperform Group U on the written and oral PD measures. It was further predicted that Group E+ would significantly outperform Group E. The rationale was that if typographical enhancement increased the likelihood of pre-adolescent learners detecting the target structures in the input, Group E+ would have more opportunities during their book flood activities to detect them than Group E, which had no such activities. Finally, it was predicted that the differences found at the immediate posttest would still be evident five weeks after the two-week typographical enhancement treatment period had ended.

Findings, passage correction task

Sixteen of the deviant forms in the passage correction task involved contexts for third person PDs. There were eight contexts for *his* and eight contexts for *her*. When mean scores were compared between groups at each testing session, they were found to be in the order predicted by the hypothesis. That is, Group E+ outperformed Group E, which outperformed Group U. Group means and standard deviations for grammatical corrections in contexts for *his* and *her* are shown in Table 2.

One-way ANOVA procedures revealed a difference approaching statistical significance for *his* [$F_{(2, 83)} = 4.20$; $p = 0.18$.)] and for *her* [$F_{(2,83)} = 4.25$; $p = 0.18$] at the immediate posttest. Post hoc Tukey procedures showed that in both cases, the differences were between Groups E+ and U. When ANCOVA procedures were carried out on the immediate posttest data using the immediate pretest scores as the covariate, differences were not significant in the case of *his* [$F_{(2,82)} = 2.42$; $p = .095$)], but significant in the case of *her* [$F_{(2,82)} = 3.61$; $p = .031$]. A Tukey post hoc test showed that the significant difference was between Group E+ and Group U. ANCOVA procedures carried out on the delayed posttest scores showed no significant between-group differences.

Trend analyses were carried out on the passage correction task. The polynomial contrasts were adjusted to compensate for the fact that the testing intervals were not equally spaced. These analyses show that certain aspects of the treatment initially boosted learning for all three groups. However, while all groups have significant linear trends, the quadratic trend is much more pronounced for Groups E+ and E than for Group U, suggesting that the immediate treatment effect is strongest for the two enhancement groups. Between the immediate and delayed posttests, all three groups continued to improve on PDs such that five weeks later, the groups performed similarly on this task.

Table 2. Study 1, Passage Correction task, mean scores out of 8: grammatical corrections of incorrect possessive determiners, contexts for his and her (Adapted from White 1996)

Pretest

Group	N	His	SD	Her	SD
E+	27	1.63	2.10	2.41	1.91
E	30	1.40	1.85	2.07	2.24
U	28	0.66	1.40	1.72	1.94

Immediate Posttest

Group	N	His	SD	Her	SD
E+	27	4.85	2.37	4.41	2.26
E	30	3.87	2.08	3.57	2.33
U	29	2.97	2.81	2.59	2.43

Delayed Posttest

Group	N	His	SD	Her	SD
E+	27	5.78	1.99	4.70	2.20
E	30	4.90	2.50	4.67	2.37
U	29	4.69	2.78	4.03	2.73

N.B. One student in Group U was absent for the pretest.

Findings, oral production task

On the oral task, nearly two-thirds of the learners were in pre-emergence stages before the typographical enhancement intervention (Table 3). Aside from one individual who was in a post-emergence stage, the other third of the learners were in an emergence stage. The typographical enhancement initially boosted performance of the E+ learners more than it did in the two other groups. At the immediate posttest, nearly half of the Group E+ learners were in a post-emergence stage, compared to about a third in Groups E and U; only 11% of the learners in Group E+ remained in a pre-emergence stage, compared to 20% and 21% in Groups E and U respectively. As was the case with the passage correction task, learners in all groups continued to make progress with *his* and *her* during the period between the immediate and delayed posttests such that at the delayed posttest, the pattern is similar in all three groups.[12] Nonetheless, only about a third of the learners had reached a post-emergence stage in which they were sorting out the distinction between the masculine and feminine forms. Most of the other learners, nearly 60%, were in an emergence stage.

---

12. During this time, the learners continued with their regular meaning-focused intensive program; Group E+ also continued the book flood.

Table 3. Study 1, Percent of Learners at Each Developmental Stage for His/Her on the Oral Production Task (Adapted from White 1996)

Pretest

Group	N	Pre-emergence Stages 1–2	Emergence Stages 3–4	Post-emergence Stages 5–7
E+	27	66	33	0
E	30	54	44	3
U	28	71	29	0

Immediate Posttest

Group	N	Pre-emergence Stages 1–2	Emergence Stages 3–4	Post-emergence Stages 5–7
E+	27	11	41	48
E	30	20	43	37
U	29	21	48	31

Delayed Posttest

Group	N	Pre-emergence Stages 1–2	Emergence Stages 3–4	Post-emergence Stages 5–7
E+	27	4	59	37
E	30	7	57	36
U	29	7	59	34

Note. One student in Group U was absent for the pretest.

A number of developmental paths were evident in the oral data, and only a few learners remained at their pretest stage throughout the study. Some learners moved forward gradually, others made rapid progress; among the latter, some went back to an earlier stage the delayed posttest stage, and some maintained their gains. The paths seemed to be related to the learner's stage just before the two-week typographical enhancement period began. Most learners who were at a pre-emergence stage on the pretest were at an emergence stage, usually stage 4 (overgeneralization of *his* or *her*) on the delayed posttests. Most who began at an emergence stage were at a post-emergence stage at the end of the study although a few individuals who had been assigned to a post-emergence stage at the immediate posttest moved back to emergence at the delayed posttest. These patterns, along with the finding that no learner stopped using gender-marked forms after *his* or *her* had emerged, suggest that emergence was a pivotal stage for learners in this study.

Interpretation
Recall that the goal of Study 1 was to find out whether an implicit type of form-focused instruction would be more effective in promoting acquisition of PDs than

the regular communicative input available in the intensive classroom and whether additional input in the form of a book flood would be even more effective. The similar end-of-study performance of the three groups on the metalinguistic and oral production tasks was not anticipated.

There are several factors that may have contributed to the finding of "no difference" among the groups at the delayed posttest. The first relates to salience. The typographical enhancement was intended to draw learners' attention to PDs. In addition, third person singular subject and object pronouns were typographically enhanced, along with *his* and *her*. Although PDs were enlarged more than the other features, some learners may have found the pages cluttered and, because their attention was divided among six different enhanced forms, PDs may have been less salient than anticipated. Another possibility is that learners' familiarity with the target forms reduced their salience. It is certain that they had already encountered *his* and *her* in their ESL classes, and the forms may not have been novel enough to attract their attention to the extent that was predicted (see Harley 1989, for a similar interpretation in a study involving grade six children in French immersion). With the contextual support available in the classroom, learners may have been able to understand messages with PDs using their L1 rule.

The second factor relates to the implicitness of the pedagogical intervention. In all three groups, considerable care was taken to avoid talking *about* the enhanced target forms. Not only was there no presentation of a pedagogical rule of thumb or corrective feedback on PD errors, but the forms that were typographically enhanced were never named or identified, nor was there any discussion of the reason for the typographical enhancement, aside from mentioning once that "these are words you have trouble with". Learners were never questioned during the study regarding what they understood to be the purpose of the tasks or of the study itself. None of the treatments drew the learners' attention to the key points of contrast between the agreement rules in English and French. Thus it may be that the enhanced input was more similar to unenhanced input than anticipated in terms of the information it did *not* provide to the learners about possessive determiner agreement in English.

Two post-hoc measures shed light on the inadequacy of such an implicit type of instruction for this target linguistic feature. The first is a questionnaire that was administered at the end of the two-week treatment to obtain information about learners' reactions to the textual enhancement. Learners' responses indicated that the enlarged words had not distracted them while they read, and some did not even remember that the texts had been enhanced! Furthermore, only a third of the learners named the enhanced forms when asked why they thought some of the letters had been enlarged. Thus it would appear that many learners were not aware of the purpose of the typographical enhancement and that it had not helped them sort out when to use *his* or *her*.

The second post-hoc measure asked the learners directly what PD rule they had induced from the treatment. In order not to alter the ongoing, presumably implicit processing of typographically enhanced input, it was necessary to wait until all other measures had been administered to investigate this. Accordingly, the day following the delayed posttests, learners were given four sentences, each describing a picture, and asked to choose whether the sentence was correct or incorrect.

Then they were asked "How do you decide whether to use *his* or *her?*". They had the option of answering in English or French. For example, one of the items was the following:

> (picture of a boy and girl sitting at a table with a loaf of bread)
> Mary and <u>his</u> brother made a loaf of bread.
> _____ Correct
> _____ Incorrect

Only 15 learners, equally distributed across the groups, stated a rule that mentioned possession or belonging or explained a pedagogical trick which indicated knowledge that agreement was between the PD and the possessor. In the example above, the following responses were considered to reveal knowledge of the rule:

> brother of Mary
> c'est son frère à elle
> Mary's brother
> an arrow drawn from *brother* to *Mary*

Instead, most learners stated a variant of the following rule of thumb: "When it's a boy, I use *his* and when it's a girl, I use *her*". Since two of the four items included a kin-different term, this rule was ambiguous as to whether the boy or girl was the possessed entity or the possessor. Some of the others said they used the strategy of looking at the noun before the PD, which would, in fact, have been a reliable rule in the four items they were asked to consider. Some of the rules and strategies were totally wrong, however:

> Je déciderais (*her*)
> I choice *her* because I'm a girl for girl it *her*
> His is *my* and *her* is *your*;
> When is a girl and you want to said "sa" in english you said "her". And the opset with "son" = "his"

Learners in Study 1 were given no help in structuring the enhanced input, nor did they have any experience or practice with explicit metalinguistic information in their communicatively-oriented ESL program. Thus, it is not surprising that most were unable to state a useful rule. Although the ability to state the relevant pedagogical rule, whether induced from the input or presented through explicit rule presentations during instruction, has not been found to reliably predict accurate performance (Green & Hecht 1992; Robinson 1996), it is possible that the inability of the majority of the learners to access a useful rule limited their performance on the passage correction task in which they would have had time to do so.

While the communicative program in place in intensive ESL did not typically include explicit form-focused instruction, prior research in this context had established that some focus on form was not only possible, but that it might also be beneficial in promoting acquisition of difficult language forms by twelve-year old francophone learners of English (see L. White 1991, regarding adverb placement and L. White et al. 1991, regarding question formation). Indeed, one interpretation of the findings is that the implicit pedagogical techniques used in Study 1 might be more suitable for younger instructed learners than for pre-adolescents. Muñoz (2007) observed that children learning second languages in the early elementary school grades use implicit learning mechanisms and consequently need massive amounts of exposure to the target language. While input flooding, typographical enhancement, and book floods provided increased exposure to the target forms, these techniques did not make use of older children's developing analytic skills and problem-solving abilities which would have allowed them to use explicit linguistic information, along with implicit learning strategies, to make more efficient and rapid progress in acquiring PDs.

In summary, the stage development analysis of the oral data, along with the passage correction results, suggests that many of the learners in Study 1 had reached a plateau at an emergence stage and would have benefited from instruction that tapped their metalinguistic skills. For instance, a different typographical technique involving arrows could have been used to make the relationship between the PD and its referent more salient and more explicit (see Doughty 1991, for a similar point). An even more explicit technique would have included a brief rule explanation, either at the beginning of the input enhancement period, or part of the way through it, to help learners structure the input. Alanen's (1995) findings on the acquisition of semi-artificial Finnish, conducted with adult learners, provide support for the benefits of combining typographical enhancement with rule explanation.

These considerations led to the decision to implement an explicit PD pedagogical intervention study with pre-adolescents.

Study 2: *Metalinguistic practice: pre-adolescent French L1 learners*

Study 2 (White & Ranta 2002) aimed to investigate whether learners who were the same age and in the same ESL program as those in Study 1 would benefit from metalinguistic instruction targeting PDs. The research question for Study 2 was the following: How does knowing the rule affect performance on oral and metalinguistic tasks in a second language? It was predicted that learners would reach higher levels of oral and metalinguistic performance if they had been taught a rule of thumb and were shown the relationship between the PD and the referent than learners in a comparison group who did not receive such instruction. Moreover, given the deceptive similarity between the French and English agreement rules, it was predicted that learners would benefit from explicit information about how the L1 and L2 rules were in fact different.[13]

Methodology
The participants were two intact intensive grade six ESL classes, referred to as the Rule group (n = 29) and the Comparison group (n = 30). Learners were the same age and in the same intensive program and school as the learners in Study 1; indeed, three years earlier, the Rule group teacher had participated as the E+ teacher, and the Comparison group teacher had taught the E Group.

The Rule group received explicit metalinguistic information about how *his* and *her* work in English, along with information that contrasted the English and French rules for PDs. The Comparison group had no explicit instruction on PDs. The Rule group was pretested the day before the PD instructional activities were introduced and posttested a week after the end of the instructional treatment. The Comparison group was tested at the time of the Rule group's posttests. On the basis of the problems with multiple testing that had occurred in Study 1, a decision was made not to pretest the Comparison group.[14] As in Study 1, the instruments were versions of the oral picture description and passage correction tasks described above. Since the instructional treatment was spread out over six weeks, versus two

---

13. For a contrastive study involving adolescent (age 16) learners, see Kupferberg and Olshtain (1996).

14. The rationale for the assumption of equivalence of groups can be found in White and Ranta (2002: 272–73). Briefly, the assumption is based on the following points: 1) the learners had been randomly assigned to their classes by the school administration; 2) formal classroom observations using the Communicative Orientation to Language Teaching (COLT) (Spada & Fröhlich 1995), as well as responses to a questionnaire (Ranta 1998), indicated that the Rule and Comparison group teachers followed the same instructional program in which oral interaction activities predominated and believed similarly that teaching grammar is not useful since children can communicate with others their age and understand the messages without grammar; nonetheless, the Rule teacher agreed to implement the instructional materials as requested and not to share them with the Comparison group teacher, who emphasized that she had no interest in teaching her students about PDs; 3) there were no significant differences between the Rule and Comparison groups on an end-of-program listening/reading comprehension test which sampled a wide range of linguistic features ($p = 0.14$).

in Study 1, there were no delayed posttests as the school year ended soon after the pedagogical intervention was completed.[15]

The instructional package was implemented as follows. Once a week, the Rule group worked through a set of materials that had been developed and piloted the previous year with two other groups of intensive learners taught by their teacher. During the first lesson, which lasted about 40 minutes, the Rule group was provided with two types of metalinguistic information about *his* and *her*: 1) learners were taught a rule of thumb (Ask yourself whose ___ is it?), and 2) their attention was directed to the difference between the possessive determiner rules in French and English, and they drew arrows to the referents to *his/her* in sample sentences in English, and to the referents to *son/sa* in sample sentences in French, as follows:

Bill and his mother are looking in his pocket.

Bill et sa mère regardent dans sa poche.

Next, they completed two short rational cloze passages with 5–7 blanks each, all requiring *his* or *her*. Every passage was contextualized by a cartoon illustrating a family situation or dilemma involving a child and members of his or her family. Working individually at first, learners filled in each blank, and drew an arrow from the possessive determiner to the referent. Next, in small groups, they justified their choices to each other and reached a group consensus.[16] This focused practice involved repeating, applying, and talking about the rule of thumb. Once a consensus was reached, the decisions were shared among groups and with the teacher, who provided feedback on the accuracy of the final decisions, and ensured that individual learners had completed the task correctly.

Learners had opportunities to refer to the rule of thumb at every stage of the activity as they talked about *his* and *her*, and as they did so, they used the metalinguistic terms *possessor, refers to, agrees with*. They enhanced their own cloze passages by drawing arrows. It is important to note that they were not required to use the target forms in communicative activities related to the pedagogical intervention. Once a week for the next five weeks, the Rule group teacher reminded the

---

15.   The instructional period was extended following suggestions that if pedagogical interventions are "parachuted in", learning outcomes may not be long-lasting (see Spada & Lightbown 1993; Williams & Evans 1998).

16.   Teachers in the school had been trained in cooperative learning techniques and had been implementing them for several years; children were accustomed to assuming roles in their groups and to using cooperative structures such as "numbered heads together" and "think-pair-share" (Kagan 1993).

learners of the rule of thumb and gave them two new cloze passages to complete as described above.

Drawing and discussing the arrows were sometimes integrated (e.g., *I put his because it's Charlie father and I put the arrow to Charlie*) although the arrows were often discussed in a separate step after consensus had been reached for all of the blanks in a passage. There are numerous instances of learners referring to the rule of thumb (e.g., *Whose father is it? It's Charlie father.*) during their discussions.

Outside of these 30-minute "shots" of explicit instruction, which were embedded within the regular communicative program, the teacher gave no additional instruction or corrective feedback on PDs. However, although there were no specific activities designed to encourage learners to use PDs communicatively, the teacher reported that after the first lesson, learners began to peer- and self-correct when *his* and *her* errors occurred during their regular oral communication activities.[17] Learners in the Comparison group had no instruction on PDs and carried on as usual with their regular communicative program.

In contrast to the intentionally implicit PD treatment of Study 1, the pedagogical intervention in Study 2 drew the learners' attention to PDs in several direct and explicit ways: every blank in the passages required a PD; the learners listened to and verbalized the rule of thumb, justifying, explaining and negotiating it, all the while relying on their own resources; they typographically enhanced the cloze passages themselves by drawing arrows to the referents; they wrote *his* and *her* in context and then read over what they had written silently and aloud in groups. The novelty and cognitive challenge of this activity may have further increased the salience of the treatment. Although these 12-year-old learners had experience using metalanguage to discuss language forms and functions in the context of their developing L1 literacy skills, they were not accustomed to talking *about* language in their English class. Furthermore, one can assume that they had never before been asked to contrast English and French language rules of thumb.

Findings

In Study 2, learners were assigned to an accuracy level according to their corrections of PD errors (*his* and *her* combined) on the passage correction task. Learners whose accuracy was below 50% were assigned to the Low level; those whose accuracy was 50–75% were assigned to the Mid level; those whose accuracy was above 75% and who attained at least 50% in kin-different contexts were assigned to the High level. They were assigned to an oral stage (Pre-emergence, Emergence, Post-emergence) as in Study 1.

---

17.   Foster-Cohen (1999: 185) sees self-corrections as an indication "of an emerging understanding of how the language system works". Although her comment relates to L1 development, it is relevant to this L2 context, as well.

Table 4. Study 2: Distribution of learners in each accuracy level on the passage correction task in percent (Adapted from White & Ranta 2002)

	Low level	Mid level	High level
Rule Group – pretest	62	14	24
Rule Group – posttest	10	38	52
Comparison Group	40	40	20

Table 5. Study 2: Distribution of learners at each developmental stage for *his/her* on the oral production task in percent (Adapted from White & Ranta 2002)

	Stages 1–2	Stages 3–4	Stages 5–7
	(pre-emergence)	(emergence)	(post-emergence)
Rule Group – pretest	38	48	14
Rule Group – posttest	0	34	66
Comparison Group	20	37	43

The effect of instruction on the Rule group's performance can be seen in Table 4 and Table 5. On the passage correction task, most (62%) of the learners obtained Low-accuracy scores on the pretest. Only 10% performed at Low-accuracy on the posttest, and half had High-accuracy scores. In contrast, learners in the Comparison group were equally distributed (40%) between the Low-accuracy and Mid-accuracy levels on the passage correction task at the end of their intensive program, with 20% performing at a High level.

On the oral task, over a third of the Rule group learners were in a Pre-emergence stage on the pretest, and only 14% were in Post-emergence. By the posttest, no learners were in a Pre-emergence stage and two thirds were in Post-emergence. In the Comparison group, 20% of the learners remained in a Pre-emergence stage at the end of their intensive program. The others were divided between Emergence (37%) and Post-emergence (43%) stages.

White and Ranta (1999) found that four developmental profiles emerged from the Rule group data (see Table 6).

1. *No change*: In the case of the four learners who had already reached the High-accuracy/Post-emergence stage on the pre-test, one cannot say that there was no development with respect to the target feature, but only that there was no change in terms of the categories.
2. *Change in oral production stage only*: Improved oral performance for some of the learners may be due to the increased exposure to *his* and *her* in the instructional input and to the opportunities to practice associating *he* with *his* and *she* with *her* in both the input and output. This could have led to the use

of enough contextually appropriate chunks containing *his* and *her* for learners to be assigned to a higher oral stage.

3. *Change in passage correction accuracy-level only*: Improved performance on the passage correction task was anticipated since the experimental instruction was metalinguistic in nature. The learners in this category, who did not also show gains on the oral task, were all at the emergence stage of oral development. Within this group, several made frequent requests for vocabulary help during the oral production task. They appeared to be devoting all their attention to expressing their ideas and may not have had enough attentional resources left to focus on *his* and *her*. Three others changed from overgeneralizing *her* on the pretest to overgeneralizing *his* by the post-test. This suggests that a restructuring of their interlanguage occurred even though the learners did not move to a higher developmental stage.

4. *Change in both oral production stage and accuracy-level*: As can be seen in Table 7, learners did not have to be at a particular accuracy level or oral production stage on the pretest to benefit from instruction. Of particular interest are two learners who went from Low-accuracy/Pre-emergence to High-accuracy/Post-emergence. On the basis of findings from Study 1, one would not have expected these Low-level learners to be "ready" for such big gains and to benefit so much from the instruction.

Table 6. Study 2: Patterns of change in rule group learners' performance with respect to *his/her* (*n* = 29) (Adapted from White & Ranta 1999)

Pattern	Number of students
No change (at ceiling on pretest)	4
Change in oral production stage only	8
Change in passage correction level only	6
Change in both oral production stage and passage correction level	11

Table 7. Study 2: Change in production stage and passage correction-level (*n* = 11) (Adapted from White & Ranta 1999)

Passage correction-level change	Oral stage change		
	Pre- to Emergence	Pre- to Post-emergence	Emergence to Post-emergence
Low to mid	1	3	1
Low to high	1	2	2
Mid to high			1

A third task, the meta-comment interview, was conducted immediately after the picture description task in order to obtain more information about the effects of instruction.[18] The aim, quite literally, was to try to "get inside the learners' heads" to find out as much as possible about the PD rules that had guided their performance on the passage correction task.

In the following excerpts, R refers to the researcher, who is reading from the student's passage, and S refers to the student, who is explaining his correction.

Example 1:
The first example shows a learner in the Rule group who used the rule of thumb as it was taught to explain her corrections. This was one of the learners who went from Low-accuracy/Pre-emergence on the pretest to High-accuracy/Post-emergence by the posttest.

> R: David's mother prepared the cake for *her* son's party.
> S: Because whose son is it? Is the mother, at the mother's.

Example 2:
Next we see a Rule group learner, Junior, who is at a High-accuracy level on the passage correction task. He uses his own version of the rule of thumb ("at who is the...?") and then adds:

> S: You go all the time at the subject before the *his* or the...

Junior was able to use this information when completing the metalinguistic task, but he was at an Emergence stage on the oral task. We might say that his declarative knowledge was not well integrated, and he relied on a strategy of overgeneralizing *his* in describing the pictures. Junior was the only student who showed an awareness of the problems that learners of French L2 face in learning the PD rule, as we can see in the next example. It is tempting to speculate that he gained this perspective through the contrastive instruction he had received.

Example 3:
> S: Because Eric is a boy. And uh is not "*her* sister". I think it's for that, uh, the people in English who try to speak in French said, uh, [ton soeur].

Example 4:
The comments of learners in the Comparison group were also revealing. The next example shows a learner who would potentially benefit from explicit instruction

---

18.   See also Lightbown and Spada (2000), regarding learner's metalinguistic thoughts.

on PDs. Benoit is intelligent and articulate, and though his performance on the two tasks is very low (Low-accuracy/ Pre-emergence), he realizes that his rule of thumb is wrong.

> S: I think, uh, I don't know, but, uh, I was thinking, *his* is for the plural
> R: Mm hm
> S: and, uh, the *her*, um, uh, is for the, the only, just one.
> R: Mm hm.
> S: Uh, I think is not that.

Example 5:
The Comparison Group learner in the final example performed at a Low-accuracy level on the passage correction task although she was at a Post-emergence stage on the oral task. Catherine's comment shows that she is operating with the French rule; this would not have been evident from the task itself as she correctly corrected the error, but we learn here that it was for the wrong reason.

> S: David is playing with *his* plane. I put *his* because plane is, how do you say [masculin]? It's for this *his* new plane.

Interpretation
Study 2 showed that pre-adolescent learners are able to benefit from form-focused instruction involving metalinguistic information and structured production practice. This explicit and contrastive instruction is associated with changes in both knowing about *his* and *her*, as demonstrated in performance on the passage correction task, and knowing how to use these forms, as demonstrated in performance on the oral production task. Learners in the Rule group outperformed learners in the Comparison group on both measures at the end of the treatment period.

Furthermore, the learning outcomes suggest that the explicit pedagogical intervention in Study 2 was more useful in promoting language development for these 12-year-old learners than the implicit intervention for learners of the same age in Study 1. Once piece of evidence to support this interpretation is that no individuals in the Rule group remained at a Pre-emergence stage at the end of Study 2, whereas there were Pre-emergence students in each treatment group in Study 1. Another is that there is no indication of an Emergence-stage plateau, which was observed in Study 1. Indeed, while approximately two-thirds of the learners in Study 1 were in an Emergence stage at the end of their intensive program, about two-thirds of those in Study 2 were in a Post-emergence stage at that time.

There are a number of possible explanations for the findings in Study 2: the rule of thumb helped Rule group learners organize the input and gave a structure to their output; their attention was directed to the target forms during the cloze task; the teacher provided corrective feedback on the accuracy of learners' responses and explanations; the arrows to the referents reinforced the L1/L2 contrast; the oral production practice and negotiation of form with peers helped make the pairing of he/his and she/her more closely associated in long-term memory and more automatic in the learners' output; the distribution of the instruction – a little bit at a time over a period of six weeks – reinforced learning. It is difficult to tease apart the features of the instruction, and indeed, it may be the combination that was effective.[19]

Study 1 and Study 2 were conducted in intensive classrooms. Although the benefits of learning an L2 in an intensive context are well documented (e.g., Collins, Halter, Lightbown, & Spada 1999; Serrano & Muñoz 2007), many learners, especially in foreign language classrooms, experience their language instruction in one or two hours a week. For this reason, it was important to investigate the applicability and effectiveness of this explicit and contrastive PD instruction in a more "typical" instructional setting where time and input are limited.

Study 3: *Metalinguistic practice: adolescent French and Catalan/Spanish L1 learners*

Whereas the two studies reported above were carried out with pre-adolescent French L1 learners, the two parallel studies that are referred to here as *Study 3* were conducted simultaneously in "regular" ESL classrooms with adolescent (age 14) French L1 learners in Quebec and Catalan/Spanish bilingual learners in Catalonia (White et al. 2007). It was necessary to carry out the study with learners in grade eight, rather than in grade six, because the overall proficiency of grade six learners in regular ESL programs is not high enough for them to be able to integrate the PD rule of thumb into their interlanguage. On the basis of previous research in regular grade eight classrooms (Pacheco 2004, in Quebec, and Pahissa 2001, in Catalonia), we considered that these learners were "ready" to learn *his* and *her* in the sense that they were able to understand and produce language containing contexts for these forms. We also knew from discussions with their secondary ESL teachers that they had not yet been explicitly taught PDs although they, like the intensive learners, had been exposed to them in the classroom input.

The principal research question in Study 3 asked whether explicit instruction involving a rule of thumb, contrastive information, and repeated contextualized practice including rule explanation would allow adolescent learners in "regular" limited-exposure programs to make progress in their use and understanding of

---

19.   See Spada, Lightbown and White (2005) for a study which aimed to investigate the specific contributions of contrastive information on the acquisition of PDs and questions by intensive learners in grades 5 and 6.

English PDs. Although gains were not expected to be as great as in Study 2, it was anticipated that the cognitive maturity of these adolescents would enable them to make efficient use of the PD instructional input such that significant improvement would be observed. The learners in Study 3 were two years older than those in Studies 1 and 2. Thus, they had two additional years of schooling in their L1. As Berman (2007: 356) notes, "the ability to relate to language beyond the basic, literal level of expression, and to regard it as an object of reflection as well as a medium of use, are milestones of later language that depend crucially on internal cognitive developments. Yet ... the fact that linguistic knowledge becomes more analytic and explicit across the school years also depends on experience with different contexts of language use and development of literacy." Of relevance here is the older learners' additional experience with decontextualized language through reading secondary-level subject-matter content material (e.g., history, science) and with learning to express themselves more clearly and accurately in writing.

A second question that was of interest to the researchers was whether the developmental framework for the acquisition of English PDs, previously found to account for acquisition by French L1 learners of English, would also account for the patterns of development of another L2 population, namely Catalan/Spanish learners of English. We know from classroom observations and conversations with ESL teachers that *his* and *her* continue to cause problems for Catalan/Spanish bilingual learners in regular programs in secondary school and that, like French L1 learners, many individuals remain in Stage 4 (overgeneralization of *his* or *her*) throughout high school. The reader will recall that the Catalan agreement rule for PDs is similar to the French agreement rule, whereas in Spanish, there is only one third person singular possessive form, *su*. We predicted that in making the *his/her* distinction, Catalan/Spanish bilinguals would rely on their knowledge of Catalan and would follow a developmental path similar to the one observed for French L1 learners of English.

Methodology

Study 3 was conducted in two intact grade eight classes in Quebec and two intact grade eight classes in Catalonia, Spain. The two contexts were similar in several ways: learners had little contact with English outside the 2–3 hours per week of instruction; they had started learning English in elementary school in regular programs for two or two and a half hours a week; English was a compulsory subject through secondary school. An important difference was the orientation of the ESL programs. In Quebec elementary schools, ESL teachers follow a government-mandated "communicative" program that emphasizes the development of oral interaction skills. Although individual reading and writing activities are added in secondary school, along with explicit form-focused instruction targeting verbs, learners are comfortable working in pairs and small groups, and, as was the case in this study, teachers typically interact with their learners in English. In Catalonia, although the official government program is communicatively-oriented, in practice, there was little oral work in the elementary and secondary ESL classes of the participants in this study; activities were often teacher-directed and textbook-based; and grammar activities were common. Learners were not accustomed to working in pairs, and the ESL teacher often interacted with the learners in Catalan, which was the language of instruction of the school.

In each context, there was a Rule and a Comparison group in the same secondary school, taught by the same teacher. The pedagogical intervention was the same one that was used in Study 2. That is, learners in the Rule group were taught the rule of thumb, including information about L1/L2 contrasts, and once a week for six weeks they worked through two cloze passages, drawing arrows to the referents, and receiving feedback from their teacher.

Findings

The findings were similar in Quebec and Catalonia and confirm that the explicit instruction on PDs was beneficial to adolescent learners in regular ESL programs. On the passage correction task, there were no significant differences between the Rule and Comparison group on the pretest. Pre- to posttest gains were significant for the Rule group, but not for the Comparison group. Significant differences on the posttest scores were in favour of the Rule group. As the number of correct corrections was small, data were reported as "percent correct" and not converted to accuracy-levels (Figures 1 and 2).

Findings on the oral production task were also similar in Quebec and Catalonia. There were no significant differences between the Rule and Comparison groups on the pretest or the posttest scores. However, the Wilcoxon matched-pairs signed ranks test showed that changes from the pretest to the posttest were significant for the Rule groups, but not for the Comparison groups (Tables 8 and 9). In the Rule Groups, the most noticeable change was movement to more advanced developmental stages. On the pretest, most of the learners were at an Emergence stage and only a few were in a Post-emergence stage; by the posttest, almost a third of the group were in a Post-emergence stage. In Quebec, all of the stage changes that occurred were in a positive direction. That is, no learner regressed at the posttest. In Catalonia, two Rule group learners regressed. Among the Comparison groups, there was more variability. In Quebec, five learners went ahead, five others went backward, and the rest stayed in the same stage. In Catalonia, only one learner went to a higher stage. All the others stayed in the same stage.

A positive relationship was observed between meta-comments and performance on the passage correction task in Quebec. That is, learners who were able to explain and apply the rule of thumb were also better able to use that knowledge to correct errors on the passage correction task. In Catalonia, however, learners

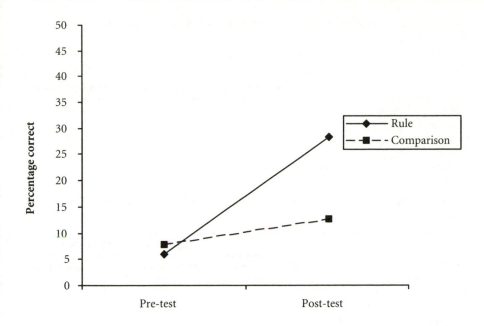

Figure 1. Study 3: Passage correction task: total correct. Grade 8 – Quebec

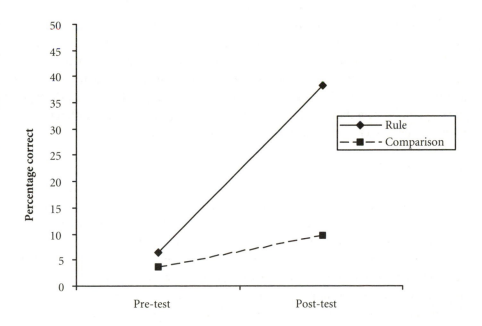

Figure 2. Study 3: Passage correction task: total correct. Grade 8 – Catalonia

Table 8. Study3: Quebec – percent of learners at each developmental stage for *his/her* on the oral production task

	Stages 1–2	Stages 3–4	Stages 5–7
	(pre-emergence)	(emergence)	(post-emergence)
Rule Group – pretest	39	57	4
Rule Group – posttest	36	36	28
Comparison Group – pretest	57	32	11
Comparison Group – posttest	64	14	22

Table 9. Study 3: Catalonia – percent of learners at each developmental stage for *his/her* on the oral production task

	Stages 1–2	Stages 3–4	Stages 5–7
	(pre-emergence)	(emergence)	(post-emergence)
Rule Group – pretest	73	27	0
Rule Group – posttest	66	10	24
Comparison Group – pretest	73	23	4
Comparison Group – posttest	68	23	9

were better at explaining than correcting. In both contexts, the meta-comment explanations of learners in the Rule groups were clearer, more complete, and more correct than those in the Comparison groups.

The second research question asked whether the findings would validate the developmental framework for the acquisition of PDs that had been created for francophone learner oral data. Study 3 confirms that the framework can also account for the patterns of development among Catalan/Spanish learners. Every learner in the Rule and Comparison groups could be assigned to one of the eight PD stages following the criteria outlined in Table 1, and significant differences in the predicted direction were found between the two groups.

Interpretation

In comparison to Study 2 conducted with grade six intensive learners, the PD gains made by the older secondary learners in regular programs were modest, though significant. This was as predicted, taking into consideration that regular program learners had only about 16 hours of exposure to English during the six weeks of PD activities, a period during which their overall proficiency gains would likely have been small. The finding that measurable improvement was observed in PD performance in such a short time suggests that the 14-year-old learners' cognitive maturity played a role. It would seem that overall, the metalinguistic nature of the instructional treatment was appropriate to the age of the grade-eight participants. Indeed, the students in both Quebec and Catalonia were accustomed to some grammar instruction in their ESL class.

Another difference between Study 2 and Study 3 is the way in which learners approached the cloze tasks. Whereas grade six intensive-program learners readily worked together in small groups to discuss and justify their choice of either *his* or *her*, the grade eight regular-program learners in both contexts were likely to complete the cloze tasks individually and then quickly compare their answers (e.g., *his* or *her*) with their assigned partners. Thus, they did not practice articulating the rule of thumb orally in the way that the younger intensive learners had done. There are several possible explanations for this. First, the Catalan learners were not accustomed to working in pairs and groups in class, and the Quebec learners did less pair work in grade eight than had been observed in the grade six classes. Not only was there less time overall in the regular program, but the teachers may have felt that individual work was more "efficient" when instructional time is limited. Second, the grade eight regular-program students may have been less motivated to follow the teachers' instructions to discuss the rule of thumb than the grade six intensive learners. They were in an English class because they had to be there, and it was a "subject" not unlike math or science. In contrast, the grade six learners had chosen to study English all day, every day, for five months, and they were generally willing to do what their teachers asked them to do. Finally, as Tarone and Swain (1995) noted with respect to immersion programs, it is difficult to get older children and adolescents to use the L2 to talk with each other as they lack the vernacular to interact in the way they are accustomed to doing in their L1 outside of class.

The difference between the way the pre-adolescent intensive learners in Study 2 and the adolescent regular-program learners in Study 3 approached the same task underlines the importance of matching the pedagogical intervention to the learning situation. While the demands of the explicit rule-focused instruction appear to have been age-appropriate in terms of the language-analytic abilities of the these older learners, a more individual type of metalinguistic practice might have been better suited to their learning style. This is an interpretation that needs further investigation.

Discussion

The findings from the studies reviewed here are a reminder that second language learning and teaching involve multiple factors that interact. One important factor is the learner's readiness for instruction on *his* and *her*. One way to view readiness is in terms of overall proficiency. In order to determine the PD referent in English, the learner must be able to process language beyond the noun phrase. Readiness is also viewed with respect to emergence of one or both of the target forms. Learners who have reached an Emergence stage and are attempting to produce *his* and *her* are more likely than Pre-emergence learners to benefit from instruction, perhaps because they have some awareness of PD gender marking. In Studies 1 and 3, learners who were at Post-emergence stages by the posttest were predominantly those who had been at an Emergence (or Post-emergence) stage on the pretest. It seems that to benefit from implicit PD instruction (Study 1), explicit instruction when time is limited (Study 3), or regular classroom input without PD instruction (comparison groups, Study 2 and Study 3), it is important to be "ready". Further support for this finding comes from Ammar (2003; Ammar & Spada 2006). She found that grade six intensive ESL learners who had performed at above 50% accuracy on a PD passage correction task at the pretest were able to make use of both implicit (recasts) and explicit (prompts) corrective feedback on PDs. In contrast those who had performed below 50% benefited most from explicit feedback.

Another way to view readiness is to consider that some learners within each group are able to make use of their analytic ability because they are maturationally ready to do so, while others may take longer to reach this point. The development of analytic ability occurs gradually, over the years of schooling, and is closely related to the development of literacy skills.

Learning style also appears to play a role. Some learners may be more ready for instruction on PDs by virtue of their analytic learning style. According to Skehan (1991:279), some learners prefer "to treat language learning as an analytic task while others regard it as a problem for memory". Wesche (1981) found that when type of pedagogy and learning style match up, adult learners make more progress. Ranta (1998, 2002) suggested that it is the more analytic learners who are able to reach Post-emergence in an implicit context, such as the input enhancement pedagogical intervention provided in Study 1, and in communicative language programs where there is little or no focus on form. Indeed, in the three PD studies discussed here, some learners in the comparison groups performed at high levels on the written and oral measures, as did some learners in the instructed groups at the time of the pretest. We can assume that these individuals were able to figure out on their own how PDs work in English. These individual differences in readiness and learning style may help to explain the different paths followed by learners who received the same pedagogical intervention as the fit between pedagogy and individual characteristics may have been better for some learners than for others.

Motivation is another factor that seems to have contributed to the findings discussed here. The motivation to learn English can be assumed to be higher in Studies 1 and 2, which were conducted in intensive classrooms, than in Study 3, which was implemented in a regular program. For one reason, participation in intensive ESL was optional; learners in the intensive classes were there by choice, and they and their parents had agreed to the extra hours of homework required to complete their academic subjects in half the year, as well as the reading and TV homework they were assigned each day during their five months in English. In contrast, the regular secondary program in Quebec and Catalonia is obligatory.[20] While we cannot say that the adolescent learners were unmotivated, they did not display the enthusiasm of the younger intensive learners towards ESL activities in general, and the pedagogical intervention of our study in particular. During the oral interviews, they were less likely to make an effort, and some even appeared to be bored.

It is important to point out that the factors of motivation and age are confounded with each other and with the factor of time. While the pedagogical activities were spread out over six weeks in Study 2 and Study 3, they represented 4 out of 120 hours of instructional time (3%) during this period in the intensive classes versus 4 out of 16 hours (25%) in the regular classes. Intensive learners had more opportunities to notice *his* and *her* in the classroom input than did the regular learners. Although, as noted above, these forms may not have been frequent in "ordinary" teacher talk, intensive teachers are known to read stories to their learners on a regular basis, and learners read other stories, as well as magazines, on their own and watch English TV at home.

This leads to the pedagogical implications of the studies reported here. Frequency in the input is not sufficient on its own to help learners move to Post-emergence stages in PD development. Study 1, which provided a typographically enhanced flood of reading material, along with a book flood in one of the enhanced groups, showed that a flood of *his* and *her* may increase learners' awareness of these forms, but without explicit instruction, most learners in this age group will not know which one to use and will overgeneralize one form in all contexts. Providing learners with a rule of thumb, along with oportunities to practice applying the rule, was shown to be beneficial for children in the age 12–14 age range. The cloze activity involved auto-enhancement through drawing arrows and further directed learners' attention to the rule and the L1/L2 differences. The group work which required explaining and justifying learners' decisions provided a kind of elaborative processing that may have helped them understand and remember how PD agreement works in English. In contexts where small group discussions are not possible, a written alternative could be implemented. For instance, learners could exchange completed cloze passages with their classmates, who would provide a written explanation of the rule that was followed or violated. In addition to practice in applying the rule, learners should be provided opportunities to listen to age-appropriate stories read aloud by their teacher or another audio

---

20.   Furthermore, in Quebec, all of the students who had been in an intensive class in grade 6 were together in an "enriched" follow-up program in grade 8, and those in the regular program were those who had not had intensive classes two years earlier.

source. Stories are often narrated in the third person and are particularly rich in the crucial kin-different contexts (*his* mother, *her* brother). Furthermore, teachers have been observed to speak more slowly and clearly when they read aloud to their students and tend not to delete word-initial *h*, thereby increasing the saliency of *his* and *her* (White *et al.* 2007).

In the research reported here, we have tried to isolate instructional variables, but in the classroom, the teacher is free to combine them in view of the learner population and pedagogical orientation of the school. As Harley (1998: 170, citing Ceci & Howe 1982) pointed out, for primary school learners, attention is dependent on the intrinsic interest of the learning activities involved. Pedagogical activities should be interesting and visually attractive; popular activities should be recycled so that they are familiar and do not have to be explained every time, thus leaving more class time for the activities themselves. This advice would be equally relevant for secondary school-age learners.

Learners need to be taught forms that are likely to be misanalyzed because of a deceptive similarity to their L1. PDs are a good candidate for explicit instruction since the rule is easy to state and has no exceptions. The stage framework can be used informally by teachers to gauge learners' development. For example, it is easy to identify learners in stage 2 as they use *your* in contexts for *his* and *her*. Learners who use only one form are at Emergence stage 4. The framework accounts for variability in performance and recognizes that learners may entertain alternative structural possibilities in their interlanguage over a long period of time. Because the form/meaning mapping is complicated by L1 interference, a lot of practice applying the rule is needed, and the pedagogical intervention should be sustained and supplemented with input containing many exemplars of the target feature.

Conclusion

A strength of this research is that different types of form-focused instruction were investigated targeting the same linguistic feature and using the same data collection instruments with pre- and young-adolescent learners in different programs (regular and intensive) and with different L1s. Each of the pedagogical interventions was extended over several weeks and was taught by the learners' own classroom teacher. The findings suggest that learners in this age group benefit from explicit form-focused instruction, but it is important to remember that the instructional context has an impact on the learning outcomes, as well.

A limitation of much classroom research, including the studies reported here, is that the long-term effects of instruction are impossible to assess, both because the learners disperse, and because other intervening variables, such as exposure to the target language, cannot be controlled. In the case of research involving PDs, we do not know whether learners go back to overgeneralizing one form after showing evidence on the posttest that they have sorted out the differences between *his* and *her*. Interactions with highly proficient adults suggest that PDs may require lifelong monitoring for individuals whose L1 is French, Spanish or Catalan. Research is needed that investigates PDs in the interlanguage of learners who had explicit contrastive information about these forms when they were children. Another important area for future research would be to find out how adult learners of English respond to the type of form-focused instruction on PDs that was found to be effective with the pre-adolescent and adolescents in Study 2 and Study 3.

Acknowledgements

I wish to acknowledge the essential contributions of my collaborators on the studies discussed here – Leila Ranta (Study 2) and Carmen Muñoz and Laura Collins (Study 3) – and to Nina Spada and Patsy Lightbown, with whom I have also collaborated on PD research, and much more. As always, Randall Halter provided his statistical expertise, for which I am grateful. I appreciate the willingness of the teachers and learners to participate in the studies, and without the help of many research assistants, the data would not have been collected, coded and analyzed. I am grateful to an anonymous reviewer, the editors, and to Cristina Garabito for useful feedback on the manuscript. Thank you, merci, gracias, gràcies.

References

Alanen, R. 1995. Input enhancement and rule presentation in second language acquisition. In *Attention and Awareness in Foreign Language Learning*, R. Schmidt (ed.), 259–302. Honolulu HI: University of Hawai'i Press.

Ammar, A. 2003. Corrective Feedback and L2 Learning: Elicitation and Recasts. PhD dissertation, McGill University, Montreal.

Ammar, A. & Spada, N. 2006. One size fits all? Recasts, prompts, and L2 learning. *Studies in Second Language Acquisition* 28: 543–574.

Berman, R. 2007. Language knowledge and use across adolescence. In *Blackwell Handbook of Language Development*, E. Hoff & M. Shatz (eds), 347–367. Malden MA: Blackwell.

Chiat, S. 1986. Personal pronouns. In *Language Acquisition* (2nd ed.), P. Fletcher & M. Garman (eds), 339–355. Cambridge: CUP.

Collins, L., Halter, R., Lightbown, P. & Spada, N. 1999. Time and the distribution of time in L2 instruction. *TESOL Quarterly* 33: 655–680.

DeKeyser, R. 2005. What makes second-language grammar difficult? A review of issues. *Language Learning* 55: 1–25.

Doughty, C. 1991. Second language instruction does make a difference: Evidence from an empirical study of SL relativization. *Studies in Second Language Acquisition* 13: 431–469.

Doughty, C. 2003. Instructed SLA: Constraints, compensation, and enhancement. In *The Handbook of Second Language Acquisition*, C. Doughty & M. H. Long (eds), 256–310. Malden MA: Blackwell.

Ellis, R. 2002. Does form-focused instruction affect the acquisition of implicit knowledge? A review of the research. *Studies in Second Language Acquisition* 24: 223–236.

Foster-Cohen, S. 2001. First language acquisition...second language acquisition: 'What's Hecuba to him or he to Hecuba?' *Second Language Research* 17: 329–344.

Foster-Cohen, S. 1999. *An Introduction to Child Language Development*. London: Longman.

Gaux, C. & Gombert, J. 1999. Implicit and explicit syntactic knowledge and reading in pre-adolescents. *British Journal of Developmental Psychology* 17: 169–188.

Green, P. & Hecht, K. 1992. Implicit and explicit grammar: An empirical study. *Applied Linguistics* 13: 168–184.

Harley, B. 1989. Functional grammar in French immersion: A classroom experiment. *Applied Linguistics* 10: 331–359.

Harley, B. 1998. The role of focus-on-form tasks in promoting child L2 acquisition. In *Focus on Form in Classroom Second Language Acquisition*, C. Doughty & J. Williams (eds), 156–174. Cambridge: CUP.

Hulstijn, J. 1995. Not all grammar rules are equal: Giving grammar instruction its proper place in foreign language teaching. In *Technical Report* 9: *Attention and Awareness in Foreign Language Learning*, R. W. Schmidt (ed.), 359–386. Honolulu HI: University of Hawai'i Press.

Hulstijn, J. H. & De Graaff, R. 1994. Under what conditions does explicit knowledge of a second language facilitate the acquisition of implicit knowledge? A research proposal. *AILA Review* 11: 97–112.

Kagan, S. 1993. *Cooperative Learning*. San Juan Capistrano CA: Kagan Cooperatiave Learning.

Karmiloff, K. & Karmiloff-Smith, A. 2001. *Pathways to Language: From Fetus to Adolescent*. Cambridge MA: Harvard University Press.

Kupferberg, I. & Olshtain, E. 1996. Explicit contrastive instruction facilitates the acquisition of difficult L2 forms. *Language Awareness* 5(3/4): 149–165.

Karmiloff-Smith, A. 1986. Some fundamental aspects of language development after age 5. In *Language Acquisition* (2nd ed.), P. Fletcher & M. Garman (eds.), 455–474. Cambridge: CUP.

Lightbown, P., Halter, R., White, J. & Horst, M. 2002. Comprehension-based learning: The limits of "Do it yourself". *The Canadian Modern Language Review* 58: 427–464.

Lightbown, P. & Spada, N. 1990. Focus on form and corrective feedback in communicative language teaching: Effects on second language learning. *Studies in Second Language Acquisition* 12: 429–448.

Lightbown, P. & Spada, N. 1994. An innovative program for primary ESL in Quebec. *TESOL Quarterly* 28: 563–579.

Lightbown, P. & Spada, N. 1997. Learning English as a second language in a special school in Quebec. *Canadian Modern Language Review* 53: 315–355.

Lightbown, P. & Spada, N. 2000. Do they know what they're doing? L2 Learners' awareness of L1 influence. *Language Awareness* 9(4): 198–217.

Loschky, L. & Bley-Vroman, R. 1993. Grammar and task-based methodology. In *Tasks and Language Learning: Integrating Theory and Practice*, G. Crookes & S. Gass (eds), 128–167. Clevedon: Multilingual Matters.

Martens, M. J. 1988. Recognition and Production of Pronouns by Francophone Learners of English as a Second Language. MA Thesis, Concordia University, Montreal.

Mah, J., Steinhauer, K. & Goad, H. 2006. The Trouble with /h/: Evidence from ERPs. Paper presented at the 8th Generative Approaches to Second Language Acquisition Conference (GASLA 2006), Sommerville MA.

Moore, M. 2001. Third person errors by children with and without language impairment. *Journal of Communication* 34: 207–228.

Munoz, C. 2007. Age-related differences and second language learning practice. In *Practice in a Second Language: Perspectives from Applied Linguistics and Cognitive Psychology*, R. DeKeyser (ed.), 229–255. Cambridge: CUP.

Pacheco, J. 2004. A Comparison of Textual Input Enhancement and Explicit Rule Presentation in Secondary One English as a Second Language Classes. MA thesis, Concordia University, Montreal.

Pahissa, I. 2001. *She Gives Him Her Elephant...and He Gives Her His Giraffe* (Course project). Barcelona: Universitat de Barcelona.

Ranta, L. 1998. *Focus on Form from the Inside: The Significance of Grammatical Sensitivity for L2 Learning in Communicative ESL Classrooms.* Montreal: Concordia University.

Ranta, L. 2002. The role of learners' language analytic ability in the communicative classroom. In *Individual Differences and Instructed Language Learning*, P. Robinson (ed.), 159–179. Amsterdam: John Benjamins.

Robinson, P. 1996. Learning simple and complex second language rules under implicit, incidental, rule-search, and instructed conditions. *Studies in Second Language Acquisition* 18: 27–64.

Serrano, R., & Muñoz, C. 2007. Same hours, different time distribution: Any difference in EFL? *System* 35: 305–321.

Sharwood Smith, M. 1981. Consciousness-raising and the second language learner. *Applied Linguistics* 11: 159–168.

Sharwood Smith, M. 1991. Speaking to many minds: On the relevance of different types of language information for the L2 learner. *Second Language Research* 7: 118–132.

Skehan, P. 1991. Individual differences in second language learning. *Studies in Second Language Acquisition* 13: 275–298.

Spada, N. 1997. Form-focussed instruction and second language acquisition: A review of classroom and laboratory research. *Language Teaching Abstracts* 30: 73–87.

Spada, N. & Fröhlich, M. 1995. *COLT: Communicative Orientation of Language Teaching Observation Scheme: Coding Conventions and Applications.* Sydney: National Centre for English Language Teaching and Research, Macquarie University.

Spada, N. & Lightbown, P. 1993. Instruction and the development of questions in the L2 classroom. *Studies in Second Language Acquisition* 15(2): 205–221.

Spada, N. & Lightbown, P. 1999. Instruction, L1 influence and developmental readiness in second language acquisition. *Modern Language Journal* 83: 1–22.

Spada, N., Lightbown, P. & White, J. 2005. The importance of form/meaning mappings in explicit form-focused instruction. In *Investigations in Instructed Second Language Acquisition*, A. Housen & M. Pierrard (eds), 199–234. Berlin: Mouton de Gruyter.

Tarone, E. & Swain, M. 1995. A sociolinguistic perspective on second language use in immersion classrooms. *The Modern Language Journal* 79: 166–178.

Trahey, M. 1992. *Comprehensible Input and Second Language Acquisition.* Montreal: McGill University.

Trahey, M. & White, L. 1993. Positive evidence and preemption in the second language classroom. *Studies in Second Language Acquisition* 15: 181–204.

Trevise, A. 1996. Contrastive metalinguistic representations: The case of 'very French' learners of English. *Language Awareness* 5: 188–195.

VanPatten, B. 1990. Attending to form and content in the input. *Studies in Second Language Acquisition* 12: 287–301.

Wesche, M. 1981. Language aptitude measures in streaming, matching students with methods, and diagnosis of learning problems. In *Individual Differences and Universals in Language Learning Aptitude*, K. C. Diller (ed.), 119–139. Rowley MA: Newbury House.

Williams, J. & Evans, J. 1998. What kind of focus and on which forms? In *Focus on Form in Classroom Second Language Acquisition*, C. Doughty & J. Williams (eds), 139–155. Cambridge: CUP.

White, J. 1996. An Input Enhancement Study with ESL Children: Effects on the Acquisition of Possessive Determiners. PhD dissertation, McGill University, Montreal.

White, J. 1998. Getting the learners' attention: A typographical input enhancement study. In *Focus on Form in Classroom Second Language Acquisition*, C. Doughty & J. Williams (eds.), 85–113. Cambridge: CUP.

White, J. 2006. Sorting Out Personal Pronouns in English. Paper presented at the American Association for Applied Linguistics (AAAL)/Canadian Association of Applied Linguistics Joint Conference, Montreal QC.

White, J., Collins, L., Trofimovich, P., Cardoso, W. & Horst, M. 2007. When positive evidence isn't evident: A multidimensional analysis of possessive determiners in classroom input. Paper presented at the Sixth International Symposium on Bilingualism, Hamburg.

White, J., Munoz, C. & Collins, L. 2007. The his/her challenge: Making progress in a "regular" second language program. *Language Awareness* 16(4): 278–299.

White, J. & Ranta, L. 1999. Learner style differences and L2 knowledge. Paper presented at the Annual Conference of the American Association for Applied Linguistics, Stamford, CT.

White, J. & Ranta, L. 2002. Examining the interface between metalinguistic task performance and oral production in second language classrooms. *Language Awareness* 11(4): 259–290.

White, J. & Turner, C. 2005. Comparing children's oral ability in two ESL programs. *Canadian Modern Language Review* 61(4): 491–517.

White, L. 1991. Adverb placement in second language acquisition: Some positive and negative evidence in the classroom. *Second Language Research* 7(2): 133–161.

White, L., Spada, N., Lightbown, P. & Ranta, L. 1991. Input enhancement and L2 question formation. *Applied Linguistics* 12(4): 416–423.

Zobl, H. 1985. Grammar in search of input and intake. In *Input in Second Language Acquisition*, S. Gass & C. Madden (eds), 329–344. Rowley MA: Newbury House.

Child SLA at home and in the community

Acquiring Japanese as a second language (JSL) in a naturalistic context

A longitudinal study of a young child from a Processability Theory (PT) perspective

Junko Iwasaki

Edith Cowan University

In recent times Processability Theory (PT) (Pienemann, 1998) has extensively supported findings from studies of a range of languages acquired as an L2, including Japanese (Di Biase & Kawaguchi 2002). Following the acquisition criteria proposed by Pienemann (1998), the current study analyses the points of emergence of verbal morpho-syntactic structures by a seven year old Australian boy who was acquiring Japanese as a second language (JSL) naturalistically. A comparison of the findings of the current study with those of the study by Di Biase and Kawaguchi (2002) shows that both child and adult learners went through a similar developmental sequence of acquisition of verbal morpho-syntax, namely category procedure, phrasal procedure and S-procedure as hypothesised by Pienemann (1998).

Introduction

Issues of natural order of language acquisition

For the last three decades it has been argued that there is a natural order for language acquisition, that is, language learners naturally proceed through similar developmental patterns. Although research about morpheme orders and developmental sequences did produce useful evidence in relation to some linguistic features within specific languages in the 1960s and 1970s, most of this type of research met strong criticism because of its apparent lack of theoretical underpinnings. This led to the emergence of more theoretically motivated researchers in the early 1980s such as those involved in the Zweitsprachenerwerb Italienischer und Spanischer Arbeiter (ZISA) project (e.g., Clahsen 1980; Meisel, Clahsen & Pienemann 1981; Pienemann 1980). However, to date only a handful of the research outcomes in second language acquisition (SLA) have been tested against a common theory.

Another important issue emerging concurrently is whether or not child learners follow the same acquisition pattern as adult learners in SLA. Aside from the results from a small number of studies (e.g., Schmidt 1983), the majority of studies conducted in the 1970s using a cross-sectional approach (e.g., Dulay & Burt 1973, 1974; Bailey, Madden, & Krashen 1974) provide indication that both children and adult learners of English as a second language (ESL) follow similar patterns of acquisition such as the acquisition of grammatical morphemes. Also, longitudinal studies conducted in the 1960s and 1970s (e.g., Cancino, Rosansky & Schumann 1978) indicate that a similar developmental path is taken by child and adult learners of ESL in acquiring negation and interrogation. However, problems with methodology (e.g., accuracy based measurements) and scope (i.e., limited linguistic features such as grammatical morphemes, negation and interrogation in English) mean the results are, in the main, not transferable. In addition, researchers (e.g., Oliver 1995, 1998; Mackey & Oliver 2002) suggest that for the young age group (8–13 year olds), too little research has been undertaken, thus there are insufficient data regarding children's L2. At the same time a comparison of the adult L2 findings with those of child L2 may have significant implications for the notion of maturational constraints (e.g., Long 1990; Hyltenstam & Abrahamsson 2003; Butler & Hakuta 2004). Therefore, testing the previous results of the adult L2 with children, preferably within the same theoretical framework, is needed.

Studies on acquisition of Japanese as a second language (JSL)

In recent years there have been numerous JSL studies, covering various aspects of the language, including syntax and morphology, but the scope of these studies has been rather narrow. The majority of the developmental sequence studies in JSL (e.g., Noro 1995; Kamura 2001a, 2001b) have been considerably influenced by empirical and descriptive studies conducted during the 1970s and 1980s, especially those conducted with English, and other European languages, as the L2 (e.g., Cancino, Rosansky & Schumann 1978; Wode 1976, 1978).

In addition, as with SLA studies in general, studies of adult learners of JSL outnumber those of child learners. This is despite the fact that there are a growing number of children learning Japanese as an L2 in Japan, and thus a strong pedagogical need for appropriate teaching of JSL to primary and lower secondary children (Yanagisawa 1995, pp. 32–35). Although researchers began to turn their attention to child acquisition of JSL in the middle of the 1990s, most of these child JSL studies focused only on a small number of linguistic forms, e.g., noun modification (Shirahata 1993) and negation (Noro 1995).

One exception to this is Ito (1997), who investigated the order of acquisition of different syntactic structures by an eight year old Russian boy. Data were collected over a period of 20 months, starting five months after he arrived in Japan without knowing any Japanese. He was placed in a mainstream class, but occasionally taken to a separate JSL class. The speech which the child produced during his JSL classes and study periods at home was audio recorded on a regular basis. An analysis was undertaken with a focus on subordination, noun modification, passives, potentials, causatives, and benefactive sentences. Ito found an acquisition order for eight grammatical structures; the benefactive verb and the potential verb *dekiru* were acquired earliest, followed by verb morphology for potential forms (i.e., *-eru/-areru*), subordination, and noun modification. Benefactive structures were acquired later. But passive and causative forms were not acquired within the time frame.

Although it is not clearly stated, it seems that the emergence criterion, based on a minimum of one occurrence in a sample, was used to determine acquisition. Therefore, it is not clear whether or not each of these linguistic features actually emerged productively. In other words, it is possible that a number of the linguistic features appeared as morphological chunks or formulae.

In summary, most of the JSL studies lack a theoretical motivation and few have used standardised methodology, which makes comparison of data from a variety of participants difficult to achieve. This also diminishes the ease with which results can be meaningfully interpreted.

Theoretically motivated studies in SLA and JSL

Recently, a growing number of more theoretically motivated SLA order studies have been undertaken in various languages, including Japanese. This line of work is based on Processability Theory (PT). PT (Pienemann 1998) evolved out of the Multidimensional Model, which was developed for initial work by the ZISA researchers investigating German as a second language (GSL). In this model, they proposed an explanation grounded in a cognitive approach for the acquisition of GSL word order and presented a variety of morpho-syntactic structures all together in each developmental stage. In PT, Pienemann successfully combined the research findings from cognitive psychology with those based on linguistic theories in order to provide a more logical explanation of the workings of the L2 cognitive processes required for each stage of language development and to extend its applicability to a wider range of morphology. More specifically, Pienemann related the processability of morpho-syntactic structure to Lexical-Functional Grammar (LFG) (Kaplan & Bresnan 1982), Incremental Procedural Grammar (IPG) (Kempen & Hoenkamp 1987) and Levelt's (e.g., 1989) speech model (see Pienemann 1998, for more detailed explanation). He suggested that the learner whose processing ability is at a particular stage can manage a certain level of exchange of grammatical information, and in turn is able to produce structures tied to that processing. The sequence in which processing sub-components can function by information exchange form a universal hierarchy for the stages of acquisition of procedural skills required by the learner.

This stepwise hierarchy of processing procedures, which is claimed to be universal, is illustrated in Table 1 in Appendix A.

Empirical evidence for this theory is provided by studies of GSL (e.g., Pienemann 1998; Håkansson, Pienemann & Sayehli 2002), ESL (Pienemann & Johnston 1985), Swedish as an L2 (Pienemann & Håkansson 1999), Italian as an L2 (Di Biase & Kawaguchi 2002) and JSL (Di Biase & Kawaguchi 2002; Pienemann, Di Biase, Håkansson & Kawaguchi 2005).

Based on LFG, and within the bounds of PT, Di Biase and Kawaguchi (2002) hypothesised the acquisition order of verbal morpho-syntax for verb inflection, the V-*te* V structure, and the passive/causative/benefactive in Japanese. They tested this by investigating the acquisition of morpho-syntax in JSL from a three-year longitudinal study of one adult learner, Lyn, and a cross-sectional study of nine adult learners who were all native speakers of English. For the longitudinal part of this study, Lyn participated in thirteen, 20–30 minute interviews at intervals of between one to two months. During the interviews, free conversation and picture tasks were used to elicit speech. The results of their study support the cross-linguistic validity of PT, because the order of the three verbal morpho-syntactic structures are in line with the acquisition order of the L2 processes predicted in PT, i.e., lexical > phrasal > interphrasal.

Motivation of the study and research questions

It is apparent from a review of the literature that to date there have been few, if any, theoretically motivated studies of acquisition of JSL by young children. This includes longitudinal and cross-sectional studies. In order to validate a theory such as PT, more empirical evidence in a variety of settings, such as for learners from different L2 backgrounds, different age groups, and different acquisition environments (i.e., whether the learner is a naturalistic or instructed language acquirer) is needed.

In the light of the previous studies of acquisition in SLA, and, JSL in particular, the following research questions are raised:

RQ1: Do developmental stages of acquisition exist in the interlanguage of a child learner of JSL?

RQ2: Do the developmental stages of acquisition by a child learner of JSL match those of adult learners of JSL?

In order to answer these questions, the current study will focus on the acquisition of three verbal morpho-syntactic structures in Japanese, namely verbal affixes, the V-*te* V structure, and the passive/causative. These structures were chosen to ensure the comparability of results between the current study and Di Biase and Kawaguchi's (2002). The results of their study, with adult JSL learners, support a hierarchy of acquisition as hypothesised in PT.

Firstly, Di Biase and Kawaguchi (2002) predict that the acquisition of verbal inflection occurs in Stage 2 as it is regarded as a lexical (i.e., non-syntactical) operation in the hierarchy of processing. According to these researchers, although Japanese verbal morphology involves attaching a variety of suffixes marking tense, aspect, politeness, polarity, causative, and so on to a verb stem, no exchange of grammatical information between the morphemes is required. This is because each morpheme "individually" adds its semantic features to the whole verb, no matter how many morphemes are added. Example 1 below from the current study shows the uses of the verbal affix -*ta* in a target like (TL) context. Here, the child, Shaun, is able not only to retrieve the concept "*hairu* (enter)" as a lemma from his mental lexicon (Stage 1), but also to attach the appropriate verbal affix, -*ta*, denoting past tense, which shows that he has acquired cognizance of information regarding the category "verb" (Stage 2).

Example 1: Suppliance of -*ta* (S1.2: A narrative of the Frog story)

> *Mizu   ni   hai-tta.*
> water   DIREC[1]   enter-PAST
> (They) entered the water.

Secondly, Di Biase and Kawaguchi (2002) predict that the acquisition of the "V-*te* V" structure requires the phrasal procedure of Stage 3, as it consists of two verbal constituents: the first verb (V1) being the infinite verb (i.e., the affix -*te* attached to the verb stem or the -*te* form of the verb) and the second (V2) the auxiliary verb. On the basis of the original meaning of V2s, a combination of these two verbs denote a variety of semantic features including the aspect of an action/event indicated in V1 (e.g., V-*te iru*: progressive/resultant state) and the benefactive meaning (e.g., V-*te ageru* [I/we do for someone], V-*te kureru* [Someone does for me/us]). Using the concept of "combinatoric TYPE" (Sells 1995, 1999), they claim that V-*te* must be followed by another V, because TYPE of V-*te* is V-sis(ter). In addition to the appropriate affixation of the stems to the two verbs, information exchange between the two Vs is needed to juxtapose them correctly, and for this the learner needs to have acquired phrasal procedural skills. The following example shows the

---

1.   List of abbreviations used throughout this paper is given in the Appendix B.

use of a sub-type of the V-*te* V structures, i.e., -*te iru* (durative/imperfective aspect marker) in a TL context. Note that the quoted part is indicated in bold.

Example 2: Suppliance of -*te iru* (S6.5: Student/teacher play)

> *Matto-kun ga   **umai** tte   yu-tte   i-mashita.*
> Matt-Mast SUBJ good QUOT say-INF ASP-POL.PAST
> Matt was saying that (I) was good.

Lastly, according to Di Biase and Kawaguchi (2002), the production of the passive, causative or benefactive requires the learner to be capable of the inter-phrasal processing procedure (Stage 4) because information must be exchanged beyond the phrase boundaries, i.e., V (or VP in the case of the benefactive) and NPs, in the grammatical encoding process. More recently, Kawaguchi (2005) updates the explanation, using the Lexical Mapping Hypothesis in the extended version of PT (Pienemann, Di Biase & Kawaguchi 2005). She states:

> This hypothesis is based on non-default mapping of semantic argument roles onto grammatical structure (technically association between argument-structure and functional-structure). In second language acquisition, learners initially map the most prominent role available onto SUBJ. The L2 learner gradually learns how to attribute prominence to a particular thematic role as well as how to de-focus or suppress a thematic role, that is, how to suppress the Agent role and promote the Patient role to SUBJ rather than mapping canonically the Agent onto SUBJ. (p. 100)

For example, before Stage 4, the learner can produce an active sentence, i.e., the agent (SUBJ) + OBJ + V in the case of Japanese, by using canonical word order (i.e., default mapping). In contrast, the production of a passive structure requires non-canonical word order, i.e., the patient (SUBJ) + the oblique agent (adjunct) + the passive form of the verb. Here, only when the sentence contains the patient marked with a particle, *ga* (SUBJ) or *wa* (TOP), and/or the oblique agent marked with a particle, *ni* (DAT), can the learner provide evidence for his/her capability of non-default mapping that requires the inter-phrasal processing procedure for Stage 4. Similarly, while the production of a non-causative sentence requires the use of canonical word order (i.e., default mapping), the construction of a causative sentence consists of the agent (SUBJ), i.e., the causer, and the oblique agent (adjunct), i.e., the causee, plus the causative form of the verb. This means that the original subject of the non-causative sentence must change to a more adjunct role (i.e., the oblique agent) in the causative sentence, which requires the learner to use non-canonical mapping. Therefore, as with the case of a passive sentence, only when the causative sentence contains the causer marked with a particle, *ga* (SUBJ) or *wa* (TOP), and/or the oblique agent marked with a particle *ni* (DAT), can the learner demonstrate that evidence for S-procedure is available. The following example shows the occurrence of the causative with both the agent marked with *ga* (SUBJ) and the oblique agent (OBLag) marked by *ni* (DAT). Note that the subordinate clause is indicated in bold.

Example 3: Occurrence of the causative with OBLag (S23.1: Free conversation)

Sorede sensee ga... **kono onna**   **ga**   **sore i-tta**   **kara...** sore
then   teacher SUBJ this   woman SUBJ that say-PAST because that
o   minna   ni   yar-ase-ta   no
OBJ everyone OBLag do-CAUS-PAST EP
Then, the teacher, because this woman said that, made everyone do it.

The study

Method

The participant

The child, Shaun, is the second son of middle class parents, both of whom speak Japanese a little but whose conversation with their children at home is always in their native language, English. He turned seven years old just before the commencement of this study. At the time of the study, Shaun had been enrolled in a primary school for Japanese children in Australia[2] for nine months. He spoke Japanese at school, where all the subjects were taught in Japanese. Whilst the child often played with his Japanese school friends after school on weekdays, he also played with Australian peers with whom he spoke English. In this way, Shaun was simultaneously developing both his L1 and L2 in two linguistically different, but natural, settings.

Shaun's family had lived in Japan for six years. When the family returned to Australia, Shaun was two years old. In his first year of primary education, Shaun went to a local Australian primary school but enrolled in the Japanese school as a first grader the following year. It was apparent that Shaun's inclination to attend the Japanese school was a result of the influence of his elder brother, Matt, who had been enrolled in the school for three years at that time. However, from an interview with Mr. Honda, his class teacher at the school, Shaun's level of Japanese proficiency had been zero when he began attending the school.

---

2. This school is a private school, which was established and approved by both the Japanese and Australian Governments. The school's aim is to provide its students with an education at a level equivalent to that in Japan and follows the curriculum prescribed by the Japanese Ministry of Education and Science (*Monbukagaku-sho*).

At the beginning, Mr. Honda had to use English to communicate with Shaun. According to the teacher's observation, Shaun readily mixed with the Japanese children and learned informal Japanese through interaction with his peers while playing. Even so, Mr. Honda recollected that it took approximately three months before Shaun produced a Japanese word spontaneously – the first being "*Yatta!* (I've made it!), and another six to seven months before Shaun started producing large quantities of Japanese. Until that time, which coincided with the beginning of data collection for this study, he still answered in English when questioned by the teacher in Japanese. It appeared that the teacher did not use explicit grammar instruction with Shaun, which would normally be the case for Japanese as a foreign language (JFL) learners. By the end of his first year at the Japanese school, which was three months after the data collection began, Shaun was using Japanese to interact at a minimal level with his peers and to respond, in a limited way, in class.

Data collection and procedure

Conversation between the child and other speakers of Japanese were tape recorded over a period of one year (24 sessions) with two follow-up sessions occurring over the next nine months. Each session lasted for approximately 90 minutes during which Shaun and other speakers of Japanese performed a range of tasks such as free conversation and communication games. These task materials included ones taken from commercial resource books for JFL or ESL teachers, a picture book with no words which has been used in previous child language acquisition research (Mayer 1969), and other communication games developed by the researcher.

The task-based elicitation method was intended to create the most spontaneous interaction possible between Shaun and his interlocutors, including his school friends, his brother, his parents and the researcher. In order to minimise task effect, eight different types of tasks, some of which were designed to elicit the use of a particular linguistic feature, were developed. Further, in order to minimise practice effect and also to avoid boredom, most of these tasks had four or five different versions; that is, a total of nineteen different regular tasks and twelve additional tasks were prepared and used over the 26 sessions. These versions were recycled to ensure the comparability of the outcomes. (See the task distribution in Appendix C.)

Data base and coding procedure

All the audio taped interactions were transcribed. These data were the basis for both quantitative and qualitative analysis. This meant that the data collection over the 26 sessions had yielded a total of 20,988 turns by Shaun and his interlocutors. Of a corpus of all these turns, 47.1 % (9,884 turns) were produced by Shaun.

As noted previously, the linguistic features investigated in the current study were those verbal morpho-syntactic structures in Japanese found by Di Biase and

Kawaguchi (2002) to exist in the interlanguage of adult JFL learners: verb inflection, the V-*te* V structure, and the passive/causative, explained below.

These three structures were isolated from the entire corpus of Shaun's utterances and were used as a basis for analysis. Inaudible or unintelligible utterances, utterances read from a textbook, diary or speech script, and utterances sung in songs were not included in the data base for quantitative analysis in the current study. However, Shaun's utterances that were not included for analysis, his interlocutors' utterances as well as notes taken by the researcher during and after each session were used as contextual evidence to support the accuracy of the transcription and the reliability of the analysis. After the exclusion of echoic, incomplete and formulaic items[3] from the data base, the remaining verb forms were coded in accordance with the rules described below.

1. Verbal affix (Category procedure – Stage 2): Each verbal affix represents a combination of tense, polarity, aspect and/or politeness. For example, -*u* marks the plain nonpast affirmative, -*ta* the plain past affirmative, -*nai* the plain nonpast negative and -*nakatta* the plain past negative. A polite version of these four affixes are -*masu*, -*mashita*, -*masen*, and -*masendeshita*. Pienemann (1998, p. 211) and Di Biase and Kawaguchi (2002) hypothesised that the emergence of verbal affixes requires the learner to acquire category procedure, which needs no information exchange. Based on Pienemann (1998), the context in which each of the verbal affixes was supplied (i.e., in a TL or non-target-like (NTL) context) was examined and marked as such. However, it is important to note that, under the emergence criteria (Pienemann 1998), affixes supplied in NTL contexts equally qualify as emergent morphemes as do the correct ones in TL contexts.

From the reduced data base, 6,764 verbal affixes were identified. If an utterance contained any verbal affix, the type of the affix was entered, and the occurrences for each affix were then totaled for each of the sessions.

2. V-*te* V structure (Phrasal procedure – Stage 3): This structure consists of an infinite verb (V1) and an auxiliary verb (V2). V2 conjugates in the same way as a

---

3. Following Wray (2002, p. 4 & 9), these refer to verbs, verb phrases, and verbal sentences – the whole of which appeared to be saved and retrieved from memory. It is important to note that 1,069 items deleted at this stage were "obvious" formulaic items. For example, 702 cases of "*chiga-u* (differ)" appeared as "No" and 73 as "different" throughout the data collection period with the exception of only one case of its varied form, "*chigai-masu* (differ-POL) observed in Session 16. The remaining 294 items deleted here included those which can be called "verbs" in terms of grammatical derivation. They appeared as part of an adverb, a greeting etc but are not defined as verbs in Japanese-Japanese dictionaries (e.g., *shi-te* [do-INF] in *kooshite* [this way: ADV]). These "verbs" always appeared in the same lexical context and in the same form. All other "verbal" structures went through emergence criteria in order to determine whether or not they were morphological chunks or formulae.

full verb, therefore it was coded as a verbal affix for Stage 2 and only the cases of V1 as part of the V-*te* V structure were counted for Stage 3.

In this study, a total of 323 V-*te* V structures were identified from the entire corpus. The procedure for the registration and calculation of the occurrences was the same as that used for verbal affixes.

3. The passives and causatives (S-procedure – Stage 4): Only 11 instances of a sentence involving the passive or causative were identified. Following Kawaguchi (2005), if an utterance contained any passive or causative, it was coded as:

1.   sufficient evidence: the passive/causative verb accompanied SUBJ/ TOP marked with a particle *ga/wa* and/or OBLag marked with a particle *ni*;
2.   insufficient evidence: the passive/causative verb accompanied neither SUBJ/TOP marked with a particle *ga/wa*, nor OBLag marked with a particle *ni*; or
3.   negative evidence (an ill-formed sentence such as the passive/causative verb accompanied SUBJ/TOP and/or OBLag marked with the incorrect particles).

While in (2) the suppliance of a passive/causative verb form only shows the acquisition of lexical operation, an ill-formed sentence in (3), in which the subject marker *ga* (or the topic marker *wa*) and the dative marker *ni* are reversed, indicates that the learner has not acquired non-canonical mapping in the passive/causative.

Method of analysis
There has been debate for some time about what should be regarded as an 'acquisition point'; whether it is emergence or TL performance. The methodology of analysis used in this study was based on the emergence criteria proposed by Pienemann (1998). While the first production of a syntactic structure was considered as justifying that the application of a syntactic rule had emerged, more stringent criteria were applied to morphological development. At least three linguistic contexts were needed to claim that a certain verbal morpheme had emerged productively, that is, not as an unanalysed morphological chunk or formulaic. For example, *hanas-u* (talk-NONPAST), *kur-u* (come-NONPAST), and *hanashi-ta* (talk-PAST) constitute two lexical variations on the same form as well as two form variations on the same lexical base in the three linguistic contexts, thus satisfying the emergence criteria. In addition, this phenomenon must have continuity throughout the data collection period. Also, the context of each incidence was qualitatively examined in relation to other incidences to see whether it occurred due to a task effect or whether counter-evidence was available. Using these distributional analyses (Pienemann 1998), lexical variation for the affix -*te* in the V-*te* V structure was also checked. To determine the emergent point for verbal syntax in Japanese, the rule developed by Kawaguchi (2005) was applied. That is, the first occurrence of a passive/causative sentence with the correct assignment of SUBJ (or TOP) and/or

OBLag (i.e., sufficient evidence) qualified as an emergence point, although it was invalidated by negative evidence (e.g., the reversed assignment of SUB/TOP and OBLag) in some cases.

It is important to note that within each stage the emergence point for a sub-type of the verbal morpho-syntactic structure (or in the case of verbal affixes at least two subtypes) represents the entire structure, even though some subtypes emerged much later than others. The reason for this is that PT predicts learn-ability derived from the development of processing procedures (Pienemann 1998, p. 209). For example, the emergent points for some verbal affixes display evidence that the learner has acquired a skill needed to produce other types of verbal affixes as well because he/she has acquired the processing procedures for verbal inflec-tion as a whole. The same applies to the V-*te* V structures and passive/causative structures. Thus, variation in emergent points for sub-types of the structures in each stage does not contravene the tenets of PT because of the impact of prag-matic and phonological factors and potentially because of task effects. Similarly, cases of some verbal affixes which emerged later than some V-*te* V structures may be explained by those factors outside PT.

After determining the point of emergence for each of the verbal affixes, the V-*te* V structure and the passive/causative, an examination was undertaken to de-termine whether or not there were any implicational relationships between these emergence points for different levels of morpho-syntactic structures. To do this, implicational scaling (Guttman 1944; DeCamp 1971, 1973) was used in the cur-rent study.

Results

Developmental stages of verbal morpho-syntax in JSL by a child learner

In this section, the first research question is answered:

RQ1: Do developmental stages of acquisition exist in the interlanguage of a child learner of JSL?

To do this, the occurrences of verbal affixes, V-*te* V structures, and passive/causative structures in Shaun's interlanguage were collated into an implicational table (see Table 3 in Appendix D). Note that all figures are based on a token count. Follow-ing Di Biase and Kawaguchi (2002), for the passive/causative structures, the figure between the slashes denotes the number of occurrences showing the provision of sufficient evidence, insufficient evidence, or negative evidence respectively.

Based on Table 2, different levels of distributional analyses (Pienemann 1998) were conducted, first at the lexical level and then at the structural level. As a result, the point of emergence for verbal affixes was determined to be at Session 1, where Shaun had more than one lexical variety each within seven different forms and, at the same time, at least one of the lexically different verbs in each of these seven forms had the same lexical verb(s) with at least one different affix. This indicates that the emergence of verbal affixes, or lexical morphology, had already begun before the first data collection session. It was also confirmed that Session 8 was the point of emergence for the V-*te* V structure as it was revealed that both Sessions 2 and 6 provided counter-evidence. Two incidences of -*te aru* in Session 7 did not satisfy emergence criteria. With regard to the passive/causative, there was one case of sufficient evidence, seven cases of insufficient evidence, and one case of negative evidence for the passive sentence, and two cases of sufficient evidence for the causative sentence. However, the case of sufficient evidence for the passive structure in Session 10 was problematic in terms of the timing of the production, which occurred immediately after the reading of a book containing a similar structure, as well as due to its co-existence with a case of negative evidence during the same session. Therefore, it was decided that Session 23, which contained the causative sentence consisting of the causative form of the verb, the SUBJ marked with *ga* and the OBLag marked with *ni*, was the point of emergence for this structure.

In order to see more clearly whether or not an implicational relation could be found among the acquisition of these three types of verbal morpho-syntax in Japanese, the interpretation of Table 3 data was summarised into a simple format (Table 4 in Appendix E) based on the application of the emergence criteria for acquisition proposed by Pienemann (1998). The dotted lines were drawn by connecting the emergence points for the three verbal morpho-syntactic structures to see whether or not they represented the acquisition stages.

The results show that the emergence points for the three types of verbal morpho-syntactic structures, i.e., verb affixes, the V-*te* V structure and the passive/causative constitute a clear implicational relationship, indicating the existence of developmental stages of these structures in Shaun's interlanguage. A calculation for the coefficient of scalability shows that it was .90. This is well above the .60 suggested by Hatch and Lazaraton (1991, pp. 210–213) as the benchmark for an implicational relationship to be statistically significant. This means that Shaun acquired the three structures following the acquisition order of the L2 processes hypothesised in PT, i.e., lexical > phrasal > interphrasal.

Developmental stages of verbal morpho-syntax in JSL by a child learner and adult learners

In this section, the second research question is answered:

RQ2: Do the developmental stages of acquisition by a child learner of JSL match those of adult learners of JSL?

To do this, a comparison was undertaken between the results of the current study and those reported by Di Biase and Kawaguchi (2002) for instructed adult JSL learners.

For purpose of comparison, following Di Biase and Kawaguchi (2002), the results for all V-*te* V structures other than -*te iru* (the V-*te* V structure marked with durative/imperfective aspect) in the current study were grouped together. In the case of verbal inflection, only verbal affixes for the eight most common verb forms from Table 3 were used for the comparison. These are affixes for the four plain verb forms, namely -*u* (NONPAST), -*ta* (PAST), -*nai* (NON-PAST.NEG), -*nakatta* (PAST.NEG), and for the four polite verb forms, namely -*masu* (POL.NONPAST), -*mashita* (POL.PAST), -*masen* (POL.NONPAST.NEG), -*masendeshita* (POL.PAST.NEG).

The results of the current longitudinal study are shown in Table 5, together with the results of the longitudinal study by Di Biase and Kawaguchi (2002) in Table 6 (See both tables in Appendix F). Note that all figures in both tables are based on a token count. Also, as with the ones in Table 4 (Appendix E), the dotted lines in Tables 5 and 6 connect the emergence points for the three verbal morpho-syntactic structures, thus representing the acquisition stages for those structures.

A comparison of the results from the current study with those of Di Biase and Kawaguchi's (2002) show that there are similar developmental stages of verbal morpho-syntax in Japanese for the naturalistic child learner and the instructed adult learners. It appears that both types of learners progressed through the three hierarchical stages of acquisition hypothesised by Pienemann (1998), lending further support to the universality of PT.

On the other hand, a close examination of the results indicates some differences in the acquisitional pattern of verb inflection. The plain form of the verbs emerged earlier than the polite form of the verbs in the current study. In contrast, according to Kawaguchi (personal communication 2004, 2007), instructed adult learners in both longitudinal and cross-sectional studies by Di Biase and Kawaguchi (2002) appear to have acquired the polite forms earlier than the plain forms. However, it is important to note that the internal order of emergence points for verbal affixes in JSL cannot be explained using Lexical Functional Grammar (LFG) within a framework of the current PT (Di Biase & Kawaguchi 2002).

Discussion and conclusion

Discussion

The results of the current study clearly indicate that a developmental sequence of acquisition of verbal morpho-syntax does exist in the interlanguage of this naturalistic child learner of JSL. This sequence matched the one predicted by PT because the order of the acquisition of the three verbal morpho-syntactic structures was lexical > phrasal > interphrasal. In addition, it was found that the order of acquisition of verbal morpho-syntax by this child, namely verbal affixes > the V-*te* V structure > the passive/causative structure, was similar to that of instructed adult learners of JSL. These results support the application of PT to characterise the JSL of an uninstructed child learner. Together with previous research, it lends further support to an order of acquisition for JSL irrespective of age or instruction. It is therefore possible that within a framework of PT, maturational constraints (e.g., Butler & Hakuta 2004) do not impact on the acquisition order of these linguistic features.

The results of the current study have relevance not only to SLA theory, as mentioned above, but also to pedagogical development.

Firstly, the results of the current study indicate that both the instructed adult learners and the uninstructed child learner of JSL acquired the three verbal morpho-syntactic structures in the same order. If these findings are supported by further research, then this may suggest that instruction does not affect the developmental sequence of these particular structures. This would endorse the claim by Pienemann (1998) that "teachability is constrained by processability" (p. 250). If supported, it suggests curriculum developers and teachers for both adult and child JSL should take account of the acquisition order of these structures, namely verbal affixes > the V-*te* V structure > the passive/causative structures, when they design and implement a syllabus for teaching JSL.

Secondly, discrepancy in the results for the points of emergence for the polite and plain form of the verbs found between the results from the current study and those from studies by Di Biase and Kawaguchi (2002) could be "the degree of freedom implied in Hypothesis Space" (Pienemann 1998, p. 233). Pienemann (1998) claims that variation observed among learners whose procedural skills are at the same stage, i.e., within the same Hypothesis Space, could be due to (1) interlanguage variation, (2) the effect of instruction on interlanguage systems, (3) task variation, and (4) types of acquisition (p. 234). It is important to note that, while a semi-structured interview called 'Play student and teacher' was conducted to elicit the use of the polite forms of the verbs in the current study, none of the tasks used in Di Biase and Kawaguchi's (2002) study were designed to elicit the plain forms of the verbs in particular. This may make a direct comparison of the results between the two studies difficult in terms of the two types of verb forms. Therefore, at this stage it is not clear which factors (e.g., pragmatic factors, and in particular the availability of the linguistic contexts for appropriate levels of speech style according to age, or task effect) were responsible for the different choice of the verb forms found between the child and adult participants in the two studies. However, there is indeed an established perception in teaching JSL that polite forms are acquired first and then plain forms (e.g., Miyaji 1990). This seems to be largely based on the complexity of inflection for certain types of verbs in the plain forms and on the assumption about contexts for adult JSL learners, taking no consideration of the different linguistic contexts available for children learning JSL. Despite the complexity of inflection for certain types of verbs in the plain form, Shaun acquired the plain forms of verbs earlier than the polite forms. This is clearly due to the ample linguistic contexts for the plain forms such as play situations that Shaun, as a seven year old child, had in his Japanese environment. In contrast, it may be that the lack of linguistic contexts for him to use the polite form of verbs means that the point of emergence for them was delayed. On the other hand, it could be that adult learners are, in general, taught the polite forms first (Miyaji 1990) and lacked linguistic contexts for the plain forms. This is clearly an area that requires much further investigation.

The existence of "the degree of freedom" (Pienemann 1998, p. 233) in fact means that this is an area where teachers may be able to differentiate the points of emergence for structures through instruction according to the age or needs of learners. Japan reportedly has over 18,000 children at primary and lower secondary levels who require JSL instruction (Kodomo LAMP 2003): if the findings of this case study are supported by further research, then order of instruction is worth careful consideration for these young JSL learners. This may also apply to Japanese immersion settings and even JSL classes at a primary school level outside Japan. Clearly more research focusing on this area is needed.

Limitations and suggestions

This study took a longitudinal case study approach to investigate the acquisition of verbal morpho-syntax in Japanese by a child learner of JSL. As with any case study, readers should be wary of generalising findings that were obtained from the data of one participant. The participant in the current study was a young naturalistic learner of JSL who lived outside Japan. This is a unique context given that most of the child learners of Japanese in Australia are learners of JFL in a classroom setting. To test the generalisability of the results of the current study, more research is needed, using more varied participants, e.g., children of various ages, and in various contexts, e.g., instructed child and adolescent JFL learners in Australia and child JSL learners in Japan, so that changes in curriculum and syllabus design in relation to the three verbal structures according to the age and need of the learners may be considered.

For example, Ito's (1997) study of the acquisition of JSL by an eight year old Russian boy indicates that the subject seemingly had acquired verbal inflection including benefactive verbs, potential verbs and verbal affixes as part of subordinate clause earlier than the benefactive structures (V-*te ageru* accompanied with

OBLang). However, at this point, a comparison of the emergence points for the three verbal morpho-syntactic structures in question in the current study to those contained in Ito's is difficult, as her study did not appear to use the same criterion for emergence of morphology nor the same scales for stages of acquisition.

Also, the data collection period of the current study was one year and nine months, which was rather short compared with the study by Di Biase and Kawaguchi (2002). Unfortunately the beginning of the acquisition of verbal inflection was missed, and therefore it was impossible to find out the internal order of some verbal affixes. Also, a longer period of data collection could have ensured a clearer continuity of the occurrences of the passive/causative structures.

Conclusion

The current study investigated the acquisition of JSL by a seven year old Australian boy who was learning Japanese naturalistically. The case study approach allowed for a close observation and detailed analysis, both quantitative and qualitative, of the child's oral production. In addition, the study was undertaken within the framework of PT. Although the limitations of this single person case study were acknowledged, unlike most of the case studies of JSL undertaken previously, the strength of the results of the current study rests in them being based on an explanatory theory, namely PT, which made possible a comparison of the results of the current study with those of the adult JSL study by Di Biase and Kawaguchi (2002). The comparison shows that the child went through a similar developmental path in acquiring verbal morpho-syntax, namely verbal affixes > the V-*te* V structures > the passive/causative structures, to that of adult learners of JSL. The findings of the current study contribute to an understanding of child acquisition of JSL from a PT perspective. The accumulation of longitudinal case studies based on a framework, both in terms of theory and analysis, like the current study is believed to lead to more meaningful and productive outcomes in the studies in the acquisition of child JSL. For this, more collaborative efforts among JSL researchers will be needed.

References

Bailey, N., Madden, C. & Krashen, S. 1974. Is there a natural sequence in adult second language learning? *Language Learning* 24: 235–244.
Butler, Y. G. & Hakuta, K. 2004. Bilingualism and second language acquisition. In *The Handbook of Bilingualism*, T. Bhatia & W. Ritchie (eds), 114–146. Blackwell.
Cancino, H., Rosansky, E. & Schumann, J. 1978. The acquisition of English negatives and interrogatives by native Spanish speakers. In *Second Language Acquisition: A Book of Readings*, E. Hatch (ed.), 207–230. Rowley MA: Newbury House.

Clahsen, H. 1980. Psycholinguistic aspects of L2 acquisition: Word order phenomena in foreign workers' interlanguage. In *Second Language Development: Trends and Issues*, S. W. Felix (ed.), 57–79. Tübingen: Narr.

Di Biase, B. & Kawaguchi, S. 2002. Exploring the typological plausibility of Processability Theory: Language development in Italian second language and Japanese second language. *Second Language Research* 18(3): 274–302.

DeCamp, D. 1971. Implicational scales and sociolinguistic theory. *Linguistics* 17: 79–106.

DeCamp, D. 1973. Implicational scales and sociolinguistic linearity. *Linguistics* 73: 30–43.

Dulay, H. & Burt, M. 1973. Should we teach children syntax? *Language Learning* 23: 245–258.

Dulay, H. & Burt, M. 1974. Natural sequences in child second language acquisition. *Language Learning* 24: 37–53.

Guttman, L. 1944. A basis for scaling qualitative data. *American Sociological Review* 9: 139–150.

Hakånsson, G., Pienemann, M. & Sayehli, S. 2002. Transfer and typological proximity in the context of second language processing. *Second Language Research* 18(3): 250–273.

Hatch, E. & Lazaraton, A. 1991. *The Research Manual: Design and Statistics for Applied Linguistics*. New York NY: Newbury House.

Hyltenstam, K. & Abrahamsson, N. 2003. Maturational constraints in SLA. In *The Handbook of Second Language Acquisition*, C. J. Doughty & M. H. Long (eds), 539–588. Blackwell.

Ito, S. 1997. Nenshoosha nihongo gakushuusha no koobun shuutoku: Juudanteki jiree kenkyuu. *Hokkaidoo Daigaku Ryuugakusei Sentaa Kiyoo* 1: 68–82.

Kamura, N. 2001a. Developmental sequence of negation in Japanese by adult Chinese-speaking learners. *Acquisition of Japanese as a Second Language* 4: 63–81.

Kamura, N. 2001b. Acquisition study of Japanese negation by Chinese-speaking learners: Focusing on past tense. *Nihongo Kyooiku (Journal of Japanese Language Teaching)* 110: 72–81.

Kaplan, R. & Bresnan, J. 1982. Lexical-Functional Grammar: A formal system for grammatical representation. In *The Mental Representation of Grammatical Relations*, J. Bresnan (ed.), 173–281. Cambridge MA: The MIT Press.

Kawaguchi, S. 2005. Processability Theory and Japanese as a Second Language. *Acquisition of Japanese as a Second Language* 8: 83–114.

Kempen, G. & Hoenkamp, E. 1987. An incremental procedural grammar for sentence formulation. *Cognitive Science* 11: 201–258.

Kodomo LAMP. 2003. Retrieved July 10, 2004 from Ochanomizu Women's University, Language Acquisition and Maintenance Project (LAMP) Web site: http://members.at.infoseek.co.jp/ocha_larp/QandA.htm

Levelt, W. J. M. 1989. *Speaking: From Intention to Articulation*. Cambridge MA: The MIT Press.

Long, M. H. 1990. Maturational constraints on language development. *Studies in Second Language Acquisition* 12: 251–285.

Mackey. A. & Oliver, R. 2002. Interactional feedback and children's L2 development. *System* 30: 459–477.

Mayer, M. 1969. *Frog, Where Are You?* New York NY: New American Library.

Meisel, J., Clahsen H. & Pienemann, M. 1981. On determining developmental stages in natural second language acquisition. *Studies in Second Language Acquisition* 3(2): 109–135.

Miyaji, H. 1990. Teenee-tai/Futsuu-tai (Polite form/Plain form). In *Nihongo Kyooiku Jiten (Dictionary for Teaching Japanese as a Second Language)*, Nihongo Kyooiku Gakkai (ed.), 233–334. Tokyo: Taishukan.

Noro, I. 1995. Daini gengo ni okeru hiteikee no shuutoku katee – Chuugokujin no kodomo no jirei kenkyuu (The acquisition of negation in Japanese as a second language: A case study of a Chinese-speaking child). *Shizuoka Daigaku Kyooiku Gakubu Kenkyuu Hookoku (Jinbun Shakai Kagaku Hen)* 45: 1–12.

Oliver, R. 1995. Negative feedback in child NS-NNS conversation. *Studies in Second Language Acquisition* 18: 459–481.

Oliver, R. 1998. Negotiation of meaning in child interactions. *The Modern Language Journal* 82: 372–386.

Pienemann, M. 1980. The second language acquisition of immigrant children. In *Second Language Development: Trends and Issues*, S. W. Felix (ed.), 41–56. Tübingen: Narr.

Pienemann, M. 1998. *Language Processing and Second Language Development: Processability Theory*. Amsterdam: John Benjamins.

Pienemann, M., Di Biase, B., Håkansson, G. & Kawaguchi, S. 2005. Processing constraints on L1 transfer. In *Handbook of Bilingualism: Psycholinguistic approaches*, J. F. Kroll & A. M. B. de Groot (eds), 128–153. Oxford: OUP.

Pienemann, M., Di Biase, B. & Kawaguchi, S. 2005. Extending Processability Theory. In *Cross-linguistic Aspects of Processability Theory*, M. Pienemann (ed.), 199–251. Amsterdam: John Benjamins.

Pienemann, M. & Håkansson, G. 1999. A unified approach toward the development of Swedish as L2: A processability account. *Studies in Second Language Acquisition* 21: 383–420.

Pienemann, M. & Johnston, M. 1985. Towards an explanatory model of language acquisition. Paper presented at the Second Language Research Forum, University of California at Los Angeles, February 22–24.

Schmidt, R. 1983. Interaction, acculturation and the acquisition of communication competence. In *Sociolinguistics and Second Language Acquisition*, N. Wolfson & E. Judd (eds), 137–174. Rowley MA: Newbury House.

Sells, P. 1995. Korean and Japanese morphology from a lexical perspective. *Linguistic Inquiry* 26: 277–325.

Sells, P. 1999. Japanese postposing involves no movement. Paper presented at AILA 1999. Also retrieved 4 July 2002, from http://www-csli.stanford.edu/~sells/

Shirahata, T. 1993. Yooji no daini gaikokugo toshite no nihongo kakutoku to "no" no kajoo seesee. *Nihongo Kyooiku* 81: 104–115.

Wray, A. 2002. *Formulaic Language and the Lexicon*. Cambridge: CUP.

Wode, H. 1976. Developmental sequences in naturalistic L2 acquisition. In *Second Language Acquisition: A Book of Readings*, E. Hatch (ed.), 101–117. Rowley MA: Newbury House.

Wode, H. 1978. The L1 vs. L2 acquisition of English interrogation. *Working Papers on Bilingualism* 11: 1–13.

Yanagisawa, Y. 1995. *Nihongo Kyooiku No Gaikan*. Nihongo Kyooiku Gakkai.

Appendix A

Table 1. Hypothesised implicational sequence of processing procedures and predicted structures

Stage	Procedure	Structural outcome	Time 1	Time 2	Time 3	Time 4	Time 5
1	Word/lemma access	"words"	+	+	+	+	+
2	Category procedure	Lexical morphemes	–	+	+	+	+
3	Phrasal procedure	Phrasal information exchange	–	–	+	+	+
4	Sentence procedure (S-procedure)	Inter-phrasal information exchange	–	–	–	+	+
5	Subordinate clause procedure	Main and subordinate clause	–	–	–	–	+

(Based on Pienemann 1998, pp. 8–9)

Appendix B

List of Abbreviations

ADV	Adverb
ASP	Aspect
CAUS	Causative
DAT	Dative
DIREC	Directional
EP	Extended predicate
INF	Infinite
MAST	Master
NEG	Negative
NONPAST	Nonpast tense
NP	Noun phrase
OBJ	Object
OBLag	Oblique agent
PAST	Past tense
POL	Polite
QUOT	Quotative
SUBJ	Subject
TOP	Topic
V	Verb
VP	Verb phrase

Appendix C

Table 2. Task distribution

Session	1 Free form Interview	2 Two-way Descriptive task	3 Two-way Locative task	4 Narrative (Picture book)	5 Narratives (Cartoon)	6 Riddles	7 Semi-structured Interview	8 Spot the difference	9 Other games
P	✓								
1	✓	✓	✓	✓		✓			Paper doll story
2	✓	✓		✓	✓	✓	✓	✓	
3	✓		✓	✓	✓	✓	✓	✓	
4	✓	✓		✓		✓			Chess, Pokemon
5	✓		✓		✓			✓	Describing people
6	✓	✓		✓		✓	✓		
7	✓		✓		✓	✓		✓	
8	✓	✓		✓			✓		Picture description
9	✓		✓		✓	✓		✓	
10	✓	✓		✓			✓		Card game
11	✓		✓		✓	✓		✓	
12	✓	✓		✓			✓		Describing people
13	✓		✓		✓	✓		✓	The Snowman
14	✓	✓		✓			✓		Picture Description
15	✓		✓		✓	✓			Card game
16	✓	✓		✓			✓	✓	
17	✓		✓		✓	✓			A Simpsons story
18	✓	✓		✓					
19	✓		✓					✓	Describing people
20	✓	✓		✓	✓	✓			
21	✓		✓		✓				Cartoon strips, Teddy bear story, Picnic stories, Picture description, Chess
22	✓	✓		✓		✓			Card game
23	✓		✓		✓	✓		✓	Japanese Monopoly
24	✓	✓		✓				✓	Describing people
25	✓		✓	✓	✓	✓		✓	
26	✓	✓		✓	✓			✓	Card game, Japanese Monopoly

Note: ✓ = that task performed in this session.

Appendix D. Table 3. The occurrences of verbal affix, the V-te V structure and the passive/causative in Shaun's interlanguage

Structure	Session 1	2	3	4	5	6	7	8	9	10	11	12	13	14	15	16	17	18	19	20	21	22	23	24	25	26
Interphrasal																										
Passive	0	0	0	0	0	0	0	0	0	1/2/1	0	0	0	0	0/2/0	0/1/0	0	0	0	0/1/0	0	0	0	0	0/1/0	0
Causative	0	0	0	0	0	0	0	0	0	0	0	0	0	0	0	0	0	0	0	0	0	0	1/0/0	0	0/1/0	1/0/0
Phrasal (V-te V)																										
-te iru	0	0	0	0	0	4	0	3	1	13	2	25	2	12	3	14	0	4	14	3	18	10	10	12	21	15
-te aru	0	0	0	0	1	0	2	0	7	1	2	0	3	2	0	1	0	1	0	1	1	0	2	2	0	17
-te miru	0	0	0	0	0	0	0	0	0	2	0	0	2	0	2	2	2	0	2	2	0	0	0	0	0	1
-te shimau	0	0	0	0	0	0	0	0	0	0	0	5	0	0	0	0	0	0	0	1	0	0	2	10	0	0
-te ageru	0	0	0	0	0	0	0	0	0	0	0	0	0	0	1	1	0	0	0	1	0	3	0	0	0	2
-te kureru	0	0	0	0	0	0	0	0	1	0	0	1	1	0	0	0	1	1	1	0	0	0	0	0	0	2
-te morau	0	0	0	0	0	0	0	0	0	0	0	0	0	0	0	0	0	1	0	0	0	0	0	0	0	0
-te iku	0	0	1	1	0	0	0	0	0	1	0	0	0	1	2	0	1	1	1	0	0	0	3	3	2	1
-te kuru	0	2	0	0	0	0	0	0	0	1	0	0	1	3	0	3	3	1	1	1	0	1	4	3	2	0
-te kaeru	0	0	0	0	0	0	0	0	0	0	1	1	0	0	0	0	0	1	0	1	1	1	0	0	1	1
Lexical (Verbal affix)																										
-u	24	58	49	22	18	33	37	20	83	22	50	28	65	35	62	57	81	70	59	42	75	50	93	65	48	97
-ta	19	23	72	45	25	35	27	40	33	39	47	36	20	38	36	60	38	40	47	42	44	47	75	49	47	63
-nai	9	43	32	17	17	16	14	10	22	6	20	12	15	17	11	17	22	12	15	20	37	9	36	15	25	25
-nakatta	0	1	0	3	1	0	0	2	0	1	2	2	2	2	1	4	3	3	2	0	4	5	2	5	2	3
-oo	0	0	0	0	1	0	0	0	0	2	1	2	1	0	0	0	0	4	0	0	1	1	1	3	4	1
-teru	6	28	13	8	9	6	11	14	42	23	36	25	37	16	34	19	19	29	22	14	36	24	34	44	30	27
-teta	4	5	1	1	0	1	0	2	2	0	4	8	5	5	1	1	0	2	12	1	3	7	3	1	4	13
-tenai	3	9	4	2	1	6	10	2	7	4	12	8	5	7	3	3	4	0	12	1	1	7	7	17	13	4
-tenakatta	0	0	0	1	0	1	0	2	2	1	0	0	0	0	3	2	0	2	0	1	3	0	0	0	0	0
-chatta	0	0	0	0	2	3	0	2	0	0	0	0	1	2	0	1	1	3	3	2	3	1	1	0	0	2
-masu	0	1	0	0	0	7	0	7	0	4	11	33	0	3	1	12	0	0	1	3	5	6	7	1	23	1
-mashita	0	0	1	0	0	14	0	8	0	3	0	26	0	15	1	17	0	2	0	3	7	3	1	4	26	24
-masen	0	0	0	1	1	1	0	0	0	1	1	0	0	4	1	0	0	0	0	0	5	2	4	1	2	0
-masendeshita	0	0	0	0	0	0	0	0	0	0	0	0	0	3	0	3	0	2	0	0	2	0	0	0	2	1
-mashoo	0	0	0	0	0	1	0	0	0	0	0	0	0	0	0	0	0	0	0	0	0	0	0	0	0	0
-temasu	0	0	0	0	0	0	0	2	0	0	10	2	0	1	0	2	0	0	0	0	0	2	0	0	3	0
-temashita	0	0	0	0	0	0	0	7	0	0	0	0	0	0	0	0	0	0	0	0	0	0	0	0	0	4
-temasen	0	0	0	0	0	0	0	0	0	0	0	0	0	0	0	0	0	0	0	0	0	0	1	0	0	0
-temasendeshita	0	0	0	0	0	0	0	0	0	0	0	0	0	0	0	0	0	0	0	0	0	0	0	0	0	0
-te (request)	0	2	0	0	0	0	0	0	0	0	0	0	0	0	0	0	0	0	0	0	0	0	0	0	0	0
-te clause	2	1	19	11	1	39	32	13	19	37	38	16	69	27	26	54	40	67	58	70	44	55	35	46	36	34
-naide (negative request)	1	0	0	0	0	0	0	0	0	0	0	2	0	0	0	0	0	1	1	0	2	3	1	1	1	0
-naide/-nakute clause	0	0	0	0	0	0	0	0	0	8	3	1	5	25	0	2	2	1	1	1	4	1	2	2	2	1
-tete clause	0	0	0	0	1	0	0	0	0	2	2	1	72	0	0	2	2	1	1	0	0	1	0	0	0	8
Other affixes	1	2	4	2	0	3	2	0	4	2	5	3	10	2	2	7	7	10	2	5	10	5	7	6	7	11

Appendix E

Table 4. The acquisition of Japanese verbal morpho-syntax by Shaun in an implicational scale

Session Structure	1	2	3	4	5	6	7	8	9	10	11	12	13	14	15	16	17	18	19	20	21	22	23	24	25	26
S-procedure (Interphrasal)	–	–	–	–	–	–	–	–	–	–	–	–	–	–	–	–	–	–	–	–	–	–	–	+	–	+
Phrasal procedure (Phrasal)	–	–	–	–	–	–	–	+	+	+	+	+	+	+	+	+	+	+	+	+	+	+	+	+	+	+
Category procedure (Lexical)	+	+	+	+	+	+	+	+	+	+	+	+	+	+	+	+	+	+	+	+	+	+	+	+	+	+

(Scalability = .90)

Appendix F

Table 5. The acquisition of verbal morpho-syntax in JSL by a naturalistic child learner

Session / Structure	1	2	3	4	5	6	7	8	9	10	11	12	13	14	15	16	17	18	19	20	21	22	23	24	25	26
Interphrasal																										
Passive	0	0	0	0	0	0	0	0	0	1/2/1	0	0	0	0	0	0/2/0	0/1/0	0	0	0	0/1/0	0	0	0	0/1/0	0
Causative	0	0	0	0	0	0	0	0	0	0	0	0	0	0	0	0	0	0	0	0	0	0	0	1/0/0	0	1/0/0
Phrasal																										
-te iru	0	0	0	0	0	4	0	3	1	13	2	25	2	12	3	14	0	4	14	3	18	10	10	12	21	15
Other V-te Vaux	0	2	1	0	1	0	2	0	9	5	2	7	7	6	6	6	8	6	4	5	2	5	11	15	3	24
Lexical																										
-u	24	58	49	22	18	33	37	20	83	22	50	28	65	35	62	57	81	70	59	42	75	50	93	65	48	97
-ta	19	23	72	45	25	35	27	40	33	39	47	36	20	38	36	60	38	40	47	42	44	47	75	49	47	63
-nai	9	43	32	17	17	16	14	10	22	6	20	12	15	17	11	17	22	12	15	20	37	9	36	15	25	25
-nakatta	0	1	0	3	1	0	0	2	1	1	1	2	1	1	0	4	3	4	1	0	4	5	2	5	2	3
-masu	0	1	0	0	0	7	0	7	0	4	11	33	1	3	1	12	0	1	1	0	5	6	7	1	23	1
-mashita	0	1	0	0	0	14	0	8	0	3	0	26	0	15	1	17	0	2	0	3	7	3	1	4	26	24
-masen	0	0	1	1	0	1	0	0	0	1	1	1	0	4	1	3	0	0	0	0	5	2	4	1	10	0
-masendeshita	0	0	0	0	0	0	0	0	0	0	0	0	0	3	0	3	0	0	0	0	0	0	0	0	2	1

(Scalability = .90)

Table 6. The acquisition of verbal morpho-syntax in JSL by an instructed adult learner

Interview number / Structure	1	2	3	4	5	6	7	8	9	10	11	12	13
Interphrasal													
Passive	0	0	0	0	0	0	0	0	0	1/0/0	0/0/1	0/2/0	0
Causative	0	0	0	0	0	0	0	0	0	0	3/1/0	0	0
Benefactive	0	0	0	0	0	0/2/0	0	0	1/0/0	1/0/0	0/1/0	0	3/2/0
Phrasal													
-te iru	0	0	0	6	2	0	2	1	1	4	2	4	5
Other V-te-Vaux	0	0	0	0	0	4	0	0	1	5	1	3	6
Lexical													
Vstem-POL (-masu)	9	18	0	11	17	2	4	5	23	13	13	16	15
Vstem-POL-PAST (-mashita)	0	1	12	12	2	20	12	2	10	20	8	20	16
Vstem-POL-NEG (-masen)	0	0	0	2	3	0	1	1	1	2	5	3	4
Vstem-POL-NEG-PAST (-masendeshita)	0	0	0	0	0	0	0	0	0	0	0	0	0

(Scalability = 1.0)
(Based on Di Biase & Kawaguchi 2002, p. 298)

Learning a second language in the family

Rosamond Mitchell and Chong Nim Lee
University of Southampton

This chapter shows how home activities can contribute to child L2 learning. The chapter draws on a longitudinal case study of a Korean family living temporarily in England. During shared L2 reading at home, and associated discussion and role play, the children developed their L2 word knowledge, their ability to explain and describe in L2, and a range of interaction skills. Sociodramatic play acting out the routines of English school life was also a popular home activity which built children's confidence and readiness for participation in 'real' school. In both types of activity, the involvement of different configurations of family members with differing levels of English knowledge provided a stimulus for creative and 'fun' use of English, as well as mutual support and flexible scaffolding which maximised all the children's opportunities to use and learn English.

Introduction and overview

There are many social circumstances in which children experience more than one language from birth, and are raised in bilingual or multilingual families where they learn to link particular languages with different significant adults and/or social situations (Kasuya 2002). Others are raised in local or regional language communities where they encounter a more powerful national language as the medium of instruction when they embark on formal schooling. Such children may be the members of indigenous groups, e.g., child L1 speakers of Quechua in the Andes who encounter Spanish in school and public life (Hornberger 1988) or Xhosa speakers in South Africa schooled through English (Prinsloo 2004). They may also be the children of newer but settled immigrant communities, e.g., child Sylheti speakers in Tower Hamlets, London who encounter English as the wider environmental language and in school (Gregory 2001).

This chapter deals with a special type of childhood L2 learning, which results from the temporary family mobility increasingly associated with globalisation of professional activity. The children in such families are confronted with the necessity of L2 learning if they are to take part in age appropriate learning, social and leisure activities. They are less visible as 'problems' in the educational system than the children of large settled immigrant minority groups, partly because of smaller numbers and temporary residence, and partly also because the professional standing and educational level of the parents are seen as buffering the children against possible problems. Perhaps as a result, the L2 learning experiences of such children have been less studied than those of disadvantaged language minorities (though see e.g., Willett (1995) for a study of ESL learning by first graders in an international elementary school in the USA, and Bongartz and Schneider (2003) for learning of German L2 by American children during a year's stay in Germany).

But what exactly are the practices within the individual, short-stay migrant family which promote their children's L2 learning and educational wellbeing more generally? This chapter explores this issue from a sociocultural perspective, by examining the experience of a particular Korean L1 family, who had relocated to live temporarily in a small city in southern England. In doing so we adopt the view of young learners as "active, competent and intentional participants" in language learning processes, expressed by Gregory et al. (2004a: 15). We acknowledge the powerful commitment of many school age children to join effectively in the community of practice of the primary school classroom, and form peer relationships there, and the consequent use of home literacy and play settings to develop ESL proficiency. We examine how ESL activity can be intertwined with a range of social relationships at home (with parent, grandparent, siblings and playmates). Overall we draw a picture of home and leisure activities as 'safe' settings where ESL skills relevant for coping with the external environment can be collaboratively developed, with distinctive contributions by each member of the family group.

A family ethnography: Introducing Susan, Amy and Diana

In this section we introduce the Korean L1 children whose ESL learning is described in this chapter, and describe the methodology used to trace their learning through a family-based longitudinal case study. The children belonged to a 'short-stay' professional family who lived in England for two years, while the mother was a student in an English university town. She was accompanied during her two-year stay by her own two children, who are here called by their English names 'Susan' and 'Amy'. Susan was aged nine at time of arrival, and Amy was aged six. Her husband remained in Korea for work reasons, but she was also accompanied by her own mother, who supported her in running the household. After five months the family in England was completed by the arrival of Diana, aged eight, also a Korean L1 speaker and the cousin of Susan and Amy. The three children were expected by the whole extended family to gain an educational benefit from this temporary 'immersion' experience in English. (For full details of participants see Lee 2005)

Mother was an English teacher by profession, who already spoke English fluently, but Grandmother did not understand any English beyond basic greetings. Susan had studied English with her mother from babyhood in Korea and had reached an intermediate level before moving to England. The other two children had attended elementary school in Korea and were already able to read and write Korean, but had received limited instruction in English. Once in England, the children were all enrolled in regular classes of the local primary school, which had only small numbers of other ESL children, including a few other Korean L1 children. Outside school they followed a busy routine including music and swimming lessons, attendance at Brownies/Guides, and occasional treats such as horse-riding. They attended a Korean church and its social activities, including formal lessons in Korean literacy. Grandmother also ensured that the children read in Korean every day, and helped them study mathematics in Korean.

Documentation of the children's ESL socialisation started around three months after the arrival of Susan and Amy in England, and continued for nine months. A wide range of data was collected almost daily. The corpus eventually included repeated picture description activities to measure the children's ESL proficiency, using pictures from a children's puzzle book (O'Hare 1990, 1991), informal comments, written notes and reports from their class teachers, writings in English produced by the children, and a detailed research journal kept by Mother. However the main dataset consisted of audio and video recordings made in home settings, documenting both L1 and L2 conversational, literacy and play activities. The individual recordings varied in length from a few minutes to over one hour, and were made on 100 separate occasions, between November 2002 and September 2003. The recorded corpus filled 60 90-minute audiocassettes, and 10 120-minute videocassettes. The equipment was operated either by Mother or by Susan, i.e., always by 'insiders' to the study, and the recorded data have three components: various home activities (reading aloud, language games, story-telling, role-playing, etc.), interviews with children about current activities (reading, writing, playing), and pre- and post-assessments to investigate spoken language development and change of learning strategies over time.

From this large and varied corpus, Lee (2005) selected two key event types: home reading, and home play. Six episodes were selected to represent each event type, with a focus on the child Amy as a central participant. Apart from this, the episodes were selected so as to represent the full timescale of the study, to include varied interlocutors with different social relationships with Amy, to include varying amounts of Korean-English codeswitching, and to illustrate use of a range of mediating tools such as books or play props. These excerpts were analysed fully in Lee (2005) using a sociocultural perspective on L2 socialisation (Lantolf 2000; Lantolf & Thorne 2006). In sociocultural theory, the development of cognition is seen as the result of participation with others in goal-directed activity. Lee's

(2005) study is particularly concerned with how routine home activities such as L2 medium shared reading and peer play offer ESL learners opportunities to notice and appropriate new language, and how participants support and 'scaffold' each others' learning. In this chapter a small number of episodes have been selected and discussed to illustrate these processes.

Family literacy and L2 learning

Official educational discourse in Western Anglophone culture values certain formal traditions of 'home reading' for all children and expects families to implement at home a range of school derived reading practices, which are widely believed to contribute to the development of schooled literacy: see e.g., discussion of English 'early years' curricula in Gregory and Williams (2001: 158–159), and in Marsh (2003). The so-called 'family literacy' movement (Hannon 1995, 2000; Jordan, Snow, & Porche 2000) has developed as a way of tackling perceived literacy deficits in the homes of disadvantaged families, primarily by engaging mothers and other carers from traditionally non-literate or low literate backgrounds in the literacy practices of the school itself. By extension, minority language families have also been assumed to have impoverished home literacy traditions, and to require encouragement to import school literacy practices into the home (Green & Halsall 2004; Gregory & Williams 2001: 159; King & Hornberger 2005). However until recently there was little research into actual home L2 literacy practices.

This gap is being remedied by a growing ethnographic literature, called 'Syncretic Literacy Studies' by Gregory et al. (2004b). These studies explore home and community literacy practices in multilingual communities, following the overall anthropological trend in literacy studies (Street 1993). One example is offered by Williams and Gregory (2001), who describe the literacy practices of both monolingual English and bilingual Sylheti/English families in Spitalfields, London, the latter influenced considerably by traditions of Koranic literacy and Bengali literacy, in addition to school models. Another is offered by Volk and De Acosta (2004) who describe home reading practices among bilingual Spanish/English families in Puerto Rico. Such studies highlight how children can draw on varied cultural and linguistic worlds to make sense of new experiences, syncretising languages, literacy and cultural practices from varied contexts.

The work of Gregory and associates is thus clearly valuable in combating 'deficit' views of disadvantaged working class and minority language families, and in demonstrating the diverse range of intergenerational literacy practices in which they engage. Most importantly, these studies show the proactive ways in which children can move between languages and manage L2 literacy experiences at home. However, they say relatively little about the specific language learning opportunities offered in home literacy events, i.e., how children come to appropriate new language and become more fluent in its use. In the next section we examine how our short-stay, professional case study family engaged in shared L2 literacy activities at home, and the scaffolded language learning opportunities which resulted.

Home L2 literacy activities around school storybooks

In the case of the Korean family, English storybooks were routinely brought home from school by the two younger children (Amy and Diana), with the expectation that these would be read and discussed with family members. The children normally read these books aloud to Mother, and discussed the story and pictures with her; sometimes they read to Grandmother and interpreted the story to her in Korean. Sometimes one child would read alone to an adult, but often the other children were present and the activity developed into a group affair. Mother took the lead in making English the main language of these interactions, but codeswitching also happened, as can be seen in the transcribed extracts which follow.

The documented activities thus fitted the general expectations of the school home reading scheme, but at times they went considerably beyond it. The detailed recordings and transcriptions allow us to examine closely how these repeated book-readings contributed to ESL development.

Developing L2 word knowledge

Firstly, and unsurprisingly, the reading sessions seemed to promote vocabulary development – there are many examples of pronunciation practice, discussion and clarification of word meaning, from the earliest recordings, as in Extract 1, where Amy is reading aloud to Mother and Susan.

(1) (Text: *Nowhere and Nothing*: Amy has been in England for 2 months 26 days)

1 Amy: What means 'lay', mummy?
2 Mother: Look at the picture. What is he doing?
3 Amy: (Giving a shrug)
4 Mother: He lies on the bed now. He lay on the bed yesterday. Now can you understand?
5 Amy: (Nodding) 누워있다 to lie. (with horizontal gesture)

Here we see Mother referring to a picture, modelling the target word in contrasting utterances, and checking Amy's understanding. In Extract 2, taken from the same reading episode, Susan and Mother collaborate to help Amy with another apparent word problem:

(2)

10	Amy:	…watching people go down [streit]. (Text: … watching people go down the street)
11	Susan:	No, go down street.
12	Amy:	No, go down [steit].
13	Susan:	See! Street.
14	Amy:	[Streit].
15	Mother:	Where is this place?
16	Amy:	Airport.
17	Mother:	Why do you think it is an airport?
18	Amy:	This helicopter, this airplane. (pointing to the flying objects in the sky)
19	Mother:	What is it? (pointing to a street light)
20	Amy:	I dunno.
21	Mother:	I think it's the street. The boy is looking out at the street. People come and go.
22	Amy:	What's [strit]?
23	Susan:	You can go out and see the street. There are many cars.
24	Amy:	Ah!. 길 road. I know the street.
25	Mother:	Now why did you read 'straight' for this word 'street'?
26	Amy:	(Points to the person who is standing in the foreground of the picture) See this man is straight (standing upright with her arms hanging straight).

In this more complex extract, we can see that Amy has been attempting to construct an overall interpretation of the text, but has used elements from the picture to support a misreading of the unfamiliar noun 'street' as the known adjective 'straight'. Susan's modelling of the correct pronunciation (lines 11, 13) does not solve the problem therefore, and clarification of the scenario is needed before Amy can appreciate that 'street' is a new, different word and grasp its meaning. Accordingly Mother redirects Amy's attention to the elements in the picture most relevant to the verbal narrative, and Susan supplies a definition of 'street'. This kind of flexible, diagnostic scaffolding helps resolve lexical problems, i.e., helps 'bottom up' text processing, but also seems to support 'top down' processing and interpretation of the overall narrative.

Developing global understanding

Further reading episodes with Mother show Amy moving to a more strategic level of L2 reading comprehension, where word decoding is less important. Five weeks after the *Nowhere and Nothing* episode, for example, Amy was recorded reading *Fred's Birthday Party (FBP)* to Mother. She is eager to read aloud and responds fairly minimally to Mother's preliminary questioning in English (a regular practice):

(3) (Text: *Fred's Birthday Party*. Amy has been in England for 4 months 18 days)

13 A: (Reading the cover page) 'This story is about Fred's birthday. How old do you think he is? When is your birthday?'

14 M: (Interrupting Amy's reading) When is your birthday?

15 A: May fourth.

16 M: May first?

17 A: Fourth.

18 M: Okay. What would you like to do on your birthday?

19 A: Eat the cake, and get the present, and open the present (chuckle), and ahmm ...

20 M: Who brings your presents?

21 A: Friends!

22 M: Friends. What do you have to do first to get presents from your friends?

23 A: Thank you!

24 M: I think you have to invite friends and then you can get some gifts from your friends. Right?

25 A: (Chuckle) Yes, Mum. (counting) Louise, Hazel, Eve, Emma, Mary Norley, Freya Norley, Megan, Olivia, ... Maria, Sophia, and Mia, eleven.

26 M: How about your boy friends?

27 A: No!

28 M: Do you have a boy friend you like?

29 A: No.

30 M: No?

31 A: Can I read please?

32 M: Yes.

33 A: (Reading the story without interruption for two minutes)

After this first reading, Amy herself attempts to initiate a discussion of the final picture that shows Fred's birthday party:

(4)

34 A: This picture is...

35 M: Wow! What is this picture about? Can you explain? What can you see there?

36 A: Umm

37 M: Do you like that picture?

38 A: Umm. ... Yes.

39 M: Why? What can you see? Who are they?

40 A: ...Fred, Stanley, Bunny and Kitty and Lucy.

41   M: What are they doing?
42   A: in the party.
43   M: They are having a party?
44   A: Yeah.
45   M: What can you see at the party ((parade))?
46   A: ...
47   M: What can you see?
48   A: Play, play, play.

However, as seen in Extract 4, at this point Amy needed supportive scaffolding to provide even a simple description, and she quickly asked to read the story aloud again.

Her confident reading suggested that her overall comprehension of this story was good, and this was confirmed a few days later when Amy wrote a story for homework which was clearly based on *FBP*. Overall this episode shows how repeated story-reading could support eventual L2 text production, even if at the time of reading there was a 'gap' between what could be read/interpreted, and what could be produced orally.

Managing L2 interaction

As we have seen in the discussion of *FBP*, Amy had her own views on the management of literacy events, and preferred to spend time on activities she could perform with confidence (reading aloud, in the case of *FBP*). As time passed, she was able to manage more diverse aspects, and other family members adapted themselves to this. Two weeks after the *FBP* episode, Amy was reading another storybook to Mother, titled *Mr. Whisper*. Again she read the story aloud with confidence. However, this time Amy appropriated a 'teacher' role, and Mother agreed to role play her 'student'. This gave Amy the responsibility for managing turn-taking, and for providing explanations and descriptions, in addition to reading the story itself. (See e.g., Aukrust (2004) for a discussion of the contribution of explanation to L2 development.) In tackling these challenges she produced considerably more extended and ambitious English utterances, along with some codeswitching.

(5)   (Text: *Mr. Whisper*. Amy has been in England for 5 months 3 days)

1   A: The story is <u>Mr. Whisper</u>. This is short but this is good...Okay, I'm gonna read this.
2   M: What is the story about...why is the name of the story 'Whisper'?
3   A: Because Mr. Whisper, not aloud his talking but a little woman, cup woman mean is ahmm cup, cup 가게주인 *shop owner* ...okay?
4   M: Who is 컵 가게주인 *the owner of cup shop*? Mr. Whisper?
5   A: No, woman.

6 M: Woman is the owner of the cup shop?

7 A: Yeah, . . .and called cup cup woman, and . . . Mr. Whisper want blue cup but he um he says to woman but, but Mr. Whisper so tired and uhm she he said something but woman can't hear, because Mr. Whisper so not aloud, so quiet.

8 M: That's why his name is called Mr. Whisper.

9 A: Yes. Okay?

10 M: Whisper means voice is so quiet and not loud?

11 A: Okay. I gonna read. . . . <u>Mr. Whisper broke his blue cup. He went to the cup shop.</u> '(in a whispery voice) <u>Do you have a blue cup?' he said with his whispery voice. Louder, I can't hear you.' said the woman. Mr. Whisper said,</u> '(in a whispery voice) <u>Do you have a blue cup?' 'Louder, I still can't hear you.' the woman said. The Mr. Whisper sout in his whis-</u> =

12 M: = <u>Shouted</u> =

13 A: = <u>shouted in his whispery voice.</u> '(in a small but yelling voice) <u>I want a blue cup!' 'I still can't hear you' said the cup woman. Your voice is too whispery. You need it, it's some big. . .</u> um. . .. There are pictures the first page.

14 M: Okay, . . .the woman asked Mr. Whisper to speak louder. =

15 A: Yeah.

16 M: = Wow (commenting on picture) Mr. Whisper has some red jacket, red like a swallow tail –

17 A: No, no, no I'll ask the coat, question. Okay? Uhm Mr. Whisper. What Mr. Whisper got in. . .uhm what . . . 한국말로 할께. *I'll do it in Korean.* Mr. Whisper 가 뭐를 입고 있지? *What does Mr. Whisper wear?*

18 M: I think –

19 A: 손들어야지? *You should raise your hand?* =

20 M: Okay. (Raises her hand)

21 A: =Yes.

22 M: I think Mr. Whisper wears some red swallow tail jacket.

23 A: Oh, this!

24 M: Yes.

25 A: and Mr. Whisper got?

26 M: . . .hair?

27 A: White hair.

28 M: Okay, white hair.

29 A: A woman got? (trying to describe the woman without waiting for the answer) Black, face grey face, black hair and some, and some, blue and some, red some, dress and some necklace white necklace and ((it's)) like this.

30 M: Okay (mimics posture of 'cup woman')

31 A: Yes. . ..Okay? then next page. Uhm, <u>Mr. Whisper sout</u> – =

32 M: =<u>shouted</u>=

33   A: =shouted in his whispery voice, 'I want a blue cup.' 'I still can't hear you.'
            said the woman. Your voice is too whispery. What you need is some big
            noisy porridge.

In Extract 5 we see that Amy is already familiar with the story and can produce
an introductory summary of it (lines 3–8). She checks the understanding of her
'student' (lines 3, 9, 31) and keeps control of turn-taking (lines 17–21). She asks
questions about the picture, first in Korean then in English (17, 25, 29), and produces a detailed description of one character herself (29). She takes account of
Mother's correction without losing the initiative (31, 32). Overall, the *Mr. Whisper*
episode shows how Amy's motivation to lead the session, and Mother's acceptance
of this, provided her with increased pragmatic and linguistic opportunities. At the
same time Mother's skill in role play provided some helpful scaffolding and linguistic modelling (e.g., for picture description, lines 16 and 30), and also promoted
Amy's attempts at story summary and explanation (lines 3–8).

Repetition and fluency development

The final literacy episode we examine here took place a couple of weeks later,
when Amy and Susan had been in England for just under six months, and Diana
for less than two months. The episode involved Mother, all three children and a
home reader brought home by Amy *(Goodbye Lucy: GL)*. With a focus on Diana,
this episode illustrates the power of 'repetition' for L2 internalisation and fluency
development (Rydland & Aukrust 2005).

The text of *GL* takes the form of a dialogue between 'Lucy', setting off to school,
and her 'Mum'. First of all, Mother encourages Diana to read aloud, and checks
her comprehension of basic vocabulary, with support from Amy. After checking
other individual words, Mother then checks Diana's more strategic understanding
of the storyline, which involves recapping the vocabulary again. Amy then reads
the story aloud, Diana makes suggestions in Korean turning it into a cooperative
role play, and Amy locates some props. However, Mother first of all draws in Susan
to model the story reading one more time; Diana echoes Susan's reading aloud as
she goes along.

The actual role play is repeated no less than six times, with the children acting in pairs and taking different parts each time. With successive attempts, more
props are added, and the children become less reliant on the storybook text. These
attempts lead to confusion at times, but overall there are clear gains in fluency and
ambition especially for Diana. Extracts 6 (second role play) and 7 (fifth role play)
show Diana's two attempts at playing the role of 'Mum', first with Amy as 'Lucy',
and later with Susan:

(6)
1   D: 'Good bye Lucy'.
2   A: 'Good bye...(giggle) Oops, I forgot something'.
3   D: °이거 다 외웠는데 *(I) memorized it all* °.
4   A: 'Mum, I forgot something. [I forgot book' =
5   D: [(giggling)   = um 'Here you are'.
6   A: 아니야 *you are wrong*.
7   M: Okay, it's okay.
8   D: 'Here it is. Good bye Lucy =   = Good bye Lucy' =
9   A: = 'good bye- =   = Good
            bye mum...Oo, oops, I forgot something. [Mum, mum I forgot
            lunch'.
10 D: [(giggling)
11 D: (continuing giggling)...'Good bye Lucy'.
12 D&A: (can't stop laughing for some time)
13 M: 해봐, 빨리 *Try it in a hurry*.... 얼른 해 *Hurry up*. 'Good bye' =
14 A: = 'Good bye mum'.
15 D: 'Good bye-' um =
16 M: =Lucy.
17 D: 잠깐만요 *just a moment*. Uh, 'good bye Lucy'.
18 A: 'Good bye mum... Oops, I forgot something'... Wha- What?
19 D: 'You've, you've got your bag, you've got your. 아니 *no*, you- you've got
            your bag, you've got, you've got your book, you've got your lunch.
            What is it?'
20 A: 'I know. I forgot my good bye hug'.
21 A&D: (giggling)
22 M: Okay, Good job!
23 D: 한번 더 해요 *Let's do it once more*.

(7)
1   D: 'Good bye Lucy'
2   S: 'Good bye mum.'
3   D: 'Oopsy, I forgot something...'
4   S: 'Mum, I forgot my book'.
5   D: 'Here you, here you is' =
6   M: =Here it is =
7   D: = 'Here you it is. Good bye Lu-. Good bye Lucy.'
8   S: 'Good bye mum. Oops, I forgot something. Mum, mum I forgot my
            lunch. Hurry Up!
9   D: Yes!... (giggles, making a gesture of finding something) °어 딨지? *Where
            is it?*°
10 S: (in a hurry) 'I forgot my lunch'.
11 D: 'Oh, urr...um, Good bye Lucy'.

```
12  S:   'Good bye mum. Oh, I forgot something'.
13  D:   (shouting) 'What? You give up, your. . . =
14  M:                                      = you've got =
15  D:   = you've got your bag, you've got your book, you've got your lunch.
         What? What is this?'
16  S:   'I know. I forgot my good bye hug.'
17  D:   (yelling and hugging Susan tightly)
```

Diana is more accurate in Extract 6, when she comments in Korean private speech that she has 'memorised' everything, and acts out her role using accurately reproduced English sentences from the story, though with some hesitations and dysfluencies (lines 15, 19). Interestingly she substitutes the sentence 'here you are' for the sentence 'here it is' found in the text (line 5), but can self-correct when criticised by Amy (line 6); presumably both these English sentences have been rote learned as chunks. In Extract 7, Diana is evidently role playing with confidence, but is less accurate; in lines 5 and 7 it seems that some analysis of these same chunks may be taking place. In line 7, for example, even after a correction from Mother, she produces a combined sentence 'here you it is', which suggests that some discrete elements have been identified within the chunks, and an attempt is being made at recombining these. But overall this episode illustrates the power of repetition and intensive recycling of limited amounts of interactive language. By the end, Diana has clearly internalised some expressions such as 'I forgot X', and new vocabulary items such as 'hug'.

Immediately following the *GL* role plays, Diana suggested that they should do the same with her own reader, a narrative storybook with a very basic verbal storyline, and no actual dialogue, but also including rich pictures elaborating on the events. After reading aloud in turn and a discussion of the story situation led by Mother, Amy started to suggest possible dialogue, and the children successfully acted out the story several times. In this episode, with no predetermined dialogue to memorise, Diana initially contributed words and phrases only. However, after repeated role play, and with some scaffolding from the others, she again succeeded in drawing on previously learned chunks, and on dialogue contributed by the other children, and produced some full, original sentences, again illustrating how flexible repetition in a supportive environment appears to 'push' language development.

Collaboration and scaffolding in L2 development

From this short account of selected home literacy events a number of key points can be highlighted. First of all it is clear that short texts with a strong narrative line and attractive, stimulating illustrations can provide a very valuable resource for modelling, repetition and internalisation of new L2 material. However, the learners need scaffolding and support when attempting to process even such 'easy' texts, not only to model forms and negotiate meanings at word and sentence level, but to ensure they stay in touch with the overall narrative schema and to locate new language within this. Flexible adult scaffolding moves between necessary focus on local L2 forms and meanings, and more global comprehension and interpretation of narrative situations; we saw how Mother adapted her scaffolding, from the early sessions when Amy needed much help with word recognition and bottom up decoding (*Nowhere and Nothing*), to later sessions when Amy could show much greater initiative, but still needed a stimulus to engage fully in discourse management and explanation (*Mr Whisper*). The inclusion of a new near-beginner learner (Diana) alongside Amy, in three- and four-way literacy events, meant Mother had to provide more differentiated scaffolding (*Goodbye Lucy*). However the children also supported each others' learning, partly by scaffolding one another linguistically. They also greatly stimulated each other imaginatively, competing for roles, developing these with props and side sequences, and engaging in jokes and language play. This play orientation sustained them through extended spells of L2 activity, when new language was modelled, repeated and internalised and known language re-used and re-sequenced, so that even within individual episodes, there is clear evidence for the activation of new L2 material and increasing oral fluency.

Play and L2 learning

Play is seen as central to all aspects of early childhood education (Bruce 1991), including first language development (Cook-Gumperz 1986; Galda & Pellegrini 1985); sociodramatic play contributes significantly to the development of children's communicative competence in L1 (Heath 1983; Saville-Troike 1989). Others have studied play among L2 learners in nursery and pre-school settings, including talk about play activities such as drawing, sociodramatic play, and word play (joking, etc.) (Cekaite & Aronsson 2004, 2005; Rydland & Aukrust 2005). L2 pretend play is seen as providing excellent scope for both self- and other-repetition, promoting involvement in L2 interaction and engagement with the perspective of others through L2 (Rydland & Aukrust 2005). L2 joking and word play also provide opportunities for developing fluency and taking control of new L2 forms (Cekaite & Aronsson 2005; Prinsloo 2004).

A more strategic view of the role of play in L2 development is expressed by Gregory et al. (2004a). They argue that play is "a context in which children are the active creators of their own development, that is, they provide their own scaffolding ... within the context of play, children often create rich, syncretic worlds drawing on the many resources in their lives" (p. 8). Crucially, L2 medium play provides contexts where learners "feel safe enough to risk experimentation" (p. 16), learning about language structure, pronunciation and cultural usage. Heath and Chin (1985) report a case study of a Korean L1 child just under 3 years old, learning L2 English, who codeswitched regularly during home play. They draw similar conclusions to Gregory et al. (2004a) regarding the need for a 'safe' zone to build up competence: "For nonnative-English speaking children whose playmates are English-speakers, the need to learn to handle dramatic play narratives must soon become painfully obvious ... SooJong did not want to risk such narratives at school and chose to try them out and practise them at home until she felt secure to try her English with playmates" (p. 164).

Playing school in L2: Susan, Amy and Hazel

The Korean family study also produced numerous instances of sociodramatic play. Here we concentrate on two examples of 'playing school', and show how this activity allows the children to take control of aspects of L2 which are vital for social and academic success outside the home.

In the first episode discussed here, Amy and Susan had been in England for almost five months, and were playing at home with Hazel, an L1 English speaker and a classmate of Amy. Hazel made an early bid to be the teacher, but Amy suggested Susan should take the role; the play continued for almost two hours, supported by suggestions from Mother, including offers of food. Susan was teacher throughout, and Hazel and Amy acted various pupils. The different activities included a spelling test and a maths lesson; Extract 8 comes from the 'spelling test'.

(8)

16	S:	Now, spelling test! You stay here, end of the room. And you, stay here!
17	H:	Wow, ((-)) I can't hear.
18	S:	because you can cheat it.
19	H:	What? (giggle)
20	S:	This is the test.
21	H:	Of course you got teeth. I haven't ...
22	S:	First one!
23	A:	Bring!
24	S:	아니야! 내가 해야 돼. No! I should do (it). Number 1!
25	A:	Bring!
26	S:	'Stephanie'! (giggle)
27	A:	Owu, I don't know.
28	H:	S-T-E-P-H- ...A-N-I-E
29	S:	Yes.
30	H:	Well done, my spelling.
31	A:	°I don't ((-))°
32	S:	and second question! Write boobabo. (giggle)

33 H: What?
34 S: Write down, 'animal'!
35 A: °animal°
36 H: (raising her hand) Uh?
37 S: Yes.
38 H: A-N-I-M-A-L
39 S: Yes.
40 A: It's too HARD!
41 S: Write down, oh no, who can tell me how spell 'Radio'?... Yes.
42 H: R-A-D- radio..-Ahmm- I-O?
43 S: Yes...Who can spell, who can say, no, who can spell 'Bag' for me?
44 H: Beg for me?
45 S: Yes.
46 A: B-A-T
47 S: No, BAG!...Yes.
48 A: B-A-G.

This extract shows Susan managing the physical environment (16–20), thinking of suitable words of varying difficulty, and checking answers. She also overrides Hazel's apparent mimicking of her accent (21 and 44), makes jokes herself (32) and sorts out Amy's confusion over roles (24). The gap in performance between Hazel and Amy is wide however, which Amy finds threatening (27, 40).

Extract 9 comes from the 'maths lesson', where the children are counting sweets and biscuits provided by Mother:

(9)
126 S: = What is then, what is two times three...yes?
127 H: Six.
128 S: Yeah. (clapping)
129 A: Oh, °I don't like you.°
130 S: O-oh, Amy. What is...no, Amy....How many, how many...how many cookies are, this mini cookies are same, one two three group?
131 A: Uh.
132 S: Yes?
133 A: Nine.
134 S: Yeah. What is three times three?
135 H: °Three times three°
136 A: (hand up) uh...
137 H: Nine.
138 S: Yeah! (clapping)
139 A: 언니 Hazel 만 clap 해주고 나는 안 해줘? *Why do you (sister) clap for Hazel, but not for me?*
140 S: How many there are, this chocolate are there? Yes, Amy!

141 A: Three.
142 S: Yeah (clapping) . . . then, how many there this chocolate and this mini things are altogether?
143 H: Four.
144 S: No, what is umm, then what is three times four? . . .Okay, Amy!
145 A: Twelve.
146 S: Yes. then, what is four times three? Four times three? . . . It's the same one.
147 H: (sound of counting) . . . four, five . . .
148 A: (hand up) Uh, Uh, Uh?
149 S: Yes, Amy!
150 A: . . .Hazel's turn, Hazel.

Here we see Susan producing a series of 'how many' questions, with Amy eagerly responding. Her numeracy skills are equal to Hazel's, and her language skills are adequate for simple counting activities. She challenges any hint of favouritism towards Hazel on her sister's part, using both private speech in English (129) and a complaint in Korean (139). However, Susan is evidently aiming to allocate turns and praise fairly (142), and Amy is sufficiently confident in this phase to offer a turn to Hazel (150). Later, Mother suggests that the children try subtraction and division, ending by eating the sweets and biscuits.

This relatively early episode shows Amy still relying on others for successful participation in L2 medium play. Her contributions are short, and she depends on Susan as 'teacher' not only to allocate turns fairly between herself and Hazel, but also to regulate the difficulty level of the spelling and maths tasks. She imitates some of Susan's expressions in private speech (e.g., line 35) and codeswitches to make a private complaint. Amy seems to find Hazel a potentially threatening presence in the game; hence her insistence that Susan should play teacher, and anxious monitoring of Susan's 'fairness'. Susan on the other hand has sufficient English to lead the activity and play 'teacher' with some skill, finding suitable questions for both her 'pupils', scaffolding Amy's comprehension, and explaining a simple mathematical procedure. Hazel is inclined to tease at first, but soon becomes engaged in the game. Presumably because of her presence, codeswitching by the Korean speakers is very limited, and both of them have an extended opportunity to rehearse straightforward school question-and-answer routines, to some extent selected by Mother, and at a pace controlled by Susan.

Playing nursery: Susan, Amy and Diana

The three Korean children were next recorded 'playing nursery' three months later, when Susan and Amy had been in England for 7 months 23 days, and Diana had also been in England for almost two months. The episode lasted for c50 minutes.

Susan began by announcing the recording details, but Amy smoothly adopted the teacher role (example 10).

(10)

1. S: Today seven May, two thousand and three. We gonna play nursery game.
2. A: Nursery game! Okay.
3. S: Yeah, play.
4. A: Okay? (gesturing) Come on, with your bag!
5. A: We gonna draw.... Come in, please. Come in.
6. S: We are at the door, Miss.
7. A: Who are you?

. . . .

34. A: Okay, can you sit down here? (to Susan) Sit down here, please. (to Diana)
35. D: Yap!
36. A: Amm, we got two girls, so, what's your name?
37. D: Hannah, Hannah Pottle Lucy, Lucy. 아니, *no*, Hannah Lucy Pottle.
38. A: Is that the first name? ...Yes?
39. S: She lives in next doors to me. ....

. . . .

46. S: What, what's your name?
47. A: Miss-, uhm. My name is Mrs. Stevenson. Says, me =
48. S: Mrs. Hood (pretend headteachers' name) says you're Miss.
49. A: = Yeah, Mrs. Stevenson.
50. S: That's nice name!
51. A: Thank you! And, and, you gonna sit down on the mat, sorry, you gonna sit down on your mat =
52. S: = Where's please?
53. A: = Sorry? ...Sit down on your mat, please. You stand up?
54. S: Where shall I sit?
55. A: With a boy or a girl?
56. S: Girl, please!
57. A: (giggle) girl! Okay! ...You sit next to Abi, please.
58. S: Hello, Abi. (jumps to her place)
59. A: No jumping, please! ... Can you ((-)) ...
60. S: Miss Stevenson? ... Can Hannah sit next to me, please?
61. A: Hannah! Go, sit down in umm next to her? Her? ((-)) ...Okay.

In this episode the children adopt imaginary characters (Amy is 'Mrs. Stevenson', Susan and Diana are pupils, 'Jasmine' and 'Hannah'), conduct an art class creating papier mâché faces, have lunch, and finish with rewards for good behaviour.

Throughout, Amy is talkative and proactive, producing 170 speech turns altogether (43%). Susan produces 135 turns (34%) and Diana 94 turns (23%). The three children codeswitch more freely than when they played with Hazel. However, they use Korean for a limited set of functions, primarily to ensure the inclusion of Diana, the weakest English speaker. Throughout, English is accepted by all three children as the most appropriate language for their various roles; though they have never attended nursery school in England, it is clear that an English nursery is being imagined.

Playing the role of teacher, Amy seems an acute observer of school life, and she now has the language ability to reproduce many small details. Extract 11 shows her not only giving task instructions, but justifying why children must learn independence, managing the movement of pupils around the school, and checking comprehension. This extract also shows awareness of the register appropriate for a teacher ('toilet' instead of 'loo', line 70):

(11)   Introduction to papier mâché task

68.   A: We gonna do this. And this is very hard work, but you have to do it because if you go to the INFANT school or RECEPTION, and you have to do your work in your own, in your self. Yes?

69   S: May I go to the loo?

70.   A: Loo? Do you know where is the loo? I mean TOILET?

71.   S: Yes. Because I have been here before.

72   A: But if you forget, can you go with Sara, please? Sara! Go with her, please! Okay? Let's go for her and . . .like. . .Yes, come in, please. . . .Okay, we gonna make hair blond. Who know what it mean hair blond? . . . Yes?

73.   S: Umm the hair is very yellowy gold.

Extract 12 shows Amy's management of prizegiving and the conclusion to the day:

(12)

375.   A: Hannah and Jas, come out please!

376.   S: Why?

377.   A: I want to do something. . . .They are new girls but they are very good. They have the prize of the, ahm, doing a making a face, and they are win Barnaby bear and yeah. Baby bear! =

. . . .

388.   D&S: (clapping) Yeahhhhh!

389.   A: Clap for her. Clap for her. . . .(clapping) And, one for you. [(sound of opening the prize) =

390.   D: = Yeah! Thank you.

391.   A: = It's just not a present. Hannah and Amy got it. You do a very good and if you are new girls, If you are new girls, you can . . . .. That's why, say something why you are happy or . . .

392. S: I'm SO happy.
393. D: Me, too.
395. A: And, you do a very good. Ding-dong. Oh, dear. Time to go home!
396. S&D: Bye.
397. A: Good bye, girls.
398. S: Bye.
399. D: Bye.

This episode involves all three girls for an extended period of time. Amy now has the language resources to carry through a leadership role successfully in English. Susan sustains the role of an English nursery pupil consistently, except for supporting Diana's participation with some Korean codeswitching (Extract 13).

(13)
167. A: Ahm, Jasmine, Jas! Can you help Hannah? Hannah help Jas. Together like this.
168. S: (to Diana) Pairs 로 한데. Pair 로 해서 어떤 Pair 가 제일 잘 만들었는지 본데. *She says that we'll do in pairs and then she'll see which pair made it best.*

Susan models English words and utterances for the others (Extract 14):

(14)   Papier mâché activity
91. A: .... We gonna do NOSE because some of you have no nose, that it will be uhm, 장애인 *a handicapped person.* =
92. S: = Disabled =
93. A: = yea, disabled.

Unlike the L2 literacy episodes discussed in Section 3, the 'play school' episodes do not have any prior written script which the children can use as a springboard for oral interaction in English. However, the routines of school are familiar for all three, and the utterances they have heard many times from teachers and fellow pupils are by this time easily available for both Susan and Amy, who both provide repetitive models for Diana. The harmony between the three girls is striking – this is a three-way collaboration to reproduce as much as possible of the interactional routines of English school. They are having fun, but the sustained commitment to use of English is reminiscent of the purposeful nature of L2 siblings' English school play noted by Williams (2004).

Home social relationships and L2 learning

This Korean family provides rich evidence concerning the distinctive contributions of different family members to L2 development in the home and related play environments. Mother played a central role in many literacy episodes. She listened and praised, she scaffolded literal comprehension, and she stimulated a range of oral activities building on the narrative material: talking about pictures, reflecting on the motivations and goals of story characters etc. She also supported play activities arising from story reading, which greatly fostered the internalisation and activation of story material and other language routines through sustained repetition and improvisation. Mother also facilitated L2 sociodramatic play, e.g., by inviting L1 English friends to the house and encouraging Susan's involvement in play episodes with the younger children, or by providing props, snacks and actual suggestions for play activities. While Grandmother spoke little English, she too regularly played some of these roles, e.g., hearing children read their English storybooks aloud, and skilfully eliciting explanations and interpretations in Korean of English stories and pictures.

However, the data also show that the children themselves are proactive participants in home L2 literacy activities. For example, as soon as Amy's English resources allowed, she was keen to take a lead, e.g., by role playing a teacher during the reading of *Mr. Whisper*, or when 'playing nursery'. These roles provided excellent opportunities for developing L2 fluency and increased control of familiar language, as seen in the 'playing school' episode for Susan, and 'playing nursery' for Amy. What is more, the presence of one or more other children with more limited L2 proficiency encouraged the 'leading' child (i.e., either Susan or Amy in 'teacher' role) to offer linguistic scaffolding, to recycle and paraphrase L2 utterances, and to find alternative ways to convey meaning, in L1 and/or in L2, if the play was to continue successfully. The benefits for both more advanced and less advanced L2 participants are self-evident.

As we have seen, 9-year-old Susan's level of literacy in English was much the highest on arrival in England. At school, she was described by her teacher as reluctant to talk to adults, though interacting well with peers. At home, she seemed to enjoy opportunities to rehearse conversational interactions in English, taking part in literacy activities arising from the younger children's reading books, and joining in sociodramatic play. Her relative cognitive and linguistic maturity showed in the linguistic scaffolding she could offer to the others, assisting them with L2 comprehension, and modelling and co-constructing utterances at appropriate levels. In sociodramatic play she was able to modify the linguistic challenge to suit her audience (e.g., the very different spellings asked of Hazel and of Amy during 'school' play). Overall she was a trusted playmate and English interlocutor for the younger children, who never seemed to resist or feel threatened by her higher level of English.

Finally, the data indicate some of the complexities of joining in an English-using friendship network. Play with native speakers can offer rich opportunities for English-medium interaction. However, it is also 'riskier' than play among L2 users, with greater language imbalances offering scope for loss of face. By the end of her stay in England, Amy was fully integrated socially with her monolingual English classmates – but the social confidence and level of English proficiency required to do this, was previously developed to a considerable extent in the 'safe' environment offered by family interlocutors at home.

Conclusion

In this chapter we have demonstrated that young L2 learners should be seen as "active, competent and intentional" participants in the language learning process (Gregory et al. 2004a). For such learners in an ESL setting, the rewards of rapid language learning are clear – successful integration at school and among English using peer friendship groups. They are intent observers of English-medium school and social routines, and bring home a considerable store of new language. The home setting then offers a supportive and non-threatening setting where the new language can be activated and fluency developed, through recycling and repetition of school-learned words, phrases and sentences, and imaginative variations on these. Picture storybooks brought home from school offer another source of L2 texts, including dialogues and simple action narratives, which can also be appropriated through repetition, recycling and variation. Imaginative role play, which re-uses familiar L2 material in new fantasy settings, and supports language with actions and play props, maintains involvement and makes the recycling of language routines fresh and entertaining. Within an L2 peer group whose members are at different stages of L2 development, new language is regularly encountered by the less proficient in a meaning oriented play context, while the more proficient get opportunities to diagnose others' language difficulties, to paraphrase, to explain and to model L2 utterances. And finally we have seen how the intimate day-to-day knowledge possessed by parents and caretakers about their children's language level, degree of self confidence and interactional preferences, allows high quality scaffolding to be provided in a flexible way, changing over time in response to children's evolving capabilities. Overall this study has allowed us to identify important dimensions of home L2 use, and the motivations which underlie it, which contribute to a more rounded and complete view of children's ESL development, and their own role in leading it.

These conclusions have nonetheless been drawn on the basis of a single family case study, and clearly need to be tested in a greater variety of circumstances. One obvious limitation to Lee's (2005) study is that all the principal actors were female, and the roles of fathers and boys in L2 family literacy development were not examined. Clearly also, this family benefited perhaps exceptionally, from Mother's high level of English and pedagogic background, and replications are needed within families of varying ESL proficiency and occupation. Also, a case study approach of this kind allows for only episodic capture of children's L2 development, which could usefully be complemented by more systematic testing and tracking of such things as the growth of vocabulary or sentence level grammar. However, even a single case study offers many hints to families and 'family literacy' programmes, about productive approaches to ESL development, which suggest rich directions for future research.

References

Aukrust, V. G. 2004. Explanatory discourse in young second language learners' peer play. *Discourse Studies* 6(3): 393–412.

Bongartz, C. & Schneider, M. 2003. Linguistic development in social contexts: A study of two brothers learning German. *Modern Language Journal* 87(1): 13–37.

Bruce, T. 1991. *Time to Play in Early Childhood Education*. London: Hodder and Stoughton.

Cekaite, A. & Aronsson, K. 2004. Repetition and joking in children's second language conversations: Playful recyclings in an immersion classroom. *Discourse Studies* 6(3): 373–392.

Cekaite, A. & Aronsson, K. 2005. Language play, a collaborative resource in children's L2 learning. *Applied Linguistics* 26(2): 169–191.

Cook-Gumperz, J. 1986. Caught in a web of words: Some considerations on language socialisation and language acquisition. In *Children's Worlds and Children's Language*, J. Cook-Gumperz, W. A. Corsaro & J. Streeck (eds.), 37–64. Berlin: Mouton de Gruyter.

Galda, L. & Pellegrini, A. D. (eds). 1985. *Play, Language and Stories: The Development of Children's Literate Behavior*. Norwood NJ: Ablex.

Green, C. R. & Halsall, S. W. 2004. Head Start families sharing literature. *Early Childhood Research and Practice* 6(2).

Gregory, E. 2001. Sisters and brothers as language and literacy teachers: Synergy between siblings playing and working together. *Journal of Early Childhood Literacy* 1(3): 301–322.

Gregory, E., Long, S. & Volk, D. 2004a. A sociocultural approach to learning. In *Many Pathways to Literacy: Young Children Learning with Siblings, Grandparents, Peers and Communities*, E. Gregory, S. Long & D. Volk (eds.), 6–20. New York NY: Routledge/Falmer.

Gregory, E., Long, S. & Volk, D. 2004b. Syncretic Literacy Studies: Starting points. In *Many Pathways to Literacy: Young Children Learning with Siblings, Grandparents, Peers and Communities*, E. Gregory, S. Long & D. Volk (eds), 1–5. New York NY: Routledge/Falmer.

Gregory, E. & Williams, A. 2001. *City Literacies: Learning to Read across Cultures and Generations*. London: Routledge.

Hannon, P. 1995. *Literacy Home and School: Research and Practice in Teaching Literacy with Parents*. London: Falmer.

Hannon, P. 2000. Rhetoric and research in family literacy. *British Educational Research Journal* 26(1): 121–138.

Heath, S. B. 1983. *Ways with Words*. Cambridge: CUP.

Heath, S. B. & Chin, H.-K. 1985. Narrative play in second-language learning. In *Play, Language and Stories: The Development of Children's Literate Behavior*, L. Galda & A. D. Pellegrini (eds.), 147–166. Norwood NJ: Ablex.

Hornberger, N. 1988. *Bilingual Education and Language Maintenance: A Southern Peruvian Quechua Case*. Dordrecht: Foris.

Jordan, G. E., Snow, C. E. & Porche, M. V. 2000. Project EASE: The effect of a family literacy project on kindergarten students' early literacy skills. *Reading Research Quarterly* 35(4): 524–546.

Kasuya, H. 2002. Bilingual context for language development. In *Talking to Adults: The Contribution of Multiparty Discourse to Language Acquisition*, S. Blum-Kulka & C. E. Snow (eds), 295–326. Mahwah NJ: Lawrence Erlbaum Associates.

King, K. A. & Hornberger, N. H. 2005. Literacies in families and community. In *International Handbook on Educational Policy*, N. Bascia, A. Cumming, A. Datnow, K. Leithwood & D. Livingstone (eds), 715–734. Dordrecht: Springer.

Lantolf, J. P. 2000. Introducing sociocultural theory. In *Sociocultural Theory and Second Language Learning*, J. P. Lantolf (ed.), 1–26. Oxford: OUP.

Lantolf, J. P. & Thorne, S. L. 2006. *Sociocultural Theory and the Genesis of Second Language Development*. Oxford: OUP.

Lee, C. N. 2005. Supporting English Learning in the Family: An Ethnographic Case Study of a Young Korean-English Learner. PhD dissertation, University of Southampton.

Marsh, J. 2003. One way traffic? Connections between literacy practices at home and in the nursery. *British Educational Research Journal* 29(3): 369–382.

O'Hare, J. (ed.). 1990. *Puzzlemania 1*. Columbus, Ohio: Highlights for Children Inc.

O'Hare, J. (ed.). 1991. *Puzzlemania 2*. Columbus, Ohio: Highlights for Children Inc.

Prinsloo, M. 2004. Literacy is child's play: Making sense in Khwezi Park. *Language and Education* 18(4): 291–304.

Rydland, V. & Aukrust, V.G. 2005. Lexical repetition in second language learners' peer play interaction. *Language Learning* 55(2): 229–274.

Saville-Troike, M. 1989. *The Ethnography of Communication*. Oxford: Basil Blackwell.

Street, B.V. (ed.). 1993. *Cross-Cultural Approaches to Literacy*. Cambridge: CUP.

Volk, D. & de Acosta, M. 2004. Mediating networks for literacy learning: the role of Puerto Rican siblings. In *Many Pathways to Literacy: Young Children Learning with Siblings, Grandparents, Peers and Communities*, E. Gregory, S. Long & D. Volk (eds), 25–39. New York NY: Routledge/Falmer.

Willett, J. 1995. Becoming first graders in an L2 classroom: An ethnographic study of L2 socialisation. *TESOL Quarterly* 29: 473–503.

Williams, A. 2004. 'Right, get your book bags!': Siblings playing school in multiethnic London. In *Many Pathways to Literacy: Young Children Learning with Siblings, Grandparents, Peers and Communities*, E. Gregory, S. Long & D. Volk (eds), 52–65. New York NY: Routledge/Falmer.

Williams, A. & Gregory, E. 2001. Siblings bridging literacies in multilingual contexts. *Journal of Research in Reading* 24(3): 248–265.

Home-school connections
for international adoptees

Repetition in parent-child interaction

Lyn Wright Fogle
Georgetown University

Studies have found that second language-learning children can benefit academically from a variety of interactions outside of traditional teacher-fronted classroom activities. However, little is known about the actual linguistic processes involved in the acquisition of academic language competence. The current study investigates the role of repetition, and more specifically the functions of self- vs. other-repetition, in productions of school-related discourse genres by international adoptees during mealtime interactions with their parents in English. Two families with four adopted children (ages 4–10) from Russian-speaking regions participated in the study. Findings suggest that parents' interactional strategies play a role in children's productions and that children use both self- and other-repetition for a variety of discourse functions related to their efforts to be competent interlocutors in family interaction. Self-repetition that leads to reformulation of utterances is seen to be a sign of discourse competence and linguistic creativity.

Introduction

Despite the general consensus that young children educated in their second languages (L2s) need to acquire the academic language necessary for school functions (Cummins 2003; Valdés 2004; TESOL 2006), few studies examine the actual processes involved in acquiring such competence. Further, some researchers and theorists question the effectiveness of traditional classrooms and classroom activities in fostering academic language skills, citing a need for English as a Second Language (ESL) students to engage in a variety of activities and interactions to gain exposure to and ownership of the language of education (Kotler, Wegerif, & LeVoi 2001; Valdés 2004; Hawkins 2005). This study examines parent-child interactions, which have been found to facilitate the development of academic competencies for children in their first languages (Michaels 1981; Heath 1983; Ochs, Taylor, Rudolph,

& Smith 1992), in adoptive families where native English-speaking parents are raising native Russian-speaking children.

In this paper I focus on the collaborative production of school-related discourse genres, e.g., narratives and explanations among others, in two adoptive families' mealtime conversations. More specifically, I identify adults' and children's use of both self- and other- repetition as a mechanism of collaborative discourse (DiCamilla & Anton 1997), which functions to facilitate the children's participation in and accomplishment of such conversational tasks. I argue that a better understanding of how repetition is used by more advanced second language learning children in everyday interactions with adults can augment our knowledge of how second language learners acquire the communicative competence (Hymes 1974) necessary for the mainstream classroom.

Literature review

Second language learning and academic language

As Valdés (2004) has pointed out, defining the term "academic English" is a difficult proposition, complicated by the fact that different language-related fields have different conceptualizations of the term. The current TESOL standards for grades pre-K – 3 in the U.S. identify discourse functions such as "comparing and contrasting information," "persuading, arguing, negotiating, evaluating and justifying," and "selecting, connecting, and explaining information," among many others as important to the development of academic achievement in all content areas for second language learners (TESOL 1997). These standards, however, at the time of writing this paper are undergoing revision that will place greater emphasis on content-based knowledge because of benchmarks set by No Child Left Behind (TESOL 2006).

Recent studies of second language-learning children have indicated that interactions outside of teacher-fronted activities can facilitate the acquisition of such classroom competencies. Kotler, Wegerif and LeVoi (2001) reported on an intervention implemented in British schools in which adult "talking partners" from the community were assigned to children in the classroom. Sixty-four English as an Additional Language students between the ages of five and eight met with adult talking partners (volunteer parents, business people, nurses, etc.) who were trained to engage the children in problem-solving activities and to use prompt cards to structure the interactions. The children who participated in this program made significant gains on both oral proficiency and literacy measures in relation to a control group.

Other studies have found that peer interaction in the classroom can also facilitate access to academic discourses and the formation of student identities (Willett 1995; Hawkins 2005). Hawkins pointed to one English language learner's proactive strategies to recruit other students in interactions that provided him access to language practice, scaffolding, and affiliations with school and schooling (three routes to English language development and learning identified by Hawkins). Hawkins concluded that teachers need to consider ways to vary participation patterns in the classroom activities so that all members of the class may, "collaboratively negotiate content- and genre- specific language and performances" (2005: 79).

While these studies show that improving academic performance for young second language learning children requires more than teaching content-relevant vocabulary or the mechanics of writing, they do not say much about the actual processes of interaction where such acquisition takes place. Hawkins notes that new perspectives on academic literacies require a reconceptualization of the notion of scaffolding and a new perspective on how to introduce and engage students in the "talking, acting, thinking and viewing inherent in the genres and discourses that are requisite for success in school" (2005: 80).

Parent-child interaction and academic language

Parent-child and family interactions have been found to be an important site of socialization into school discourses for first language-learning children (Michaels 1981; Heath 1983; Ochs et al. 1992) According to Ninio and Snow (1996), young children learn to take others' perspectives through collaborative interactions with caring interlocutors, thereby gradually achieving autonomy in such discourse activities as storytelling. In a study of middle class families with school-age children, Ochs et al. found that theory building, or the construction of scientific discourse, started at home at the dinner table through the co-narration of stories in which, "family members draw upon and stimulate critical social, cognitive and linguistic skills that underlie scientific and other scholarly discourse" (1992: 37). Integral to this process, according to Ochs et al., was the familiarity that existed between family members that created a shared expectation for making meaning out of everyday events. There are few studies that examine such parental scaffolding of a child's discourse production in an L2; however, in adoptive families where parents and children do not share a first language (L1), such interactions may be fruitful sites of exposure to academic discourses as in traditional monolingual families.

Repetition in language learning

In studies of second language acquisition, repetition has been seen to play a role in learners' grammatical development through the acquisition of formulaic sequences (Hatch, Peck, & Wagner-Gough 1979; Wray 1999) and learners' use of language play or private speech as a route to internalization of new forms (Lantolf 1997; Broner & Tarone 2001). Repetition has also been studied in the form of recasts or feedback to learners' utterances given by interlocutors (Lyster 1998; Long 2006) and, from a sociocultural perspective, has also been noted to be a key mechanism in scaffolding. DiCamilla and Anton (1997), for example, identified repetition as the mechanism that allows second language learners engaged in a collaborative task to create a "cognitive space" to work and build more complex productions.

For first language-learning children, repetition has also been found to play an important role in meeting not only the linguistic goals, but also the interactional and social goals of children and their interlocutors. Ochs Keenan, for example, found that repetition functions above and beyond simple imitation to provide the child a means to appear to be a competent interlocutor in interaction with his or her caregiver:

> We can say that in repeating, the child is learning to communicate. He is learning not to construct sentences at random, but to construct them to meet specific communicative needs. He is learning to query, comment, confirm, match a claim and counterclaim, answer a question, respond to a demand, and so on. (1977:133)

Furthermore, in a study of the use of diminutives in native Spanish-speaking parent-child interactions, King and Melzi (2004) concluded that parents' use of imitation of their children's diminutive forms developed a sense of mutual participation and even an affective bond between parent and child. Repetition between adults and children, therefore, can be seen as a communicative resource to meet a number of social goals.

Second language-learning children have also been found to use repetition in multiparty (classroom) discourse in order to gain participation. In a study of a five-year-old Arabic-speaking child in a nursery school classroom in Italy, Pallotti (2003) examined "appropriations" of others' speech as a communicative strategy and showed how others' utterances were incorporated into the child's own utterances to participate in the classroom discourse. In Willett's (1995) study, such repetition also played an important role in providing a means through which the three Limited English Proficient girls could participate in classroom activities and at the same time boost their proficiency, and importantly, construct identities as competent students.

These studies focused primarily on the learner's repetition of others' utterances; however, self-repetition can also play a role in meeting such interactional goals. Merritt (1982) found that self-repetition was one way that children get the teacher's attention and participate in multiparty discourse. Further, Ochs Keenan (1977) argued that self-repetition provides a means by which children can establish cohesion in discourse without the use of pronominal reference or more complicated referential expressions. In this way self-repetition serves both social and linguistic goals for the child.

These studies suggest that repetition, both by children and their adult inter-locutors, could play an important role in the type of scaffolding and oral produc-tions noted to be of value in building academic language competencies discussed above. However, we don't know enough about how repetition is used in interac-tions between young second language learners and adult interlocutors or what the varying roles of self- and other- repetition are. Rydland and Aukrust (2005) in-vestigated the latter question in a quantitative study of second language-learning children's use of different types of repetition in explanatory discourse with peers. By examining free play interactions of 24 Turkish-Norwegian bilinguals interact-ing in their second language (Norwegian), Rydland and Aukrust found that the use of self-repetition was positively correlated with the children's frequency of verbal participation and that use of "complex" other-repetition (i.e. repetition of other's utterances with some type of modification or expansion) was positively correlated with the children's academic language skills. This study concluded that other-repetition is more cognitively complex than self-repetition. However this conclu-sion is drawn from quantitative results alone. We don't know if self-repetition can function in a similar way to other-repetition for second language-learning children in some cases. Further, studies of repetition in second language-learning children's productions have involved primarily peer interactions; although, adult-child dis-course and the nature of scaffolding in adult-child interactions may be different (Philp and Duchesne this volume).

The current study presents a qualitative analysis of family mealtime inter-actions in which second language-learning children engage in interactions with their parents in their L2. These interactions require the children to accomplish certain discourse tasks such as telling stories about their day, giving instructions about a craft activity, and writing an oral letter to a grandmother among others, as well as to engage in other academic-related discourse activities such as explain-ing, evaluating, and justifying their contributions to the conversation. In these episodes, repetition is seen to be a strategy that children use to meet a variety of interactional challenges associated with the participation structures of the fam-ily mealtime and the demands of taking the parents' point of view. Through the analysis a more holistic view emerges of how repetition is used by more advanced second language-learning children in the process of acquiring the communicative competence necessary for school.

Methods

Participants

Two families out of a pre-existing pool of 11 adoptive families (Fogle 2006) were selected for and agreed to participate in the current study. Each family consisted of two adopted siblings, ranging in age from eight to three at the time of arrival, with the children in Family One being slightly older than those in Family Two. The current study focuses on the two children who were closest in age, Sasha from Family One and Arkadiy from Family Two, ages eight and six respectively at the start of the study. Sasha was the younger of two boys, while Arkadiy was the older brother to a younger sister. Sasha had arrived in the U.S. and had been enrolled in a public charter school for about 13 months at the start of the study. Arkadiy had arrived in the U.S. and had been homeschooled (with some interruptions, according to interviews with his father), for about 11 months.

Sasha and Arkadiy both lacked exposure to literacy and schooling prior to arrival in the U.S. John, the father from Family One, reported in an initial interview one year prior to the start of the current study that Sasha was learning to read and write for the first time in English. Kevin, the father from Family Two, reported that Arkadiy could count to 10 in Russian and write his name, but had no other apparent literacy skills at the time of arrival. Both parents reported that the boys had been too young to enter the first grade in Ukraine or Russia, which normally begins at age seven, and therefore had no prior exposure to schooling. Sasha had spent less time (approximately one year total) in the orphanage or institution than Arkadiy (approximately three years total), based on the fathers' interview reports.

Family One spoke Russian at home for approximately the first six months after the children's arrival, according to John. John had studied university level Russian prior to the children's arrival and felt comfortable using Russian with the boys. He reported that the boys had been exposed to Ukrainian and seemed to speak a mix of Ukrainian and Russian with each other, but were able to communicate with John exclusively in Russian. It is also possible that the boys were from a trilingual background because their biological father was noted to be of Central Asian, rather than Ukrainian, origin. Detailed information on the children's language

Table 1. Child demographics

Family	Children	Gender	Age	Age of Arrival	Date of Arrival	DOB	Grade
1	Dima	M	9;11	8;10	9/25/04	11/30/95	3
	Sasha	M	8;1	7;11	9/25/04	9/20/97	2
2	Arkadiy	M	6;8	5;10	12/20/04	2/18/99	Homeschool
	Anna	F	4;3	3;6	12/20/04	7/31/01	Nursery school

backgrounds was not available to John, and the older son Dima did not remember what language was used with his biological father when asked by John in a later mealtime recording. Kevin and Meredith, the parents in Family Two, spoke only English and reported using only limited phrases in Russian with their children. Arkadiy was not exposed to any additional languages other than Russian prior to his arrival in the U.S.

In both families the father was the primary caregiver for the children. Family One was a single-parent home, and Family Two was a dual-parent home. Information about the parents may be found in Table 2. All of the parents were European American, and the families were comparable in socio-economic status with John self-employed as a psychotherapist and Meredith holding a government attorney position. Family One resided in an urban townhouse, while Family Two lived in a single family home in the suburbs. Education levels were also comparable for the parents. Although the children in Family Two spent more time at home with their father, their mother Meredith was present during most of the family mealtime recordings.

Table 2. Parent demographics

Family	Parent	Age	Education	Occupation	Other languages
One	John	50	MA (2)	Psychotherapist	French, Russian
Two	Kevin	31	JD	Stay-at-home Father	none
	Meredith	28	JD	Staff Attorney	none

Data collection

Parents were asked to choose one week out of each month to conduct four individual recording sessions – two dinnertime sessions and two bookreading, homework, or other literacy-related events – for a duration of six months. The researcher met with both fathers for monthly ethnographic interviews, which were conducted approximately one week after the recordings were returned to the investigator. This paper examines three mealtime interactions for both families (Table 3).

Table 3. Mealtime recording times in minutes

Month	Family 1	Family 2
1	28	21
2	34	19
3	25	13
Total	87	53

Analysis

For this paper, one mealtime recording from each of the first three months of the study were selected on the basis of length for each family and transcribed (six total recordings). Mealtimes were chosen in order to look primarily at conversational interaction, and the first three months were chosen because a change in parent strategies (specifically questioning practices associated with scaffolding in story-telling or other extended discourse activities) was noted in Family Two by the end of month four. While this change is certainly of interest, the focus of this paper will be on the differences in the two families, which are most evident in the first three months of recording.

The six mealtime interactions were transcribed and initially coded generally for instances of "extended discourse" (i.e., for discourse in which the child pro-duces several turns in a row with minimal assistance [Ninio & Snow 1996: 172]) and more specifically for discourse type (e.g., narrative, explanation, planning dis-course, language play, etc.). For the purposes of this paper, narratives were defined as two or more temporally sequenced events told together (Ochs & Capps 2001). Explanations were identified as talk that makes a logical connection between ob-jects, events, or concepts (Beals & Snow 1994). The data were then examined for instances of communication breakdowns and corrective feedback. Finally, data were coded for question forms, prompts, and repetitions, which were examined qualitatively for speaker and function.

Repetition is identified as any lexical item or phrase repeated in part or in whole within the discourse unit identified (e.g., narrative, explanation, definition, etc.). In some cases the whole mealtime interaction was examined to see if repeti-tion occurred outside of the immediate discourse being analyzed. Such instances will be discussed in detail in the following section.

Parent-child interactions

Data gathered from interviews indicated that the parents participating in the study had different strategies and made very different educational and linguistic choices for their adopted children from the outset. John, a single father, had learned Rus-sian and used only Russian at home for the first six months at which time he reported that the children had led the switch to English. His children attended a public school with an ESL program. John also reported using simplified speech in English and providing explicit corrections of his children's language produc-tion. Meredith and Kevin, in contrast, spoke only a few words of Russian and had decided to homeschool their oldest son Arkadiy for at least his first year in the U.S. Kevin and Meredith reported a belief in not correcting their children or modifying their own speech for the benefit of their children's comprehension – suggesting that the children will just "pick up" English. In the following sections, I will present data first from Family One and then Family Two.

Family One: Sasha

As in other studies of family discourse (e.g., Blum-Kulka 1997; Ochs & Capps 2001; Abu-Akel 2002) the parent (John) in Family One initiated many of the children's stories and reports about their day through elicitations. These elicitations often involved other-repetition, and in this way John established a framework for the provision of more information and the establishment of lexical cohesion in the narrative (Michaels 1981). Other typical features of Family One's mealtime inter-actions included a routine in which each family member discussed one bad thing and then one good thing about the day in turn and a pattern of frequent inter-ruptions of the younger child Sasha by his older brother Dima. These features are evident in Excerpt 1.

Excerpt 1: Good thing

1	John:	Dima did you – Sasha did you say your good thing?
2	Sasha:	I don't <know> [?].
3	John:	What was your good thing?
4	Sasha:	I <said> [!] that.
5	John:	I forget.
6	Sasha:	I got to play # uh recess instead of <dance> [!].
7	Dima:	Oh yes.
8	John:	You did recess instead of dance?
9	Dima:	Yes.
10	Sasha:	Yeah because uh [Miss – Miss] +/.
11	John:	[And that's a good thing?]
12	Dima:	Miss Clarkson wasn't there.
13	John:	Oh.
14	Dima:	Kind of recess we got to play indoor recess.
15	John:	Dima.
16	Sasha:	[and] +/.
17	Dima:	[Another] piece of pizza the smaller than the other one.
18	Sasha:	And the uh something [good is]
19	Dima:	[plea:se]
20	Sasha:	that I <rested> [?] – [uh – uh raced] +/.
21	Dima:	[yeaoooh]
22	John:	Guys guys guys guys oh!

23		phw phw.

23   phw phw.
24 Sasha: That I raced +/.
25 John: It's getting kind of loud.
26 Sasha: that I raced Inigo and I might <n> [?] won.
27   But I was the last one and Inigo!
28   So I was jumping and I uh took another jump and almost there,
            but I uh slipped and fell and I sprained my ankle.
29 Dima: A – in soccer?
30 John: I – [you know] +/.
31 Sasha: [No]!
32 John: I think you might've twisted your ankle, but I don't think you
33   sprained it [if you] –
34 Sasha: [Uh-uh]
35 John: if you sprained it you would not be able to run up and down the
            hill like you did.
36 Sasha: I know but uh I fell.
37   The floor was hard.
38   I fell and then I hit my knee <really> [!] hard.
39 John: Ow!
40 Dima: Ahw!
41   p-dup-p-du ahw!
42 Sasha: Hurts.
(See Appendix for transcription conventions)

In the first section of this episode (lines 1–10), John uses repetition to prompt Sasha to expand on his utterance, "You did recess instead of dance?" This other-repetition establishes mutual engagement in the storytelling activity. However, John takes a slightly different turn in line 11 when he asks Sasha, "And that's a good thing?" This question suggests that missing dance class is not an appropriate topic for the "good thing" narrative. Ochs et al. (1992) call such questions "challenges to ideology" in which interlocutors are required to revise their interpretation of an event by taking another's point of view. We see here that this challenge is issued by the use of repetition (the adult's self-repetition) and results in Sasha losing his turn to his older brother. Sasha attempts to explain, "Miss – Miss...," but Dima again interrupts, "Miss Clarkson wasn't there," and revises Sasha's statement, "Sort of recess...," which serves to lessen the value of the statement and presumably make it more acceptable to John. Here we see that Sasha encounters a variety of conversational challenges: mainly that he is required to contribute content that is acceptable to his father and he is interrupted by a more competent older brother.

In the second half of Excerpt 1, however, we see how Sasha takes part in the storytelling activities at mealtime so that his contribution is not interrupted and is acceptable to his father. In line 18, Sasha reintroduces his "good thing" narrative and this time successfully completes it. He does this primarily through the use of repetition. To begin, he appropriates part of his father's prompt, "and something good is..." This prompt is present in the local discourse (i.e. in his father's first utterance), but is also part of a larger family routine that occurs at most mealtimes. Therefore it is an established way to take an extended turn in the family conversation. Sasha then uses self-repetition for a variety of functions to build the story: to correct his pronunciation (from "<rested> [?]" to "raced"), to hold his turn during interruption ("I raced, I raced"), to achieve lexical cohesion ("Inigo"), and finally to revise his narrative one more time in response to a second challenge from his father who questions his use of the word "sprained".

Sasha concludes his story with a final event in line 28, 'I uh slipped and fell and I sprained my ankle." John, however, objects to this conclusion, repeating the phrase "sprained ankle" and suggesting the revised "twisted ankle." Sasha argues further: "I know but...>" and then uses self-repetition of his own previous conclusion from line 28 with some revision and reformulation, most notably omitting the sprained ankle, to make it more acceptable: "I know but uh I fell. The floor was hard. I fell and then I hit my knee <really> [!] hard". This conclusion achieved the involvement from his father and brother he was seeking in the response, "Ow!".

In Excerpt 1 John requires that Sasha pay attention to the words he is using, know what they mean, and revise his contributions so that the content is acceptable. In terms of academic language, Sasha is learning important aspects of taking part in multiparty conversations, holding the floor, being relevant and precise with language, and attending to metalinguistic factors such as word meanings. Sasha meets the demands of this interaction primarily through self-repetition.

In Excerpt 2, however, Sasha relies on other-repetition in a more unassisted production of extended discourse.

Excerpt 2: Dear *Babushka* 'Grandma'

1	John:	So # after we're done dinner, you can finish the movie.
2	Dima:	Ok!
3	Sasha:	Mmhmm
4	John:	And then after you finish the movie we'll see how the time is, but
5		if we have time I'd like to # uh I don't think we're going to have time.
6	Sasha:	What?
7	John:	I'd like to start making an outline about things you could tell Babushka.
8	Sasha:	Uh like a – uh – uh – for Babushka, then draw a circle around it uh put uh like +/.
9	Dima:	That's a web!

10	Sasha:	Yeah.
11		A web.
12	John:	Oh, so is that how you would do it?
13		Make a web?
14	Sasha:	Yeah.
15	John:	+^ Ok.
16	Dima:	Outline is not a web.
17	Sasha:	In my – uh – in my +/.
18	John:	Yeah.
19		A web goes like out in all directions
20	Dima:	Mmhmm
21	John:	An outline sort of goes boom boom boom boom boom.
22		They're both very good ways to # capture ideas.
23	Sasha:	Catch ideas.
24	John:	Catch ideas.
25		Have you caught any ideas lately?
26	Sasha:	Yeah.
27	John:	Like what?
28	Sasha:	Like, Dear Babushka,
29		I hope you have a nice time there.
30		I'm sorry that I'm not there but I love you so much and # uh we could come there soon +/.
31	Dima:	We don't think about you all the time.
32		[Just kidding.]
33	Sasha:	[W- we could] – we could come there sometimes it – # there and we think about you – and I – and Sasha thinks about you all [!] the time.
34	John:	Mmhmm.
35		Do you?
36		[Do you] think about her a lot?
37	Dima:	[Mmm] !
38	Sasha:	Mmhm.

Here Sasha provides an alternative to writing an outline (i.e. a web) and actually produces the letter to his Ukrainian grandmother in oral form, both productions suggest he is establishing his own authority with school-related activities in this interaction. Interestingly, Sasha uses the same other-repetition strategies discussed above to reinstate his turn in the conversation by repeating his father's phrase, in a reduced form, "catch ideas," in line 23. Although this reduced repetition of "capture ideas" could be considered an instance of language play or rehearsal, it also has an interactive function as it allows Sasha to take another turn in the conversation and allows John to expand Sasha's contribution further by repeating the

phrase a second time. Dima further contributes to the letter with an ironic statement in line 31, "We don't think about you all the time." Sasha incorporates this
statement into his own production, but makes changes so that it meet the needs
of his intended audience (i.e. both his grandmother, the recipient of the letter, and
his brother and father, the immediate interlocutors). Here Sasha revises Dima's
utterance through a string of self-repetitions that involve changing the pronoun
"we" to "I" to third person "Sasha" so that Sasha singles himself out in opposition
to his brother and subsequently changes the form of the verb (from "we think"
to "Sasha thinks"). These changes require not only manipulation of grammatical
forms but also the capability to see different perspectives of the letter – both the
point of view of the reader and the point of view of the collaborative letter-writers.
Interestingly, it is through repetition and then reformulation of Dima's utterance
that Sasha establishes his own independence and identity in this task.

In a discussion of the functions of repetition in discourse, Merritt (1994) concludes that reformulations may provide a window onto creativity to language.
In both Episodes 1 and 2 we see that Sasha uses repetitions of himself (and his
brother) to revise meanings and contribute to the conversation by taking the point
of view of the other interlocutors or the intended audience. These findings are in
line with those of Rydland and Aukrust (2005) who found that older second language learners who were more academically proficient used more other-repetition
in explanations than those who were less academically proficient. However, here
we see that self-repetition can function in the same way as other-repetition to
make subtle revisions to a narrative that, in this case, make the production acceptable to the audience. Sasha's ability to creatively use repetition points to his
competence in the language and with the discourse genres in which he is participating; however, it is also shaped by the interactional challenges that he faces (i.e.
his father's rejection of some statements and his brother's interruptions) as well
as his own efforts to establish an identity and independent voice in the family
conversations.

Family Two: Arkadiy

The members of Family Two (Kevin, Meredith, Arkadiy and Anna) typically engaged in defining and explaining episodes more than narratives or reports about
the day (perhaps because the family members spent more time together than
in Family One or the children were a bit younger). The children often led the
family conversations by asking questions of their parents. More communication
breakdowns or requests for clarification occurred in this family's discourse. These
features can be seen in Excerpt 3.

In Excerpt 3 the family collaborates to produce a narrative about a play episode
that had happened earlier in the day. The first part of the "narrative" takes the form

of a sort of guessing game (other instances of question-answer games are found in Family Two's data), which begins 38 lines prior to the data given here with Anna asking the question, "Who was – wa – I was in fight?" (Meredith gives the answer in line 2 here.) The excerpt given below starts with Arkadiy's continuation of the question-answer game.

Excerpt 3: Monsters

1	Arkadiy:	Mama?
2	Meredith:	Showlin Kristen [=! whispers]
3	Anna:	<Owlin> [?] Kristen!
4	Meredith:	Mmhmm. <Yes, Arkadiy> [?].
5	Arkadiy:	At the <play park> [?] I been th – papa been uhm # Tomais?
6	Meredith:	Mmhmm.
7	Arkadiy:	And who else?
8	Kevin:	Who else was I big guy?
9	Arkadiy:	Tomais and was Aldegard?
10	Kevin:	I was also the Monster Count.
11	Arkadiy:	Mm-mm!
12		I forgot Monster Count and +...
13	Kevin:	++ Monster Baron
14	Arkadiy:	Mmuhmm
15	Meredith:	That's a lot of monsters.
16	Arkadiy:	Yeah, I killed 'em all.
17		It wasn't hard at all.
18	Meredith:	With swords?
19	Arkadiy:	No.
20		I tickled them.
21	Meredith:	Ahhah.
22		[The secret – the] secret weakness.
23	Arkadiy:	[on the feet and] +/.
24	Kevin:	[Yeah], he's found a new weakness.
25	Arkadiy:	[Yeah].
26		I – I – I tickled when I take off the socks.
27		I tickle him.
28	Meredith:	Ahhah.
29	Arkadiy:	Huhah.
30	Meredith:	How did you discover that weakness?
31	Anna:	Mama I xxx +/.
32	Arkadkiy:	I thought it and it worked so I did it.
33	Meredith:	It worked?
34		Heroes have to be very cunning to figure these things out.

Meredith changes the direction of this narrative in line 15 with the evaluative statement, "That's a lot of monsters." Her subsequent questions, like John's above, provide a framework for Arkadiy to build his narrative; however, they notably do not employ repetition of Arkadiy's utterances. In fact, the only other-repetition noticeable in the second part of this narrative is between the parents Meredith and Kevin who repeat the word "weakness." Other-repetition has been noted to play a role in establishing intersubjectivity between speakers, and here we see that this intersubjectivity is established mainly between the parents of Family Two even though Arkadiy is an active participant in the conversation.

Here Arkadiy uses much the same strategy as Sasha did above when he faces interruption from another interlocutor. He repeats himself across several turns (lines 20–27) which allows him to hold his place in the conversation: "I tickled them…on the feet. I tickled when I take the socks off. I tickle him." These three turns look like language play or rehearsal. The result of this play is twofold – on the one hand it serves an interactive purpose to hold his turn at talk, on the other hand the repetition extends Arkadiy's narrative by providing a slot for new information. Here Arkadiy changes the tense of the verb (perhaps signaling a change in function in the narrative – from simple past to a habitual function – i.e. "This is what I did today" vs. "This is what I usually do in that situation"). He also changes the object of the verb, "them" vs. "him", and adds the adverbial phrase "when I take the socks off."

Meredith responds by recycling part of the previous conversation with her husband in a question to Arkadiy, "How did you discover that weakness?" While this is a prompt for Arkadiy to expand on the story, the intersubjectivity between speakers is not established and Meredith does not emulate the form of Arkadiy's contribution (as in John's prompt in Episode 1, "You did recess instead of dance?"). This makes Arkadiy's next turn more challenging. He needs to know what the word "weakness" means, and he needs to provide an explanation of his mental processes leading up to the tickling. Arkadiy approximates an explanation, "I thought it, and it worked." But this does not answer Meredith's question directly. She responds with a repetition and then an expansion, providing a sort of model for the sort of answer she was expecting, "Heroes have to be very cunning to figure these things out," and evaluation of the actual event. If, as DiCamilla and Anton (1997) suggest, interactional assistance or scaffolding depends on repetition, we can imagine that Meredith's prompts and questions could have been more effective in drawing an explanation from Arkadiy if they included some type of repetition of his previous utterances and therefore stayed within his apparent zone of proximal development (i.e. to expand on the discussion of tickling rather than moving toward a discussion of the more abstract concept of "weakness").

In Excerpt 4 we will see how Arkadiy makes use of other-repetition with limited assistance from other interlocutors.

Excerpt 4: Handprint wreath
Earlier in the conversation Meredith had announced that the family would make a handprint wreath for Christmas that afternoon. Meredith reintroduces the topic here.

1	Meredith:	xxx a handprint wreath.
2	Kevin:	Which is?
3		I mean it sounds – I mean # it sounds like a highly technical term hand, print, wreath.
4	Kevin:	Like pictures of hands?
5	Meredith:	[We're going to take our hand]
6	Kevin:	[xxx hand write]?
7	Meredith:	We're going to put our hand on construction paper.
8		We're going to trace around our hands.
9	Anna:	Oh!
10	Meredith:	And we're going to cut out the tracing.
11		And then we're going to glue them # in a big circle to make a handprint wreath.
12	Anna:	Mama you know what?
13	Kevin:	Very interesting.
14		[Never heard of it].
15	Anna:	[xxx, mama]?
16	Arkadiy:	Mama I – I know what to do.
17	Meredith:	It's xxx difficult.

<Interruption from Anna>

29	Arkadiy:	Mama?
30		I know something # we can do # if you want.
31	Kevin:	What's that?
32	Arkadiy:	We can put our hand and trace it.
33	Meredith:	Mmhmm.
34	Arkadiy:	And then after we're done tracing it we can put round it a big circle.
35	Meredith:	That might make it easier to cut out.
36	Kevin:	Mmhmm
37	Anna:	Yeah.
38	Meredith:	We could do it that way.
39	Arkadiy:	Mmhmm
40	Kevin:	It might be a good idea actually.
41	Meredith:	Cause then we can just cut out the big circle rather than cutting out the [xx fingers].
42	Anna:	[Mama have] to get a paper xx to – to take the window things # <off> [!], right?

43 Meredith: The window decorations, yes.
44   We'll need a xxx.
45 Arkadiy: Because then we just draw a hand and cut it out and that way
               we can put inside of the xx # of the circle.

In this excerpt Arkadiy contributes to the planning/explanatory discourse initiated by his mother, i.e. how to make a handprint wreath, and he appears to propose a new way to make the wreath, which is accepted by both parents as "a good idea." However, close inspection of the actual language produced by Arkadiy suggests that although his ideas are accepted as new and different, they are in fact altered repetitions (mainly reductions) of his mother's previous utterances. Figure 1 shows Arkadiy's repetitions side-by-side with his mother's statements, the intervening turns are omitted.

With some changes, omissions and reductions, Arkadiy replays his mother's instructions for making a handprint wreath over multiple turns in lines 32–45. There is one main difference between Arkadiy's version and his mother's, however. This occurs when Arkadiy suggests "We can put round it a big circle," rather than, "We can glue them in a big circle." We can't know if Arkadiy intended to make a difference in meaning with his utterance (maybe he didn't hear or couldn't remember the word *glue*, maybe he associated the word *round* with *circle*, or maybe he meant to propose a new idea). However, this slight modification has helped him to appear to be a competent interlocutor with something new to contribute to the conversation (i.e., cutting out a circle is easier than cutting out the hand with fingers) even if his intention wasn't to propose a new way to make the wreath. In fact, upon close inspection, the novelty of the contribution appears suspect when Arkadiy seems to contradict himself later in line 45 by saying, "We just draw a hand and *cut it out*." Here Arkadiy comes closer to his mother's original instructions (to cut out the hands and glue them in a circle), and perhaps the practice with the instructions that he had in the earlier production helped him approximate his mother's discourse more closely in the second go.

Line	Mother's utterance	Line	Arkadiy's utterance
7	We're going to put our hand on construction paper.		
8	We're going to trace around our hands.	32	We can put our hand and trace it.
10	And we're going to cut out the tracing.		
11	And then we're going to glue them # in a big circle: to make a handprint wreath	34	And then after we're done tracing it we can put round it a big circle.
41	Cause then we can just cut out the big circle rather than cutting out the xx fingers.	45	Because then we just draw a hand and cut it out and that way we can put inside of the xx # of the circle.

Figure 1. Arkadiy's repetition of his mother

In Excerpt 4 Arkadiy uses chunks of language produced by his mother in the immediate discourse to find a way to contribute to the conversation. He establishes himself as an authority on the family activities in this way and takes on the appearance of being a competent interlocutor. This is a circular process however to some degree, Arkadiy has developed strategies to overcome the lack of conversational assistance in the family discourse, but his strategies are so effective that they do not provide access to conversational assistance. Arkadiy has learned to emulate the discourse produced around him, but he does not have the opportunity to expand on his own productions or revise his repetitions in such a way to make changes to meaning that have been noted to be important for classroom discourse (such as analyzing, arguing, and making connections).

In contrast to Arkadiy's above performance, Excerpt 5 presents an episode that occurs about 50 lines prior to Excerpt 4 in which Arkadiy is not successful in demonstrating his expertise. Here, Meredith proposes making snowflakes for the windows, but does not provide instructions. Instead of making up instructions or proposing a way to make the snowflakes himself, Arkadiy complains that he will not be able to do it because he doesn't know how. Anna, Arkadiy's sister, seems to compete with Arkadiy here as she is familiar with such craft activities from nursery school; whereas Arkadiy is exposed to such activities primarily at home.

Excerpt 5: Snowflakes

1   Meredith: The other thing we have to do # at some point, is we need snowflakes to put – you [remember] +/
2   Anna: [Mmhmm]!
3   Meredith: how we had the leaves up here?
4   We're going to do snowflakes.
5   Arkadiy: But when?
6   Meredith: Maybe we could do that after # quiet time.
7   Arkadiy: But mama I can't do it because I don't know how.
8   Meredith: Well, I'll show you.
9   Anna: And I know!
10   Mama I know how to do [it].
11 Arkadiy: [Be]cause in case I get wrong # then # it will not be good.
12 Anna: Mama?
13   Mama?
14   You know what?
15   [I know how to] +/.
16 Meredith: [Finish – finish] chewing first.
17 Arkadiy: Mama?
18   I can't <making my own> [?] snowflakes.
19   Only leafs.

The fact that Arkadiy is not willing to venture an explanation of how to make a snowflake without prior instruction (and even fears the outcome of the activity) suggests the extent to which he relies on prior discourse to express new information in family conversations and perhaps build his own linguistic competence.

Discussion

How do young second language learners acquire the communicative competence necessary for educational settings? Recent discussions have suggested that a variety of experiences are needed to lead to these type of academic competencies, many of which take place outside of traditional teacher-fronted activities (Kotler, Wegerif, & LeVoi 2001; Valdés 2004; Hawkins 2005). This study has found that young children adopted from abroad by English-speaking parents engage in episodes of collaborative discourse at home that expose them to discourse genres associated with school practices such as narratives, explanations and other literacy-related events.

Self- vs. other-repetition

In specific, this study has examined the varying functions of self- and other- repetition in collaborative discourse between adults and children. While other-repetition was found to be an important aspect of scaffolding when used by adult interlocutors to establish intersubjectivity with children, both self- and other-repetition were found to be important communicative resources for second language learning children in accomplishing complex conversational tasks. A comparison of the two learners' use of repetition in this study found that both boys used other-repetition to gain new turns at talk and used self-repetition to maintain turns at talk when interrupted. However, in cases where assistance was not readily available, for both children, the repetition of discourse routines (such as the bad thing/good thing routine) or chunks of "local" discourse (as in Arkadiy's repetition of his mother or Sasha's use of his brother's line in the letter) provided a means through which children can scaffold their own participation (as found in Pallotti, 2003). Further, self-repetition allowed for revising utterances and providing more information to meet interactional demands. The more competent English user in this study, Sasha, was seen to use reformulations or revisions of his own and others' utterances in a creative way that allowed him to establish an individual identity in the interaction. These reformulations were most often prompted by challenges from Sasha's interlocutors, suggesting that parental strategies or interactional obstacles (such as interruptions from an older sibling) can serve to push a learner's production.

Further, the findings in this study suggest that the multiple functions of self-repetition in particular should not be overlooked by second language researchers. Sasha's use of self-repetition in response to challenges from his father and brother points to the nuanced ways in which learners may build on their own previous utterances to reformulate and revise their contributions to meet their interlocutor's point of view while at the same time establishing an independent meaning, and subsequently, identity. While previous studies of scaffolding in first language development have found that children whose caregivers prompted or challenged them during storytelling events were more likely to avoid storytelling activities (see Ochs & Capps 2001), findings from the present study suggest that prompting and challenging can require a child to reformulate contributions in such a way to establish a shared perspective on the event being discussed (see also Ochs et al. 1992). Moreover, these challenges as well as responses to challenges, as in the case of Sasha and John, rely on repetition. Merritt (1994) indicates that it is precisely these types of repetition discourse analysts (and I would argue second language researchers) should be interested in.

Limitations

This study has focused on aspects of the micro interaction between adoptive parents and children to explain two boys' differential linguistic performances; however, other explanations may be given. While neither Sasha nor Arkadiy attended school or possessed the ability to read and write in his native language at the time of arrival, Arkadiy was younger than Sasha and had spent a longer time in the orphanage in his early years according to parental reports. These factors have been suggested to play a role in international adoptees' early learning experiences and relative school performance (Glennen & Bright 2005). However, in a study of two adopted Vietnamese brothers' language acquisition (ages 10 and 12), Sato (1990) concluded that factors other than age and cognitive development played a role in the boys' different outcomes, such as experiences with English literacy in the classroom. In the micro analysis presented in this study, we can find some evidence of how parental interactional strategies and the children's post-adoption language ecologies (including the influence of schooling, siblings, and home literacy) affect their linguistic productions.

Because this study does not directly investigate the boys' performance in school, we don't have a clear understanding of how the interactions that occur at home influence those inside the classroom and vice versa. At the end of this study, Kevin and Meredith had decided to enroll Arkadiy in a local public school. He was placed in the first grade in agreement with school administrators even though he would turn eight during the school year. Sasha was reported to have caught up to his grade level (2nd) in reading; although, he still had difficulties as the assignments got more complicated. A further limitation to this study is that it does not consider the boys' own perspectives on how they took part in the family interactions and how they viewed themselves as learners, students, and family members. As Hawkins (2005) notes, we cannot truly understand the identity work that goes on for young second language learners until we have a better understanding of how they themselves view these processes.

Conclusion

Although many studies have concluded that learners move from reliance on repetition in interaction to gradual autonomy of production and less repetition in second language acquisition, this study suggests that some complex forms of repetition (i.e. reformulations) may be a marker of discourse competence. Repetition, after all, is a linguistic universal (Merritt 1994) that is ubiquitous to social interactions and serves greater discourse functions than those often identified by researchers interested in language learning (see for example Tannen 1990). As research in second language learning moves beyond investigating scaffolding as a means for lexical or grammatical development to a site of socialization into discourse competencies, investigating the more nuanced uses of strategies such as repetition in learner discourse takes on new importance. Further, as we consider what types of experiences and interactions second language-learning children need to develop academic competencies, we need to know more about what makes certain interactions more successful than others for young learners. Finally, the findings from this study suggest that a challenging and engaging interactional environment that involves individual attention from adult interlocutors can provide fertile ground for second language learners to make the most out of their communicative resources.

References

Abu-Akel, A. 2002. The psychological and social dynamics of topic performance in family dinnertime conversations. *Journal of Pragmatics* 34: 1787–1806.

Beals, D. E. & Snow, C. 1994. 'Thunder is when the angels are upstairs bowling': Narratives and explanations at the dinner table. *Journal of Narrative and Life History* 4(4): 331–352.

Blum-Kulka, S. 1997. *Dinner Talk: Cultural Patterns of Sociability and Socialization in Family Discourse*. Mahwah NJ: Lawrence Erlbaum Associates.

Broner, M. & Tarone, E. 2001. Is it fun? Language play in a fifth-grade Spanish immersion classroom. *The Modern Language Journal* 85(3): 364–379.

Cummins, J. 2003. BICS and CALPS: Origins and rationale for the distinction. In *Sociolinguistics: The Essential Readings*, C. B. Paulston & G. R. Tucker (eds), 322–328. Malden MA: Blackwell.

DiCamilla, F. J. & Anton, M. 1997. Repetition in the collaborative discourse of L2 learners: A Vygotskian perspective. *The Canadian Modern Language Review/La Revue Canadienne des Langues Vivantes* 53(4): 609–633.

Fogle, L. W. 2006. 'These are not kids with ESL': Examining adoptive parents' talk about second language learning and their internationally adopted children. Paper presentation, Sociolinguistics Symposium 16 (SS16), Limerick, Ireland.

Glennen, S. & Bright, B. 2005. Five years later: Language in school-age internationally adopted children. *Seminars in Speech and Language* 26(1): 86–101.

Hatch, E., Peck, S. & Wagner-Gough, J. 1979. A look at process in child second-language acquisition. In *Developmental Pragmatics*, E. Ochs & B. Schieffelin (eds), 269–277. New York NY: Academic Press.

Hawkins, M. 2005. Becoming a student: Identity work and academic literacies in early schooling. *TESOL Quarterly* 39(1): 59–82.

Heath, S. B. 1983. *Ways with Words: Language, life, and work in communities and classrooms.* Cambridge: Cambridge University Press.

Hymes, D. 1974. *Foundations in Sociolinguistics.* Philadelphia PA: University of Pennsylvania Press.

King, K. A. & Melzi, G. 2004. Intimacy, imitation and language learning: Spanish diminutives in mother-child conversation. *First Language* 24(2): 241–261.

Kotler, A., Wegerif, R. & LeVoi, M. 2001. Oracy and the educational achievement of pupils with English as an Additional Language: The impact of bringing 'talking partners' into Bradford schools. *International Journal of Bilingual Education and Bilingualism* 4(6): 403–419.

Lantolf, J. P. 1997. The function of language play in the acquisition of L2 Spanish. In *Contemporary Perspectives on the Acquisition of Spanish*, Vol.2: *Production, Processing, and Comprehension*, W. R. Glass & A. T. Pérez-Leroux (eds), 3–24. Somerville MA: Cascadilla.

Long, M. 2006. *Problems in SLA.* Mahwah NJ: Lawrence Erlbaum Associates.

Lyster, R. 1998. Recasts, repetition, and ambiguity in classroom discourse. *Studies in Second Language Acquisition* 20: 51–81.

MacWhinney, B. 2000. *The CHILDES Project: Tools for analyzing talk.* 3rd edn. Mahwah NJ: Lawrence Erlbaum Associates.

Merritt, M. 1982. Repeats and reformulations in primary classrooms as windows of the nature of talk engagement. *Discourse Processes* 5: 127–145.

Merritt, M. 1994. Repetition in situated discourse – Exploring its forms and functions. In *Repetition in Discourse: Interdisciplinary Perspectives*, Vol. 1, B. Johnstone (ed.), 23–36. Norwood NJ: Ablex.

Michaels, S. 1981. Sharing time: Children's narrative styles and differential access to literacy. *Language in Society* 10: 423–42.

Ninio, A. & Snow, C. 1996. *Pragmatic Development.* Boulder CO: Westview Press.

Ochs, E. & Capps, O. 2001. *Living Narrative.* Cambridge MA: Harvard University Press.

Ochs, E., Taylor, C., Rudolph, D. & Smith, R. 1992. Storytelling as a theory-building activity. *Discourse Processes* 15: 37–72.

Ochs Keenan, E. 1977. Making it last: Repetition in children's discourse. In *Child Discourse*, S. Ervin-Tripp & C. Mitchell-Kernan (eds), 125–138. New York NY: Academic Press.

Pallotti, G. 2003. Borrowing words: Appropriations in child second language discourse. In *Ecology of Language Acquisition*, J. Leather & J. van Dam (eds), 183–202. Dordrecht: Kluwer.

Rydland, V. & Aukrust, V.G. 2005. Lexical repetition in second language learners' peer play interaction. *Language Learning* 55(2): 229–274.

Sato, C. 1990. *The Syntax of Conversation in Interlanguage Development*. Tübingen: Narr.

Tannen, D. 1990. *Talking Voices: Repetition, Dialogue, and Imagery in Conversational Discourse*. Cambridge: Cambridge University Press.

TESOL. 2006. TESOL revises PreK-12 English Language Proficiency Standards. Teachers of English to Speakers of Other Languages, Inc. http://www.tesol.org/s_tesol/sec_document.asp?CID=1186&DID=5349 (accessed June 26, 2007).

TESOL. 1997. ESL standards for Pre-K-12 students: Grades Pre-K-3. Teachers of English to Speakers of Other Languages, Inc. http://www.tesol.org/s_tesol/sec_document.asp?CID=113&DID=314&rcss (accessed June 26, 2007).

Valdés, G. 2004. Between support and marginalization: The development of academic language in linguistic minority children. *Bilingual Education and Bilingualism* 7(2/3): 102–132.

Willett, J. 1995. Becoming first graders in an L2: An ethnographic study of L2 socialization. *TESOL Quarterly* 29(3): 473–503.

Wray, A. 1999. Formulaic language in learners and native speakers. *Language Teaching* 32(4): 213–231.

Appendix

Transcription Conventions adapted from CHAT (MacWhinney 2000)

+...	incompletion of utterance
+/.	interruption of utterance
+^	quick uptake by speaker
++	other completion of previous utterance
–	speaker retraces or false start
[ ]	words in brackets overlap
#	pause of two seconds or less
xx or xxx	unintelligible word or words
[?]	best guess at word or words in angle brackets
[!]	word is stressed

Language transfer in child SLA

A longitudinal case study of a sequential bilingual

Eun-Young Kwon and ZhaoHong Han
Teachers College, Columbia University

In this chapter we report on a 26-month longitudinal study of a Korean-speaking child acquiring L2 English in the United States (AoA: 3;6). Focusing on negation, plural, and possessive marking, we examined the nature of language transfer as a function of changes occurring in the participant's L1 and L2. We subsequently found bidirectional transfer in the child's placement of the negator, reverse transfer in certain plural constructions, and a delay in the acquisition of possessive marking that is attributable to the lack of a corresponding feature in the participant's developing L1. Importantly, this pattern of transfer appears to arise from the waxing and waning of the child's L1 and L2.

Foster-Cohen (2001) suggests a sliding-window approach to understanding child second language acquisition (SLA). She views development as a continuum along a variety of axes, including but not limited to age, cognitive maturity, and proficiency, which are interrelated such that waxing along one axis may coincide with waning along another. Adopting the "sliding window" notion as its conceptual backdrop, this chapter reports on the longitudinal study focusing on language transfer as a function of changes occurring in the child's L1 and L2. Transfer was herein defined as a process in L2 acquisition (L2A) whereby one language influences the other. This is dubbed substratum transfer when the influence comes from the L1 and reverse transfer when the influence comes from the L2 (Odlin 1989).

Transfer in child L2A

In the domain of child SLA, it is not uncommon that researchers see language transfer as largely irrelevant – except as random and isolated incidents (Dulay & Burt 1974; Gillis & Weber 1976; McLaughlin 1978; Selinker & Lakshmanan 1993). Selinker and Lakshmanan (1993), for example, took the theoretical position that SLA in young children is based on UG and target language (TL) input and hence follows a process similar to L1 acquisition. Even so, a number of empirical studies have suggested that transfer in child SLA is far less rare (or limited in terms of domain) than is often held (Odlin 1989). Even in the domain of morphosyntax, which is supposedly non-susceptible to crosslinguistic influence, evidence exists to the contrary. For example, Wode (1981), in a study examining the L2 English of four German children aged four to nine, identified reliance on L1 to be an "integral part" of L2 acquisition and that occurs systematically. In a UG-based study, Whong-Barr and Schwartz (2002) found that, like L1 English-speaking children, Japanese (mean age: 7;8) and Korean-speaking child learners of L2 English (mean age: 8) overgeneralized the to-dative double-object forms, but that only the Japanese children did so for the for-dative as well. This difference within a broadly common developmental pattern was interpreted as evidence of L1 transfer.

Where child L2 acquisition of English negation, plural -s and possessive -'s – the target linguistic forms in the present study – is concerned, there is evidence for L1 transfer as well – notwithstanding the fact that these grammatical forms have been universally found to follow a natural developmental sequence (negation)[1] or order of acquisition (plural -s and possessive -'s).[2] First, with regard to negation, Hansen (1983; see also Lakshmanan 2006) studied acquisition, loss, and reacquisition patterns in the L2 negation of two L1 English-speaking child learners of Hindi-Urdu (ages 2;1–5;0 and 3;9–7;6). Overall, both children evidenced

---

1.   The term *developmental sequence* refers to the passage of learners through a series of (in most cases) progressively more target-like manifestations of a given feature, each of which predominates at a given stage of development. The sequence for L2 English negation, which is similar yet not identical to that identified for L1 (Klima & Bellugi 1966), has four stages:

1) External negation (i.e., no or not is placed at the beginning or end of the utterance, as in 'No (you) playing here');
2) Internal negation (i.e., the negator – no, not or don't – is placed between the subject and the main verb, as in 'You no talk');
3) Negative attached to modal verbs (e.g., 'I can't play that one); and
4) Negative attached to auxiliary verb (e.g., 'She didn't believe me.' 'He didn't said it'). (R. Ellis 2000, p. 100)

Duration in these stages can differ across individual learners. For the purposes of this study, the duration of a stage is defined as those months for which the associated manifestation accounts for a statistical majority of recorded tokens for the feature in question.

2.   The order of acquisition in English morphemes was extensively studied in the 1970s. Despite lingering methodological issues (see Goldschneider & DeKeyser 2001), considerable support emerged for the L1 order found by Brown (1973), viz., present progressive -ing, in, on, plural -s, past irregular, possessive -'s, uncontractible copula, articles (a, the), past regular -ed, 3rd person singular regular -s, 3rd person singular irregular, uncontractible auxiliary, contractible copula, contractible auxiliary, and the L2 order found by Dulay and Burt (1974), viz., articles, copula, progressive -ing, simple plural -s, auxiliary, past regular -ed, past irregular, long plural -es, possessive -'s, 3rd person singular.

bell curves in which placement of the negator initially approximated L1 norms, gravitated toward targetlike syntax, and then receded back to the L1-influenced structure once the family returned to an English-speaking environment. That the non-targetlike structures were in fact instances of transfer is supported by their absence from the negative utterances of Hindi-Urdu child learners with an L1 (Telugu) that is typologically distinct from English for this feature (Sharma 1974).

Evidence of L1 transfer in negation can also be found in studies of Korean and Japanese child learners of L2 English. Shin (2001) reported that her participants, 40 elementary, 40 middle, and 23 high school students in Korea, exhibited a developmental sequence for negation that coincided with the universal sequence; however, all groups, especially the elementary school students (Stage 1) were prone to using post-verbal negation in their L2 English, a feature of their L1 not typically found in other learners of English. Transfer of this kind also showed up in Koike's (1980) longitudinal study of three Japanese children learning English as the L2. Similar to Korean, Japanese allows post-verbal negation.

With regard to possessive marking, Fathman (1975) compared Korean and Spanish learners of English (N=120) aged 6 to 14 and found, *inter alia*, that they differed significantly in marking possessive -'s, with the Korean children achieving higher accuracy scores on the Second Language Oral Production English (SLOPE) test than their Spanish peers. This difference is ascribable to L1 influence: Korean employs a post-nominal morpheme that corresponds to the English possessive -'s (obligatory in writing), whereas Spanish marks possession by means of a periphrastic construction equivalent to the English *Noun+of+Noun*.

Korean children's advantage in acquiring the possessive morpheme, as a result of positive transfer from the L1, has also been noted in contrast to their disadvantage in acquiring the plural morpheme, as a result of negative transfer. Pak (1987), examining the acquisition of English grammatical morphemes by five-to-twelve-year-old Korean children living in Texas, observed that the indefinite article, the third person singular -s, and plural -s presented the greatest difficulty, all being considered grammatical morphemes by the classic morpheme order studies. Of relevance to note for the purposes of the present study is that Pak's participants acquired the possessive morpheme before the plural morpheme – a violation of the universal order of acquisition (Dulay & Burt 1974). The same finding was reported in a study by Shin and Milroy (1999) of the bilingual development of Korean-American children attending first grade in New York City. Here not only did the acquisition of the possessive morpheme occur prior to the plural morpheme, but there was also a reverse transfer of the L2 plural marking into the L1. Further evidence of the "possessive before plural" sequence can be found in Jin (2003), who looked at the use of determiners by Korean child learners of English in two different age groups (mean age 6;2 and 8;1). Interestingly but not surprisingly, in a longitudinal study, Hakuta (1976) also found that his five-year-old L1

Japanese participant, Uguisu, acquired the possessive -'s before the plural -s. In both the Korean and the Japanese case, the violation is attributable to L1 influence: Korean and Japanese are alike in that they both have obligatory marking for possessive but optional – in fact, infrequent – marking for plural nouns.

Summing up, although evidence of transfer in child L2A is not as abundant as in adult L2A, it nevertheless exists, and as far as negation, the plural -s, and the possessive -'s are concerned, it manifests in three ways: (a) deviation from the universal sequence, (b) adoption of an L1 feature, or (c) relatively superior deployment of a particular L2 feature. Moreover, just as in adult SLA, the crosslinguistic influence in child SLA may arise from L1-L2 similarity (i.e., as in possessive marking) as well as from difference (i.e., as in plural marking) and may occur both ways, from the L1 to the L2 and vice versa.[3] Thus, as Odlin (2003) has argued, "cross-linguistic influence may be inevitable ... when a second language begins to develop and ... after processes of primary language acquisition are well underway" (p. 470). It is clear, however, that in the literature on child L2A, the issue of transfer has by and large been treated as tangential. This may have to do with the general conception of its limitations noted at the beginning of this section. More pertinently, however, the study of transfer is methodologically challenging, even with adult learners. In the case of child learners, transfer, if it occurs, is inextricably entwined with endogenous developmental processes. Next, we briefly discuss (a) methodological issues in transfer research and (b) Foster-Cohen's (2001) sliding window hypothesis, as both provided motivation for the present study.

Methodological issues

Although transfer has been a perennial issue in L2A and has thus led to a plenitude of research, methods for determining transfer have not been entirely satisfactory (Jarvis 2000). One approach focuses on what is abundant in learners' output, typically utilizing quantitative analyses of elicited, group data. Another approach looks at less quantifiable facts such as avoidance of structures in individual participants. The former, though by conventional accounts a reliable method, may lead to re-

---

3.   That bidirectional transfer may occur in sequential bilinguals should come as no surprise, as this phenomenon has been documented both in late bilinguals, i.e., post-puberty onset L2 learners (e.g., Pavlenko 2000; Pavlenko & Jarvis 2002) and in simultaneous bilinguals (e.g., Döpke 2000). However, acquisitional processes in sequential bilinguals who start learning the L2 before L1 acquisition is complete have generally been understudied. *Inter alia*, such learners may still be acquiring or have yet to acquire certain complex or late-acquired structures in their L1, making their encounter with the corresponding structures in their L2 a first-time experience (see Lakshmanan 2006).

sults that are superficial and premature, as critics have noted (see e.g., Odlin 2003; Weinreich 1953). By way of illustration, Schachter's (1974) study, undertaking both quantitative and qualitative analyses of the data, offers compelling evidence that the influence of the L1 on the L2 can be implicit: learners may avoid certain L2 syntactic constructions for which there are no (identical) counterparts in their L1. Importantly, this phenomenon of avoidance emerged not from a simple tally of errors but rather from qualitative analysis. Han's (2000) longitudinal study points to a different kind of implicit influence of the L1 on the L2 that, likewise, would not lend itself to a quantitative analysis: her two participants, both native speakers of Chinese, were prone to using the English passive construction as a surrogate for an unmarked, topic-comment syntactic structure and discourse function in the L1.

At the same time, the qualitative approach can be said to sacrifice generalizability, due to the small sample size often employed and, in many cases, the lack of statistical evidence for a pattern in the observed phenomena. Nonetheless, transfer has generally, if not universally, been conceded to be an idiosyncratic phenomenon. Hence, as Odlin (2003) has aptly noted, "a great deal of language contact research does not – and sometimes cannot – use statistics" (p. 451). Even so, the two approaches need not be construed as diametrically opposed. Again, as Odlin has pointed out, "the evidence for crosslinguistic influence takes many forms ... no single data collection procedure will necessarily provide better evidence about transfer" (p. 451). Such has indeed been the option sought by current transfer research. In particular, efforts have been made to diversify the types of data, e.g., naturalistic and elicited, and to lengthen the duration of the study, the aim being to obtain unambiguous evidence (see e.g., Han 2000, 2001). The latter is particularly important when it comes to investigating transfer in child SLA, a much more dynamic process than that of adult SLA.

The sliding window hypothesis

It is precisely this changing nature of child language acquisition that Foster-Cohen (2001) stresses in her sliding window proposal. For Foster-Cohen, the focus of language acquisition research, be it on the L1 or the L2, should be on the continuities rather than the discontinuities, because, as she puts it, "if we focus on the continuities between L1 and L2 and within L2, the discontinuities take care of themselves" (p. 342). She explains:

> Take, for example, two points in time, say at five years of age and at 12 years of age (and there are, of course, an infinite number of such points). We can then ask for each point where the child is in relation to a range of different developments: metalinguistic development, lexical development (of words and of lexical phrases), critical period(s) for L2, theory of mind development, reasoning development,

as well as all the usual linguistic structural developments. If you draw, in even a rough graphic way what we know about the rising and falling capacities in each of these areas (and there are many others that are relevant), you reveal a complex and different pattern of capacities at each age. As you slide the window over the age span from zero to 20 ... You do not find sharp cut-offs. You simply find different configurations of capacities and skills. (p. 342)

From this line of reasoning, it follows that linguistic changes do not occur in isolation but in complex combinations, and as part of a larger human developmental system, involving multiple domains (cf. N. Ellis & Larsen-Freeman 2006). Hence, empirical research on language acquisition should not only be longitudinal in nature, if the goal is to reveal changes (or lack thereof), but also more inclusive than it has been in its database to incorporate information culled from related developmental domains.

Purposes of the present investigation

The present study examines L1 transfer that occurs in child L2 acquisition. Its purpose is three-fold: (a) to establish evidence of transfer in relation to three linguistic features: negation, possessive, and plural marking, (b) to document changes in the quantity and quality of transfer, and last but not least, (c) to examine the relationship between transfer and changes in the L1 and the L2 in light of the sliding window hypothesis. Specifically, the following questions were asked:

1. Is there evidence of transfer in the participant's L1 (i.e., Korean) and/or L2 (i.e., English)?
2. If so, what type of transfer is it?
3. Is there a relationship between transfer and changes that occur in the L1 and the L2?

These questions were addressed through examining a two-year longitudinal database of the naturalistic oral production of a child L2 learner. Details are given in the Method section.

Typological comparison of Korean and English

Negation

English negation is achieved by placing the negative particle *not* or *n't* after the first auxiliary element.

English: **aux + not + V**

(1)   Mary does *not* eat.

Korean, on the other hand, has two possible negative constructions: pre-verbal and post-verbal. These are sometimes called short and long negation, respectively, and can be used interchangeably. In preverbal negation, the negator *an* ('not') or *mos* ('can't') is placed before the verb. In post-verbal negation, the verb is nominalized using the particle *-ci* followed by one of the above negative particles and the verb *hata* ('to do'), the most common realization using *an + hata* in the contracted form *anhta*. Thus, for the affirmative sentence in (2), both (2a) and (2b) represent possible negations.

Korean: **an/mos + V; V+ -ci+ an/mos + hata**

(2)   *Mary-ka   muk-ta.*
        Mary-NOM   eat-DECL
        'Mary eats.'

   a.   *Mary-ka   an   muk-ta.*
          Mary-NOM   NEG   eat-DECL
          'Mary does not eat.'

   b.   *Mary-ka   muk-ci an   h-ta.*
          Mary-NOM   eat-CI NEG   do-DECL
          'Mary does not eat.' (Kim 1974)

Plural -s. English forms regular plurals by generally attaching *-s* to the end of nouns, which are sometimes preceded by an unspecific or specific quantifier, as illustrated in (3a) through (3c).

English: -s

(3)   a.   John gave *a book* to Mary.
        b.   John gave *books* to Mary.
        c.   John gave *some books* to Mary.
        d.   John gave *two books* to Mary.

Conversely, Korean nouns, such as *chaeck* 'book,' are generally not marked for plurality. Although a post-nominal plural marker, *-tul*, does exist, it is never used with specific quantifiers (e.g., *two books*) and optionally but seldom used when the quantifier is unspecific or absent. Hence, the Korean utterance shown in (4a), in which the noun is not marked for plurality, could correspond to any of the English sentences (3a) to (3d). Korean does, however, employ one of several classifiers, most commonly *kae* but also *kwen, mali,* etc., after specific quantifiers. Therefore, whether the specific quantifier was *one, two*, or a higher number, an utterance such as (3d) would almost always be rendered in Korean by inserting a classifier, *kwen*, after the quantifier, that is, without using the plural marker, as in (4b).

Korean: (-tul)

(4) *John-i   Mary-eke   chaek(-tul)-ul   cu-os-ta.*
     John-NOM Mary-DAT book(-PL)-ACC give-PAST-DECL
     'John gave Mary book(s).'

a. *John-i   Mary-eke   chaek   tu   kwen-ul   cu-os-ta.*
    John-NOM Mary-DAT book two CLASS-ACC give-PAST-DECL
    'John gave Mary two books.' (Jin 2003)

Possessive -'s. English marks possession using either post-nominal -'s or the periphrastic construction, *noun +of + noun*, with the first noun denoting 'possessed' and the second noun 'possessor.' The two options are illustrated in [5a] and [5b].

English:

(5) a.   Mommy's car
     b.   The car of Mommy

Korean, on the other hand, has a post-nominal possessive particle -*ui* that is obligatory in writing but typically absent in speech, as illustrated in [6]. This morpheme is acquired late by L1 learners of Korean, usually emerging between the ages of four and five (Ha 2001). Although Ha cites evidence from pronoun use to suggest that Korean children have at least a rudimentary concept of possession from about age twenty months, they typically form nominal possessive constructions using target-like word order without the particle.

Korean:

(6) *Umma(-**ui**)   cha*
     Mommy(-POS) car
     'Mommy(-'s) car' (Kang 2001)

Method

Participant

The participant was a Korean female child, named Sooji, who was born in Korea and who arrived in the United States at the age of 3;6. Sooji is best characterized as a "sequential bilingual," i.e., a child who "is exposed to one language first and the second language sometime later" (Bhatia & Ritchie 1999, p. 584). Sooji is distinguishable not only from "simultaneous bilinguals," who start their linguistic experience by learning two languages at the same time, but also from older child L2 learners. One potentially significant difference between the two is the fact that sequential bilinguals are exposed to the L2 before their L1 is fully acquired.

Following Bae (1995), Sooji's oral proficiency in her L1, Korean, was slightly above average for her age. For example, while most Korean children at age 3;6 can only produce one-clause utterances, Sooji produced two-clause utterances, including embedded and relative clauses. Except during and shortly after her summer visit to Korea in 2004, Sooji's L1 proficiency declined across the study period (2003–2005) in terms of length of utterance, complexity, and accuracy.

Before her arrival in the United States, Sooji had limited exposure to English via children's songs and animated films in English. Once in the United States, Sooji attended a six-hour Pre-K day program, five days per week, with English as the only language of instruction (March 2003 to June 2004), followed by a similar kindergarten program (September 2004 through the close of data collection in April 2005). Throughout this time she lived in New York with her mother and sometimes her maternal grandmother, who spoke only Korean with each other and with Sooji in the home (Phase I; see Table 1). After completing Pre-K in June 2004, however, Sooji spent two months in Korea (Phase II; see Table 1), returning to the United States at the end of August 2004 at age 4;11 and residing there with her mother until the end of the study period (Phase III; see Table 1).

Database

Naturalistic data were collected from March 2003 through April 2005. They included (a) audio and video recordings of two hours of observation per week made in school or at home when Sooji interacted with her peers, (b) field notes on Sooji's spontaneous production at home, outside the observation sessions, and (c) informal interviews with Sooji.

Data analysis

Jarvis (2000), garnering disparate insights from previous transfer research, proposed a unified approach to establishing evidence of transfer. On this approach, three types of comparisons are made: (a) within-group (i.e., comparing the IL data of participants with the same L1), (b) between-group (i.e., comparing the IL data of participants with different L1s), and (c) within-group (i.e., comparing the participants' IL and L1). If these comparisons show respectively intra-L1-group homogeneity, inter-L1-group heterogeneity, and intra-L1-group congruity (i.e., between the L1 and the IL), then it is safe to conclude that L1 transfer is

Table 1. Linguistic environment by month of study

Phase	Month	Milestones in Type and Extent of Input
	1	Arrival in United States (L2 environment);
	2	Pre-K begins (6 hrs./day L2 only);
	3	Grandmother accompanies from Korea
		(strong L1 presence at home)
	4	Summer School begins (8 hrs./day L2 only);
	5	Trips to Washington and Disney World
	6	(L2 predominates);
Phase I		Grandmother returns to Korea (less L1 at home)
	7	Pre-K begins at new school (6 hrs./day L2 only)
	8	
	9	Grandmother returns to United States
	10	(strong L1 presence at home)
	11	
	12	Grandmother returns to Korea (less L1 at home)
	13	
	14	Grandmother returns to United States
	15	(strong L1 presence at home)
	16	
Phase II	17	Participant visits Korea with mother and grandmother
	18	(near-exclusive L1)
Phase III	19	
	20	
	21	
	22	Participant returns to United States
	23	with mother only;
	24	Kindergarten begins (6 hrs./day L2 only)
	25	
	26	

in operation. Although this approach was born out of, and hence, is suited for, group-based research, we adapted it to our case study, by comparing:

a. the participant's IL with that of other learners of similar age and at similar stage of development whose L1 is either Korean or Japanese,
b. the participant's IL with that of other learners of similar age and at similar stage of development whose L1s are other than Korean and Japanese, and
c. the participant's IL and L1.

More specifically, for (a) and (b), naturalistic utterances containing the targeted features were compared to relevant data from 32 published studies, of which 16 had participants whose L1s were either Korean or typologically similar to Korean (e.g., Japanese) and 16 whose L1s were typologically disparate from Korean (e.g., Spanish; see Appendices A & B). The participants in many of these studies were similar in age to Sooji. Then, for (c), Sooji's utterances were compared to her L1 and, where different, to the standard form of the language. These comparisons made it possible to identify tokens of transfer. These tokens were subsequently analyzed to determine the frequency and distribution of substratum (from the L1 to the L2) and reverse (from the L2 to the L1) transfer.

Results

Negation

A chronological summary of Sooji's use of negation in her Korean and English appears in Table 2.[4] As can be seen, when she arrived in the United States, at age 3;6, Sooji was using both pre-verbal (see [K1]) and post-verbal negation (see [K2]) in nativelike fashion in L1 Korean. After the first month of the study, however, she was observed to use the post-verbal construction in her L1 only once (see Discussion). Otherwise, she used pre-verbal negation exclusively, even during her visit to Korea (see Table 1).

The data for Sooji's L2 English, on the other hand, showed four distinct though not clear-cut stages of development (see Note 1). In Stage I (Months 1–2), Sooji placed the negator *no* at the end of the utterance, as in [E1–9].[5] In Stage II (Months 3–12), the negators *no* and *not* were moved to sentence-internal positions, as illustrated in [E10–13]. In Stage III (Months 13–20), the negator was attached to modal verbs, as in [E14–17]. Finally, in Stage IV (Months 21–26), Sooji employed target-like negation with auxiliary plus negator, although she did not always mark number and tense correctly, as shown in [E18–21].

Of the four stages of utterances shown in Table 2, only those belonging to Stage I were coded as L1 transfer. These [E1–9] were produced in the first three months of the study, and all feature external negation in sentence-final position. This is non-targetlike in English on two counts: (1) the negator follows the verb and (2) the negator follows the object. In Korean, however, where the standard word order is S[O]V, post-verbal negation is inevitably sentence final. Thus, the

---

4.   "K" stands for Korean and "E" for English.

5.   Since they were coded as LT, all Sooji's utterances containing negators from this stage were included, except for one-word utterances and those containing (initially) formulaic expressions like "I don't know." For Stages II–IV, four utterances were chosen to illustrate each stage.

Table 2. Sooji's use of negation*

Input Conditions	L1 (Korean)	L2 (English)	
	(K1) Manjeo bonikka **an** teukeoweyo. (3;6) *Touch so not hot.* (=I touched it and it was not hot.)		
	(K2) Elmo-ka chaeck-eul ireoke mani poko chiwuji an**asseyo.** (3;6) *Elmo book this many read clean not.* (=Elmo read so many books and he did not clean up.)	Stage I (E1) Catherine is Sooji friend *no*. (E2) Catherine: Catherine likes Sooji. Sooji: No. Sooji *no*. (=Sooji doesn't like Catherine.) (E3) I the friend *no*.	(3;7) (3;7) (3;7)
Phase I (Months 1–16 in the U.S.)		(E4) Smetha, I your friend *no*. (E5) I jacket *no*. (E6) I the Sponge Bob Greby no. (E7) I want this one *no*! (E8) I'm the friend your *no*. (E9) This one *no*.	(3;7) (3;7) (3;7) (3;8) (3;8) (3;8)
		Stage II (E10) No stand there! (E11) I *no* can do it. (E12) You're *not* can do. (E13) I'm *not* talking you.	(3;8) (3;10) (3;11) (4;3)
	(K3) Ajikdo **an** chollyeoyo. (4;5) *Still not sleepy.* (=I still am not sleepy.) (K4) *Aekimal-ika **an** malieyo. (4;6) *Baby talk not talk is.* (=It's not baby talk.)	Stage III (E14) I can*not* found it, Mommy. (E15) We can*not* open by wereself.	(4;6) (4;7)
Phase II (Months 17–18 in Korea)	(K5) Na-neun iche **an** paekopayo. (4;11) *I now not hungry* (=I am not hungry now.)	(E16) I *don't* did that.	(4;10)
Phase III (Months 19–26 in the U.S.)		(E17) I will *not* fell down. Stage IV (E18) My mommy *don't* like Sponge Bob Square Pants. (E19) It didn't made a sense. (E20) Why did you *didn't* saw? (E21) That's why I did *not* saw it.	(5;2) (5;2) (5;2) (5;4) (5;5)
	(K6) Massage **an** choahaeyo? (5;6) *Massage not like* (=Don't you like massage?)		

* ⟹ indicates substratum transfer and ⟸ indicates reverse transfer.

following inter- and intra-group comparisons support Korean as the source for [E1-9] (see also Table 3).

Intra-L1-group homogeneity. External negation at the end of the sentence is exemplified in the early acquisition of L2 English by speakers of languages that are typologically similar to Korean. The youngest participant in Koike (1980), a five-year-old speaker of Japanese, showed this structure in her earliest attempts at English negation (e.g., "This is *no*," "Girl is *no*"), as did several of the Korean L1 child learners of various ages in Shin (2001) (e.g., "Rain *no*," "Girl *no*," "Buy *no*").

Inter-L1-group heterogeneity. For speakers of L1s that are typologically distant from Korean, their Stage I utterances appear to be marked by placement of the negator in sentence initial rather than sentence final position (Butterworth 1972; R. Ellis 2000; Schumann 1979; Shapira 1976).

Intra-L1-group congruity. As shown in Table 2, at the beginning of the study period Sooji was observed using both the pre- and post-verbal forms available for standard Korean negation, though the latter disappeared from her L1 speech in the first month. Neither of these constructions allow the negator to precede the object. Thus Sooji's Stage I negation in L2, in which she placed the negator at the end of the sentence, reflects her L1 rule system.

Table 3. Evidence of transfer for negation

Type of Utterance Compared [Participant's Data]	Criterion 1 (intra-L1-group homogeneity)	Criterion 2 (inter-L1-group heterogeneity)	Criterion 3 (intra-L1-group congruity) [Participant's Data]
(E3) I the friend *no*. (3;7)	Girl is *no*. (Koike 1980)	*No* is correct. (Butterworth 1972)	Pre-verbal: (K1) Manjeo bonikka **an** tteukeoweyo. (3;6) *Touch so not hot.* (=I touched it and it was not hot.) Post-verbal: (K2) Elmo-ka chaeck-eul ireoke mani poko chiwuji anasseyo. (3;6) *Elmo book this many read clean not.* (=Elmo read so many books and he did not clean up.)
	Rain *no*. (Shin 2001)	**No** *is too little.* (Shapira 1976)	
L1 Transfer Supported	YES	YES	YES

Interestingly, while the above analysis made substratum transfer evident, it also revealed reverse transfer (i.e., L2 transfer) in concert with changes happening in Sooji's L2 system. The reverse transfer, as manifested in [K3–6] (Months 12–24), outlasted the data collection period, thereby showing stabilization. Importantly, both types of transfer occurred in connection with Sooji's predominant exposure to English, her L2.

Plural -s. Table 4 summarizes plural marking in Sooji's Korean and English. First, with regard to her Korean, at the beginning of the study period, Sooji exhibited nativelike use of plural. This included targetlike use both of plural constructions marked with the morpheme -tul, as in *chinku-tul* [K8], and of complex constructions in which quantifiers and classifiers were used, as shown in [K7] and [K9]. In Months 24–26, however, only three of these latter constructions were recorded, the word order of which all deviated from native speaker norms in ways that show reverse transfer, as in [K11–13].

As with negation, Sooji's use of English plural showed identifiable stages.[6] In Stage I (the first 19 months), she did not use the plural -s morpheme (see [E23–28]) in obligatory contexts.[7] In Stage II, beginning in Month 20, Sooji began using the plural -s regularly on English nouns, and for several months thereafter, she even overgeneralized the use of this morpheme, supplying it not only with nouns that require irregular or zero plural in the TL but once even with a Korean noun used in an English utterance [E32]. Finally, in Stage III (Months 24–26), no such overgeneralizations occurred and all recorded use was consistently targetlike. However, as evidence of her correct use of irregular plurals was found only later, the assignment of Sooji's L2 plural use immediately after her last recorded overgeneralization to the stage of "consistent targetlike use" must be

---

6.   As in Table 2, examples in Table 4 were chosen to provide a representative sample; here, however, the number of English examples for each of the three stages is more or less proportional to their relative duration.

7.   Non-marking at this stage might be evidence of transfer, since in Korean (and Japanese) nouns are not marked for plurality in many contexts in which marking is obligatory in English (Martin 1992). Indeed, the published data surveyed included a similar-aged learner of English with L1 Spanish, which has plural -s marking, who showed a high level of initial accuracy (Robertson 1986). By contrast, at the initial stage the four German children studied in Wode (1981), whose L1, like Spanish, *consistently* marks plural on most nouns (using a variety of patterns, including -s for loan words), marked some English nouns with -s in *both* sg. and pl. and others in neither. Thus, a claim for transfer in our subject requires additional systematic comparisons; moreover, Sooji had used the plural marker -tul in Korean before she arrived in the United States, meaning that, whatever its distribution in her input or production, unlike possessive marking (see below), plural marking was attested in her L1 system.

Table 4. Sooji's use of plural*

Input Conditions	L1 (Korean)	L2 (English)
Phase I (Months 1–16 in the U.S.)	(K7) Kaekuri-ka ne kae isseoyo. (3;6) *Frog four classifier are.* (=There are four frogs.) (K8) Mikuk chinku-*tul*-i jakku "heart" keuraeyo. (3;6) *American friends again heart say.* (=American friends pronounce it "heart.") (K9) Tu kae-man pwasseoyo. (4;7) *Two classifier only saw.* (=I only saw two [books].)	Stage I (E22) How many *cookie*? (3;9) (E23) This is a two *chair*. (3;11) (E24) It's three little *pig*. (3;11) (E25) Are you close your *eye*? (4;3) (E26) You had *eye*. (4;3) (E27) It means you and grandma – two *mommy*. (4;9)
Phase II (Months 17–18 in Korea)	(K10) Se kae-man isseoyo. (4;12) *Three classifier only are.* (=There are only three [stickers]).	(E28) Count all this thing. (4;10)
Phase III (Months 19–26 in the U.S.)	(K11) Se kae chaek juseyo. (5;6) *Three piece book give please.* (=Give me three books, please) (K12) Tu kae sa tang juseyo. (5;6) *Two piece candy give please.* (=Give me two candies, please) (K13) Se kae ureum-ika mukeumyun baeka apayo. (5;7) *Three piece ice [cream bar] eat if, stomach hurt.* (=If you eat three ice cream bars, your stomach will hurt.)	Stage II (E29) I have four hand*s*. (5;2) (=I have four fingers.) (E30) How many *childrens*? (5;2) (E31) Look at the beautiful *deers* (5;3) (E32) Mommy, I need *saekchongis*, marker*s*, string*s*, and straw*s*. (5;5) Stage III (E33) I love book*s* muchier than Joshua. (5;6) (E34) Why you cannot see no pictures? (5;7) (E35) Where are the book*s* that I buyed in my school? (5;7)

* ⇐ indicates reverse transfer.

considered provisional. Moreover, in the final two months of the study three utterances [K11–13] Sooji's in L1 Korean were recorded that may also be considered "overgeneralizations" of English plural constructions.

   Thus, of the utterances listed in Table 4, only the three Korean utterances were transfer-related, as confirmed by the following comparisons (see also Table 5).

Intra-L1-group homogeneity. Shin and Milroy (1999) cited word order similar to that employed by Sooji in [K11–13] from L1 Korean speech data produced by

Table 5. Evidence of transfer for plural -*s*

Type of Utterance Compared [Participant's Data]	Criterion 1 (intra-L1-group homogeneity)	Criterion 2 (inter-L1-group heterogeneity)	Criterion 3 (intra-L1-group congruity) [Participant's Data]
(K11) se kae chaek *three piece book* (=three books) (5;6)	tu sikye *two watch* (=two watches) (Shin & Milroy 1999)	chaek se kwen *book three piece* (=three books) (Standard Korean)	(E29) four hand*s* (5;2)
L2 Transfer Supported	YES	YES	YES

sequential bilingual learners of L2 English of similar age and age of arrival to Sooji (see Appendix A).

Inter-L1-group heterogeneity. Due to lack of baseline data in the literature on the L1 Korean speech of sequential bilinguals with an L2 that is typologically distinct from English – the ideal group to contrast to Sooji in this regard, standard Korean is used for comparison. Concerning [K11–13], standard Korean word order would call for *chaek se kwen juseyo* (literally, *Book three pieces give please*), *sa tang tu kae juseyo* (literally, *Candies two pieces give please*), and *ureum se kae-reul mukeumyun baeka apayo* (literally, *Ice [cream bar] three piece eat if, stomach hurt*). These formulations differ from Sooji's recorded utterances.[8]

Intra-L1-group congruity. The word order used by Sooji in [K11–13] corresponds to that of the L2 rather than to that of the L1. If we disregard the classifier (translated as "piece"), which has no counterpart in English, we can see that Sooji placed the specific quantifier (the cardinal number) before the noun. In Standard Korean, the order of these elements would be the reverse.

Possessive -*'s*. Table 6 provides a summary of Sooji's use of the possessive -*'s*. As shown, Sooji did not use the possessive morpheme in her L1 prior to her arrival in the United States or during the study period [K14–18]. Likewise, she consistently

---

8.   Shin (2005), citing J, Lee (1995) and K, Lee (personal communication), notes that monolingual Korean children sometimes overgeneralize the use of *kae*, which is not appropriate for all nouns, but cease to do so earlier than bilingual children with L1 Korean. In her study of Korean child learners of L2 English (AoA < 5), Shin observed the same English-like word order in the treatment of Korean plurals noted here. Shin did not quantify the occurrence of this usage among her ten subjects (see Note 4 above); however, she speculated that it might represent reverse transfer.

Table 6. Sooji's use of possessive -'s*

Input Conditions	L1 (Korean)	L2 (English)
	(K14) Sooji kutu (3;6) *Sooji shoes* (=Sooji's shoes)	(E36) Smetha grandma (3;7)
Phase I (Months 1–16 in the U.S.)	(K15) umma seonsaengnim (3;7) *Mommy teacher* (=Mommy's teacher)	(E37) Mickey bed (3;11)
	(K16) na wangja (4;5) *I prince* (=My prince)	(E38) family nose (4;6) (E39) Mommy tummy (4;7)
Phase II (Months 17–18 in Korea)	(K17) umma chaek (4;12) *Mommy book* (=Mommy's book)	(E40) Daddy car (4;10)
Phase III (Months 19–26 in the U.S.)	(K18) umma saeng il (5;8) *Mommy birthday* (=Mommy's birthday)	(E41) Campbell noodle soup (5;1) (E42) Mommy day (5;7)

* ⇒ indicates substratum transfer.

showed no sign of using the possessive -'s in obligatory contexts in her L2 production [E36–42]; instead, she used the juxtaposition of *Noun (possessor)* + *Noun (possessed)*, as in [E36–42].

Thus, Sooji's treatment of the possessive -'s in her L2 manifested only a single stage, one characterized by the absence of the morpheme, as in her L1. The following comparisons provided support for interpreting this correspondence as a transfer effect (see also Table 7).

Intra-L1-group homogeneity. As noted earlier, a number of previous studies of acquisition of English possessive and plural marking by Korean and Japanese children have revealed a deviation from the universal order; that is, the participants acquired the possessive -'s before the plural -s. In Sooji's case, however, it was the reverse. In other words, Sooji appeared to follow the universal order, as did the three to four-year-old participant in Jung's (1985) longitudinal study. While methodological differences may have led to the different findings, it is important to recall that Sooji did not acquire Korean possessive marking (see Table 6). In consequence, her L1 failed to confer the supposed advantage to her L2 acquisition.

Inter-L1-group heterogeneity. Dulay and Burt (1974) claimed a "universal" status for the acquisition of the plural *-s* before the possessive *-'s* in English (L1 *and* L2), based, in part, on evidence from child learners with Spanish as the L1. As noted earlier, Spanish is typologically distinct from Korean in that it does not have a post-nominal possessive-marking morpheme; instead, it uses a possessive construction equivalent to the English *Noun (possessed) + of + Noun (possessor)* construction. Comparison of Robertson's (1986) four-year-old participant with the five-year-old child discussed in Hakuta and Cancino (1977) indicates that L1 Spanish child learners of English variously make use of the *Noun (possessed) + Noun (possessor)* construction, with or without a preposition *of*, and the *Noun (possessor) + Noun (possessed)* construction, with or without the marker *-'s*. However, both of these participants did begin to use the possessive *-'s* marker, importantly, in the course of studies of shorter duration than the present one, whereas Sooji appeared to 'stabilize' at the *Noun (possessor) + Noun (possessed)* construction.

Intra-L1-group congruity. Although, as Ha (2001) observed, the possessive form is almost never used by L1 Korean speakers under age four, as confirmed by its absence in Sooji's Korean, there is nevertheless striking similarity in Sooji's manner of marking the possessive in Korean and in English (see Table 6). In both cases, she invoked the same construction of *Noun (possessor) + Noun (possessed)*.

In summary, our analysis of the naturalistic data yielded 11 instances of transfer. Eight of them involved substratum transfer (i.e., from the L1 to the L2) affecting word order in Sooji's L2 English negation, all in the first three months of the study. The other three involved reverse transfer (i.e., from the L2 to the L1) affecting her use of plural in L1 Korean, this time in the *last* three months of the study. Additionally, transfer effects were noted with respect to constructions that Sooji did *not* employ. First, the fact that Sooji did not use the possessive *-'s* mor-

Table 7. Evidence of transfer for possessive

Type of Utterance Compared [Participant's Data]	Criterion 1 (intra-L1-group homogeneity)	Criterion 2 (inter-L1-group heterogeneity)	Criterion 3 (intra-L1-group congruity) [Participant's Data]
(E42) Mommy day (5;7)	Daddy car Mommy school (Jung 1985)	truck Jennifer a tractor Daniel the bottle of my sister (Robertson 1986) frog de Freddie Freddie's frog (Hakuta & Cancino 1977)	(K18) umma saeng il *Mommy birthday* (=Mommy's birthday) (5;8)
L1 Transfer Supported	YES	YES	YES

pheme in her L2 English throughout the study period was in part related to her lack of acquisition of possessive marking in her L1. Second, Sooji's loss of post-verbal negation in L1 Korean after the first month of the study was partly related to her predominant exposure to English, her L2, which supports only pre-verbal negation.

Discussion

The present study set out to investigate transfer in a sequential bilingual learner of Korean and English. The participant's naturalistic production data were analyzed for stages in the development of three morphosyntactic features, and the results were subsequently compared to relevant data from published studies as well as to her L1 to see if there was any "intra-L1 group homogeneity," "inter-L1-group heterogeneity," and "intra-L1-group congruity" – the three evidential facets of transfer (Jarvis 2000). Answers were thereby obtained to the questions we posed at the outset of the study, repeated below for convenience:

1. Is there evidence of transfer in the participant's L1 and/or L2?
2. If so, what type of transfer is it?
3. Is there a relationship between transfer and changes that occur in the L1 and the L2?

First, there is evidence of both substratum and reverse transfer. Specifically, Sooji showed a four-stage developmental pattern of negation that is familiar to English L2 learners with a variety of L1s, except that in Stage I she placed the negator in sentence final position. As noted earlier (see Note 1), "typical" Stage I L2 English negation involves placement of the negator in sentence *initial* position (Butterworth 1972; Shapira 1976; Schumann 1979; R. Ellis 2000). Sooji's placement of the negator in sentence final position not only coincided with the word order for negation in her L1 but is also corroborated in the L2 English use of other speakers of Korean and Japanese. It thereby constitutes unambiguous evidence of substratum transfer. Moreover, Sooji did not appear to persist in the *no + V* stage of development; in fact, the *no + V* construction, as in *No stand there!* [E10] and *I no can do it* [E11], occurred only twice more in the data over a two-month period (3;9–3;11). Following Schumann (1979), the brevity of this stage is attributable to the L1 featuring post-verbal negation (see also Gerbault 1978; Ravem 1974; Wode 1978).

Further evidence of substratum transfer was observed in Sooji's possessive marking in both the L1 and the L2. Here Sooji consistently used, in her L2, the same construction that she used in her L1, viz., *N (possessor) + N (object possessed)*, rather than the other L2 syntactic option, which is not available in Korean.

In this case, it is seemingly difficult to decide on the direction of influence, since the behavior was non-targetlike in both cases. However, the fact that child learners of L2 English with L1 Spanish were able to acquire the English possessive -'s in a fairly short time, whereas Sooji remained "stuck" with that one construction for quite a long time appears to suggest that her L1, though not yet fully-developed vis-à-vis the target feature, had an impact on her L2 acquisition.

The evidence of reverse transfer, on the other hand, manifested itself in (a) the disappearance of post-verbal negation from Sooji's use of her L1 followed by exclusively preverbal negation and (b) the word order of quantifiers and classifiers that Sooji employed when marking plural in her L1. Importantly, both incidences were found in the context of continued exposure to the L2 (Phase 1 and Phase 3, respectively; see Table 1). However, a single exception was noted in the context of a resurgence of L1 input (see Table 1). Specifically, in Month 16, two months after her grandmother rejoined the family in New York, Sooji said *Yi donu-sseun dal-euji anchiyo*? "This doughnut sweet not?" (4;9). The "delayed effect" of this change in environmental conditions on Sooji's performance is reminiscent of her mani-festation of reverse transfer in plural marking five months after her return from Korea (see Table 4). Moreover, a similar effect can be seen in Sooji's "backsliding" to substratum transfer in her L2 negation in Month 13. This was observed twice, within one and one and a half months respectively *after* a period in which Sooji had been receiving L1 input from her grandmother at home: *When he was clean up he doing* not *the good work* (4;6); *Yitai want to* not *that* (4;6). However, changes in language dominance may be gradual or delayed in their manifestation; for exam-ple, although her visit to Korea began at the end of Month 16, it was not until the start of Month 18 that Sooji began to make substantial use of Korean in her speech.

In combination, the types of evidence cited above bring to light a complex relationship between transfer and changes in the L1 and the L2 in child SLA (Research Question 3). First, substratum transfer is apparent in the domain of morphosyntax in the early stages of acquisition, when the L1 is stronger than the L2, but later disappears. Such a pattern has been reported for other early child L2 English learners (Hakuta & Cancino 1977; Robertson 1986), although data are not available to confirm whether these participants also began to manifest reverse transfer as their L2 English began to dominate over their L1 Spanish and Japanese. Such reverse transfer, however, was observed in our longitudinal study (see Figure 1), as noted above. In one instance (i.e., the disappearance of post-verbal nega-tion in Sooji's L1 after Month 1 [K2]), the reverse transfer appeared to be due to a major functional shift in the balance of input exposure in favor of the L2 (see Table 1 and Figure 1), and thus to the influence of exclusively preverbal negation in English. In the other instance (i.e., plural marking, Months 24–26), the reverse transfer occurred late, at which time the participant's L2 had become functionally adequate and hence dominant. These two incidences, along with the occurrences

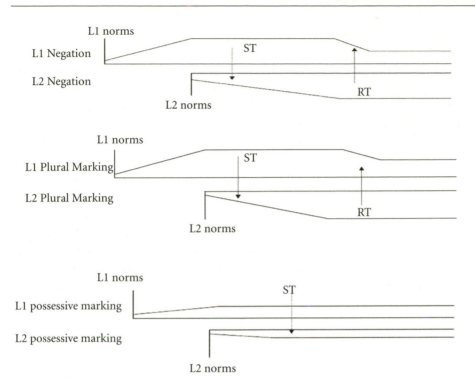

Figure 1. The sliding window between Sooji's L1 and L2 and its relation to transfer (ST = substratum transfer; RT = reverse transfer)

of substratum transfer, point to transfer as a dynamic process in child SLA, which, in turn, demonstrates Foster-Cohen's notion of a "sliding window," as graphically illustrated in Figure 1.

As shown in Figure 1, Sooji's L2 acquisition vis-à-vis the three linguistic features had a differential point of departure in that it began at a time when she had fully acquired negation and plural marking in her L1 but only partially acquired possessive marking. To some extent, this subsequently determined the rate and scope of her L2 acquisition, which exhibited the following sequence:

(7)   Negation > plural > possessive

Sooji's acquisition of English negation outpaced that of plural. In contrast, her acquisition of possessive stabilized prematurely, at her initial stage of zero marking. Although substratum transfer occurred at the early stage of her learning in two of the target features (i.e., negation and possessive), it persisted in the case of possessive, whereas it was superseded by reverse transfer in the case of negation.

Both the substratum transfer and the reverse transfer are attributable to the fact that at a certain point in Sooji's developmental process, one language became representationally and functionally stronger than the other, in accordance with changes in the linguistic environment. The window slid, as it were, several times in the 26 months of the study period. For example, in Months 17–18 Sooji made a summer trip back to Korea and the change of linguistic environment had a noticeable impact on Sooji's L1 use. In Month 18 and for several months thereafter, she – not surprisingly – made more frequent use of Korean than she had at any time since the fourth month of the study. Interestingly, however, rather than showing a resurgence of substratum transfer, as might be expected, she showed reverse transfer at this time, though not in the selected features. Thus, during this period Sooji included subjects and objects in many L1 utterances from which Korean speakers, even young children, typically omit them. For example, Sooji said *Na-neun paeko-payo*, "I am hungry" (4;11), when the context would call for *Paekopayo*, "Hungry". In Month 19, shortly after her return from Korea, Sooji began attending an all-day English-only kindergarten. Her L2 input at this time included frequent repetitions of constructions that emphasized the distinction between single and multiple objects. Counting activities also reinforced the use of English singular and plural constructions. As noted (see also Table 4), Sooji began to overgeneralize the use of the plural *-s* in English in Month 21 and subsequently transferred English plural constructions to Korean in Months 24–26 [K11–13].

The sliding window hypothesis, which postulates interactions among various "axes" of development, can help us to predict not only the onset and direction of transfer (see Figure 1), but also features that are likely to emerge. For example, a prediction can be made with regard to Sooji's L2 acquisition of possessive marking: provided continued, predominant exposure to English, Sooji will acquire the possessive *-'s* before the *noun+of+noun* construction. This is so not only because of the similarity of the morphological option to that which she used in her first language, but more importantly, because the syntactic option is more cognitively challenging than the morpholological option, a difference that is highly significant when the participant's age is taken into account. Furthermore, it is predicted that when Sooji fully acquires the possessive *-'s*, her L1 possessive marking will benefit from "reverse transfer," given, of course, further exposure to the language.

The question still remains: What gave rise to the above noted L2 sequence (see [7])? Input characteristics, such as frequency and perceptual salience (see, e.g., Larsen-Freeman 1975; Goldschneider & DeKeyser 2001) may provide an explanation. In her linguistic environment Sooji probably heard negation more frequently than the other forms. Negation is also perceptually more salient as it is realized through a free rather than a bound morpheme. Moreover, negation is functionally more useful than plural and possessive, and cognitively, the least challenging. Another explanation lies in the typological similarity/dissimilarity between the two languages. There is more similarity for negation, but less for plural and even less for possessive – at least in the spoken language (see earlier section "Typological

Comparison"). Hence, although similar structures in the L1 and L2 do not necessarily undergo positive transfer, it appears that the more similarity there is, the
easier the learning may be, as predicted by the Contrastive Analysis Hypothesis
(Lado 1957). This second explanation is arguably more powerful than the first,
since L1 influence has been frequently found to override the influence of input
frequency and salience (passim the L2 literature).

Conclusion

Embracing a broader notion of development than is traditionally entertained,
the present study, by virtue of its longitudinal approach, has shed valuable light
on transfer in the morphosyntactic domain of child SLA. Among other things,
the study uncovered a correlation between substratum transfer (i.e., possessive
marking) and L1 dominance and a correlation between reverse transfer (i.e., negation and plural marking) and L2 dominance. This relationship between transfer
and changes in the L1 and the L2 lends support to Foster-Cohen's (2001) claim
that simultaneous language development may involve reciprocal relationships of
advance and decline in language proficiency.

However, these findings should be taken as suggestive for the following reasons. First, they were based on observations of one child learner. For one thing,
the linguistic environments and the changes therein that Sooji experienced may
not be generalizable to those of many child learners, not to mention potential differences on many other fronts, such as cognitive capabilities. Second, the findings
came from a database that consisted exclusively of snapshots of Sooji's naturalistic oral production. It is possible, then, that some of her utterances may have
reflected behavioral rather than cognitive changes. Furthermore, with such kind
of database, it is difficult if not impossible, to pinpoint the time at which changes,
cognitive and/or behavioral, begin to occur. That is to say, even longitudinal naturalistic data are insufficient for capturing the process of change. A similar point
was made recently by N. Ellis and Larsen-Freeman (2006) when commenting on
the limitations of corpus data:

> [A]ttested data cannot tell us what transpired in the language up until the con-
> struction of the text, nor where it is destined. While this may seem obvious, and
> forgivable, from a complexity theory perspective, by limiting our investigations to
> attested language, we miss the perceptually changing, perceptually dynamic nature
> of language (Larsen-Freeman, in press). (p. 575)

A way to improve the methodology of the present study would be to *elicit* data
from the participant longitudinally – using a variety of tasks – in parallel to naturalistic data collection. Studies of individuals and small groups that follow this

approach would provide greater richness of detail than either cross-sectional or purely naturalistic longitudinal studies, while retaining most of the advantages of both. However, given their small sample size, increasing the generalizability of the findings would still depend largely on collective efforts to conduct multiple case studies of individuals in comparable (and disparate) acquisitional conditions. In other words, the detail and depth of understanding achievable through such studies will translate most convincingly into generalizations to the extent that findings converge.

Research on child L2 acquisition is still scarce and sparse, and as a consequence, the general understanding of its process remains piecemeal. However, precisely because of its numerous intricacies child SLA deserves adequate and systematic attention. Given its 'hybrid' nature (i.e., between child first language acquisition and adult second language acquisition), child SLA is a unique test case of theories pertaining to the mechanism, process and outcome of first as well as second language acquisition. Among its prospective findings, research on child SLA may potentially elucidate the continuity of language acquisition (and for that matter, human development), as a whole.

References

Adams, M. S. 1974. Second Language Acquisition in Children: A Study in Experimental Methods: Observation of Spontaneous Speech and Controlled Production Tests. MA thesis, University of California at Los Angeles.

Agnello, F. 1977. Exploring the pidginization hypothesis: A study of three fossilized negation systems. In *Proceedings of the Los Angeles Second Language Research Forum*, C. Henning (ed.), 224–234. English Department (TESL), University of California at Los Angeles.

Bae, S. Y. 1995. *Korean Child Language Development*. Seoul: Hankuk EoneoByoungli Hakhoi.

Barker, L. 1975. Describing the Transitional Dialects of Second Language Learners. MA thesis, Goddard College.

Bhatia, T. & Ritchie, W. 1999. The bilingual child: Some issues and perspectives. In *Handbook of Child Language Acquisition*, W. Ritchie & T. Bhatia (eds.), 569–643. New York NY: Academic Press.

Brown, R. 1973. *A First Language*. Cambridge MA: Harvard University Press.

Bruzzese, G. 1977. English/Italian secondary hybridization: A case study of the pidginization of a second language learner's speech. In *Proceedings of the Los Angeles Second Language Research Forum*, C. Henning (ed.), 235–245. English Department (TESL), University of California at Los Angeles.

Butterworth, G. A. 1972. A Spanish-speaking Adolescent's Acquisition of English Syntax. MA thesis, University of California at Los Angeles.

Cancino, H., Rosansky, E. J. & Schumann, J. H. 1978. The acquisition of English negatives and interrogatives by native Spanish speakers. In *Second Language Acquisition*, E. Hatch (ed.), 207–230. Rowley MA: Newbury House.

Döpke, S. 2000. The interplay between language-specific development and cross-linguistic influence. In *Cross-linguistic Structures in Simultaneous Bilingualism,* S. Döpke (ed.), 79–104. Amsterdam: John Benjamins.

Dulay, H. C. & Burt, M. K. 1974. Natural sequences in child second language acquisition. *Language Learning* 24: 37–53.

Ellis, N. C. & Larsen-Freeman, D. 2006. Language emergence: Implications for applied linguistics. *Applied Linguistics* 27(4): 558–589.

Ellis, R. 2000. *The Study of Second Language Acquisition.* Oxford: OUP.

Fathman, A. 1975. Language background, age and the order of acquisition of English structures. In *On TESOL '75: New Directions in Second Language Learning, Teaching and Bilingual Education,* M. K. Burt & H. C. Dulay (eds.), 33–43. Washington DC: TESOL.

Foster-Cohen, S. 2001. First language acquisition … second language acquisition: 'What's Hecuba to him or he to Hecuba?'. *Second Language Research* 17: 329–344.

Gerbault, J. 1978. The Acquisition of English by a Five-year-old French Speaker. MA thesis, University of California at Los Angeles.

Gillis, M. & Weber, R. M. 1976. The emergence of sentence modalities in the English of Japanese-speaking children. *Language Learning* 26: 77–94.

Goldschneider, J. M. and DeKeyser, R. M. 2001. Explaining the "natural order of L2 morpheme acquisition" in English: A meta-analysis of multiple determinants. *Language Learning* 51: 1–50.

Ha, K. J. 2001. *Language Acquisition and Development.* Seoul: Kookhak Jaryowon.

Hakuta, K. 1976. A case study of a Japanese child learning English as a second language. *Language Learning* 26: 321–351.

Hakuta, K. & Cancino, H. 1977. Trends in second language acquisition research. *Harvard Educational Review* 47: 294–316.

Han, Z-H. 2000. Persistence of the implicit influence of NL: The case of the pseudo-passive. *Applied Linguistics* 21: 78–105.

Han, Z-H. 2001. Fine-tuning corrective feedback. *Foreign Language Annals* 34: 582–599.

Hansen, L. 1983. The acquisition and forgetting of Hindi-Urdu negation by English-speaking children. In *Second Language Acquisition Studies,* K. Bailey et al. (eds.), 93–103. Rowley MA: Newbury House.

Jarvis, S. 2000. Methodological rigor in the study of transfer: Identifying L1 influence. *Language Learning* 50: 245–309.

Jin, J. D. 2003. Acquisition of L2 English DP by Korean children. *Reading Working Papers in Linguistics* 7: 77–101.

Jung, D. B. 1985. The acquisition of the English language by a Korean child. *Bilingualism* 2: 133–182.

Kang, B. M. 2001. The grammar and use of Korean reflexives. *International Journal of Corpus Linguistics* 6: 134–150.

Kim, Y. K. 1974. Variation in Korean negation. *Eohak Yeonku* 10: 1–21.

Kjarsgaard, M. M. 1979. The Order of English Morpheme Category Acquisition by Vietnamese Children. PhD dissertation, Arizona State University.

Klima, E. S. & Bellugi, U. 1966. Syntactic regularities in the speech of children. In *Psycholinguistic Papers,* J. Lyons & R. Wales (eds.), 183–208. Edinburgh: EUP.

Koike, I. 1980. Second Language Acquisition of Grammatical Structures and Relevant Verbal Strategies. PhD dissertation, Georgetown University.

Lado, R. 1957. *Linguistics across Cultures.* Ann Arbor MI: University of Michigan Press.

Lakshmanan, U. 1993. "The Boy for the Cookie": Some evidence for the nonviolation of the case filter in child second language acquisition. *Language Acquisition* 3: 55–91.

Lakshmanan, U. 2006. Child second language acquisition and fossilization puzzle. In *Studies of Fossilization in Second Language Acquisition*, Z. Han & T. Odlin (eds.), 100–133. Clevedon: Multilingual Matters.

Larsen-Freeman, D. 1975. The acquisition of grammatical morphemes by adult ESL students. *TESOL Quarterly* 9: 409–420.

Lee, J. 1995. Hankuke Supunlyusaui Uimi Punseok [A Semantic Analysis of Korean Numeral Classifiers]. MA thesis, Sangmyung Women's University.

Makino, T. 1979. English Morpheme Acquisition Order of Japanese Secondary School Students. PhD dissertation, University of New Mexico, Albuquerque.

Martin, S. E. 1992. *A Reference Grammar of Korean: A Complete Guide to the Grammar and History of the Korean Language*. Rutland VT: Charles E. Tuttle.

McLaughlin, B. 1978. *Second Language Acquisition in Childhood*. Hillsdale NJ: Lawrence Erlbaum Associates.

Milon, J. P. 1974. The development of negation in English by a second language learner. *TESOL Quarterly* 8: 137–143.

Odlin, T. 1989. *Language Transfer: Cross-linguistic Influence in Language Learning*. Cambridge: CUP.

Odlin, T. 2003. Cross-linguistic influence. In *The Handbook of Second Language Acquisition*, C. Doughty & M. Long (eds.), 436–486. Oxford: Blackwell.

Pak, Y. 1987. Age Differences in Morpheme Acquisition among Korean ESL Learners: Acquisition Order and Acquisition Rate. PhD dissertation, University of Texas at Austin.

Pavlenko, A. 2000. L2 influence on L1 in late bilingualism. *Issues in Applied Linguistics* 11: 175–205.

Pavlenko, A. & Jarvis, S. 2002. Bidirectional transfer. *Applied Linguistics* 23: 190–214.

Ravem, R. 1974. Second Language Acquisition: A Study of Two Norwegian Children's Acquisition of English Syntax in a Naturalistic Setting. PhD dissertation, University of Essex.

Robertson, H. S. 1986. The Order of Acquisition of Fourteen Grammatical Morphemes in English by a Native Spanish-speaking Four-year-old Learning English in a Naturalistic Setting. PhD dissertation, The University of Texas at Austin.

Schachter, J. 1974. An error in error analysis. *Language Learning* 24: 205–214.

Schumann, J. 1976. Second language acquisition: The pidginization hypothesis. *Language Learning* 26: 390–408.

Schumann, J. 1979. The acquisition of English negation by speakers of Spanish: A review of the literature. In *The Acquisition and Use of Spanish and English as First and Second Languages*, R. Andersen (ed.), 3–32. Washington DC: Teachers of English to Speakers of Other Languages.

Selinker, L. & Lakshmanan, U. 1993. Language transfer and fossilization: The "Multiple Effects Principle." In *Language Transfer in Language Learning* (rev. ed.), S. Gass & L. Selinker (eds.), 197–216. Amsterdam: John Benjamins.

Shapira, R. G. 1976. A Study of the Acquisition of Ten Syntactic Structures and Grammatical Morphemes by an Adult Second Language Learner: Some Methodological Implications. MA thesis, University of California at Los Angeles.

Sharma, V. 1974. A Linguistic Study of Speech Development in Early Childhood. PhD dissertation, Agra University.

Shin, Y. S. 2001. A Study on the Learning of English Negation for Korean Students. PhD dissertation, Korean national university of education, Chung Buk.

Shin, S. J. & Milroy, L. 1999. Conversational code-switching among Korean-English bilingual children. *International Journal of Bilingualism* 4: 351–383.

Shin, S. J. 2005. *Developing in Two Languages: Korean Children in America.* Clevedon: Multilingual Matters.

Shirahata, T. 1988. The Learning of English Grammatical Morphemes by Japanese High School Students. PhD dissertation, The University of Arizona.

Stauble, A. E. 1978. Decreolization: A model for second language development. *Language Learning* 28: 29–54.

Stauble, A. M. 1984. A comparison of a Spanish-English and a Japanese-English second language continuum: Negation and verb morphology. In *Second Languages: A Crosslinguistic Perspective,* R. Andersen (ed.), 323–533. Rowley MA: Newbury House.

Weinreich, U. 1953. *Languages in Contact.* The Hague: Mouton.

Whong-Barr, M. & Schwartz, B. 2002. Morphological and syntactic transfer in child L2 acquisition of the English dative alternation. *Studies in Second Language Acquisition* 24: 579–616.

Wode, H. 1978. Developmental principles in naturalistic L2 acquisition. In *Second Language Acquisition: A Book of Readings,* E. Hatch (ed.), 101–117. Rowley MA: Newbury House.

Wode, H. 1981. *Learning a Second Language: An Integrated View of Language Acquisition.* Tübingen: Narr.

Young, D. I. 1974. The Acquisition of English Syntax by Three Spanish-speaking Children. MA thesis, University of California at Los Angeles.

Appendix A: Selected studies of Korean and Japanese learners of English

Study	L1	Number of partic-ipants	Age at First Exposure to L2	Duration	Features Exam-ined	Results
Milon (1974)	Japanese	1	7	7 months	Neg.	Long *no V* stage
Fathman (1975)	Korean Spanish	200	6–15	Cross-sectional	Pl.	Pl. Poss.> Poss.
Barker (1975)	Korean Chinese Spanish	1 1 3	University level	5 weeks	Neg.	*no V* used only by Spanish L1s.
Hakuta (1976)	Japanese	1	5	1 year	Neg. Pl. Poss.	Non-existent *no V* stage; Poss.> Pl.
Gillis & Weber (1976)	Japanese	2	6:11–7:6	5 months	Neg.	Short or non-existent *no V* stage
Hakuta & Cancino (1977)	Japanese Spanish	1 1	5	13 months 8 months	Pl. Poss.	Poss. > Pl. by Japanese L1 Pl. > Poss. by Spanish L1
Makino (1979)	Japanese	777	13–15	Cross-sectional	Pl. Poss.	Pl. > Poss.
Koike (1980)	Japanese	3	5:00–12:6	31 months	Neg. Pl. Poss.	Non-existent *no V* stage; Pl. > Poss. (2 cases) Pl. = Poss. (1 case)
Stauble (1984)	Japanese Spanish	6 6	30-85	1 month	Neg.	Short *no V* stage Long *no V* stage
Jung (1985)	Korean	1	3:6	10 months	Pl. Poss.	Acquisition order not reported
Pak (1987)	Korean	40 children 40 adults	5–12 25–38	Cross-sectional	Pl. Poss.	Poss.> Pl.
Shirahata (1988)	Japanese	31	High school	Cross-sectional	Pl. Poss.	Poss. > Pl.
Shin & Milroy (1999)	Korean	12	6–7	Cross-sectional	Pl. Poss.	Poss.> Pl.

Appendix B: Selected child L2A of English studies

Study	L1	Number of participants	Age at First Exposure to L2	Duration	Features Examined	Results
Butterworth (1972)	Spanish	1	13:0	3 months	Neg.	Long *no V* stage
Dulay & Burt (1974)	Spanish Chinese	60 55	6–8	Cross-sectional	Pl. Poss.	Pl. > Poss.
Ravem (1974)	Norwegian	1	3:9	10 months	Neg.	Short *not V* stage
Adams (1974)	Spanish	10	4:11–5:9	3 months	Neg.	Long *no V* stage
Young (1974)	Spanish	2	5	9 months	Neg.	Long *no V* stage
Schumann (1976)	Spanish	5	5:00–33:00	10 months	Neg.	Long *no V* stage
Shapira (1976)	Spanish	1	22	2 years	Neg.	Long *no V* stage
Agnello (1977)	Greek	1	42	3 hours of speech	Neg.	Long *no V* stage
Bruzzese (1977)	Italian	1	40	3 hours of speech	Neg.	Long *no V* stage
Wode (1978)	German	4	3:11–8:11	1 year	Neg.	Short or non-existent *no V* stage
Cancino, Rosansky, and Schumann (1978)	Spanish	2 children 2 adole-scents 2 adults	5 11&13 25&33	10 months	Neg.	Long *no V* stage
Stauble (1978)	Spanish	2	10	10 months	Neg.	Long *no V* stage
Gerbault (1978)	French	1	4:6	10 months	Neg.	Short or non-existent *no V* stage
Kjarsgaard (1979)	Vietnamese	45	7–14	Cross-sectional	Pl. Poss.	Pl. > Poss.
Robertson (1986)	Spanish	1	4	8 months	Neg. Pl. Poss.	Long *no V* stage; Pl. > Poss.
Lakshmanan (1993)	Spanish	1	4:6	8 months	Neg.	Long *no V* stage

Index

In the series *Language Learning & Language Teaching* the following titles have been published thus far or are scheduled for publication: